Small-Scale Mining,
Rural Subsistence and
Poverty in West Africa

Small-Scale Mining, Rural Subsistence and Poverty in West Africa

Edited by
Gavin M. Hilson

PRACTICAL ACTION
Publishing

Published by Intermediate Technology Publications Ltd
Schumacher Centre for Technology and Development
Bourton on Dunsmore, Rugby,
Warwickshire CV23 9QZ, UK
www.practicalactionpublishing.org

ISBN 1-8533-9-6354 (paperback)
ISBN 978-1-85339-6359 (paperback)
ISBN 1-8533-9-629X (hardback)
ISBN 978-1-85339-6298 (hardback)

First published in 2006

A catalogue record for this book is available from the British Library.

Since 1974, Practical Action Publishing has published and disseminated
books and information in support of international development work
throughout the world. Practical Action Publishing (formerly ITDG
Publishing) is a trading name of Intermediate Technology Publications Ltd
(Company Reg. No. 1159018), the wholly owned publishing company of
Intermediate Technology Development Group Ltd (working name Practical
Action). Practical Action Publishing trades only in support of its parent
charity objectives and any profits are covenanted back to Practical Action
(Charity Reg. No. 247257, Group VAT Registration No. 880 9924 76).

Index preparation: Indexing Specialists (UK) Ltd
Typeset in Trade Gothic and Stone Serif
by S.J.I. Services
Printed by Replika Press Pvt. Ltd

Contents

    Victor A. B. Davies

    Analytical framework   165
    Diamonds and poverty   168
    Diamonds and the civil war   175
    The post-conflict era   176
    Conclusions   180

15. Reflections on the political economy of artisanal
    diamond mining in Kono District, Sierra Leone   181
    Estelle Levin

    An overview of diamond mining in Kono   182
    A political economy of contemporary artisanal diamond production   187
    Illegal mining   203
    Monitoring and disciplining the industry   204
    Conclusion   207

16. Perspectives on diamond mining and public health
    in Akwatia, Ghana   211
    Kaakpema Yelpaala and Saleem H. Ali

    Methodology   211
    Diamond mining in Ghana: an overview   212
    Mining, environmental health, and economic development   213
    Diamond mining and health challenges in Akwatia   213
    HIV/AIDS and mining in Akwatia: a looming problem?   215
    A framework: the need for more robust understanding of the
        links between environment and health challenges in Akwatia   216
    Conclusion   217

17. Socioeconomic, environmental and policy implications
    of alluvial diamond mining in the Birim
    diamondiferous field, eastern Ghana   219
    Frank K. Nyame and S. K. A. Danso

    Study area and methods   220
    Socioeconomic and environmental factors   221
    Policy issues   225
    Conclusion   226

18. 'Live and let live': The relationship between artisanal/
    small-scale and large-scale miners at Abosso Goldfields, Ghana   227
    Anthony Kwesi Aubynn

    Purpose of engagement and data   228
    Prevailing situation and the need for a change in approach   229
    Abosso Goldfields and neighbouring ASM   231
    Impact of 'Live and let live' policy   235
    Conclusion   238

Foreword

Ian Smillie

This book fills important gaps in knowledge about West Africa. Ostensibly about artisanal and small-scale mining (ASM), it is, in fact, a book about development, an aspect of development that most development organizations have simply ignored.

The book starts with a recent history of artisanal mining in West Africa, but it is worth going back a bit further than the last century. When the Portuguese first arrived in West Africa in the 15th century, they were amazed at the quality of brass-casting they found, and refused to believe that the brilliant art work of Ife and Benin had not been influenced, or even produced, by ancient Greek or Roman travellers. The lost-wax method of brass casting is an old one, known in many societies; but such was the quality of work in West Africa that the Portuguese took African craftsmen with them to introduce and expand the technology in Brazil.

There are sites in West Africa with evidence of an iron industry dating back as far as 500 BC, coinciding with the development of the Iron Age in the UK. The earliest sites in Ghana date from the second century AD, and by the 15th century, iron had become a common village industry there, producing a range of agricultural implements and weapons. When 15th-century European traders arrived in search of gold, they gave a spur to the iron industry, as new tools were needed for mining; but as the European taste for gold increased and as slaves were added to the list of exports, more and more textiles, agricultural implements, tools and firearms were imported. Under the influence of these imports, iron production gradually declined, and by the early 20th century it survived only in remote areas of northern Ghana, little more than a crude cottage industry. Iron technology was lost, but ironically the lost-wax method of bronze casting, which in most other societies disappeared, has survived in West Africa. No longer an essential or important technology, it continues largely through handicraft sales. The greatness of the past age is sometimes recalled, however, in the auction rooms of Europe and North America: a small Benin bronze plaque recently fetched US $500,000 at a Christie's auction in New York and another Benin bronze realized •456,000 in 2004 at a Sotheby's auction in Paris.

The lost-wax technique may not have been lost, but almost everything else was, and the African development in metallurgy that might have paralleled Europe's was gradually reduced to a variety of activities defined as artisanal. The most alarming consequences of underdevelopment in Africa's artisanal mining sector are much more recent: the diamond wars that raged like a holocaust across Angola, the Democratic Republic of the Congo and Sierra Leone through most of the 1990s and into the current decade.

Alluvial diamonds, washed by 50 million rainy seasons down rivers and across plains, are not like those found in Botswana, Canada or Russia. Those can be fenced, and in any case, require major investments in technology and heavy equipment. Alluvial diamonds, however, mined today by more than a million diggers across vast swathes of the African countryside, are more amenable to artisanal techniques. They are also more amenable to unscrupulous buyers, criminals, money launderers, smugglers and, in the end, the rebel armies who have sought them out in order to buy weapons.

The combined United Nations peacekeeping efforts in Sierra Leone, Liberia and Côte d'Ivoire have never cost less than US$1 billion a year since 2000; the UN peacekeeping budget in the DRC alone was US$1 billion in 2005–6. These peacekeeping missions and the wars that made them necessary are a consequence of illicit diamonds, and in the DRC by other artisanally mined minerals. Yet, efforts by donor organizations and development agencies to correct the problems in the artisanal mining sector amount to considerably less than 1 per cent of that amount per year: 'an ounce of prevention is worth a pound of cure' or so the old saying goes. In this case, however, the real-life equivalent would be more like a ton of cure against a pitifully few ounces of meaningful prevention.

Many development organizations shy away from extractives. Few have an interest in mining, especially the rough and tumble world of artisanal mining. Artisanal mining in Africa, however, is not first and foremost about mining. It is about livelihoods. It is, in fact, about seven of the eight Millennium Development Goals (MDGs), because it is directly related to children, women and poverty. Artisanal mining centres are not just magnets for the poor and focal points for crime and social disruption, they are vectors for malaria and HIV/AIDS. Artisanal mining ignored is environmental sustainability ignored, and if the truth be known, could be the focus of the eighth MDG as well: a global partnership for development. This is the aim of the newly formed Diamond Development Initiative (DDI), which grew out of the Kimberley Process Certification Scheme for rough diamonds. Understanding that regulation alone has never worked to control the artisanal diamond fields of West Africa, the DDI, a unique partnership among governments, NGOs and the diamond industry, is adopting a developmental approach that focuses first and foremost on the miners themselves and their communities. In the long run, better remuneration, better conditions and better alternatives are more likely to make a real difference in the artisanal mining sector than more rules, more antipathy and more peacekeeping.

The contributions in this book line up well with the thinking behind the DDI, and will help to strengthen the case it is making to governments, donors, the private sector and civil society. The book helps to shed important new light on an old problem, one that will not go away until it receives the developmental attention it needs, and that it most certainly deserves.

Ian Smillie
Partnership Africa Canada Ottawa, Canada

Acknowledgements

The idea for this edited work emerged in late 2003 during informal discussions with Dr Brigitte Bocoum of the African Development Bank. In addition to Dr Bocoum, the editor would like to thank everyone who provided valuable feedback, inspiration, advice and criticisms during the course of the book's development: James Haselip, Professor John Monhemius, Dr Clive Potter and Dr Tamsin Cooper at the Imperial College of Science, Technology and Medicine; Dr Kieron Stanley, Dr Andrew Flynn and Professor Terry Marsden at Cardiff University; Professor Barbara Murck at the University of Toronto; Professor Marcello Veiga at the University of British Columbia; Dr Thomas Akabzaa at the University of Ghana; Jeffrey Davidson at the World Bank; Rickford Vieira at the WWF Guianas; and Robert Yakubu and Ben Aryee at the Minerals Commission, Ghana. The editor would also like to give special thanks to Toby Milner and the staff at Practical Action Publishing, whose support, patience and commitment made this initiative possible. On a personal note, the editor is grateful for support received throughout from Andrea Dempster, Andrew Hilson, Mike Hilson, Vikram Gulati, Ricky Seghal, Vishal and Bhavish Nayee, Dr Daniel Weisser and Peter Stephens. This book is dedicated to the academics and researchers committed to making a difference on the ground in the artisanal and small-scale mining sector.

List of figures

List of tables

Acronyms and abbreviations

ACP	African, Caribbean and Pacific Group of States
ADMS	Alluvial Diamond Mining Scheme
AGC	Ashanti Goldfields
AGL	Abosso Goldfields
ALG	Authority of Liptako-Gourma
AMREF	African Medical Relief Foundation
APC	All People's Congress
APRODEB	Action pour la Promotion des Droits de L'enfant au Burkina
ASM	Artisanal and small-scale mining
BDM	Banque de Développement du Mali
BGL	Bogoso Goldfields
BRGM	Bureau de Recherches Géologiques et Minières
BUMIGEB	Bureau des Mines et de la Géologie du Burkina Faso
CASM	Communities and Small-Scale Mining
CAST	Consolidated African Selection Trust
CBMP	Comptoir Burkinabé des Métaux Précieux
CEDAW	Convention on the Elimination of All Forms of Discrimination Against Women
CFAFr	CFA Franc (African Franc Zone currency)
CMC	Chiefdom Mining Committee
CMH	Commission on Macroeconomics and Health
CONAPEM	National Corporation of Small-Mine Artisans and Operators
CSIR	Ghana's Centre for Scientific and Industrial Research
DDI	Diamond Development Initiative
DEMPEC	Direction des Exploitations Minières à Petite Echelle (Directorate of Small-Scale Mine Exploitation)
DFID	Department for International Development
DGMGC	Directorate General of Mines, Geology and Quarries
DNGM	National Directorate for Geology and Mines
DSA	Debt Sustainability Analysis
ECOMOG	West African Multilateral Armed Force
ECOWAS	Economic Community of West African States
EIA	Environmental Impact Assessment
EPA	Environmental Protection Agency

EU	European Union
FAO	Food and Agriculture Organization
FFr	French Franc
GCD	Ghana Consolidated Diamonds
GDP	Gross Domestic Product
GGDO	Government Gold and Diamond Office
GIE	Economic Interest Group
GMI	Global Mining Initiative
GPMB	Groupement Professionel des Mines du Burkina
GSR	Golden Star Resources
HIPC	Heavily Indebted Poor Countries
IDA	International Development Association
IFIs	International Financial Institutions
IIED	International Institute for Environment and Development
ILO	International Labour Organization
IMF	International Monetary Fund
IPEC	International Programme on the Elimination of Child Labour
IRM	Industrial Rocks and Minerals
IUCN	International Union for the Conservation of Nature and Natural Resources (now known as World Conservation Union)
KPCS	Kimberley Process Certification Scheme
MDGs	Millennium Development Goals
MMR	Ministry of Mineral Resources
MMSD	Mining, Minerals, and Sustainable Development Project
MPRI	Mining Policy Research Initiative
MRTF	Mineral Resources Trust Fund
NACP	Ghana National AIDS/STI Control Programme
NCC	Nigeria Coal Corporation
NDC	National Democratic Congress
NDMC	National Diamond Mining Company
NGO	Non-governmental Organization
NMC	Nigerian Mining Corporation
NPP	New Patriotic Party
NPRC	National Provisional Ruling Council
OBGRM	Office Beninois des Recherches Géologiques et Minières
PAMPE	Project for the Promotion of Traditional Mining and Environmental Protection
PDA	Peace Diamond Alliance
PDRM	Program for Mineral Resources and Development
PGR	Prestea Gold Resources
PMMC	Precious Minerals and Marketing Corporation
PNDC	Provisional National Defence Council
PRSP	Poverty Reduction Strategy Paper
PSIA	Poverty Social Impact Assessment
RUF	Revolutionary United Front

SAP	Structural Adjustment Programme
SDA	Sustainable Development Agreement
SGMC	State Gold Mining Corporation
SL	Sustainable Livelihoods
SLST	Sierra Leone Selection Trust
SME	Small- and Medium-Sized Enterprise
STD	Sexually Transmitted Disease
TMPAG	Traditional Medical Practitioners Association in Ghana
UDHR	Universal Declaration of Human Rights
UEMOA	Union Economique et Monétaire Ouest Africaine
UN	United Nations
UNCED	United Nations Conference on Environment and Development
UNCRC	United Nations Convention on the Rights of the Child
UNCTAD	United Nations Conference on Trade and Development
UNDESA	United Nations Department of Economic and Social Affairs
UNDP	United Nations Development Programme
UNECE	United Nations Economic Commission for Europe
UNEP	United Nations Environment Programme
UNICEF	United Nations International Children's Emergency Fund
UNIDO	United Nations Industrial Development Organization
UNOMIN	National Association of Mine Operators in Mali
USAID	United States Agency for International Development
WCED	World Commission on Environment and Development
WFCL	Worst Form of Child Labour
WHO	World Health Organization
WSSD	World Summit on Sustainable Development

Contributors

Anthony Kwesi Aubynn studied at the Universities of Ghana, Helsinki, Tampere and Oslo. He is currently Corporate Manager of Public Affairs and Social Development at Gold Fields in Ghana. His research interests include mining and sustainable development, mineral economics and democracy in Africa.

Blaise Zida is with the Bureau de Recherches Géologiques et Minières in France.

Catherine Greffié is with the Bureau de Recherches Géologiques et Minières in France.

Christopher J. Hilson is in the Department of International Relations, Faculty of Arts and Science, University of Toronto. His main research interest is the political economy of sub-Saharan Africa.

Collins Anim-Sackey holds BSc (Hons) and MPhil degrees in Chemical Engineering and Mining Engineering, respectively, from the Kwame Nkrumah University of Science and Technology (KNUST), Kumasi, Ghana. He also holds a Certificate in Project Planning and Management from the Ghana Institute of Management and Public Administration (GIMPA), Accra. He currently works as a senior chemical engineer at the Ghana Minerals Commission in Accra.

Dialla Konate is founding director of DSM Consulting in Mali, and an adjunct Professor at Ecole Nationale d'Ingénieurs et Faculté des Sciences et Techniques, Université de Bamako, Mali. He studied at McGill University in Canada, and the Pennsylvania State University in the United States.

Eric Jaques is with the Bureau de Recherches Géologiques et Minières in France.

Estelle Levin received a BSc in Geography from the University of Edinburgh and a Master's degree in Human Geography from the University of British Columbia, Canada. She recently completed a seven-month internship in the Communities and Small-scale Mining Secretariat at the World Bank in Washington, DC.

Frank Kwakyi Nyame is a Lecturer in the Department of Geology, University of Ghana. He received his PhD in geochemistry from Okayama University, Japan.

Gavin M. Hilson is a Lecturer at the Institute for Development Policy and Management (IDPM), University of Manchester. He received his PhD from the Imperial College of Science, Technology and Medicine.

Jean-François Thomassin is with the Bureau de Recherches Géologiques et Minières in France.

Kaakpema Yelpaala specializes in a broad range of health and development issues, including HIV/AIDS, health systems, capacity-building for rural community-based organizations and public-private partnerships. He is the founder and president of the US-based international health organization Network for the Improvement of World Health.

Karen MacDonald is an environmental lawyer, consultant and research associate in Environmental Law at Imperial College London. Her research interests include environmental human rights and procedural environmental rights, particularly those related to the Aarhus Convention and environmental assessment processes. She received her LLB degree from the University of Hull, and her LLM degree from the University of London.

Mario Billa is with the Bureau de Recherches Géologiques et Minières in France.

Matthew Gibb is a doctoral candidate in the Department of Geography, Rhodes University, South Africa. His research interests are broadly placed within the areas of globalization, locality-based development, rural livelihoods, and sustainable development.

Miriam Anike Lawal received her MSc in Energy Studies at the University of Dundee in Scotland. Her main research interest is artisanal mining in Nigeria, particularly relevant poverty and livelihoods issues.

Natalia Yakovleva is currently a research associate at the BRASS Research Centre, Cardiff University. Her research interests include corporate social responsibility, environmental reporting and community development in the mining industry, particularly in the gold- and diamond-mining sectors. She received her Bachelor's degree in Economics from the Yakutsk State University in Russia, and her PhD in Environmental Studies from the University of Sunderland, UK.

Richard K. Amankwah is a Senior Lecturer at the Tarkwa School of Mines, Kwame Nkrumah University of Science and Technology, Ghana. He received his PhD in Mining Engineering from Queen's University in Canada.

Sabine Luning is an Associate Professor at the School for Asian, African and Amerindian Studies, Leiden University, the Netherlands. Her research interests include gold markets and artisanal gold mining, particularly in Burkina Faso.

Saleem H. Ali teaches environmental planning and conflict resolution at the University of Vermont's Rubenstein School of Natural Resources. He holds a PhD in Environmental Planning from the Massachusetts Institute of Technology.

Sandra Pardie is in the Department of Geology, University of Ghana. Her main research interest is the environmental impact of artisanal mining in West Africa.

Seth K.A. Danso is a Professor of Soil Microbiology at the University of Ghana. Professor Danso received his PhD in Soil Science from Cornell University, Ithaca, New York.

Tilo Grätz completed his undergraduate studies at the Free University of Berlin and received his PhD in Sociology from Bielefeld University. He is currently a Research Fellow at the Max Planck Institute for Social Anthropology in Halle.

Victor A.B. Davies is a Lecturer in Economics at Fourah Bay College, University of Sierra Leone. He is currently a doctoral candidate in the Department of Economics, Oxford University. His research interests include conflict economies, natural resources, foreign aid and the political economy of development.

Introduction: resuscitating the policy and research agenda for artisanal and small-scale mining

Gavin M. Hilson

In May 1995, at the International Roundtable on Artisanal Mining hosted by the World Bank, a consensus was reached that artisanal mining was a poverty-driven activity taken up by individuals with few, if any, employment alternatives. Apart from bringing to the fore the potential problems associated with the industry's rapid expansion worldwide, the seminar highlighted the global donor community's commitment to providing financial support to regularize informal mining activities. Bank officials in particular underscored their interest in this 'poverty-driven activity...[in light]...of the organization's mandate to alleviate poverty' (Barry, 1996: 1).

Yet, poverty as it applies to artisanal and small-scale mining (ASM) has hitherto been given low priority on the research and policy agendas of multilateral and bilateral development agencies. Prolonged neglect of the sector's poverty and broader socioeconomic issues has, in a number of cases, rendered promising policy and support initiatives ineffective. The reality is that the relationship between poverty and ASM is far more complex than policymakers at donor agencies and multilateral institutions care to admit. For example, further analysis beyond the generalization about poverty-driven activity has revealed that many artisanal miners now find themselves trapped in a vicious cycle of impoverishment, fuelled by, among other things, indebtedness to corrupt gold and diamond buyers, minimal land tenure, inefficient equipment and the absence of sustainable support services. Moreover, in response to the expansion of ASM, now understood to be linked to wider unemployment issues in the developing world economy, a number of stakeholders have called for the implementation of equitable policies to facilitate the rapid regularization of operations; a more formalized sector, they argue, could promote entrepreneurial activity for agricultural and public-sector workers whose livelihoods have been disrupted heavily by structural adjustment policies.

It is the independent research carried out by ethnographers, sociologists, geographers and anthropologists, and not the work sponsored by multilateral lending institutions championing developmental assistance for ASM, that has both uncovered and provided extended analysis of the many faces of poverty in ASM. In recent years, the International Labour Organization (ILO) has worked exhaustively to inform the donor community of the need to improve understanding of the underlying social and interrelated poverty dynamics of ASM communities: in its landmark report, *Social and Labour Issues in Small-Scale Mining*, it is noted that to date, 'for the most part, emphasis has been on finding technical solutions to mining and processing problems, with scant heed being paid to the underlying economic, labour and social issues' (ILO, 1999).

'When assistance…is being developed and implemented,' argues Norman Jennings, Senior Industrial Specialist in the Sectoral Activities Department of the ILO, 'due consideration should be given to other issues – legal, financial, technical, cultural and political – that affect it' (Jennings, 2000: 3). Jennings (1999: 2) highlights the many shortcomings of the approaches being taken to regularize and deliver support to ASM:

> An ad hoc approach to small-scale mining has constrained efforts to: promote better organization and work practices; increase the productivity of small-scale mines; and lessen the adverse labour and social effects. Erratic policy and decision-making has led to confusion among administrators and managers of both large and small mines and has sometimes caused conflict at mining locations – between large and small mines and between small-scale miners and regulators. A lack of coordination in the provision of external assistance has not helped. No wonder that bringing order to small-scale mining is a problem.

The work of the ILO was acknowledged in the ASM report of the Global Mining Initiative (GMI), which notes that the 'implementation of technical changes, modifications and improvements…[in ASM]…in almost any case requires detailed knowledge of the cultural, social, economic and organizational context of the miners' (Hentschel et al., 2002: 40). The donor community, however, has responded poorly to the ILO's efforts: it has become apparent that multilateral and bilateral development institutions dismiss this crucial knowledge as insignificant, evidently content with providing financial support for projects which emphasize the technological aspects of operations with comparatively minimal focus on underlying poverty and social issues.

Without sufficient knowledge of the technical capabilities and anthropological characteristics of target populations, how can appropriate technologies be identified? Similarly, in a sector now recognized globally to be heterogeneous in terms of the skill and educational levels of its participants, its degree of mechanization and the nature of its practices overall, why are funds being used to implement licensing schemes and support services without carefully studying target populations beforehand? We need look no further than the mechanized technology installed in rural stretches of Ghana under the auspices of the World Bank Mining Sector Environmental Project, where equipment that has broken down or has gone unused is now being used to air-dry villagers' clothes. Similarly, consider efforts made to facilitate the adoption of mercury retorts and sluice boxes in countries such as Zimbabwe, Guyana and Bolivia, which have been unsuccessful because of miners' discomfort with using equipment designed in the developed world.

What is even more frustrating for researchers carrying out important social and anthropological work on ASM is that staff from multilateral and bilateral development agencies have entrusted a small group of consultants with the task of resolving the sector's policy problems and implementing key projects touted to help achieve broader development objectives, particularly the UN Millennium Development Goals. Often overlooked amid the mad scramble started by the issuance of a World Bank, the Department for International Development (DFID) UK or European Union (EU) tender is the fact that the majority of these consultants, apart from being somewhat distracted by the desire to forge additional contracts for their global consultancies, are mining engineers, who though technically skilled, often lack the requisite training to manage social and policy support projects for ASM. Moreover, many choose to ignore anthropological research findings, the analysis of which would go a long way towards designing more sustainable policies and support services for small-scale miners. Researchers labour for months upon years in the field studying the dynamics of mining communities; they are in a far better position to assess critically the suitability of say, a draft piece of legislation or technology.

Of major concern is the influence that the consultants wield: apart from implementing important projects, most now advise multilateral development banks, bilateral development agencies and host governments on approaches to ASM project support. Many organizations are being seriously misled by consultants' contentions that ASM is suffering from research fatigue and is in need of immediate action on the ground. On the contrary, ASM has been, and continues to be, plagued by *inappropriate* research, a main reason why the millions of dollars in development aid injected into the sector to date have yielded few positive results. By detaching themselves from the social and anthropological research agenda completely, these consultants are simply perpetuating what has become a questionable global support facility for ASM.

There are a number of other issues of major concern. The most significant of these are as follows:

- Why, given the poverty alleviation mandates of multilateral development institutions and aid agencies, do international ASM seminars continue to have poor grassroots representation from developing countries themselves? Concerns have been voiced about attendees from Africa, Latin America and Asia, particularly representatives from NGOs, lobbying on behalf of artisanal miners, disrupting negotiations and discussions in an effort to further their agendas. Paradoxically, in having minimal representation from developing countries, it is the organizers of these international workshops – principally, the lending agencies themselves – who are implementing their own agendas.
- The majority of ASM support projects continue to be managed and administered at organizations' headquarters by people who rarely travel to

the field, and not through their regional offices. In certain cases, consultants go to lengths to establish relationships with the top executives of mining companies or a donor agency, in order to ensure that local units have minimal project participation. The resulting centralized and non-participatory mode of project governance impairs the quality of research and delivery of support. In these cases, top executives, who are based outside the host country and conduct minimal fieldwork, manage the project, and local, more specialized units are excluded. Why are lending agencies not involving their country personnel, who are clearly more familiar with conditions on the ground?

- The state of the industry's support system is such that individuals championing the poverty alleviation mission, and who have forged close ties with the organizations issuing contract tenders, are now being touted as industry experts and chairing international plenaries. Exactly how this has come about is unclear but it most certainly minimizes any chance for objectivity.

- Of the few social and anthropological research projects that have been sponsored by multilateral and bilateral development agencies in recent years, most have been concentrated in the more established, well-researched ASM regions of countries, and not more remote areas. These efforts certainly do no justice to the ILO's repeated call for improving understanding of the social dynamics of ASM communities. Despite organizations' assurance of their cognizance of the sector's heterogeneity, most appear reluctant to stretch their resources in order to ascertain the ways in which this holds true.

These realities shed considerable light on the very nature of the global ASM support facility today: despite the diligent efforts of the ILO to facilitate people-centred research, the delivery of support continues to be driven from the top down, in many ways reflecting the nature of development assistance as a whole. The ineptitude of ASM research and policymaking strategies today is only rivalled by the fruitless, costly efforts made during the 1970s and 1980s to host international conferences aimed largely at devising universal definitions of 'artisanal' and 'small-scale mining'.

The contributors to this book are committed to helping bridge this research gap created by the international donor community's prolonged neglect. The book uses a case study of the Economic Community of West African States (ECOWAS) to improve understanding of the social dynamics of informal mining communities. Specifically, through detailed analysis of West Africa's rapidly expanding ASM communities, authors capture the essence of the poverty problem in the sector; the drivers behind miners' increased participation in the industry; and the nature of their struggles.

The book is divided into three sections. The first, 'Artisanal and Small-scale Mining in West Africa', is comprised of reviews designed to provide scope and essential background on the region, that is, ECOWAS, being examined. The second section, 'Country case studies: Francophone West Africa', presents findings from fieldwork conducted in ASM communities in French West African countries, including Benin and Burkina Faso. The final section, 'Country case studies: Anglophone West Africa', provides parallel case study analysis from English-speaking West African countries, including Ghana, Nigeria and Sierra Leone.

The aim of this book is to trigger a change in the approaches taken by multilateral and bilateral development institutions towards ASM policymaking, research and support. For ASM consultants profiting under the pretext of executing the World Bank's, the United Nations Development Programme's (UNDP) and DFID's poverty alleviation agendas and misleading organizations at the expense of already marginalized artisanal miners, the burning question remains: how can conditions improve in this industry if underlying socioeconomic issues are not properly understood?

Part I

Artisanal and Small-scale Mining in West Africa

CHAPTER 1
An overview

Gavin M. Hilson

The geographical focus of this book is ECOWAS; the topic of study is the ASM industry – specifically, its association with poverty. Before proceeding, it is necessary to provide essential background analysis on the region, and the sector and themes being examined.

There is consensus among policymakers that ASM is a poverty-driven sector of industry, employing individuals with few, if any, alternative income-earning opportunities. While not making a direct link, many of the early reviews of ASM certainly alluded to the industry's intimate association with poverty. Davidson (1993: 316), for example, argued that 'artisanal mining has become the principal livelihood for millions of miners and their families...[and that]...during periods of environmental and economic stress, it has met the needs of a much wider population, to whom it has provided the wherewithal sufficient to stave off further hardship'. Similarly, Jennings (1994: 12) noted that small-scale mining is generally characterized by 'poor working conditions... [with]...problems of safety and health and environmental degradation abound'. The link was officially recognized in Washington at the International Roundtable on Artisanal Mining, 17–19 May 1995, where, framed in the context of the World Bank's poverty alleviation mandate, it was noted that 'small-scale, informal miners – although they may be better off than many of their counterparts – are poor...to a large extent, informal mining is a poverty-driven activity' (Barry, 1996: 1).

ECOWAS provides an ideal platform for exploring further the link between poverty and ASM, and examining in greater depth many of the industry's pressing social and environmental problems, most of which continue to be poorly understood and inappropriately tackled. The unprecedented industry mechanization and privatization experienced in the region over the past 20 years has been responsible for significant redundancies, layoffs and rural displacement. According to the latest Human Development Report (UNDP, 2005), aside from Ghana and Togo, all of ECOWAS is characterized as 'low human development'. In fact, with the exception of Cape Verde and Nigeria, ECOWAS exclusively consists of Heavily Indebted Poor Countries (HIPC).[1] The dire unemployment situation now seen throughout most of the region has been instrumental in fuelling the rapid, and often anarchic, expansion of informal, small-scale activities, particularly mining.

Recognizing the severity of the unemployment problem, several West African governments have come to acknowledge that if formalized effectively, ASM not only has the potential to alleviate significant rural poverty but at the same time, can also make valuable contributions to foreign exchange. The host of ASM support projects, regulatory frameworks, policies and infrastructure implemented in the region in recent years is testament to this realization. Key examples include the following:

- In 2004, the Federal Government of Nigeria and the World Bank negotiated a US$120 million loan to assist with the development of the country's solid mineral sector. The work will establish, among other things, a basis for poverty reduction and rural economic renewal in selected areas of the country through the development of ASM.
- In Ghana, significant work has been undertaken in the areas of geo-prospecting, institutional strengthening and licensing for ASM as part of the US$13.7 million Mining Sector Development and Environment Project, launched in 1995. The outputs of the project, which include an assortment of support services, today serve as benchmarks for neighbouring countries working to regularize ASM.
- UN agencies operating in Sierra Leone and Liberia, locations long victimized by civil violence, a chief driving force of which was artisanal diamond extraction and illicit sales, are now working on a limited basis to help regularize indigenous diamond mining regions.
- In Burkina Faso, some US$4.2 million from the US$20 million World Bank Mining Sector Capacity Building and Environmental Management Project (18.6% of the total project cost) has been budgeted for regularizing ASM. Funds have been, or are in the process of being, used for studying the socioeconomic, environmental and geological characteristics of ASM communities; establishing training centres for miners; and disseminating improved equipment.

Worldwide, there has been a propensity to implement ASM support from the top down rather than the bottom-up, which, more often than not, has rendered promising projects ineffective: without careful analysis of target populations, operations and local conditions, how can appropriate technologies and industry support services be designed? The aforementioned and parallel development work being planned in West Africa stands to suffer the same fate if community issues continue to be dismissed. Using the case of ECOWAS, this book aims to facilitate a radical change in the way in which policies and support services are implemented for ASM by underscoring the importance of improving the understanding of target populations, local settings and industry dynamics. The book brings together a rare collection of country case studies on ASM, the research for which was undertaken by individuals who are based in the field and/or who have received subsistence funding for their work. It is research of this nature that donor agencies and advising consultants continue to overlook, research which is a prerequisite to strengthening ongoing and planned industry support.

It is instructive, however, to first provide an overview of the location under study and introduce the issues being examined. This section of the book is devoted to this task, providing vital background analysis and raising important topics for discussion. The first chapter of this section (Chapter 2), by Christopher Hilson, provides an essential historical overview of West Africa, painting a picture of how we arrived at this point and laying the foundation for subsequent chapters. In Chapter 3, Gavin Hilson revisits general discussions on ASM and impoverishment, examining how poverty has propelled the expansion of informal mining in West Africa. Framing the discussion against the background of theoretical analysis on this issue, the author also explains why the region's ASM operators remain trapped in a life of poverty.

For readers unfamiliar with the social and environmental problems associated with ASM, Matthew Gibb provides a comprehensive review of key industry sustainable development issues, with emphasis on West Africa, in Chapter 4. The chapter brings together some of the key contemporary arguments, debates and definitional challenges surrounding informal mining, focusing upon its socioeconomic influences and impacts on the physical environment. In Chapter 5, Sandra Pardie and Gavin Hilson look at how an increased dependence on mercury, used to amalgamate gold, has fuelled further poverty in West African ASM communities. The authors argue that regional governments have seriously overlooked mercury's role as an agent of poverty.

In Chapter 6, Richard Amankwah and C. Anim-Sackey examine one of the most serious problems plaguing the ASM sector today: conflicts between illegal, informal operators and large-scale mining companies. The authors identify causes of such conflict, describe some of the initiatives being taken by certain large-scale miners operating in West Africa to improve relations with small-scale miners, and prescribe recommendations for improving relations between these parties. The final chapter of this section (Chapter 7), by Karen MacDonald, analyzes the aims and scope of international environmental and human rights law in relation to ASM communities in West Africa. It provides an interesting insight on the potential use and application of key agreements from these areas in reducing regional poverty and ameliorating interrelated social and environmental impacts in the sector.

The discussions and issues raised in this section of the book set the stage for the country case study analysis presented in Parts 2 and 3.

CHAPTER 2

Poverty and economic development in West Africa: a historical analysis

Christopher J. Hilson

To recap centuries of the development and emergence of what is today an extremely profitable region for multinational mining corporations would not only be overwhelming but rather inappropriate in terms of the greater purpose of this book. All aspects of world history encompass a loose series of events which can be strung together to represent a seemingly arbitrary interconnectedness; this situation renders itself no different. The objective of this chapter, therefore, is to briefly review the development of North–South trade in West Africa, with emphasis upon mineral extraction, and the rise of the ASM sector. The overall aim of the chapter is to provide an overview of the development of the mining sector, framed in the context of trade and economic policy, in West Africa, the geographical area of focus of this book. Following this historical analysis, Chapter 3 analyzes in greater detail the link between poverty and ASM in contemporary West Africa.

The West African economy in the early nineteenth century

During the nineteenth century, West Africa experienced a series of political developments that resulted in increasing political and economic integration with the respective 'occupying' European settlements. Though formal colonialism occurred in the 1880s and 1890s, terming European involvement as 'occupation' prior to this period is inappropriate.

A series of French, British, Dutch and Danish trading forts were scattered along the coast at the time, but much of the West African interior was still under indigenous control (most of present-day Ghana was under Ashanti suzerainty around 1800). In their detailed account of West African history, Ajayi and Crowder (1987: 380) explain that 'the concept of the stagnant "subsistence economy"...has been more or less jettisoned by those concerned with early West African history' and that 'archaeological evidence...confirms the existence of surpluses in pastoral and agricultural societies'. Indigenous West African manufacturing was fully functional and it is widely recognized that the success of these economies had been longlived up to this point. A complex system of trade was at full capacity by the mid-nineteenth century and had produced elaborate social stratification and labour specialization.

Abolition and economic change in the West African economy

The nineteenth century was a unique phase in the history of West Africa, as it marked the division between the period of the transatlantic slave trade and that of colonial rule. In this sense, it is more of a transition phase, characterized by the gradual infusion of abolition. The first attempt at abolition initiated by British legislature in 1807, which made it illegal for the kingdom's citizens to engage in the slave trade, was not highly successful in practice (Law, 1995: 32–5). Moreover, centuries of trade had fostered a deeply rooted and sophisticated system of exchange (both indigenous and Afro-European); consequently, the period often experienced higher levels of trade than before 1807. The French followed with a similar declaration in 1818. Despite initial discouragements to the industry, it had minimal effect: 482 French slaving ships sailed to West Africa between 1814 and 1834 (Klein, 1998: 19).

The development of West African indigenous economies during the precolonial period was a direct extension of the slave trade: due to the intricate Afro-European network of the export of slaves both within the continent and across the Atlantic, these communities traded in exchange for European industrial goods. In this manner, while satisfying European demand for labour in the New World and indigenous demand for manufactured goods (a relentlessly developing industry in the West), the trade effectively subverted the development of any sort of African secondary or manufacturing industry. Most notable is the reality that African chiefs regarded slaving as the most profitable means of purchasing modern European arms.

The impact of abolition on the development of West African economies in the nineteenth century can be seen in the second phase of its implementation: what scholars have denoted the emergence of 'legitimate commerce' (Ajayi and Crowder, 1987: 383). Precolonial economic interaction in Africa can be separated into the following two basic spheres: an interior and often termed continental economy, which here is of lesser significance but existed nonetheless as a multitude of complex relationships between *jihad* states and interior chiefdoms; and a coastal economy, which by mid-century was experiencing a strong second anti-slave movement partly as an evangelical movement but more directly as an economic flexion of the European industrial muscle. Historians call it the period of legitimate commerce, not merely as a suggestion that slave-based trade was in exclusive remission (on the contrary, the exchange of slaves would continue well into the twentieth century) but based on the emergence of a coastal Afro-European exchange of justifiable commodities such as coal, salt and cocoa. Law (1995: 3) underscores the importance of this new legitimate commerce: 'military chiefs who had dominated the slave trade were less able to control the new trade in agricultural produce, because the latter was readily open to participation by small-scale traders and farmers whereas the slave trade strengthened the elite, the peanut trade put money, and thus guns, in the hands of peasants'.

This period, therefore, rather than the period of colonial rule, facilitated the beginnings of the modern economic history of West Africa: it was now a short step for West African small-scale producers of cocoa, tin and gold to be linked to the world economy. The slave trade was a large-scale operation for entrepreneurs and rulers of great states in the western Sudan; the emergence of a new side to the coastal economies enabled family labourers and small-scale producers to be much more far-reaching than the Atlantic slave trade ever had been (Klein, 1998: 1–3; Law, 1995: 11–15). The success and growth of small-scale operations in the mid-1800s can be explained by cheap and readily available land and the small quantity of venture capital required for opening new operations. Moreover, agriculture and mine sites employed family labour and featured simple, traditional tools. There was little scope to engage in economies of scale amid a population starved of appropriate technology and industrial machinery (Hopkins, 1973: 125). Overall, the conditions provided few barriers to entry for farmers wishing to engage in small-scale operations to a point where, generally speaking, cash crops were worked by large numbers of migrant labourers and land was for the first time beginning to gather commercial value (Ajayi and Crowder, 1987: 384).

The West African economy and the basis of colonialism

The discussion of the new economy must be understood alongside its impact on the implementation of formal colonial rule, or what can be deemed the imposing influence it generated on behalf of the European powers; moreover, there was visible impact on both indigenous and expatriate communities, which caused formal colonial rule to become an eventuality.

First, indigenous traders formerly engaged in slave export developed an affinity for trade in legitimate goods, developing alongside the aforementioned expanding community of small-scale producers. The latter's growing power with respect to the export trade cultivated an overall increase in their political significance, whereby a broad capability of economic meritocracy was surfacing towards the second half of the century. This new capacity is personified by the notorious Ja Ja, a former slave who rose to establish his own kingdom and became a figure of extreme economic significance in Bonny in the 1860s (Law, 1995: 1, 5). The resulting situation, unquestionably part of the extremely intricate web of indigenous society, was one of expanding social mobility and importance granted to small-scale producers. Rulers now sought the wealth of these farmers and miners in the form of taxes or rather subsidies which, barring any disagreement from the newly emerging capitalist class, contributed to the overall expansion of indigenous states. This gave rise to a good range of opportunities for African traders in that their labour resources could be widely employed in the small-scale mining and harvesting sectors. For example, their efforts could be used in the allocation of exports and the eventual distribution of manufactured goods. Hopkins (1973: 147) illustrates this increasingly expansive indigenous side of the economy: 'it might be useful to think of the economic aspects of this cycle in terms of the theory of the firm, whereby a successful company expands, takes over its rivals, and achieves a local monopoly, only to find that its dominance is undermined from within, as managers leave to start their own businesses, and challenged from outside, as new competitors move in to try and secure a share of the monopoly profit'.

For a while, it seemed that Europeans and African states could coexist, but the above account of economic development had foreign implications as well, namely in facilitating an influx of expatriates to West Africa in the late 1800s. Most notable are the contrasting origins of the newcomers with those of previous generations: where Europeans had once been explorers first and traders second, these arrivals were strictly for wholesale purposes (Hopkins, 1973: 148). One particular European-initiated development, the advent of the steam-ship, was greatly responsible for these arrivals. In 1851, the African Steamship Company was formed, followed by the British & African Steam Navigation Company in 1868 (Hopkins, 1973: 149). Similar developments were made at French posts with the formation of the Fabre-Fraissinet line in 1889. One illustration should be made, and that is that the increased volume of European traders on the coast did not assist them in trade. Trade occurred with a second development, the conversion of local currencies to metropolitan currencies, which enabled newcomers to immediately engage in exporting or importing (hitherto strange currencies had forced new traders to associate themselves with well-established firms in order to become both exporters and importers) (Carney, 1971: 236–9). Indigenous traders would now be strongly encouraged to deal in sterling or francs. Therefore, the prevailing increased European economic interests influenced local government (and, effectively, the governments in London, Paris and to a lesser extent, Berlin) and played a large role in establishing formal colonial rule. With the emergence of African traders of legitimate commerce, European interests were not served as they had been before; moreover, and for the purposes of this chapter, formal colonialism can be seen as the product of an emerging class of capitalist African small-scale producers.

Taxation and colonialism

By 1913, the French possessed the majority of what would become present-day Senegal, Burkina Faso, Guinea, Mali, Côte d'Ivoire, Niger and Benin; the British established their rule over roughly modern Ghana, Sierra Leone and Nigeria. It must be understood that during the years before the first world war (and, for obvious reasons, for a substantial time during that period), there was prolonged indecisive government, a direct consequence of European rule in a region about which they understood very little. The following two different types of government began emerging at this time. First, there was the French approach, characterized by a high degree of control by Paris over French administrative officers in the colonial hierarchy, and furthermore over African chiefs. Second was the British approach, characterized by indirect rule (developed by Frederick Lugard), whereby white administrative officers focused on maintaining peace, while natural rulers reserved the power to allocate tax revenues and administer local courts as per historical and cultural traditions.

In both colonial spheres, the trend was an overall shift from short-term military alliances to local administration by Europeans powers. Central to both governing powers' doctrine for colonialism was the self-help system of governance, as illustrated in Earl Grey's 1852 dictum that 'the surest test for soundness of measures for the improvement of an uncivilized people is that they should be self-supporting' (Hopkins, 1973: 190). There was doubtless a motive of imperial capitalization between these words, but nonetheless the principle of self-support was apparent throughout all of French and British West Africa during the colonial period, and, as such, local officials were required to generate revenue through taxes. It is not difficult to imagine that local taxation was a major topic of discussion throughout the period, especially from the African point of view. It was imposed in a threefold manner: indirect taxes on import-export trade, indirect taxes on railways and other government services, and direct taxes on village communities and individuals. As explained by Ajayi and Crowder (1987: 504), between 1895 and 1902, 15 per cent of tax revenues in French West Africa were spent on servicing debts, 26 per cent on administrative costs, with only 19 per cent going to local investment, agriculture and transport, which in turn impeded the development of local industries and infrastructure. In many cases, as in the Upper Senegal and Niger region, the need for revenue often disregarded the uneven distribution of resources. Communities unable to generate sufficient revenue based upon export and import levels became impoverished, a manifestation of higher direct taxation. Though in British West Africa, direct taxation was not implemented until 1919, import duties served as the largest source of a budget based on 33 per cent European salaries and 25 per cent education, health and transport services.

Innovation and colonial exploitation

Woolf (1968) explains that British and French imperialism in the early and mid-nineteenth century began respectively as spectacle and statement. Imperial growth for the British under Disraeli included such notions as dominion, power and prestige, and war, ships and men; in France, the acquisition of empire abroad translated as a declaration of recovery from the Napoleonic wars (1793–1815). However, from the 1880s and into the twentieth century, the label had completely changed: motives now became dominated by notions such as spheres of influence, and markets and tariffs.

As mentioned previously, before 1880, the economic environment was more favourable for African miners and farmers: markets were generally restricted, with indigenous small-scale producers generally flourishing in the absence of the steamship and the intervention of metropolitan currencies, which would come to largely favour expatriate firms (Hopkins, 1973: 203–4). The turn of the century initiated this period of colonial exploitation. As was the case in the nineteenth century, industrial innovations carved revolutionary change into the West African economy. This was manifested in the form of two major instruments of transportation. The first was major railways, developed in Senegal, the Gold Coast and Nigeria in the 1880s and 1890s and extending further inland. The second innovation was the expanding motor-vehicle industry, which provided for faster, cheaper and lighter vehicles. There were 16 motor vehicles in French West Africa in 1913; this number had reached 10,000 by 1940 (Hopkins, 1973: 195–7).

Expatriate firms and Europeans in general had hitherto been positioned primarily in the coastal region, reflecting the previous period of informal relations with the interior and more unfamiliar regions, and overall the reality that transportation was highly restricted. As one observer of early nineteenth-century West Africa put it, 'Europeans travel in two ways, either by sea in a canoe, or by land in a hammock' (McPhee, 1971: 106). The construction of roads and railways inland, however, subverted this reality as firms began setting up bases further inland, merely an extension of the consensus that inward expansion opened up potential for new trades (such as mining). In an attempt to consolidate the capital required for such inward movements, many small firms were driven out of business as the larger ones merged to a point where, by 1930, three large firms remained: the United Africa Company, the Compagnie Française de l'Afrique Occidentale and the Société Commerciale de l'Ouest Africain (Hopkins, 1973).

Essentially, what emerged out of these changes was an oligopoly of European firms (though it must be noted that these firms were still price-takers, and that their abilities to lower the costs of production through effective economies of scale yielded a substantially greater profit compared with that of small-scale producers). African traders were therefore slowly driven out of the import-export system, a product of the resulting smaller and a more interconnected West Africa. In addition, these oligopolies coordinated themselves with banks and shipping companies, making it essentially impossible for Africans to acquire loans or obtain credit. The situation presented itself as follows: infrastructure development was entirely paid for by the African worker through taxation, while expatriate firms benefited entirely from this development since construction was based upon resource-demand expectations in metropolitan centres. To worsen matters, expatriate amalgamation successfully isolated and excluded indigenous firms and small-scale producers, forcing migration to labour-intensive areas.

The emergence of West African mining companies in the twentieth century

It is against this background that the region's mining sector experienced unprecedented expansion during the late nineteenth and early twentieth centuries; however, two clarifications must be made. The first is that European involvement in the mining sector was relatively non-existent prior to colonial rule. As Hopkins (1973: 44) explains, although iron, gold and salt (primary minerals) and tin, copper and silver (secondary minerals) were mined on a recognizable scale during the precolonial period, these commodities were chiefly worked by indigenous operators and traders. In fact, European influence in this area at the time centred on stimulating the already existing and well-established small-scale mining industry and obtaining minerals through trade. Second, mineral distribution in West Africa is sparse and inconsistent. For example, iron ore deposits in the mid-twentieth century were dispersed along the western coast in Sierra Leone, Guinea and Liberia, but thinned noticeably eastward to Nigeria, at the confluence of the Niger and Benue rivers (Morgan and Pugh, 1969).

As mentioned earlier, the rise of legitimate commerce perpetuated the emergence of a new class of African traders, who made their presence felt on the world market. There is no doubt of the level of participation of indigenous traders in the mining sector in precolonial West Africa. Two basic reasons can be extracted for expatriate involvement in the mining sector. The first is that World War I exhausted world economies at a level never seen before. In this manner, the war accelerated the development of major industrial necessities, particularly coal, limestone, tin, manganese and bauxite. Moreover, with a decrease in overall European imports, African colonial administrators were forced to resort to greater exploitation of local resources. Second, it was the various technological influences that shaped the development of significant European mining interests by the time of colonial rule. Firms that desired to expand inland consolidated themselves with other firms, for very basic venture-capital necessities. With significant rail and automobile improvements, these inward expansions allowed for new resource discoveries, which precipitated the rise of multinational mining companies. Primary examples include: the Ashanti Goldfields Corporation (est. 1897), the Sierra Leone Development Corporation (est. 1929), the Consolidated African Selection Trust (est. 1932, later to become the Sierra Leone Selection Trust in 1935) and the Amalgamated Tin Mines of Nigeria Ltd (est. 1939). Had colonial policy regarding expatriate participation in the economy been more unenthusiastic, European involvement in the mining sector might have been largely offset. Moreover, as technological developments enabled expatriate interests to increase inland, colonial officials struggled to subvert these developments with the industrial necessities brought on by 1914. It can be said that the positive effects in extending the European presence inland could be seen in the discovery of new resources, among them coal and iron, both of which are essential to industrial development.

The West African economy during the interwar period

The period 1919–39 is often seen as the epitome of French and British colonial rule in West Africa: colonial domination through business administration. The period was characterized by African economic acquiescence in the face of European exploitation, as rebellions occurred less frequently and military superiority was generally accepted. Moreover, the latter was symbolized by a shift in colonial administration from military governance to civilian administration. This section of the chapter outlines the link between poverty and colonialism before independence, and therefore lays the foundation for examining present-day realities.

Economic and social policies can be used as evidence for illustrating the disadvantages granted to Africans during the interwar years. First, in the aftermath of European atrocities between 1914 and 1919, French and British administrators made it a priority to ensure that the majority of exports and imports of their colonies were transacted with the metropolitan country. The state of the colonial economy thus became represented by the level of exports and imports transacted with the home country, supplanting any traditional economic theories which measured economic productivity as a function of the total value of production in a region, measured in terms of GDP (Ajayi and Crowder, 1987: 594). A manifestation of this concept was visible in both countries' issuance of new forms of currency tied to their home currencies. This not only prevented any other country from trading with the colony (as is in the tradition of colonialism) but more importantly, forced African traders of all kinds to deal in these currencies (as tax collection required equivalencies in currencies backed by either sterling or francs). This tradition would continue into the period of independence (Church, 1966: 18–19). Second, liberal economic capabilities allowed expatriate interests to prosper at the expense of small-scale producers. This was largely seen in banking, navigation and judicial processes, all of which ensured control of the economy by expatriate firms. Earlier research has demonstrated the de facto existence of European oligopolies on the African continent. Ajayi and Crowder (1987: 529) illustrate further the control of domestic factors by foreign interests:

> These firms took action to ensure – through collusion concerning prices both of imports and exports, through agreements not to compete in one another's major spheres of interest and other monopolistic and discriminatory practices – that African businessmen were effectively eliminated from the import-export trade and that the African producer and consumer did not enjoy the benefit of a competitive market in relation to either the price of his exports or the price of the imported goods he bought.

Just as there had been few barriers to entry for African traders in legitimate commerce, so the emerging European powerhouse in West Africa dates back to this era of liberal trade policies which characterized colonialism. What cannot be ignored is the effect informal domination had in causing low wage rates; moreover, acting in a suspiciously monopolistic manner, firms effectively drove African competition out of the market and established lower, fixed wage rates. What worsened the situation was that colonial administrations fixed taxes such that they encouraged Africans to either increase cash-crop or mineral production, or seek employment from expatriate firms (Ajayi and Crowder, 1987).

A third link between West African poverty and colonialism can be seen in the collection and transportation of minerals and crops. Previously, the transportation of goods was exclusively in the hands of Africans, who knew the regions well, spoke the local languages and could therefore negotiate wherever required. This role made a gradual transition to expatriates, and to a lesser extent, Levantines, Indians and Greeks. The West African Shipping Conference, which broadly functioned as a monopoly of the shipping and transportation industry, extended higher rates for shipping goods to non-members (also an example of price-fixing previously mentioned). With the growing demand for goods within the African continent (a direct impact of expanding methods and modes of transportation), traders operating outside these groups gained little benefit from these developments.

Fourth, all efforts were made to reduce African involvement (at the firm and small-scale level) in processing mineral and cash-crop harvests. When railroads and roads extended into the interior regions of West Africa, what occurred essentially was a resource drain from the interior regions to the coast, with little or no encouragement for the development of local manufacturers. This was basically a replication of the patterns of African industrial development in the nineteenth century – or lack thereof – which was hindered by trade with Europe for industrial goods. Notable examples of such discouraging practices with respect to the development of secondary industries include the groundnut and textile industries. In the case of the former, farmers were discouraged from removing shells locally on the pretext that it could be done more efficiently elsewhere; the latter industry, a hallmark of the traditional West African economy, was opposed on the basis that cheaper imported textiles could be obtained from the metropolitan countries. Higher living standards were visibly offset by the reality that profits were claimed and held in offshore accounts.

Ghana, independence and gold: a case study

The preceding discussion provides insight into the economic side of repression at the height of European colonialism. Overall, there is scarce evidence to suggest that colonial officials sought to develop the West African economy to the benefit of Africans. The greater purpose of this chapter has been to sketch economic development in West Africa from the mid-nineteenth century onwards. Moreover, it has recaptured the general trends at the expatriate and small-scale level in the context of formal colonial rule. This case study focuses on the emergence of the gold-mining industry in Ghana in the 1950s and 1960s, setting the stage for discussions later in the book.

The major theme of economic independence in Ghana can be summarized by increased state intervention in the economy. Herbst (1993: 19–20) identifies the independence period in Ghana with the worldwide trend of state intervention, which characterized the 1960s. This was obviously manifested in monetary policy. Though the early years of independence witnessed a retaining of assets backed 100 per cent in sterling, by the 1960s a state-owned bank had been established, the Ghana Commercial Bank, which broke into the monopoly enjoyed by Barclays Bank DCO and the Standard Bank of West Africa (Carney, 1961: 63–5). In this sense, independence initiated a trend of monetary sovereignty, in which by the early 1960s a fiduciary component of £12 million had been created in the money supply. In mining, similar trends prevailed. At the time of independence in 1957, gold mining was still largely in the hands of foreign companies, which included such foreign enterprises as Amalgamated Banket Areas, Ariston Gold Mines, Ashanti Goldfields, Bremang Gold Dredging, Ghana Main Reef and Konongo Goldmines. However, gold production in Ghana had gradually declined before independence. As Hilson (2002g) explains, in 1950, the value of the gold output in the-then Gold Coast was merely two-thirds of what it had been 10 years earlier; furthermore, whereas 50 gold-mining operations were functional in the 1930s, only 11 were operating at the time of independence. What this meant was that state intervention in a now independent economy was necessary in order to salvage the remains of a wounded gold industry. By 1966, the majority of the gold-mining operations were nationalized to a point where, with the passing of the Minerals Act (Act 123) in 1962, Ghanaian minerals were formally declared the property of the country and controlled by the presidency (Hilson, 2002g).

What was at work during this period was the shift from tension between large-scale firms and small-scale miners during the colonial period, to similar conflicts between nationalized and foreign enterprises and small-scale miners in the era of independence. It could be effectively argued that governmental bodies, which have channelled most of their energies into revitalizing and encouraging large-scale mining in recent years, have greatly overlooked the needs of Ghanaian small-scale miners. Moreover, small-scale mining today exhibits many of the same sufferings it has experienced in the past. Accounting for a small proportion of overall gold exports in Ghana, the industry is seldom regarded as legitimate, despite its formal recognition in 1989, when the Small-Scale Gold Mining Law was implemented by the government. In 1990, the state-operated Precious Minerals and Marketing Corporation made 30 per cent of its US$20.4 million in sales from gold bought from small-scale operators (Berry, 1995). Though the issue is largely cultural, it has severe implications for small-scale miners whose immediate source of wealth largely depends on extracting gold. The ongoing disputes between large-scale and small-scale miners are at the most basic level disagreements over property rights and land use. In addition, as governmental and international agencies' interests lie largely in further opening up West African economies to European and American large-scale companies, small-scale miners are experiencing similar links between poverty and their trade as in previous generations.

Conclusion

In West Africa, the causal link between poverty and small-scale mining can be traced back to colonial rule. The nineteenth century witnessed the emergence of a new class of Africans capable of making their presence felt on the world markets in many industries. The era of colonial rule formalized relations between expatriate firms and governments in the region, rendering it increasingly difficult for African miners and farmers to prosper. Similarly, with inland European expansion, this period ushered in the emergence of large-scale mining operations. At root here are the same disputes which exist today between large-scale and small-scale miners, an issue examined further in Chapter 6. This chapter has provided essential background on the link between poverty and small-scale mining operations evident today in West Africa. It sets the stage for the analysis of poverty and ASM in contemporary West Africa presented in Chapter 3.

CHAPTER 3
Poverty and artisanal mining in West Africa

Gavin M. Hilson

This chapter explores the link between poverty and informal mining in West African states. According to crude census estimates, West Africa's ASM population now exceeds 1 million. In Ghana, an estimated 300,000 men, women and children are involved in gold, diamond, sand and salt mining at the artisanal level; in Mali, gold washing has been practised for centuries and remains a primary occupation for as many as 1,200,000 people; and in Niger, the total ASM workforce is reported to be about 442,000, of whom at least 250,000 are youths aged under 18 (Aryee, 2003a; Keita, 2001; ILO, 1999). As is the case throughout the developing world, in West Africa, ASM is predominantly a poverty-driven occupation. According to Grätz (2003a: 198), in Northern Benin 'by and large, miners benefit from gold mining because there are only few possibilities of earning a cash income in this region'. Similarly, in Ghana small-scale mining is prevalent in areas which, in addition to exhibiting high levels of poverty, also feature a shortage of alternative employment opportunities (Aryee, 2003a: 403). It is against this background that this chapter examines the state of ASM in West Africa, and explains why its participants remain *trapped* in a life of perpetual poverty.

Poverty in West Africa: an overview

In the 1980s, a number of publications emerged (Piachaud, 1987; Walker, 1987) that highlighted the challenges associated with defining and measuring poverty universally. Hagenaars and Devos (1988: 211) attributed this problem to the inherent difficulties associated with identifying with precision the poor segments of a society and the inability of policymakers to pinpoint effectively the aggregation of its income gaps – a necessary prerequisite for constructing indices capable of measuring disparities in wealth. However, the authors reasoned that most definitions of poverty emphasize one or more of the following themes: having less than an objectively defined, absolute minimum; having less than others in society; and the feeling that there are insufficient resources to succeed.

The World Bank's 'Understanding and responding to poverty' website (2004a) furthers this view, noting that poverty is 'hunger... is lack of shelter...is being sick and not being able to see a doctor...is not being able to go to school and not knowing how to read...is not having a job, is fear for the future, living one day at a time...is losing a child to illness brought about by unclean water...is powerlessness, lack of representation and freedom'.

In accordance with the Bank's assertion that poverty 'has many faces', this chapter adopts a broad definition in its assessment of the relationship between ASM and impoverishment in West Africa. For the purposes of the discussion, poverty is assumed to be any barrier to prosperity and conditions characterized by a lack of resources and opportunities, a lack of empowerment, and a shortage of support systems.

Poverty is now rampant throughout most of Africa (see Table 3.1); in 1991, the continent's combined debt was estimated to be US$176 billion (Logan and Mengisteab, 1993). Nearly half of Africa's population subsists on a daily wage of less than US$1, some 200 million people suffer from malnutrition, and only 60 per cent have access to fresh drinking water (Van Koppen, 2003). In sub-Saharan Africa in particular, few, if any, countries are free of persistent poverty which, over the past 15–20 years, has been exacerbated by a number of geopolitical and socioeconomic factors, including HIV/AIDS, violent civil warfare and depleted foreign exchange. As is furthermore pointed out by Rukuni (2002), the region is characterized by a heavy food imbalance, widespread environmental degradation, excessive drought and deforestation. Conditions have particularly deteriorated in the rural regions of sub-Saharan Africa, where poverty levels are now 50–77 per cent (Karekezi, 2002).

In ECOWAS, a geopolitical region which occupies 25 per cent of Africa's land area, contains 34 per cent of its population and contributes 15 per cent of its GDP (Jones, 2002), poverty has induced, among other things, widespread migration. As Lydie and Robinson (1998: 471–3) explain, patterns of circulatory migration are now commonplace throughout West Africa, fuelled largely by mass unemployment and/or government persecution:

> In Burkina Faso, it has been estimated that about 60 per cent of men have been migrant labourers at some time in their working lives. In the region of Ziguinchor in Senegal, 80 per cent of men aged 18–40 go to the coast each year to find work. In Niger, between 25 percent and 80 per cent of men aged 18–40 go to the coast each year to find work...In West Africa...Liberia [had] been stricken by civil war since 1989. More than 800,000 of the 2.4 million inhabitants have fled to exile, mainly to Guinea, Côte d'Ivoire, Sierra Leone, Ghana and Nigeria.

Persistently poor conditions have also induced a major brain drain in West Africa. In his comprehensive study of West African states, Adepoju (2002: 6) examines this problem at length, noting that 'highly skilled migrants, including doctors, paramedical personnel, nurses, teachers, engineers, scientists and technologists have moved from Ghana, and recently Nigeria, to virtually all African countries, attracted by relatively higher salaries and better working and living conditions'.

Table 3.1 Indicators of social and economic development in selected West African countries

Country	GDP per head (US$), 2002	% of population earning <US$2 per day, 1990–2001	Adult illiteracy rate (%)	Prevalence of child malnutrition (% of children under 5)	Access to fresh water (%)	Ranking on UNDP Human Development Index (out of 175 countries)
*Burkina Faso	220	85.8	75.2	34	42	173
*Côte d'Ivoire	610	49.4	50.3	21	81	161
Ghana	270	78.5	27.3	25	73	129
*Guinea	410	N/A	N/A	33	48	157
*Mali	240	90.6	73.6	N/A	65	172
*Mauritania	340	68.7	59.3	32	37	154
*Niger	170	85.3	83.5	40	59	174
*Nigeria	290	90.8	34.6	41	62	152
*Senegal	470	67.8	61.7	18	78	156
Togo	270	N/A	41.6	25	54	141

Sources: UNDP, 2003a; World Bank, 2004b.
*Denotes 'Low Human Development'.

As is the case in most of the developing world, throughout ECOWAS, poverty has been exacerbated by Structural Adjustment Programmes (SAPs). Shortly after declaring independence, a number of West African states experienced countless military *coups d'états*, extended periods of economic mismanagement and widespread political corruption, which collectively caused their economies and social service infrastructure to rapidly deteriorate. Moreover, worsened terms of trade led to 'shortages of foreign exchange, production bottlenecks, and negative economic growth' (Peabody, 1996: 824). On the brink of financial collapse, the majority of West African governments negotiated loans with the international financial institutions (IFIs), that is, the IMF and the World Bank.

The monies dispensed by the IFIs to developing countries in recent decades, however, have generally had several conditions attached. These have included commitments to devalue currencies; expand production, particularly exported goods (in turn shifting labour and capital from non-traded to traded commodities); and change government institutions and economic policies, or simply divest state-owned operations, and concurrently promote privatization and foreign ownership (Peabody, 1996: 824). In 1980 alone, the IFIs orchestrated the implementation of 15 adjustment programmes in Africa, forged an additional 156 agreements with continental governments in the 1980s, and oversaw another 94 partial monetary allocations between 1990 and 1996 (Riddell, 1997).

As Crisp and Kelly (1999: 534) explain, proponents of SAPs have argued that reforms 'return developing economies to growth and check exorbitant rates of inflation': the freeing of exchange rates should decrease the costs of goods produced for the international market; devaluation should curtail imports; and financial liberalization, trade liberalization and deregulation are expected to facilitate increased private-sector investment. Although this formula appears prescriptive, theoretically, for resurrecting an economy, the liberalization policies implemented under reform have failed to empower low-income groups, in many cases, lowering country living standards overall. The rapidity with which SAPs have been implemented throughout sub-Saharan Africa in particular has resulted in significant job losses and diminished government control. Moreover, by hastily divesting state assets and privatizing large segments of industry, governments have essentially put their economies in the hands of foreign multinationals.

Geo-Jaja and Mangum (2001: 33) argue that overall, the experiences with SAPs in sub-Saharan Africa 'comprise another of a series of expensive, nonlocalized, inadequate, and inappropriate development strategies imposed as an experiment...leading to dependency and underdevelopment, and culminating in unemployment and impoverishment'. In Nigeria, for example, the Shagari government negotiated a loan with the IMF in the 1980s because of the growing crisis in its economy, brought on by decreased oil prices and fiscal mismanagement; IMF executives demanded the implementation of a number of policies before the loan was awarded (Walker, 2000: 155). These included reduced government spending, privatization of public sector assets, liberalized trade through the removal of tariffs, and removal of subsidies and government controls on imports. These changes, however, eventually resulted in the dissolution of the Nigerian Cocoa Board, in turn causing a price war between Nigerian and non-native (Syrian and Lebanese) exporters, who tried to gain control of the cocoa trade. The cocoa boom of 1987–8 was largely offset by a heightened inflationary environment, increased prices of farm implements and expensive labour, all of which were brought on by the SAP. Furthermore, at the conclusion of the cocoa boom, many farmers found it difficult financially to maintain their operations.

In Côte d'Ivoire, which had the highest debt per head in sub-Saharan Africa in the early 1990s, attempts to restore macroeconomic imbalance during the first phase of its adjustment programme (1981–7) plunged the economy into recession. As Ridler (1993) explains, under reform, the country experienced a decline in its terms of trade: the index figure of 110 in 1985 fell to 100 in 1987 and to 80 in 1990, in response to world prices for cocoa and coffee, two of its major exports. The SAP has had a significant impact on farmers' welfare, and in the country as a whole, real household expenditure declined by over 30 per cent over the 1985–8 period, during which time the fraction of the population that was poor rose from 30 per cent to 45.9 per cent (Grootaert, 1995). The

Ivorian rice economy was also undermined by an overvalued exchange rate, resulting in 'high rates of implicit taxation of producers due to official pricing policies that effectively subsidised consumption of cheap import rice', in turn leading to increased rice imports (Jutting, 2000: 68).

In Ghana, as explained by Owusu (2001: 389), 'workers' salaries have not kept pace with the devaluation and inflation' during the adjustment period. As is further explained by Hutchful (2002: 90), total employment in the large- and medium-scale formal sector (enterprises with 30 or more employees) has decreased considerably since the inauguration of the SAP. Employment in the sector, which was 464,000 in 1985, fell to 394,000 in 1987, and even further to 186,000 in 1991, 'a decline of almost 60 per cent in five or six years'. Policy reforms in the agricultural sector, which have 'focused preponderantly on rehabilitation of the cocoa industry and reform of its marketing system' (Hutchful, 2002: 67), have resulted in the elimination of some 80,000 job positions on the Cocoa Board alone. Moreover, schemes allegedly put in place to improve efficiency in the public sector have also had a devastating effect on job creation and levels of employment: between 41,000 and 45,000 civil servants were immediately 'redeployed' (29,000 were dismissed in 1988, and the remaining, in 1989), over 20,000 state-enterprise employees were laid off, and hundreds of private-sector employees lost textile and manufacturing jobs as a result of import liberalization (Weissman, 1990: 1626).

Mining, structural adjustment and poverty in West Africa

The mining sector has featured prominently in the SAPs implemented in a number of countries in sub-Saharan Africa, including Ghana (gold), Guinea (bauxite), Tanzania (gold) and Zambia (copper). In the 1980s and 1990s, numerous state-owned mines in the region were exorbitantly inefficient because of acute capital shortages and prolonged use of inappropriate technology. Policymakers at the IFIs, therefore, advised certain African governments to privatize mines; many became convinced that the liberalization of mineral exports would rapidly resurrect their economies. Since 1990, the World Bank alone has administered more than US$2.75 billion in loans and guarantees to African governments in support of projects emphasizing the liberalization and deregulation of the extractive industries (Pegg, 2003).

This financing notwithstanding, there is growing consensus that the privatization of state-owned mines and accompanying expansion has failed to sufficiently raise living standards in sub-Saharan Africa; the evidence for this claim is compelling. For West Africa, analysis by Weber-Fahr (2002) shows that the mining countries that have opened their mineral economies to foreign investment recorded minuscule GDP per capita growth during the 1990s (Table 3.2). Subsequent analysis by Ross (2001) and Pegg (2003) shows that the loans awarded to the governments of sub-Saharan Africa for mining projects have caused protracted indebtedness. Today, 34 of the region's countries are classified as HIPC by the Bank.

Overall, the mines developed and redeveloped in West Africa under reform have failed to generate sufficient downstream economic growth and jobs. In broader terms, this phenomenon – namely, the inverse correlation between economic growth and natural resources abundance in many developing countries – is known as the 'resource curse'. As Mikesell (1997: 192) explains, the resource curse is paradoxical because mass production of natural resources provides immediate foreign exchange, is generally the initial source of all development, attracts foreign capital and skills, and provides raw materials for processing and a market for manufactured products. Apart from experiencing tiny economic growth since implementing reforms, in the West African countries that have privatized their mining sectors, including Ghana, Guinea, Mali, Niger and Burkina Faso, the resource curse, manifested as a series of resource booms, has caused real exchange rates to rise, and labour and capital to migrate to booming mineral industries from other potentially productive sectors.

In revising their codes for the purpose of attracting foreign investors, West African governments have been advised by IFI policymakers to emphasize the following:

- Security of tenure: ensuring that a holder of mineral rights is provided guaranteed access to a parcel of land for a reasonable period of time, has exclusive entitlement to the minerals within that plot and has the right to transfer exploration rights.
- System for granting mining titles: implementation of a systematic process for awarding mining titles.
- Maintaining an open-title registry: the requirement of the titles registry to be open to the public, which would enable private investors to readily determine available land.
- Environmental issues: commitment to environment protection and regulation.
- Competitive and stable fiscal regime: the specific type of fiscal regime a country adopts is imperative, as it directly affects each party's share of the benefits derived from the minerals being exploited.

Critics such as Campbell (2003a, 2003b), however, argue that such changes made to mineral policy have in most cases created too attractive an investment climate for foreign investors, delivering considerably fewer benefits to the local economy. For example, in Ghana, although reforms have facilitated a sevenfold increase in gold production in the past 20 years, an estimated 71 per cent of extracted product and accompanying revenues now lie in offshore accounts (Campbell, 2003a). In Burkina Faso, codes have 'reduced corporate taxes on mining companies, and exempted mining equipment and materials from import duties for the duration of the development phase and through the third year of commercial production' (Pegg, 2003: 19). The mine taxation scheme now in place in Burkina Faso, which features a contract tax for commercial and industrial professionals (IMFPC), an employer and apprenticeship tax (4 per cent levy on wages for nationals and 8 per cent for expatriates) and a 2.5 per cent building and property tax, allows 'for exemption [from these taxes] for the first half of a mining project's life, up to a maximum of seven years' (Forster and Bills, 2002: 198). In neighbouring Mali, the government has made a concerted effort to model its mining code after that of Ghana's. The country's SAP 'produced a revised tax code that exempts foreign mining companies from taxes on profits for five to eight years, depending on the size of their investment' (Pegg, 2003: 19). The revised mining codes in Burkina Faso, Mali and Ghana all offer a low royalty rate of 3 per cent.

In Liberia, a series of tax breaks have also been implemented to attract foreign investment in the mining sector. As explained by Elder (2002), mine production royalties have been set relatively low (3–10%), US dollar offshore escrow accounts are permitted to foreign mining companies, and low annual surface rental rates have been established (US$0.80/acre). In Guinea, the national SAP 'coincided with negotiations during 1985–7 to restructure the pricing formula for exports of unprocessed bauxite' (Campbell and Clapp, 1995: 431), and through restructuring, an export levy of US$13 per metric tonne on bauxite ore was removed. These new mining agreements have made the Guinean economy more susceptible to fluctuations in the international aluminium market, and have reduced taxation payments in the medium term.

The perpetual expansion of predominantly foreign-owned large-scale mining operations has made it exceedingly challenging for indigenous artisanal and small-scale mining groups to secure viable plots of land. In recent years, West African governments have sought to formalize resident artisanal mining activities. Policies and licensing arrangements for artisanal mining, the participants of which hitherto have not been required to adhere to any regulatory structure, are, however, extremely bureaucratic, in many cases further marginalizing rural communities. It is becoming increasingly apparent that such schemes were implemented as part and parcel of policy strategies aimed at increasing investors' confidence by demonstrating to prospective large-scale mining companies that measures were being taken to regulate perceived chaotic artisanal mining activities.

Table 3.2 GDP growth in selected West African mining countries

Country	Relevance of mining for exports, 1990–9 (%)	Average GDP/per head growth, 1990–9 (%)
Guinea	84.7	1.42
Niger	70.6	− 1.50
Sierra Leone	50.0	− 6.31
Mauritania	46.0	0.55
Mali	40.0	0.69
Togo	37.7	− 1.27
Ghana	34.0	1.55
Senegal	10.3	0.53

Source: Weber-Fahr, 2002: 17.

Artisanal mining and poverty in West Africa

Experts are in general agreement that the most rudimentary mineral extraction activities in developing countries are driven by poverty. Labonne (2003: 131), for example, argues that 'because artisanal mining is largely driven by poverty, it has grown as an economic activity, complementing more traditional forms of rural subsistence earnings'. The seminal report of the Mining, Minerals, and Sustainable Development (MMSD) Project, 'Breaking New Ground', similarly notes that ASM is a 'livelihoods strategy adopted primarily in rural areas [and] in many cases...represents the most promising, if not the only, income opportunity available' (MMSD, 2002a: 314).

It was Nöetstaller (1996) who first conceived the idea of the poverty-ASM nexus, maintaining that artisanal miners were, in fact, trapped in a vicious cycle of poverty exacerbated by the regulatory failure, impoverished policy and social instability that has intensified under reform. Gilam (1999) has since updated Nöetstaller's original diagram (see Figure 3.1) for the purpose of framing the debate in the context of sustainable livelihoods. It is against this background that the discussion that follows explores the link between poverty and artisanal mining in West African states; in doing so, each of the factors featured in Nöetstaller's graph is examined and expanded upon. The analysis demonstrates that in West Africa, SAPs have not only driven an increasing number of individuals to take up artisanal mining as an occupation – a direct consequence of employment reductions in other segments of the economy – but have also further marginalized indigenous mining communities, even in cases where regulatory frameworks and support services have been implemented specifically for small-scale mining.

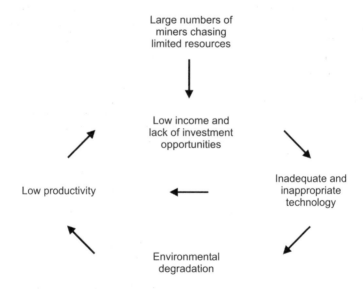

Figure 3.1 Depiction of the poverty-artisanal mining trap *Source*: Gilam, 1999.

Large numbers of miners chasing limited resources

As is the case throughout much of the developing world, in West Africa, artisanal mining – particularly, precious metals and gemstone extraction – is seen as a 'rush' activity. Experts often compare the chaotic unregulated gold and diamond rushes of the recent past to the migration patterns of the opportunistic gold diggers of the old American West.

Despite many claims to the contrary, artisanal miners have since become less anarchic in their pursuits of economic deposits. In West Africa, this is perhaps best exemplified by the degree of organization exhibited by so-called illegal mining contingents. For example, in the Perma Region of North-Western Benin, 'miners work in teams headed by a team leader, *chef d'équipe, chef de trou* or *patron* who has the informal right to exploit a shaft or a certain plot of land' – a right which 'is simply appropriated without any official license for the period of exploitation' (Grätz, 2003a: 195). Keita (2001: 12–13) alludes to similar circumstances in Mali:

> From the outside, gold washing appears to be an unorganized or even anar-chic activity. In fact, gold washing follows closely the organizational forms of village community and family structures...based on a set of customary prescriptions accepted by everyone [which] form coherent and original systems. Their originality is deeply marked by the community spirit, which is a vital element for customary rule as a source of law. Sites have their own regulations that all gold washers accept in advance when they come to settle there. Access to sites is open to all, on condition that they respect the regulations in force. Violations are subject to sanction. Characterized by customary practices, gold washing is so rigorous that any offence committed on the site is mercilessly punished. The following activities are forbidden on working sites: sex and theft; access of shoe-repairers and introduction of dogs; work on sites on Mondays.

Improved organization is also evident among the transient illegal *galamsey* mining populations of Ghana, which are comprised of a series of small gangs, each featuring a gang leader and a network of labourers with designated specific tasks (Hilson and Potter, 2003).

Nöetstaller's inclusion of the criterion 'large numbers of miners chasing a limited resource' in his poverty model was in all likelihood in reference to artisanal operators migrating chaotically to land possessing abundant reserves of gold and precious stones. However, findings from research undertaken on ASM over the past 10 years suggest that it is the unavailability of land, and not the deposit itself, that represents the limiting factor in this context. Specifically, under adjustment, the demarcation of concessions to predominantly foreign-owned large-scale mining operations has restricted the movement of indigenous opportunistic artisans, hence limiting their access to economic mineral deposits. In Ghana, the location of the first SAPs implemented in sub-Saharan Africa, hundreds of concessions have been awarded to mineral exploration and extraction companies: at the end of 1998, some 237 companies were prospecting for gold alone, and another 23 had been granted mining leases (Aryee, 2001). As a direct result of the growth experienced in the large-scale mining sector, numerous communities have been uprooted, particularly in the Tarkwa locality, as well as hundreds of previously undisturbed *galamsey* villages. Surrounding countries such as Mali and Burkina Faso have only recently amended their mineral codes in an attempt to attract foreign investment in large-scale mining. With mining giants such as the Anglo-Ashanti Group beginning to secure exploration and mining concessions in these countries, displacement similar in magnitude is likely to occur.

In short, with large-scale mining now in the picture, it is no longer a case of artisanal miners flocking in chaotic, rush-like fashion to areas of mineralization, and working unsustainably until reserves are exhausted. Rather, it is a case of the movement of artisanal miners being restricted because of an increased presence of large-scale mine concessions, which, in turn, has limited the number of deposits they can realistically access.

Low income and lack of investment opportunities

What types of incomes are earned in the artisanal mining industry? In the MMSD publication 'Global Report on Artisanal Mining', the authors note that artisanal mining is generally characterized by a 'low level of salaries and income' (Hentschel et al., 2002: 5). Jennings (1998) furthermore notes that the wages paid to illegal miners by concession holders are generally low, and are often awarded after the end of a work contract.

In West Africa artisanal mining is also a poorly paid occupation with few investment opportunities. The claim made by Appiah (1998) that a small-scale mineworker in Ghana earns as much as US$7 each day (US$1,820 annually) is not representative of the region's artisanal mining earning potential. Although precise salary data are unavailable, repeated reference to peoples' unwillingness to abandon low-income farming in favour of mining suggests that earnings are not necessarily consistent. For example, in a survey of 500 children working at artisanal mines in Burkina Faso (in ILO, 1999), two-thirds of respondents believed they were in an unstable employment situation. In Mali, it was noted in a consultancy report (AIRD, 2002: 32) that artisanal miners are willing to 'make special efforts' during the period between harvest and the start of the next planting season if gold prices increase but at the same time, are 'not ready to quit agriculture in favour of gold production work' and therefore 'confine traditional gold production to a secondary role as a source of additional income'. Based upon calculations made by Keita (2001), the average daily wage in the country's gold-washing workforce is approximately US$1.25. In Benin, Grätz (2003a: 198) reports that a major problem in the artisanal gold-mining industry is that 'potential earnings are not steady and difficult to predict' because individuals compete for access to mountainous areas, have limited knowledge of local geology and operate in locations of variable mineralization.

In the majority of West African countries, there are not only few opportunities for artisanal miners to supplement their incomes, but industry support is also minimal. In Ghana, for example, where there is a network of agricultural banks and support schemes in place for small-scale farmers, financial institutions refuse to provide loans to even licensed mine operators, who have been granted security of tenure on a demarcated plot of land for between three and five years. Lawal (2001: 7) reports a similar situation in Nigeria, where 'provisions for short- and long-term finance and long-term saving instruments attractive to the local markets are lacking'. When it is possible to secure financing from banks, interest rates are typically too high for prospective small-scale miners. This, along with the country's high national interest rate (8.2%), has deterred investment in the sector.

Reflecting on how a lack of 'external assistance to the traditional mining sector can have lasting effects without the active support and participation of governments', Keita (2001: 23) notes that in Mali, the ad hoc approach taken by the authorities towards formalizing artisanal mining has contributed to the impoverished state of the industry today. In Burkina Faso, where 'artisanal miners do not have the means and business people are hesitant to get involved in such operations, being more used to low-risk investments which offer immediate results', economic improvements will depend 'on the capacity of the state to establish financing mechanisms through local banks and other financial institutions to help artisanal miners' (Gueye, 2001: 3). Even the momentum of promoting alternative livelihoods in artisanal mining, highly regarded as one of the most promising support-related initiatives pursued in the industry to date, is somewhat superficial, as it presupposes that operators are willing to relinquish their professions altogether. To date, few of the alternative livelihoods programmes implemented for ASM, including the UN's effort in Ghana, have achieved positive results.

To summarize, not only do most West African artisanal miners earn paltry wages, but there is also little in the way of additional financial support in the form of grants and loans for improving their living conditions.

Inadequate and inappropriate technology

A case is made in several influential texts (UN, 1996a; UN, 1996b; ILO, 1999) that ASM sites generally feature exorbitantly inefficient equipment, resulting in substantial losses of earnings for the subsistent operator. In Ghana, for example, it was claimed in a recent study by Iddirisu and Tsikata (1998) that the technology used at artisanal gold mines is on average only 30 per cent effective, which is not surprising given the widespread usage of such rudimentary implements as jute matting, inner-tyre tubing and homemade sluices. Aryee (2003a: 390) corroborates these claims, arguing that in Ghana, artisanal mining and processing methods 'have not significantly changed over the years', with most operators relying 'solely on traditional/manual methods of mining, still inclined to use simple implements such as shovels, pick-axes, pans, chisels and hammers, as well as windlasses to haul ore from deep pit working'. There is also widespread use of inefficient equipment in Burkina Faso, where Gueye (2001) reports that the 'major obstacles to efficient and effective mining' include the application of inadequate ore treatment methods (typically resulting in the extraction of only 30% of available gold) and maladapted extraction techniques. In Mali, Keita (2001: 15) reports that mineral excavation using artisanal implements rarely results in the extraction of more than 50 per cent of potential reserves. In the case of gold, losses as high as 75 per cent for a placer deposit and 90 per cent for a lode are common, with outputs rarely exceed 2–3 cubic metres per person per day.

The problems associated with using inappropriate equipment are exacerbated by an impoverished policy; specially, in the majority of West African states, the policies and legislation in place for artisanal miners are piecemeal. Lawal (2001) argues that this is a serious drawback in the Nigerian case because it signifies that the sound development of ASM is not a national priority, which sends the wrong message to individuals operating outside the legal bracket. Keita (2001:23) notes that in Mali, the policies and strategies destined to promote small-scale mining are also 'not bold enough', and have therefore failed to sufficiently rectify problems such as site disorganization and environmental degradation. Certain governments have what appears to be contradictory ASM policy. A case in point is Ghana, where government officers do not provide support or advice to any miner unless he or she has secured a licence to mine on a small scale. At the same time, however, licensed government gold buyers do not discriminate when it comes to purchasing minerals, issuing payments to both licensed and illegal miners. Poorly designed and enforced policy provides the industry's participants with limited direction, but more significantly, dissuades prospective operators from adhering to regulatory frameworks altogether.

In addition to featuring dilapidated equipment, sites are also generally highly disorganized. Although as already explained, hierarchically, artisanal mining groups exhibit a notable degree of organization, the uncertainty of the gold yield and the panic associated with pinpointing sufficiently mineralized areas often lead to anarchic behaviour on-site. For example, in Mali, while traditional gold washing follows a well-established model of organizing work, there is no production plan followed on-site (Keita, 2001), which causes widespread confusion. Despite being organized in a series of gangs, Ghana's *galamsey* gold miners, who work without a licence and have no concessions of their own, operate uncontrollably inside the concessions of large-scale mining companies or in areas prohibited for mining, such as forest reserves. Aryee et al. (2003) reports that such miners are highly disorganized, and operate in a hit-and-run manner, often initiating confrontations with both state law enforcement agencies and the security personnel of large-scale mining companies. Some 15–20 years ago, reports surfaced that in Burkina Faso, during the aftermath of the serious droughts that induced widespread poverty in rural areas, populations began exploiting gold deposits for incomes. However, because activities were disorganized, there were several accidents in the field, a problem which continues to plague the industry today (Gueye, 2001).

The widespread illegality in the sector reflects the ineffective nature of government policy: despite the existence of licensing schemes and sector-specific regulations in most West African countries, the fact that the majority of the region's artisanal miners continue to operate without a licence suggests that governments are providing minimal support to the industry vis-à-vis large-scale mining. In countries such as Ghana, certain artisanal miners choose to evade regulations altogether because of diminished confidence in the government to address, among other things, technology and support-related needs.

Environmental degradation

Acute shortages of financial assistance, widespread application of rudimentary equipment and a lack of government support have made the environment a secondary concern in the ASM sector. According to broad analyses of the industry, because operators endure long, laborious shift work in order to earn sufficient income to purchase a daily ration of food for their families, it is not surprising that most neglect the important health-related and environmental concerns of mineral extraction and processing. For example, one of the most serious environmental and health-related concerns in the industry is the haphazard handling of mercury in the gold-processing circuit. Although efforts have been made for well over 15 years to raise awareness of the need to handle mercury appropriately, miners continue to use it without any respiratory or hand protection. Moreover, the repeated use of inefficient equipment, along with the perpetual hit-and-miss activity that occurs in areas where geological potential has yet to be determined, results in considerable land degradation and water pollution. Miners and their families generally reside in close proximity to these deteriorated landscapes, often consuming contaminated vegetation matter and water.

Pollution from ASM has been identified as a major problem in several West African countries. Gueye (2001) lists a number of the environmental impacts of artisanal mining activities in Burkina Faso. These include:
- the creation of embankments, which degrade arable lands;
- the clearage of shrubs and trees, the wood from which is used to construct huts and sheds in mining zones, and to build supports in wells, construct ladders and for cooking; and
- dust (e.g. crushing, digging, sluicing) and gas from chemical products (nitric acid), major sources of air pollution.

In Dumasi, an important artisanal gold-mining region in Ghana, Babut et al. (2003) found elevated concentrations of mercury in the sediments and fish samples collected within the locality, as well as downstream. These findings corroborate claims made by Aryee et al. (2003: 135), who note that many of Ghana's rivers and streams are now 'polluted by solid suspensions and mercury, which are commonly discharged into resident water bodies during the sluicing process and amalgamation, respectively'. The authors further claim that

> A common practice of small-scale gold miners in Ghana is the burning of gold amalgam in the open air. This practice produces mercury fumes, which are released into the atmosphere. In some instances, the burning of amalgam is conducted in poorly ventilated rooms, exposing miners to the dangers of mercury contamination. [Aryee et al., 2003: 135–6]

In Mali, high concentrations of gold washers and the land requirements of their houses place considerable strain on forests and topsoil. Mercury is also a major concern, particularly in alluvial regions, where an estimated 40 per cent (of mercury), in the form of metal balls or steam, is released into surrounding rivers and sediments (Keita, 2001).

What is perhaps even more tragic in West Africa in particular is the continued neglect of regional governments. Lawal (2001) faults the Nigerian government's inadequate policies and neglect of educational issues for the widespread environmental degradation prevalent at ASM sites. In Ghana, despite having constructed district centres to help address ASM concerns more effectively, many important decisions continue to be made in Accra by policymakers unfamiliar with the artisanal mining landscape. For example, the procedures that must now be followed to secure a small-scale mining licence are bureaucratic, and often subject the subsistence operator to considerable delays. This has dissuaded prospective miners from registering altogether; most have reverted to their environmentally degrading hit-and-miss practices. Similar problems have surfaced in Mali, where 'most assistance projects emphasize technical aspects at the expense of the vital needs of communities and populations in mining zones' (Keita, 2001: 23). Governments, however, cannot be singled out as the sole perpetrators of promoting ineffective ASM policy, as aid agencies and multilateral lending institutions, which are supposedly on the cutting edge of development research, have done little to influence policy direction positively.

Throughout ECOWAS, the environment is clearly another important element of the artisanal mining-poverty nexus.

Low productivity

When Nöetstaller (1996) developed his artisanal mining poverty model, only a handful of governments in the developing world appeared to recognize the socioeconomic importance of the industry. At the time, few governments were making any attempt to control the outward flow of minerals extracted on a small scale and the revenues accrued from their sale. Kambani (1995) identified the implications of ignoring these activities, indicating that governments were losing significant quantities of precious minerals from smuggling, and therefore, potentially important contributions to foreign exchange. The majority of West African governments, including those in Ghana, Burkina Faso and Mali, have since attempted to streamline regulations to prevent the illicit marketing of minerals. The results have generally been positive.

However, artisanal miners are not necessarily processing insufficient amounts of gold or diamonds, as Nöetstaller's artisanal mining poverty nexus implies. To some degree, the industry's production is inhibited by the continuous application of inefficient equipment, widespread disorganization on-site and geological uncertainty; but these shortcomings aside, the majority of artisanal miners, based on the amount of mineral product they process, should be able to generate sufficient income to improve their living standards. The message conveyed in the general ASM literature is that operators tend to squander their earnings, wasting substantial proportions of their incomes on prostitution, alcohol and drugs. While this may hold true, what cannot be overlooked are the paltry payments artisanal gold miners often receive for their product. Nöetstaller's (1994) claim that a proliferation of illicit mineral marketing occurs when the difference between the market and the selling price exceeds 5 per cent is inapplicable in situations involving highly remote and itinerate people. In such cases, gold buyers are free to quote 'bush' prices, and in many instances, have devalued product by as much as 50 per cent. A case in point is Ghana, where more than 800 licensed buyers travel to the remotest reaches of the country to purchase product from artisanal miners. Despite being required to pay 98 per cent of the market price for both gold and diamonds, buyers rarely pay anywhere near this amount. Moreover, because artisanal miners frequently secure loans from buyers, many feel obliged to sell them their product, even if it is at a discounted price.

To summarize, in the context of West African states, the final aspect of Nöetstaller's artisanal mining poverty nexus, low productivity, is inapplicable; it is more a case of artisanal miners receiving inequitable payment for their labour.

Conclusion

This chapter has examined the impoverished state of artisanal mining activities in West African states. Speaking abstractly, a number of texts (UN, 1996a; UN, 1996b; ILO, 1999) have labelled ASM a poverty-driven activity. Based upon empirical evidence, such is the case throughout ECOWAS, where there are now well over 1 million artisanal miners in operation.

Upon further investigation, not only have the majority of the region's artisanal miners been driven to the industry because of a lack of alternative employment but most remained *trapped* in a life of poverty. The poverty-ASM nexus devised by Nöetstaller (1996), updated by Gilam (1999), was used to explain this phenomenon. Specifically, the restrictions imposed on subsistence mining activities under reform, the inability of miners to secure finances, the use of inappropriate technology, limited awareness of environmental issues and inequitable payments for mineral products have perpetuated a vicious cycle of poverty in the West African ASM sector.

CHAPTER 4

Artisanal and small-scale mining in West Africa: an overview of sustainable development and environmental issues

Matthew Gibb

For thousands of years, ASM in its various guises has been an important building block of societies around the world, contributing to the spread of trade routes and growth of empires. In this manner, mining has formed the basis of many West African nations' economies for countless centuries, as evidenced by the ancient kingdoms of Mali, Songhai and Timbuktu, which supplied gold and gemstones to the Middle East and the coastal empires along the Horn in exchange for equally precious commodities (Keita, 2001; d'Souza, 2002). Although the march towards industrialization and modernity in other places witnessed the formalization, mechanization and consolidation of mineral extraction in the Western world, artisanal mining activities located on the fringes of today's global economy in many of these same areas have remained, to a large degree, much the same. Bigger, in this case, is not necessarily better, but millions of people in the developing world continue to eke out a living at conceptually primitive mines: according to recent estimates, the ASM sector provides direct employment to as many as 13 million people in some 55 countries (Hinton et al., 2003b). It is perhaps the fact that ASM activities are often located in remote and inaccessible areas of similarly forgotten countries that they have, until only recently, been invisible or overlooked as important economic contributors to national coffers and sources of local growth potential (Tráore, 1994; Hentschel et al., 2002).

Recently, however, there has been a flourish of interest in ASM, and a rush on the part of scholars, development agencies and international governing bodies to carry out research aimed at defining, quantifying and improving operations; and, for the sake of uniform and globalized management of such activities, identifying means for licensing, regulating and monitoring the sector (Danielson and Lagos, 2001; Carnegie, 2002; Andrew, 2003; Boers, 2003). The growing fascination with ASM parallels the wider post-structuralist and counter-globalization discourse relating to notions of localization theory, which has development analysts looking to the locality as the fountain from which the now-stylized clichés of holistic, bottom-up, community-based or socioeconomic development will flow (UNDESA, 2003). The expansion of ASM is often viewed as an excellent means for diversifying rural economies. Upon closer inspection, however, underlying tensions such as damages to the environment and resource mismanagement, as well as the unavailability of accurate industry statistics, threaten to undermine its credibility as a precursor to national and locally based socioeconomic development. Thrown into the mêlée is the now quite extensive and vocal debate on the sustainable or non-sustainable nature of informal mining, which calls into question the pros and cons of issues relating to income generation, local economic development and alternative rural livelihoods compared with long-term environmental degradation, questionable health and safety standards, concerns about child labour and land conflicts (Hilson, 2001a; de Mowbray, 2002; UNDESA, 2003; World Bank, 2003a).

It is against this background that this chapter provides an overview of sustainable development issues in West Africa's ASM sector. The main objective is to bring together some of the key contemporary arguments, debates and definitional challenges surrounding informal mining, with particular emphasis on its socioeconomic influences and impacts on the physical environment. This review provides a synthesis of the writings of such authors as Keita (2001), Gueye (2001), Hilson (2001b) and Hilson (2002c), as well as research outputs from the MMSD Project, the World Bank and the UN, all of which have had heavy hands in organizing international workshops on ASM (World Bank, 1994, 1995, 2003a; UNECA, 2002a, 2002b).

Defining ASM

Internationally, one of the biggest conceptual headaches has been setting the boundaries of what is actually implied when discussing ASM, and establishing an all-purpose definition that can be applied not only to West African countries, but also to countries everywhere featuring this type of activity. Labonne and Gilman (1999: 1) offer a very basic and simplistic summation of commonly held understandings of informal mining: 'Although there is no formerly recognized definition of artisanal mining...artisanal mining is characterized mainly by the absence or low degree of mechanization, low safety standards, poorly trained personnel, large influx of migrant workers, low pay scale, low productivity, chronic lack of capital, illegality due to mining without concession rights, little consideration of environmental impact and unknown mineral reserves'.

Most national governments have set their own standards and upper limits as to what they legally consider to be ASM. As Keita (2001) explains, industry seminars held in the capitals of many of West Africa's francophone countries have yielded a preliminary list of qualifying guidelines to be taken into account when formulating national ASM policies. These include:
- type of equipment, level of mechanization, and technology used;
- production levels;
- physical size of the deposit;
- importance of the investment; and

- organizational and management structure of the mine.

According to various sources, the number of people engaged in artisanal mining ranges from a single person up to eight, nine or 10 salaried employees, but may include many more if unpaid family members are taken into consideration; on the other hand, in the small-scale mining industry, the number of people employed is generally capped at 100. Together, daily production does not tend to exceed 200 tonnes (Paul et al., 1997; Dreschler, 2001; Hilson, 2002a). There are over 40 different minerals extracted on an artisanal and small scale in developing countries (Hilson, 2002d).

As Gueye (2001: 5) explains, in Mali, artisanal mining is defined as 'any operation which extracts and concentrates mineral substances drawn from primary/secondary outcropping or sub-outcropping deposits using manual or traditional methods and procedures'. Small-scale mining is characterized by 'any permanent small mine equipped with a minimum number of fixed installations, using semi-industrial methods based on a primary discovery of a deposit with an annual production not exceeding a certain tonnage of the marketable product'. In the case of gold, Malian authorities consider an operation to be small in scale if it has a production capacity below 500 kg of gold per year. Burkina Faso also adheres to the same definitions of ASM (Gueye, 2001). In Ghana, small-scale mining is defined by concession size: as stipulated in the Small-Scale Gold Mining Law, it is 'any mining activity not involving substantial expenditures in areas not exceeding 25 acres' (World Bank, 1995: 7)

A global overview of ASM

ASM operations dot the landscape of many of the planet's least developed countries. From Latin America, through Indochina to sub-Saharan Africa, residents of individual nation-states are turning in increasing numbers to ASM in search of work. The quantity of published materials recording this trend has exploded in recent years, with the MMSD Project joining other authors in sponsoring major fact-finding missions on small-scale mining in some of the most unlikely places (Hollaway, 2000; Zamora, 2000; Aspinall, 2001). In addition, countries such as Brazil (do Nascimento, 2001), India (Chakravorty, 2001), Ghana (Hilson 2001b, 2002c; World Bank, 2003b) and China (Gunson and Jian, 2001; Andrews-Speed et al., 2002) continue to feature strongly in the ASM literature. From these publications and other more general investigations, the larger picture begins to unfold, and the magnitude of the informal mining sector on a global scale becomes clearly visible.

Depending on different sources, it is now estimated that, internationally, up to 100 million family or household members depend on ASM and/or its downstream benefits for their livelihoods (Andrew, 2003). Table 4.1, adapted from a variety of sources, provides estimates of ASM employment in selected countries. In Brazil and China over 1 million and 3 million, respectively, are engaged in informal mining (UN, 1996b). In Africa, ASM provides direct

Table 4.1   ASM employment in selected developing countries

Country	Estimated employment
China	3,000,000
Brazil	1,000,000
India	500,000
Democratic Republic of the Congo	500,000
Tanzania	100,000
Mali	100,000
Sierra Leone	100,000
Burkina Faso	60,000
Guinea	60,000
Ghana	30,000
Angola	30,000
Zambia	30,000
Zimbabwe	30,000
South Africa	20,000
Niger	15,000
Ethiopia	10,000
Central African Republic	10,000
Senegal	3,00
World total	6,345,000

Sources: UN, 1996b; Gilman, 1999; Hilson, 2002d.

employment to 3.2 million–4 million people; overall, 6 million–28 million Africans depend on the sector for their livelihoods (d'Souza, 2002). Although Table 4.1 suggests that fewer people are employed in this area, various authors now concede that the global ASM workforce has been seriously underestimated. For example, in Burkina Faso, a UN report shows that there are 60,000 workers, whereas Gueye (2001) estimates that there are 100,000 miners at 200 different sites supporting 200,000 people. Similarly, Keita (2001) estimates that there are 200,000 small-scale miners operating in Mali, a figure which the UN places at 100,000. Hilson (2001b) corroborates the notion that there are 30,000 registered scale-scale miners in Ghana, but adds that there could be an additional 170,000 illegal artisanal miners.

It is believed that the number of people drawn to ASM will triple by 2010 (d'Souza, 2002).

An overview of ASM in West Africa

The rapid expansion of the ASM industry has been fuelled by a number of factors and is symptomatic of much larger fluctuations in the global economy that have preceded a re-organization of the global mining industry (Campbell et al., 2003). For many, entry into the informal mining sector represents an attempted escape from chronic poverty; for others, it is an attractive alternative avenue of employment during the dry season or in times of industrial downsizing; and for others still, it is an opportunity to diversify their livelihoods and move away from, for example, the dangers associated with low and declining agricultural commodity prices (Jennings, 1999). In West Africa, these are among the numerous reasons why many people are turning to ASM.

The contemporary escalating shift to ASM began about 25 years ago but has accelerated since 2000, so much so that activities are now considered essential components of non-farm diversified rural economies (Wels, 1983; Spiropoulos, 1991; Gilman, 1999; Hilson, 2002a). Due to global climatic changes, droughts in places such as Burkina Faso and Mali in the 1980s, falling prices for commercial crops, crop failure and land degradation in many communities, informal mining, regardless of size, has even come to replace traditional rural farming and agricultural occupations (Tráore, 1994; Gueye, 2001; Keita, 2001). In Cameroon, volcanic activity has pushed people off the land towards ASM, while in Sierra Leone, armed conflict has left people with few options other than informal mining, which for many is a last resort (d'Souza, 2002).

Worldwide reduction in demand for particular minerals, an ensuing decline in prices and decreased investment in the formal large-scale mining sector have also fuelled the rapid expansion of ASM. In the wake of imposed adjustment policies in the 1980s, corporate downsizing and the growing economic crisis in Africa as a whole, redundant large-scale mine and industrial workers turned to ASM in search of incomes for their families (Gilman, 1999; Hilson, 2002a; UN, 2003).

In the majority of cases, people are driven to this form of activity because there are few alternatives. Hilson (2002a: 6) describes the reality of many rural Africa dwellers:

Perhaps the biggest stimulus to participation in small-scale mining activity is the lure of quick enrichment and financial and social independence that comes with it. Wages are comparatively higher than employment in construction or agriculture, making work in this sector financially appealing. Further, small-scale mining provides employment for many retrenched workers from large-scale mines, which in turn has increased income levels and raised living standards.

As reinforced by the UN in a report to the Secretary-General in 1996, 'small-scale mining should be viewed and approached from the broader view of socio-economic development and poverty eradication' (UN, 1996b: 20). Although poverty is rampant in most developing countries, it is the localities in which ASM operations are generally found that are particularly impoverished and in dire need of assistance. Andrew (2003) points out that small-scale mining is usually located in the poorest, most remote and rural peripheries of a country, far from regional and national capitals and industrial centres.

The quality of tools and the primitive nature of the techniques used by operators deny them further opportunities to increase the amount of income that they could otherwise earn from their sites. The equipment used is readily available or is often manufactured on-site and tools, which are extremely basic, include shovels and buckets (Tráore, 1994). Mining procedures are typically rudimentary and inefficient, thereby resulting in excessive wastage of resources; miners are also generally unaware of environmental and safety regulations (Zamora, 2000; Andrews-Speed et al., 2002). For instance, in Mali, Ghana and Burkina Faso, it is not uncommon to see artisanal miners using basic implements such as hammers, pickaxes, shovels, wood ladders, ropes, buckets, calabashes and plastic bags, and transporting ore via cart, wheelbarrow, pail and donkey (World Bank, 1995; Gueye, 2001). Hilson (2001b, 2002d) notes how in some places, as a result of using these rudimentary implements, miners only extract 20–30 per cent of the gold from excavated ore.

The number of people dependent upon ASM and deepening economic inequalities worldwide have given rise to numerous international conferences, seminars and roundtables that have focused upon the intricacies of the sector and identified ways in which to improve operations. Hentschel et al. (2002) explain how in 1991–2003, delegates at the meetings charted in Table 4.2, including a seminar in the Cameroonian capital of Yaoundé, met with the goal of approximating and harnessing the socioeconomic dynamism of ASM for national economies as well as local host communities. The vision statement of the Yaoundé Seminar will invariably shape the direction of the sector and the international donor community for years to come. It expresses the desire to

Table 4.2 International ASM conferences, seminars and workshops

Year	Location	Host institution	Discussion topic
1991	Calcutta	National Institute for Small Mines	Issues of small-scale mining
1993	Harare	United Nations	Guidelines on small/medium-scale mining
1995	Washington D.C.	World Bank	Artisanal mining
1996	Calcutta	National Institute for Small Mines	Issues of small-scale mining
1997	Vienna	United Nations Industrial Development Organization	Global pollution and artisanal gold mining
1999	Geneva	International Labour Organization	Labour issues and small-scale mines
2000	Ouagadougou	World Bank	African mining symposium
2002	Yaoundé	United Nations	Sustainable livelihoods and ASM
2003	Maputo	World Bank	ASM as a tool for rural development

Sources: Davidson, 1993; Hentschel et al., 2002.

'contribute to sustainably reduced poverty and improve livelihoods in African artisanal and small-scale mining communities by the year 2015' (UNECA, 2002a).

The issues discussed at these meetings included different methods of regulation and formalization strategies; child and female labour; strategies for administering financial, organizational and technical support; and environmental, health and safety concerns. From these debates, an increasingly topical debate has erupted: some factions see ASM as an important ingredient of rural livelihoods, whereas others see it as being particularly detrimental to sustainable development. As Hilson (2002a: 6) explains, it was at the Harare Seminar on Guidelines for Development of Small and Medium Scale Mining in 1993 that representatives definitively decided that the positive economic spinoffs associated with ASM outweighed the negatives, that it 'collectively makes important contributions to national economies, and provides economic stability to thousands of indigenous people residing in rural areas'. Conversely, Gilman (1999: 1), writing on behalf of the Sustainable Livelihoods Division of the UNDP, focuses heavily on the lawlessness, health problems and the questionable long-term feasibility associated with ASM, and is joined by those who explain that the sector is highly damaging to the surrounding environment of the host communities.

The future of the ASM policy environment, as determined by authorities and multilateral development agencies, is therefore unclear. Will the sector be championed as a means of affording jobs to millions who would otherwise be unemployed, or will it continue to be condemned for its part in the destruction of the natural environment?

Legislation and guidelines for ASM in West Africa

In West Africa, the regulatory frameworks implemented for ASM over the last century have generally fallen within the legislative domains of wider natural resources ministries responsible for, among other things, water affairs, energy production and general mining issues. In certain countries, such as Burkina Faso, colonial authorities set aside particular areas to be exploited solely by artisanal miners, although the majority of ASM-specific legislation was not passed until the 1980s. In many respects, it has been predominantly because of the sector's environmental pollution that has led many West African governments to draw up a range of licensing and regulatory guidelines.

Such national institutional bodies and laws as the Directorate of Small-Scale Mining (Burkina Faso), The Small-Scale Gold Mining Law (Ghana) and the Project for the Promotion of Traditional Mining and Environment Protection (Mali) seek specifically to maximize the benefits of ASM while minimizing its negative impacts. Each miner is theoretically required to obtain some form of licence (Ghana), mining title or administrative authorization (Burkina Faso), or gold washer's card (Mali) from the relevant government department. The aim of these is to ensure that extracted minerals, particularly gold and diamonds, are not smuggled from the country via the black market, but rather sold directly to government agents, which, in turn, affords the government certain profit-making allowances. In terms of protection for the environment, recent legislation requires would-be miners to fulfil certain stipulations before they receive their licence. These include (Gueye, 2001; Hilson, 2001b; Keita, 2001) the following:

- assurance of compliance with existing national environmental regulations;
- proof of consultation with indigenous peoples and local populations;
- a submission of an environmental impact study;
- a submission of a programme for environmental management and conservation;
- the provision of measures to deal with a potentially environmentally damaging accident;
- a submission of a plan for the rehabilitation of exploited areas; and
- a declaration that following its closure, the mine site will be secure.

As has been the case throughout the world, although rules and regulations may be inscribed in government documents, it does not necessarily mean that they are being adhered to. The cost of obtaining a licence, the numerous forms that require completion and the wait for their final approval, in addition to the general inconvenience involved in carrying out this process, means that many miners are simply choosing to ignore current legislation (Hilson, 2001b). This has become a trend with many West African miners, as evidenced by the region's growing illegal mining contingent. Non-compliance in this regard has further contributed to problems of environmental deterioration and lost revenue for national governments.

ASM and its implications for socioeconomic development

For centuries, ASM has been financially rewarding for the countries of West Africa. It is in the context of the contemporary global economy, however, that the extent of its wealth generation and contribution to national economies, in part through increased topic-related research and documentation, has become more apparent. Keita's (2001: 11) report calculates that each of Africa's 1.2 million gold washers produces an average daily amount of 0.16 grams of gold, which would cumulatively amount to 42 tonnes of gold a year, fetching a value in excess of US$300 million.

There is no question that with an income amounting to hundreds of millions of dollars, ASM has a positive impact on the economies of many West African countries. The total volume of minerals extracted by the sometimes hundreds of thousands of people employed in the sector has meant that they often have the capacity to corner large percentages of national export earnings and are even found in the top five national money-making industries. Gueye (2001), in his report on ASM in Burkina Faso submitted to the MMSD Project, established that the gold produced by artisanal miners now constitutes the third largest national export after cotton and leather, contributing to 10 per cent of GDP. From 1986 to 2000, artisanal miners produced nearly half of the 26 tonnes of pure gold in Burkina Faso, which was worth CFAFr50,000 million (Gueye, 2001). In Ghana, Hilson (2002c) reports that artisanal and small-scale miners were able to turn out over US$117 million in gold and US$98 million in diamonds between 1989 and 2000. In Mali, gold production accounted for 95 per cent of the country's mineral exports and 20 per cent of total exports in 1994. Just under half of the US$67 million produced from mining that year originated from the informal mining industry (van Oss, 1995; Mobbs, 1997). In 1999, artisanal and small-scale gold miners in one region of Mali alone contributed US$22 million to the national economy. Although Kambani (1995) reveals that the impact of ASM on national economies is questionable, in part due to illegal trading activities, in many cases, such as in Ghana, government middlemen have been able to recoup mining revenue that would have otherwise been lost via clandestine smuggling by paying miners a more equitable percentage of world prices (World Bank, 1995; Hilson, 2002c).

Collectively, the millions of US dollars generated by artisanal and small-scale mines, especially in the precious metals and minerals sector, make important contributions to foreign exchange, aggregate domestic savings, help to balance trade vis-à-vis neighbouring countries, provide stability to central reserve banks and help states diversify their income sources (Hilson, 2002b; Villas-Bôas and Barreto, 2002; World Bank, 2003a). The ASM actor is regarded as a crucial factor in stemming the flow of thousands of unemployed rural persons to cities and putting mounting pressures on already constrained economic resources and limited employment opportunities (McMahon and Davidson, 2000; Hilson 2002a). Thus, ASM reinforces more widespread, albeit not necessarily equal, distribution of economic growth, industrial development, opportunities for enhanced revenue generation and employment prospects in these countries.

It is often at the local level, however, where ASM has the greatest impact. In a modern international context that calls on communities to look inwardly to sustain local development, ASM represents one of the few options for generating employment using otherwise untapped natural resources. Because, as Tráore (1994) has ascertained, start-up costs are relatively low and there are quick tangible results to be had, ASM is an excellent means of promoting poverty alleviation and improving standards of living. In addition, artisanal mines are usually locally owned, implying that income is retained locally, which leads to increased domestic savings and improved economic empowerment within a given area (Andrew, 2003; Andrews-Speed et al., 2002).

On account of its ability to often act as a catalyst for economic growth or recovery for localities, ASM has the further potential to spark additional entrepreneurial endeavours, including equipment manufacture, tool repair, transportation, and food service and catering. In countries such as Ghana and Mali, where precious metals are the focal point of ASM, among the downstream beneficiation opportunities likely to be found are with a range of metalworkers or jewellers, who process gold on-site and offer their crafts directly for sale to local peoples (Hilson, 2001b).

From a socioeconomic perspective, ASM feeds into a larger global movement of socially and economically disenfranchised people becoming more proactive and self-reliant in initiating poverty-alleviating strategies of their own (de Mowbray, 2002). In this way, ASM has, for many, become a multifaceted empowering process that has brought both individual and shared opportunities to numerous localities throughout West Africa. It has also played a major role in highlighting the advancement of women within these areas, which is what Labonne (1996) describes as an important 'economic stepping stone' for many of them. Although only 5 per cent of ASM operators and entrepreneurs in Gabon and 35 per cent in Guinea are female, in the larger countries where activities are more formalized, women play a more central role in the industry. For example, in Ghana and Burkina Faso, up to 45 per cent of ASM workers are women and in Mali, where women have long played a valuable role in the social organization of ASM mining, this number is as high as 50 per cent (d'Souza, 2002; Keita, 2001). In some cases, such as in Tourba in northern Burkina Faso, the promotion of women in the management of small-scale mining enterprises has been specifically emphasized by the government (Gueye, 2001).

Depending on its degree of formality, small-scale mining might have the capacity to contribute to the development of local social infrastructure and encourage socially responsible mining practices. In the Bouda region of Burkina Faso, health facilities have been established at certain mine sites, while in Essakane, there is evidence of a reduction in the number of children involved in mine-related activities (Gueye, 2001). In the Sadiola gold-mining region of Mali, a specially targeted project has helped to introduce a school and an adult learning institution, as well as provide assistance in the operation of a community health centre (Hentschel et al., 2002).

There is also evidence that ASM can improve social problems traditionally associated with poverty-stricken communities. Hilson (2002a) notes that small-scale mining helps to reduce, in some way, a reliance on crime as a coping strategy and helps curb suicides among economically disempowered individuals. At the same time, however, in especially crowded ASM areas, child labour and human rights problems are compounded by increased alcohol and drug abuse, a degradation of morals, rising incidents of prostitution and sexually transmitted diseases and higher crime rates (Keita, 2001; UNECA, 2002a). In other regions, additional concerns include land disputes and conflicts between miners and indigenous peoples (Hilson, 2002e, 2002f, 2003; Bayah et al., 2003).

ASM and environmental impacts

One of the hottest topics in the sustainable development debate is the preservation of the physical environment and the safeguarding of natural resources for future generations. It is perhaps this contemporary focus on sustainable development and the media hype that has followed a recent string of Earth Summits and sustainable development dialogues that has landed ASM in the hot water in which it finds itself today. Just as there is no doubt that the millions of dollars of output produced in the ASM sector has had fundamental effects on the national and local economies of West African states in the many years that it has been in practice, there is also little doubt that the negative environmental consequences have been equally monumental (Hilson, 2002b; Aryee et al., 2003).

Located in a particularly drought-ridden region of the continent that is already subjected to overgrazing and a depletion of plant life, the countries of West Africa are at risk of further deforestation from the expansion of ASM. Trees and bushes are rapidly being felled to be used for supports at mines, housing for mineworkers and fuel. Deforestation of this sort has led to a continued degradation of arable regions in Burkina Faso, and has exacerbated the desiccation of land, releasing large quantities of dust particles, which have caused a range of respiratory problems among mineworkers (Gueye, 2001). In Mali, Keita (2001) explains that the local belief that the largest gold nuggets are found between the roots of trees has caused an even greater destruction of vegetation. The continuous search for bigger and better deposits of gold has pushed miners to frequently move to new locations, leaving behind abandoned and unprotected mine shafts and processing sites, destroying even more otherwise productive land, and creating potentially dangerous snares for animals and local residents (Keita, 2001).

Much of the environmental damage caused is of a chemically induced nature. In Ghana, Mali and Burkina Faso, the soil and water in the immediate as well as general vicinity of gold-washing areas are generally highly contaminated (Hilson, 2001a). Mercury, oils, acids and other chemicals used in the extraction of gold infiltrate soils, posing numerous health concerns for miners. During the various phases of mineral processing, up to 40 per cent of the mercury used in certain amalgamation techniques can escape containment and enter local river systems, tainting local fish supplies and causing damage to the food chain (Keita, 2001; Hinton et al., 2003b). Some miners have been known to discard tailings and other effluents directly into water bodies. These are further spoiled by the introduction of topsoil runoff no longer held in place along river embankments because of deforestation, which, in turn, influences turbidity and salinity levels, threatening delicate plant life and aquatic fauna.

The collection of physical waste is another area of major concern in the ASM sector. The amount of garbage churned out by hundreds of thousands of miners has left the countryside blighted with household waste, plastic bags, spent batteries and derelict mine infrastructure (Hentschel et al., 2002). This visible pollution is added to the already pit-marked, mine dump-filled and scarred landscape, and is complemented by the noise pollution contributed by hundreds of generators (Aryee et al., 2003).

Despite the legislation that has recently overseen the semiformalization of small-scale mining in West Africa, which has among its aims and objectives curbing the environmental damages caused by activities, the legacies of years of continued exploitation, ignorance, inability to comply and blatant disregard on the part of miners, added to the powerlessness and ineffectiveness of faraway government bureaucracies to enforce these regulations, has meant that ASM continues to function at the expense of the environment (Hilson, 2002d).

What does this mean for ASM?

Despite the hundreds of millions of dollars being injected into the national and local economies of the developing world, the darker side of ASM seems to be getting the entire industry into trouble. In addition to the main counterpoints of environmental degradation and unsafe mining practices, the principal arguments used by the United Nations Department of Economic and Social Affairs (UNDESA), which rightly recognizes the long-term repercussions of ASM, originate in its quasi-illegal nature and the negative social impacts it is perceived to have on surrounding communities (Gilman, 1999; UN, 2003). Due to its continued informality and the proliferation of ad hoc approaches taken to regulate operations, there is the added belief that in many cases, there are too many would-be entrepreneurs concentrating on too small an area, mismanaging or wasting limited resources, hampering optimum productivity, promoting the exploitation of child labour and contributing to the break-down of the social fabric of many communities (Gilman, 1999; UNECA, 2002a). Many authors have also noted that mine-related land-use conflicts are on the rise between some miners and indigenous peoples not engaged in this activity themselves (Hilson, 2002e; MMSD, 2002a; Andrew, 2003). In this case, rather than helping to fight crime and boost civic participation or the morale of local populations, the UN reports an apparent clandestine and lawlessness associated with ASM, the supposed higher crime rates it is associated with, issues concerning prostitution and the spread of HIV/AIDS, as well as drug and alcohol abuse among mine employees (UNECA, 2002a; World Bank, 2003a).

What this boils down to is that some are of the opinion that ASM does not, in fact, contribute to the long-term sustainable development of rural communities (UNDP, 2003b). The main reason for this claim is the belief that the significant numbers of people entering this sector, the fact that most have insufficient technical and business skills, the existence of a weak technology base, widespread undercapitalization, the absence of regulatory coordination and inadequate monitoring will eventually lead to overproduction, wastage and an exhaustion of local resources, thereby exacerbating social problems. The United Nations (UN, 1996b: 20) does, however, recognize this duality of ASM in rural development. In its aforementioned 1996 report, it states that 'small-scale mining should be viewed and approached from the broader view of socio-economic development and poverty eradication', and in its more recent 2003 report, Poverty Eradication and Sustainable Livelihoods, it is proclaimed that 'paradoxically, the financial windfall of ASM does not visibly contribute to lasting poverty reduction and sustainable livelihood' (UN, 2003: 1). Gilman

(1999: 2), on behalf of the United Nations, stresses that two of the UNDP's chief strategies to deal with this paradox are the 'necessary generation of alternative livelihood opportunities' and to 'formalize artisanal mining'.

Jennings (2000) explains that the task ahead is to bring ASM into the mainstream, an undertaking that will be particularly daunting as thousands of artisanal miners will be required to switch occupations to unidentified alternative livelihoods. Undoubtedly, miners would explore different options if available in their immediate surroundings. Many authors have recognized this seemingly futile search for alternative sources of income which, at best, can only provide sustenance to a handful of ex-miners, and are now looking into how best to ameliorate the existing set-up of ASM (Hilson, 2002d). Whether or not this includes supporting initiatives that will boost the profitability of mines through skills training or microlending while introducing more environmentally friendly techniques and technology, evidence suggests that the long-term and overriding goal of any project should ultimately be geared towards contributing value-added benefits to existing operations.

For this to occur, it will require the concerted commitment of local stakeholders, numerous levels of government, non-governmental organizations (NGOs), supranational governing bodies and, first and foremost, the cooperation of artisanal and small-scale miners themselves. The recent outpouring of documented research has shown that many authors and organizations are beginning to recommend different ways and means of enhancing the ASM sector (UN, 1996a, UNECA, 2002a). From the national government's perspective, this would include not only establishing laws but also enforcing guidelines on licensing, monitoring, health and safely requirements, environmental standards and land rights issues (Hilson, 2002a, 2002b). Additional ways in which authorities can be of assistance include providing technological support and facilitating access to affordable loans. NGOs also have the potential to assist in improving the standards of living of rural miners through social services such as education and health care. In many ways, they can increase awareness among local miners concerning health and safety, marketing, technological skill and credit (UN, 1996a). Furthermore, some NGOs have conducted baseline studies, provided more appropriate technologies and even conducted field demonstrations on how to use new, better or environmentally friendlier techniques. NGOs can also help to organize miners' associations and establish local or regional mining centres where people can solicit business advice. Hinton et al. (2003b) argue that any ASM support strategies and assistance must be economically beneficial, simple and expedient: 'for an artisanal miner, this means a method must be fast, easy, and cheap...an artisanal miner will not pay out a dollar for a piece of equipment or technique that does not return two dollars' (Hinton et al., 2003b: 102).

Again, this idea of being stuck between a rock and a hard place comes to the fore of ASM issues and activities. On the one hand, there is recognition that something needs to be done to curb the accelerating environmental destruction of host communities and initiate measures to heighten the sustainability of the informal mining sector overall. On the other hand, the number of people involved in this sector, the vast amounts of income being generated, and the inability or reluctance of miners to change their ways or comply with international recommendations have meant that many of the same damaging activities will likely continue and perhaps intensify. McMahon and Davidson's (2000) declaration that 'artisanal and small-scale mining is here to stay' holds true, which makes the implementation of improved support strategies imperative.

Conclusion

An overview of the literature on case studies of ASM in West Africa and around the world reveals the true nature of the sector's socioeconomic and environmental impacts. In some cases, accounts of environmental violations and criminal activities overshadow the notion of poor people doing it for themselves and making a living for their families. Until informal mining communities and resident miners are in a position to put into practice the recommendations put forth by myriad sources, they will remain international pariahs, and the promised potentials of ASM will remain unrealized.

As long as poverty persists in West Africa and there is a quick buck to be made in the informal mining sector, or any other money-making activity for that matter, people will be drawn to it regardless of the dangers posed to themselves and the environment. The conclusions reached by Andrews-Speed et al. (2002: 48), that 'central government may be able to argue cogently that the aggregate costs incurred by small-scale mining far outweigh the benefits at a national scale; but the balance of costs and benefits at the local level may be quite different', are vital to the realization that ASM is a necessary evil for much of the rural poor. Proposals to encourage the identification of alternative livelihoods for these people seem to overlook that ASM is, in fact, the only employment option for those engaged and/or is the most profitable.

In conclusion, ASM has proceeded largely untouched for many centuries but has since experienced rapid growth, with an increasing number of people engaged in the activity, more and more minerals being extracted, and profits being generated at such a rate that it has piqued the attention of many who have sought to scrutinize its socioeconomic contributions and examine its relationship with the physical environment. While this discovery of ASM has engendered a sequence of internationally hosted conferences espousing grand theories, critical analyses, policy recommendations and proposed plans of action, these conceptual wranglings continue to impact very little upon the daily lives of the ordinary informal miner. Unless national governments and the international community provide real solutions that take into account Hinton et al.'s (2003b) suggestion that miners will only work to improve their practices if it is profitable to do so, then it is quite likely that ASM will carry on in the same fashion as it has for many years to come.

CHAPTER 5

Mercury: an agent of poverty in West Africa's small-scale gold-mining industry

Sandra Pardie and Gavin M. Hilson

The environmental and health-related impacts of mercury use in the small-scale gold-mining sector have received considerable attention in recent years. Backed by millions of dollars in research support, the scientific community has shown time and time again that areas characterized by intensive artisanal gold-mining activity generally contain elevated levels of mercury. In most cases, such contamination is attributed to careless handling, low levels of environmental awareness and/or the absence of appropriate environmental safeguards.

Although considerable attention has been paid to measuring and monitoring mercury releases and the resulting contamination at artisanal and small-scale gold mines worldwide, the social impacts of amalgamation (for an explanation of this process, see below) remain largely unexplored. A case is often made that mercury amalgamation is the preferred practice in the sector because it is a reliable and portable means for concentrating and extracting gold from low-grade ores (Lacerda, 1997; Lacerda and Salomons, 1998). This accessibility and convenience notwithstanding, what is often overlooked in such simplistic analysis is the socioeconomic burden imposed by mercury.

This chapter argues that an increased dependence upon amalgamation techniques has perpetuated poverty in West African ASM communities. Overall, mercury has been seriously overlooked as an agent of poverty in the sector, and should be a featured element on Nöetstaller's (1996) ASM-poverty graphic (introduced in Chapter 3). Several distributional, production and health-related factors in mercury use and handling have exacerbated poverty in subsistence mining communities; recent rises in the unit cost of mercury, as well as its increased scarcity, have magnified these problems. Analysis in the literature is combined with findings from recent research undertaken in Ghana to illustrate how a heavy reliance upon mercury has been a major driving force behind the rampant poverty in many of the region's artisanal gold-mining communities.

Mercury contamination in the ASM industry: a focus on West Africa

Individuals working within, or downstream of, ASM regions can become readily exposed to metallic mercury in two ways. The first is through the amalgamation process itself, when mercury is mixed with wet sluice containing gold-aggregated sediments; this is generally carried out without any hand protection. The second route is through inhalation, specifically, the inhalation of mercury vapour produced when amalgam is burned to purify gold. The amalgam is typically burned over an open flame, releasing significant quantities of mercury fumes into the atmosphere. In some cases, the burning of amalgam is conducted in poorly ventilated rooms.

Releases of inorganic mercury, in both liquid and gaseous forms, are transformed by bacteria into toxic methylmercury, which subsequently bioaccumulates in soils, water, plants and animal tissues, increasing in concentration at the higher trophic levels of the food chain. Methylmercury has proven to be a major health threat to a host of species, including humans. It readily crosses the walls of the gastrointestinal tract, accumulating in the envelopes of nerve cells, causing neurological damage. Other manifestations of acute mercury poisoning include neuromuscular malfunctions, ranging from the numbing of the extremities to loss of eyesight; tremors and paralysis; and depressions and other behavioural disturbances.

Over the past 15–20 years, several researchers (Akagi et al., 1995; Appleton et al., 1999; Taylor et al. 2005) have examined at length the health-related impacts of mercury use in the ASM sector. Studies have generally aimed to quantify contamination levels in various environmental media and human tissues, and have helped to identify major exposure pathways. In West Africa, the majority of studies on mercury contamination and ASM have been carried out in Ghana, where an estimated 10 per cent of gold is produced on an artisanal and small scale (Yakubu, 2003a). The earliest analyses (Amegbey et al., 1994; NSR, 1994) were carried out in the localities of Dumasi and Tarkwa, where it was reported that vegetation, streams and crops contained elevated concentrations of mercury. During subsequent studies (Golow and Adzei, 2002; Golow and Mingle, 2003), samples of soil, elephant grass, mudfish and fern collected from farms in Obuasi and Dunkwa-Offin were observed to contain exceptionally high levels of mercury, and showed signs of persistent bioaccumulation. More recent studies of mercury contamination in Ghanaian ASM regions include Bonzongo et al. (2003), who investigated mercury concentrations in selected mine-impacted watersheds; Bannerman et al.'s (2003) assessment of mercury pollution in the Ankobra River, which flows through the major gold-mining localities in the Western Region of the country; Serfor-Armah et al.'s (2004) baseline analysis of mercury pollution in the mining town of Prestea; and Donkor et al.'s (2006) study of mercury speciation in the Pra River.

Ghana was also the beneficiary of a comprehensive UNIDO study on mercury, heralded by many local policymakers as groundbreaking analysis. As one officer put it, 'this UNIDO project we made on mercury...we have really improved much as a result'. While advertised as having multiple phases, the main thrust of the project was impact analysis, specifically, assessment of mercury contamination in ASM regions through extensive soil, sediment, fish, chicken, vegetable, surface water and groundwater sampling. The findings, reported in Babut et al. (2003), suggest that the environs of the study sites are contaminated.

Research carried out by Keita (2001) in Mali, Gueye (2001) in Burkina Faso, and Grätz (2003a) in Benin suggests that mercury contamination is a pressing problem throughout ECOWAS. The dearth of literature on mercury contamination in other West African states, however, does not necessarily mean that parallel 'effects-based' research is urgently required. For over 20 years, scientists have received hundreds of thousands of dollars in funding to undertake repetitive research on mercury in different ASM communities worldwide. The work being carried out in this area continues to yield near-identical conclusions: that within the areas where mercury is being used to amalgamate gold and/or emitted carelessly, various environmental media have become contaminated (Hilson, 2006a). At the same time, more pressing social and anthropological concerns are being seriously neglected in the policy and research agendas. Are miners aware of mercury's toxicity? How is mercury being distributed? What precautionary measures are being taken to minimize emissions? One issue that has been overlooked entirely is how an increased reliance upon mercury has exacerbated impoverishment in ASM, a sector, as highlighted in Chapter 3, which is already recognized to be intimately linked with, and driven by, poverty. This chapter examines the implications of this dependence in West Africa.

Mercury: an agent of poverty in West African ASM?

It is the intention of this section of the chapter to explain how a dependence upon mercury has proved to be a curse for the participants of the region's ASM sector. First, with limited outlets available to purchase mercury, miners have had to resort to acquiring supplies of the metal from licensed gold-buying agents (many are also licensed to sell mercury). Buyers, therefore, are in a position to supply mercury in exchange for processed gold at discounted prices; this, in turn, deprives miners of badly needed finances. Second, overexposure to mercury, which has serious health implications, deteriorates the quality of life of poverty-stricken communities even further. Finally, it is worth noting that the support facility that has sought to correct these and related problems has been ineffective at best, causing indigenous ASM populations to lose confidence in assistance programmes. The facility has not necessarily exacerbated poverty in this context, but has certainly done little to offset it.

Impact of intermediaries

While a considerable amount of effort has been made to assess, and inform the wider public of, the environmental implications of amalgamation, minimal research has been undertaken to identify, with precision, how mercury reaches small-scale gold miners. In fact, apart from recent work undertaken as part of the Global Mercury Project,[1] few if any studies have been carried out to improve knowledge of the roles of the various actors involved in the distribution of mercury in developing countries; the lack of information governments possess in this area is worrying.

In an attempt to capture the gold produced in the ASM sector, several governments have acted to improve local mineral-purchasing services. Generally, mine ministries have commissioned a series of buyers to travel to producing areas to purchase gold from miners; this has been the case throughout gold-rich West Africa. In Burkina Faso, for example, the Gold Purchase Counter, which at one time was the 'only body allowed to purchase, process and market gold', employed technicians to purchase product from artisanal mine sites, and granted authorization cards which permitted local buyers to purchase gold that could be resold to holders of gold marketing cards (Gueye, 2001: 19). Similarly, in Ghana, the Precious Minerals and Marketing Corporation (PMMC) today employs 800 licensed buyers, who travel throughout the country purchasing gold from artisanal and small-scale miners (Hilson and Potter, 2003).

Few, however, realize just how much influence gold buyers wield. In a number of cases, buyers are the chief suppliers of mercury, which, in turn, puts miners at their mercy when it comes to selling gold: mercury is often supplied upfront by individual buyers with the condition that gold is sold back to them, often at drastically reduced prices. In Tanzania, for example, gold buyers, who provide mercury, transportation services, food and tools, and deduct these expenses from the price of gold, are often considered to be unfair, retaining an inflated percentage of profits (Hinton and Veiga, 2004). In Zimbabwe, most miners also obtain mercury from private gold buyers, as they do not have the option to purchase mercury from other sources. Here, buyers offer miners a production agreement 'whereby the mercury is provided (rationed) for free by the private buyers but, in exchange, the miners have to sell the gold for US$7.5/g to the private buyers instead of selling for US$8.2/g to the government buyers' (UNIDO, 2005: 14). Work carried out under the Global Mercury Project has helped to underscore the corrupt practices of buyers.

A parallel pattern is emerging in West Africa. In Ghana, many PMMC agents are notorious for quoting a bush price for gold to the miners who have borrowed funds from them and/or to whom mercury has been provided conditionally. The situation is perhaps most pressing in Ghana because many buyers have become full-fledged financiers and sponsors of ASM activities. One illegal miner emphasized this during a personal interview, explaining that 'we [the miners] use them as sponsors...they help us buy this pump, mercury and some other equipments, then we sell the gold to them'.[2] A similar situation persists In Mali, where 'smaller local buyers sometimes have "special" close links with gold washers (loans to buy food) and pay prices which are difficult to control' (Keita, 2001: 11). For example, on 8 February 1991, when the world market price for gold was Ffr31/gram, the prices paid to Malian miners were Ffr17.50/gram for gold powder and FFr20 for nuggets (Keita, 2001); this problem continues to plague operators at the Kiénéba site in particular.

There is emerging evidence that gold buyers are fuelling the vicious poverty cycle which now characterizes ASM, especially at operations in sub-Saharan Africa. By supplying mercury, which is becoming increasingly scarce, to gold-mining communities, buyers are able to manipulate prices to their benefit and deprive miners of badly needed cash. Yet, despite emerging concern, surprisingly little research has been carried out to expose further the corrupt practices of buyers. There is particular need for work to be undertaken in gold-rich West Africa, where, outside of Ghana, little is known about the amounts of money being withheld from miners. What is even more worrying is the apparent contentedness local policymakers have with the power now wielded by gold buyers, who, through increased monopolistic control of mercury sales, have been influential in preventing miners from escaping acute impoverishment.

Health, mercury and poverty

As already mentioned, overexposure to mercury also leads to a deteriorated quality of life. Over the past 15–20 years, the scientific community has carried out extensive analyses of mercury use in ASM regions worldwide, proving repeatedly that through overexposure to mercury, miners subject themselves to a variety of health risks. Representatives from NGOs, governments, universities and multilateral institutions have used this research to inform mining communities about these risks – albeit with varying degrees of success. Convincing gold-mining people of mercury's toxicity remains a challenge worldwide, from the resistant *garimpeiro* populations in Brazil, to the more easily persuaded artisanal gold miners of West Africa.

In ECOWAS, perhaps more so than any other region of the developing world, ASM is characterized by rudimentary implements, and, apart from the occasional pump and crusher, is virtually devoid of machinery. In fact, the difference in the level of sophistication between, for example, a small-scale mining operation in Guyana and Ghana is remarkable. Whereas the former features excavators, tailings ponds and mercury abatement equipment, the latter is associated with pickaxes, shovels and a variety of rudimentary implements used for processing and concentration, including the 'inner tyre tube', a rudimentary means of concentrating ore using the inner tube of an automobile tyre. With this contrast in mechanization comes a sharp difference in labour: because West African sites are more rudimentary, there tends to be a higher concentration of labourers engaged in arduous manual work for menial wages.

This has serious health and interrelated economic implications. One officer in Accra used the case of female labour to illustrate how the backbreaking nature of ASM not only takes its toll physically but also financially: 'Look…they [women] go home and buy paracetamol and buy all these drugs to take for medication. They get 16,000 [cedis] a day and maybe spend about 5000 on drugs because they have pains all over'.

Worse still, such intensive manual work weakens the immune systems of miners, making them even more susceptible to disease and illness, particularly malaria, a serious ailment present in virtually every ASM community world-wide. The symptoms of mercury poisoning, however, are similar to malaria: fever, dizziness, pains and nausea. Miners often purchase malaria medication, unaware that they are suffering from mercury poisoning. Overexposure to mercury also weakens the immune system further, making miners and dependents even more susceptible to other ailments and necessitating the purchase of costly medicines.

A lack of environmental awareness at the community level has certainly impeded improvement, in turn worsening problems on the ground. As Hinton et al. (2003a: 618) explain, 'artisanal miners generally have limited access to information concerning the risks associated with Hg [mercury] in marginalized artisanal mining communities, a situation often exacerbated for women due to socio-cultural inequities'. This is a major concern in Burkina Faso, where 90 per cent of all mineral-processing activities are carried out by women (Gueye, 2001), as well as Mali, where a half of the ASM labour force is female, and 90 per cent of mineral processing activities are undertaken by women (Keita, 2001). In Ghana, miners were observed to be both unaware and/or unconvinced of mercury's toxicity. One government official argued during an interview that this is owed largely to indigenous *galamsey* being 'semi-illiterate and…their perception about the health impacts of mercury…[being] very low…not knowing much about it, and so…[not caring] much about it'. This was confirmed during visits to mining regions, where several miners were observed to be handling mercury without appropriate respiratory and hand gear, and 'sucking' the amalgam sponge:

> I do not know it [mercury] poses health problem. Am not aware mercury is toxic and do not know it has any health effects…After panning, to obtain the amalgam, I put the amalgam in a handkerchief and suck the excess mercury from the amalgam for reuse. [*galamsey* miner].

Although inappropriate handling of mercury occurs throughout rural Ghana, there are several promising signs that information is reaching certain communities,[3] and importantly, that individuals appear willing to take suggestions on board. One *galamsey* operator noted, 'we [miners] have hand gloves', and another explained that 'when you are burning the gold, you have to go out from the room [so] it does not get in your lungs'. Another miner reported having constructed enclosed 'furnaces' to burn amalgam, which 'disperse' noxious fumes downwind, 'away from the family and children'. In fact, the child factor proved to be an effective means of convincing many Ghanaian *galamsey* about the severity of mercury: miners were more receptive to the possibility of taking precautionary measures when informed that overexposure to mercury could impair a child's development (Hilson, 2006a). There are now several reports which provide detailed accounts of child labour in other West African ASM regions (ILO, 1999; Alfa, 1999; Delap et al., 2004). In Niger, Burkina Faso and Mali, where child labour features prominently in the ASM sector, governments are advised to also use the child factor to persuade industry leaders and foremen to engage in best-practice mercury management.

Technological assistance

Are donor agencies working to improve awareness of mercury's toxicity in ASM communities, as well as to introduce technologies to minimize emissions? Clearly, another overlooked aspect of the mercury-poverty issue in the sector is technology failure. More specifically, why have millions of dollars in donor aid failed to facilitate marked improvements in mercury management? This phenomenon warrants an explanation: while not necessarily driving poverty in ASM communities, mercury support and educational projects have certainly failed to equip operators with the requisite know-how to improve their lives.

The difficulties with disseminating environmental knowledge through middlemen, by far the most effective means of reaching miners, have left one-on-one training and technology transfer as the most viable options for resolving the mercury contamination problem. Although technologies can certainly be readily deployed to minimize miners' exposure to mercury, donor agencies and host governments have struggled with this task, largely because of the hitherto fixation on designing technologies in Western countries, refusing to interact with target populations and selling equipment at unrealistic prices. This has proved to be a recipe for disaster: levels of acceptance and adoption have been low, and in the process of such cavalier implementation, substantial sums of donor aid have been wasted. Government, UN and World Bank officials, who are often quick to blame miners' lack of cooperation on low levels of equipment uptake in the area of mercury management, have failed to take stock of the success of the many projects that have emphasized implementation of local solutions. For example, in Papua New Guinea, the inexpensive 'tin fish tin' mercury retort, constructed from local scrap tuna tins with which local people are familiar, has proved far more palatable than the expensive, fragile UNIDO retort, designed by engineers in Vienna. The latter has been promoted extensively in Ghana, particularly under the UNIDO project, but with minimal success.

The tendency to overrate local UNIDO efforts and parallel projects has not helped the situation; in fact, the confidence officials appear to have in donor-driven initiatives in mercury education and support is disconcerting. For example, the UNIDO programme in Ghana, one of the most comprehensive mercury abatement project launched in ECOWAS to date, continues to receive high praise from officials, despite being laden with problems. During interviews with two government officers, the work carried out in mercury monitoring and the efforts made to minimize emissions through dissemination of retorts were discussed extensively. What was not mentioned was, as another stakeholder explained, that 'the government is selling it [retorts] at 500,000 cedis', or that the retort itself is fragile, inefficient and often burns out. Why would a miner even consider purchasing an inappropriate piece of equipment? More importantly, how can the government expect an impoverished operator to mobilize the US$50 required for its purchase? There is now reason to believe that ASM communities, repeatedly the recipients of such ad hoc intervention and ineffective assistance, are growing increasingly wary of government support, and with good reason.

The fact remains that the UNIDO project was a debacle, focusing primarily on the effects of mercury contamination, rather than identifying ways in which to alleviate miners' dependency upon mercury and reduce their exposure to the metal during amalgamation. It is imperative that mercury scientists and social scientists carrying out research in West African ASM communities go beyond the conventional analysis of mercury pollution, and begin incorporating anthropological issues in their work. The mercury contamination problem is now well understood; it is high time that researchers begin working directly with communities to educate operators about the health implications of amalgamation, and to identify and develop appropriate local-level technological solutions.

Conclusion: alleviating poverty in mercury-dependent ASM communities

This chapter has examined how an increased dependence upon mercury in West Africa's ASM sector has perpetuated poverty in local communities. Miners are generally at the mercy of gold buyers, who are also licensed to sell mercury; by withholding supplies, buyers are in a position to quote bush prices for gold, which deprives impoverished mining groups of badly needed income. Reliance upon mercury has also brought with it a host of health problems, imposing an unquantifiable cost: treatments must be purchased for resulting illnesses, as well as for dealing with sicknesses caused by the weakening of the immune system brought about by overexposure. It was also judged necessary to examine the technological assistance factor, simply because hundreds of thousands of dollars in donor aid for the alleviation of mercury pollution in the ASM sector have rarely materialized into anything meaningful on the ground. The global fixation on assessing contamination levels in environmental media, species and riverine populations in ASM regions, which has spilled over into West Africa, has impeded efforts to determine how the environmental impacts of mercury are perceived on the ground and for developing appropriate educational programmes for communities. As evidenced by the UNIDO project in Ghana and parallel efforts, there appears to be a reluctance on the part of Western researchers and engineers to study target ASM populations.

To curtail dependency upon mercury in West African ASM communities, research funds must first be released to develop alternatives to amalgamation. The EU, currently the largest producer of mercury, has set a 2011 deadline to ban exports (of mercury), which would be catastrophic for the region's impoverished small-scale gold miners: at present, there are no suitable alternatives to amalgamation, and with the minimal progress that has occurred here over the past decade, there is little reason to believe that plausible options will be available by 2011. Vieira (2004) cites a number of alternative mercury-free mineral-processing strategies, including gravity separation, improved sluicing and Gemini tables. Plans were made by staff at the University of Ghana to demonstrate these technologies in Ghana in 2006; local consultants are also in the process of piloting improved technologies in Burkina Faso. It is imperative that this work is carried over into Mali, Benin and Guinea, where ASM research as a whole is in an embryonic state. In each case, however, demonstration activities must involve the host communities themselves: local knowledge and solicited feedback from operators are the keys to devising appropriate solutions to the mercury problem in the region's ASM sector. As Hinton et al. (2003b: 100) explain, 'technical alternatives derived from formal mining, or developed specifically for ASM, must be thoroughly examined, pre-tested, appropriately modified and successfully transferred...before ASM is likely to transform into an environmentally sound and socio-economically sustainable activity'.

There is also a need to disseminate appropriate mercury retorts. There has been a propensity, not only in the case of Ghana and surrounding countries but in the developing world as a whole, to design retorting apparatuses in the West and promote mass implementation without assessing feasibility. This has resulted in low levels of adoption. More favourable results have, however, been achieved where equipment has been designed using local materials with which target groups are more familiar. In these instances, there has been a recognizable level of interaction with the community. For example, as noted above, during the recent AusAid study on ASM in Papua New Guinea, retorts were constructed using scrap tin. Consumption of tinned fish occurs throughout Papua New Guinea; tins are a principal waste product. The 'tin fish tin' model features a small tin (the top removed), in which the amalgam cake is placed. A second, larger tin is placed atop the first tin; the dish is filled with damp ashes or sand, and is placed over a fire. The mercury becomes trapped in the damp sand, is panned out and can be reused (Crispin, 2003). A similar procedure, involving two buckets and a bowl filled with water, is now popular in Chinese gold mining regions (Hinton et al., 2003b). These local-level solutions have had a far greater impact than the campaigns sponsored by multilateral donor agencies, which have sought to promote untested, and often expensive, retorting technologies.

On the educational front, there is a need for West African governments and donor bodies to adopt more pragmatic instruments for disseminating information on mercury to mining communities. As the areas in which operations occur are often remote, the aids used must reflect this. Commenting upon research carried out in Suriname, Heemskerk and Oliveira (2004: 38) note that 'the most important limiting factor in disseminating information to the interior is access: many media and communication forms are not available or function properly in the interior'. The authors recommend, given this limitation, that radio – generally, the most accessible and popular medium for receiving information in developing countries – is used as a principal outlet for communication. Radio broadcasts on mercury have already proved effective in Ghana, where many miners indicated during personal interviews that they had first heard about the lethality of mercury during a national broadcast in 2004, and have since taken various measures to address the problem.

Portable videos have also been found to be effective. As Crispin (2003) explains, in Papua New Guinea, the Outreach Program run by the Small-Scale Mining Branch of the Department of Mining produced a series of videos, one of which is entitled 'Mercury use in small-scale mining'. A solar-powered video and television player was developed, which the training team used to show a film on mercury in several remote villages. A similar initiative was taken in Ghana:

> They dramatized the use of mercury and we have a video of it, so these officers will, they get a TV set then put on the video and he (the local government officer) knows the whole community is there to watch. Then, after that, he explains to them what has happened in the community and tells them how mercury is: it's very poisonous. Then, he educates them. [Senior government officer, Accra]

The only flaw in the exercise was that it was only part of a training programme for legal small-scale gold miners. It is recommended that West African governments adopt a similar strategy of educating operators, but that they do not discriminate between registered (legal) and illegal miners when using video media, because generally it is the latter who are in need of the most training and education. Moreover, by working in illegal mining regions as well, authorities help to arm the more transient clandestine operators with important knowledge, which could go a long way towards reducing mercury pollution. As Heemskerk and Oliveira (2004: 39) note, 'a large screen in the center of the village is likely to attract a large audience'.

Illustrative material, particularly comics and brochures, should be distributed by government officers to village heads, miners and community dwellers (Veiga, 1997a,1997b). The low levels of literacy prevalent in many ASM regions worldwide limit the effectiveness of written material. In Papua New Guinea, illustrative booklets were produced with accompanying written explanations in both English and Tok Pisin, a local dialect (Crispin, 2003). Mine operators 'may be especially targeted with cartoon brochures' (Heemskerk and Oliveira, 2003: 34) because 'if posters or cartoon brochures are used, pictures rather than words should convey the message' (Heemskerk and Oliveira, 2004: 39). It is also imperative that assistance groups convey the appropriate message, which, in many cases, has not proved to be simply highlighting the environmental and health-related impacts of careless mercury handling. As Veiga et al. (2006) and Hinton et al. (2003b) report, when certain small-scale mining groups in the Latin American region were informed that acute mercury exposure results in impotency, it caught the attention of the most resistant of operators. As explained above, the child factor has been shown to be the most effective means of getting the message across to Ghanaian miners, and promises to have a similar effect throughout ECOWAS.

To summarize, considerable work has been undertaken to quantify mercury contamination levels in communities, not only in West Africa but also throughout most of the developing world; continued and repeated analysis in this area provides minimal additional information. Improving knowledge of conditions on the ground and the capabilities and views of operators would enable West African governments and donor bodies to design and implement more effective mechanisms for resolving the mercury dependency problem, which is proving to be another important factor in the region's ASM-poverty nexus.

CHAPTER 6

Fostering cooperation between small- and large-scale gold-miners in West Africa

Richard K. Amankwah and C. Anim-Sackey

Conflicts between artisanal and small-scale miners, on the one hand, and the management and security personnel of large-scale mines, on the other, are pervasive in several parts of the developing world. The prevailing view is that large-scale and artisanal and small-scale mining cannot coexist. It is argued in this chapter, however, that these important members of the mining community can work together.

The objectives of this chapter are to provide a brief overview of ASM in West Africa, and to identify some of the major causes of conflict between the region's mining parties. The chapter will look at case studies and initiatives taken by certain large-scale miners operating in West Africa to improve relations with small-scale miners. The chapter concludes by prescribing recommendations for further improving relations between the region's ASM and large-scale mine operators.

ASM in West Africa: historical and contemporary perspectives

West Africa has been a major gold-mining area for many centuries, with activities dating back to the beginning of the fifth century. According to historical data, in 1325, Emperor Kankan Moussa of Mali embarked on a pilgrimage to Mecca, armed with about 8 tonnes of gold. It is also known that during the period 1490–1600, 254 tonnes of gold, representing about 35 per cent of the world's gold output at the time, was produced in the territory that is now Ghana; regional output from 1601 to 1800 alone was 370 tonnes.

This gold was produced solely by artisanal and small-scale means (Ghana Publishing Corporation, 1970; Kesse, 1985; Keita, 2001); large-scale mining did not commence in West Africa until the late 1800s. Despite the major advances made by multinational mining companies in recent years, small-scale gold-mining is still widespread throughout the region. Today, the sector employs thousands of people in such countries as Ghana, Burkina Faso, Guinea, Mali and, to a lesser extent, Benin (Figure 6.1).

According to the ILO (1999), worldwide, between 11.5 million and 13 million people are employed directly in the ASM sector. Though this number keeps

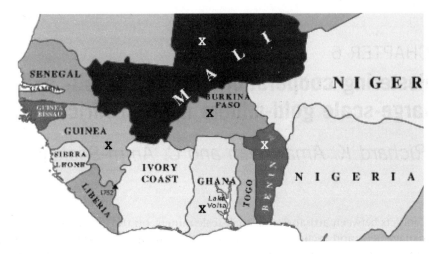

Figure 6.1   West African countries showing the widespread ASM areas (marked 'x')

increasing, it is difficult to obtain reliable population estimates because of the rural character of the sector and the migratory nature of its operators. The ILO has estimated that between 1989 and 1999 the ASM workforce increased by 20 per cent. Based upon the research carried out under the MMSD Project, West Africa's ASM population was at least 500,000 strong in the late 1990s (MMSD, 2002a).

The legislation of each West African country differs in its definitions of an artisanal mine and a small-scale mine. These differences notwithstanding, ASM generally comprises activities characterized by low tonnage of material and rudimentary levels of technology. Operations have low overheads due to the application of inexpensive equipment. Miners acquire concessions or arrogate concessions to themselves in areas where deposits are rich, but too small to justify investment in the infrastructure and equipment necessary for large-scale operations.

The ASM sector has had a significant impact on the livelihoods of many individuals and communities, as it provides both part-time and full-time employment; in some cases, it is the only source of income available. In the rural communities where ASM occurs, activities have reduced rural exodus, promoted local economic development and alleviated poverty. Through ASM activity, basic skills develop, and due to the low barriers to entry in terms of capital needs and formal educational requirements, operations provide excellent outlets for indigenous entrepreneurs.

Drivers of conflicts between ASM and large-scale mining parties

In most developing countries, such as those in West Africa, mining projects involve three major stakeholders: a large-scale miner, central or local government and the local community (Barry, 1997). The groups of people found in local or host communities include occupational, residential and indigenous parties; each is affected differently by changes to the social system induced by a mining project. Residential parties in this context are those living in the host community but with no ancestral ties to the land (MMSD, 2002a).

In rural areas, a great percentage of people in host mining communities are either small-scale miners or subsistence farmers. Conflicts generally arise in these communities when the exploitation of mineral resources is not managed in a sustainable manner, and there is a consequent loss of livelihood, extensive damage to the environment and an inequitable distribution of benefits (WCED, 1987; MMSD, 2002a). Poor communication between large-scale mines and affected communities has also been identified as a key driver of conflicts (Hilson, 2002e).

Generally, before large-scale mines acquire concessions, artisanal and small-scale miners are working in the same area. These miners are the unglorified pathfinders to many gold deposits, using local knowledge to pinpoint economic mineral reserves. Usually, licensed small-scale miners are given very short mining leases to prevent them from holding on to concessions. These miners migrate frequently and often abandon their own concessions for extended periods while working illegally on other concessions perceived to be richer. When foreign mining companies with the potential to carry out mechanized, large-scale activities arrive in a country, they are typically awarded concessions, which often encompass concessions held by licensed small-scale miners. These plots are subsequently transferred to the former as soon as the leases of the latter expire. This step is generally not only meant to earn more foreign exchange for the central government but also ensures that viable mining lands are not left unexploited. In many cases, small-scale miners return and continue to work illegally on portions of concessions held by large mines, leading to conflict.

As part of their social responsibilities, large-scale mines often promise displaced small-scale miners jobs but due to the highly mechanized setup of modern mines, few employment opportunities are created. With few employment avenues available, people continue to work as illegal miners. Clandestine operations are now widespread: according to a survey conducted in 28 countries by the ILO, 5–80 per cent of small-scale mining activities fall in this category (ILO, 1999), although this is likely an underestimation.

A critical assessment of relations between ASM and large-scale mine parties in West Africa

Amankwah and Anim-Sackey (2004) examined some of the initiatives being taken by the management of four mining companies in Ghana to improve relations with small-scale miners in host communities. The following section provides an update on the situation in Ghana, detailing the steps taken by companies to forge partnerships. Though small-scale mining is now ubiquitous throughout rural West Africa, the discussion concentrates on Ghana, which hosts most of the region's large-scale mines, Guinea, Burkina Faso and Mali.

Ghana

Ghana Goldfields and Bogoso Goldfields (BGL) are two large-scale mines that have permitted small-scale miners to work on their concessions at Abosso and Tarkwa, and Bogoso and Prestea, respectively. In 1996, when the Abosso Mine concession was a subsidiary of Rangers of Australia, the company set aside an area for seven small-scale mining groups displaced as a result of the transfer of the mining lease from the latter to the former. Some 700 miners were organized along the lines of statutory laws in the Mining Regulations tributor system (Ghana Publishing Corporation, 1970). Within a period of three years (1996–9), the small-scale miners had produced and sold 86.7 kg (2,803 oz) of gold (Amankwah and Anim-Sackey, 2004). Gold Fields took over the mine in 2001 but the new management continued to foster the level of cooperation already established. After exhausting the mineralized zones in the area allotted to them, however, the small-scale miners moved to another section beyond their boundaries. Unfortunately, this was an area earmarked for large-scale operations by Gold Fields, and their activities have since become illegal due to their unwillingness to return to the area allocated. More research and increased interaction with the host community is needed to identify a sustainable relocation plan or alternative livelihoods project.

In 1999, Gold Fields relinquished a portion of its concession to the government to be licensed to the Akoon Small-Scale Mining Cooperative Society. The underground operation run by the cooperative has been inactive since 2003, however, due to the flooding of work areas. The cooperative has been seeking a partnership with an investor who would provide funds to purchase pumps to drain the flooded portions of the concession and reset the working area, but a candidate investor has not yet been found.

In 2000, ASM operators working on the mineral concession of BGL rejected a portion of the concession allocated to them at Dumasi, Bogoso, because of its perceived poor gold mineralization. These miners opted to move to another area, which they believed to be more mineralized, and immediately began mining for gold without the permission of BGL. It took a team of soldiers and policemen to drive them away from their new site. Since then, the security situation has prevented work on that portion of the concession.

In June 2005, more than 500 people from Prestea, Himan, Bondaye and other communities surrounding Bogoso poured on to the streets of Prestea to demonstrate against surface mining by BGL. Some of the demonstrators attempted to enter a nearby pit that security officers were guarding. The security men fired warning shots and tear gas, wounding seven of the demonstrators. The matter is still under investigation and at the time, the community gave the mining company a 21-day ultimatum to stop all mining activities at Prestea (*Ghanaian Chronicle*, 2005a).

Despite the fact that small-scale miners continue to work on lands demarcated for them on BGL's concession in Prestea, it appears that the relationship between Gold Fields and its host communities is better than that of BGL. Perhaps it may be necessary for Golden Star Resources, the majority owner of the BGL concession, to review its community relations policies, adopt a more proactive strategy and consider upholding some of the agreements forged when the section of the concession in Prestea was under the management of Prestea Gold Fields.

Many of the mechanisms deployed by large-scale mines to broker peaceful negotiations with ASM operators and occupants of surrounding communities have deteriorated, resulting in hostile relationships in areas such as Bogoso and Prestea, and Obuasi, which host BGL and Anglo-Ashanti Gold's operations, respectively. In an attempt to curb the rampant pilfering of ores from its concession, Anglo-Ashanti was reported to have threatened to shoot on sight any artisanal/small-scale miner who entered the company's concession. In June 2005, one ASM operator died after receiving injuries on Anglo-Ashanti's concession. There are conflicting reports as to how he died: the family of the deceased and the medical officer who carried out the autopsy on the dead man allege that he died of gunshot wounds, but the mine security officers indicated that he was wounded when spikes on top of a metal gate pierced his stomach. Investigations into this incident are still ongoing (Ghana News Agency, 2005).

Guinea

As in Ghana, illegal small-scale gold mining in Guinea is referred to as *galamsey*; a large percentage of these miners work on the mineral concession of Anglo-Ashanti at Siguiri. ASM was practised in the area long before the concession was demarcated to Anglo-Ashanti. Though mine management at Siguiri has permitted ASM activities on a section of their concession, illegal operators encroach on other parts of the plot.

According to one mining engineer at the mine site, there is little farming and schooling in the area. Consequently, about 7,000 *galamsey* operators from the six surrounding villages and other settlements in the district travel to the site every day to mine for gold. Of these, 10 per cent are children and 75 per cent are women. Though mine security personnel usually drive the *galamsey* away from the active mine sites, there have not been any major conflicts reported between the two parties.

Burkina Faso

Burkina Faso has abundant mineral resources, including gold, but these are yet to be exploited to an appreciable extent. There are currently several exploration and prospecting companies and a small group of mining companies working in the country. The presence of few large mines has given the state more control over national gold production, and therefore, artisanal and small-scale miners are well organized (Gueye, 2001).

Generally, there exist good relations between artisanal and large-scale miners in Burkina Faso. This is mainly due to the fact that the country's Mining Code states that a permit for artisanal mining does not allow its holder to obtain a mining title, nor does it prevent research from being carried out on the surface area covered by the permit. When a mining title covering the same surface area is granted, the artisanal mining permit will not be renewed, although by law, the artisanal miner must be compensated by the holder of the mining title. As discussed by Gueye (2001), the government moves to resolve complaints and remove artisanal miners whenever large-scale miners complain about their presence in their territory.

Despite the relatively serene relations between miners in Burkina Faso, if large-scale operators continue to take over concessions held by ASM operators, these could deteriorate to the extent to which it has in parts of Ghana. For example, when OreZone, a Canadian junior exploration company, began exploration work at Seguenega, it was realized that thousands of small-scale miners or *paillers* were already mining in the area. These miners included indigenes and individuals who had migrated from other parts of the country, driven by severe drought and crop failure. With over 2,000 small-scale miners on their hands, the challenge currently facing OreZone is how, with its limited resources, to equitably resettle such a large group of people.

Mali

In 1997, Anglo-Ashanti (then AngloGold) opened a large open-cast mine at Sadiola in western Mali, where traditional artisanal gold mining has long been practised. At the time the mine commenced operation, managers were challenged to address a host of environmental problems, including land degradation caused by the activities of small-scale miners; this eventually led the company to resettle the inhabitants of two communities, Sadiola and Farabakouta, which host the mine. As a means of compensating the local communities, Anglo launched the Sadiola Gold Mining Project with the intention of extending assistance to artisanal miners, promoting community development and diversifying the local economy. The project began with public consultation, involving traditional groups and representatives from local NGOs, to help identify target groups and potential partners for the project (Keita, 2001).

The efforts made under the auspices of the Gold Mining Project resulted in the establishment of the Sadiola Mining Cooperative. The cooperative is supported by a programme of technical assistance, which emphasizes geological analysis and the identification and testing of mining equipment. Moreover, the project has led to the creation of a community development fund, support for a school and the establishment of health and learning centres for adults.

The project has also supported small enterprises such as bakeries, woodwork shops, jewellers, metalwork shops and – specifically for women – market gardening, dye and soap-making businesses. Overall, the project has affected some 500 people in four communities, and has stimulated local entrepreneurial activity and purchasing power. Interestingly, the number of people engaged in artisanal mining at the Sadiola site is declining rapidly because of the better commercial opportunities available through trade with workers at the large-scale mine.

Possible ways forward

From the case studies examined above, it appears that Ghana is one country where illegal mining (*galamsey*) activities are on the rise and where, as a consequence, conflicts between small- and large-scale miners have intensified. It is therefore necessary for stakeholders such as the management of large-mines, leaders of the host communities and small-scale mining groups, and government representatives to step up efforts to foster cooperation at both the local and national levels. It is unacceptable for ASM operators to encroach on the mineral concessions of large-scale mines with impunity. For example, it has been reported that at Anglo-Ashanti's Obuasi mine, some ASM operators dig pits very close to ongoing operations and link them to various levels underground. Some of these illegal pits threaten the stability of dam walls. It is, however, equally disturbing when a company's policy is to shoot on sight encroaching ASM operators.

Anybody who has carried out research on relations between artisanal, small- and large-scale miners will acknowledge that there are no simple solutions to resolving conflicts. Several strategies have been proposed to manage the conflict between the participants of these important segments of the developing world economy. Andrew (2003) classifies these as: government initiatives; mining company initiatives; and stakeholder interests. The author also suggests mediation as a process to manage conflicts between mining parties. The traditional West African legal and social system already utilizes mediation in the resolution of thorny issues between various groups; it could readily be extended to the present subject as well.

An integrated and transparent approach that emphasizes the participation of local and central government, mining companies and local community leaders, and which features a mediator where necessary, could yield enormous benefits. For example, as was noted earlier, small-scale miners rejected a piece of land given to them by BGL management because the grade of ore (in the demarcated plot) was perceived to be uneconomical. This could, however, be confirmed or disproved by both the mining company and the government through prospecting or sharing with *galamsey* the information detailed on the maps of the area and the grades of cores drilled there. Such assurance could persuade miners to work within the boundaries of the demarcated area. In the long term, the local and central government could use portions of the royalties accrued from the large-scale mining operation in the community to purchase or rent mining processing equipment that could be utilized to improve the operations of the small-scale miners on the ceded land.

A number of large-scale mining companies have proposed alternative livelihood projects such as livestock rearing, poultry farming and cloth (batik, tie and dye) production. Though these would create jobs for a larger number of people in the mining communities, artisanal and small-scale miners generally do not show an interest because in their opinion, these occupations are less lucrative and they have no means of surviving until products are ready for the market. The challenge, therefore, is to put into operation integrated farming ventures that have the potential to sustain workers from the outset. To reduce the social pressure exerted, mining companies could consider this as part of their social responsibilities. Companies, however, must ensure that there is a clear business case for this.

It is generally accepted that both ASM operators and large-scale miners stand to benefit from increased cooperation. Developing a win-win relationship requires significant understanding and patience. As each community is unique in terms of needs and livelihood systems, and although all demands cannot be met, enhanced dialogue between both artisanal and small-scale miners and other members of the local community at an early stage of development of a large-scale mining venture could help build important bridges. Where necessary, mediators and facilitators should be utilized, and agreements must be documented.

CHAPTER 7

Artisanal and small-scale mining in West Africa: achieving sustainable development through environmental and human rights law

Karen MacDonald

It is time to face an uncomfortable truth: the accustomed model of development has been fruitful for the few, but flawed for many. A path to prosperity that ravages the environment and leaves a majority behind in squalor will be a dead end. The world today needs to usher in a season of transformation, a season of stewardship.

Kofi Annan, United Nations Secretary-General, World Summit on Sustainable Development, 2 September 2002

This chapter analyzes the aims and scope of international environmental and human rights law in relation to ASM communities in West Africa. It provides insight into the potential use and application of key agreements in reducing poverty and ameliorating interrelated social and environmental impacts in the sector, arguing that the formalization of operations could contribute significantly to poverty reduction and sustainable development. The chapter is structured as follows: first, links between the environment, human rights and development in ASM, including sustainable development; second, international environmental law approaches to achieving poverty reduction in ASM, the role of the Millennium Development Goals (MDGs) and the World Summit on Sustainable Development; third, international human rights law and environmental law approaches to some key ASM concerns, including poverty; fourth, the right to development, land-use conflicts, licensing, security of tenure for indigenous and traditional communities and the right to self-determination; and fifth, women and children. This is followed by a short examination of current ASM regulations and practices in ECOWAS, and concludes with some suggested next steps.

According to the UNDP (2003b: 1), it is estimated that more that 20 million men, women and children depend on ASM for their subsistence. For example, the ILO (1999) stated that part-time small-scale mining in Niger employed approximately 132,000 people; when small-scale quarries are included, the total small-scale mining workforce amounted to about 442,000. Further, 60 per cent of Ghana's mining labour force is employed at small-scale mines (Hilson, 2001b: 6). Estimates state that ASM accounts for 20–25 per cent of the world's non-fuel mineral production; generates close to US$2 billion in gold and gems in Africa alone; produces more that US$200 million worth of gold in more than six countries; and is responsible for 15 per cent of all diamond production, valued at US$1.2 billion (Jennings, 2004).

In recent decades, international environmental and human rights law have generated numerous norms, binding agreements and soft law principles. These are potentially of relevance to the sustainable and ethical development of ASM in West Africa, and may contribute to establishing the very stewardship to which the UN Secretary-General aspires. There follows an analysis of legal frameworks that might be useful when considering the regulation of ASM as a means for reducing poverty and addressing related environmental and social concerns within the framework of sustainable development.[1] Examples of issues associated with ASM that can potentially be addressed by international environmental law and/or international human rights law frameworks include the cross-sectoral, interrelated issues of environmental degradation; occupational health and safety; public participation in decision-making; poverty; land claims; indigenous persons' rights; environmental rights; health issues; gender inequalities; child labour; and conflicts.

The chapter examines several international agreements promulgated under the auspices of the UN. In this context, it is important to appreciate that the preamble of the 1945 United Nations Charter states, among other things, that the UN was formed:

> to reaffirm faith in fundamental human rights, in the dignity and worth of the human person, in the equal rights of men and women;…to establish conditions under which justice and respect for the obligations arising from treaties and other sources of international law can be maintained; to promote social progress and better standards of life in larger freedom, to employ international machinery for the promotion of the economic and social advancement of all peoples.

The UN's aspirations have frequently been asserted through international laws regularly generated by global negotiations and the consensus-making processes that attend UN membership. Such agreements are relevant for advancing our arguments in that they can provide a framework from which regional and national-binding legislation can be advanced. As member states of the UN,[2] representatives from ECOWAS are present at such negotiations, participate in the international law-making process and are in a position to influence not only the development of international law but also their own legislation and policies.

International environmental and human rights law in ASM: an overview of the issues

Linking environment, human rights and development in ASM

Small-scale mining means different things to different people. To some it is dirty, dangerous, disruptive and should be discouraged. To others it is profitable, productive, or simply the only way out of poverty (ILO, 1999).

This alliterative statement summarizes perfectly the variants at play when attempting to regulate ASM practices. Many individual concerns are central to ASM practices but remain coterminous. According to Hentschel et al. (2002: 1), 'the [ASM] sector is perhaps better known for its high environmental costs and poor health and safety record. Many continue to view ASM as dirty, unprofitable and fundamentally unsustainable'. ASM practices undertaken 'by individuals, groups, families or cooperatives [often operate] with minimal or no mechanization, often in the informal (illegal) sector of the market...the informality of [which] may have negative effects on the social, environmental and fiscal regimes of a country or region' (Hentschel et al., 2002: 5, 11).

Nevertheless, 'national governments are becoming increasingly aware of the sector's importance as both a means of poverty alleviation and a generator of national income' (Hentschel et al., 2002: 13). In these statements, we see that formal regulation of the ASM sector is tasked with reconciling. However, the reconciliation has been difficult in mining states the world over, including developed, developing and least-developed countries. As Smith (1998: 244), a Nigerian environmental lawyer and scholar, observes, 'the paradox of humans' struggle for survival, their economic activities, and the collective strive towards economic growth and national development is that they are, like the warp and weft in the tapestry, generally enmeshed in environmental complexities'.

Primary natural resource extraction, of which ASM is an example, is full of these environmental complexities. It is without doubt that environmental concerns are raised during the course of mining activities, whether large-scale mechanical operations or small-scale artisanal ventures. They are also interwoven with many other social issues, some of which are considered below. Often, developing countries, particularly those in sub-Saharan Africa, 'are characterized by poverty as a result of which people are compelled to over-exploit natural resources' (Smith, 1998: 248). The regulation of ASM practices as a means of poverty reduction should therefore aim to achieve integrated and balanced environmental, social and economic goals. At a minimum, international environmental and human rights law can offer one approach for addressing some of the environment and poverty-related issues of ASM.

It is necessary to analyze how such international laws work. International environmental and human rights laws have largely been created by states through several declarations, treaties and other subsidiary means. Declarations, which are a large focus of this chapter, are expressions of intention and declare obligations (environmental or rights-related) that states create for themselves and aim to fulfil. Declarations are often flexible and broad, described frequently as soft law,[3] and tend to provide goals to aim for as opposed to precise, rigid targets and requirements found in treaties or hard law. For our environmental law purposes here, we are concerned with soft law declarations, as there are not yet any international environmental hard law agreements that regulate ASM practices or that address its environmental and poverty issues.

There is a certain utility to soft law agreements. Giving states the flexibility or scope for interpretation and implementation in a declaratory text is often a means of attaining the support of governments in terms of advancing those common international goals that require national action. Soft law can be adapted to suit the situation of the country, as long as the general objective is being aimed for.

This can be contrasted with requiring states to meet the hard law treaty requirements that would be potentially threatening in terms of the financial, technological and other means (particularly in the case of environmental law) needed to achieve compliance. Further, noting that international environmental law rests on the doctrine of the sovereignty and equality of states (though such sovereignty is not absolute – for example, states are required not to cause environmental harm beyond their own borders), individual states would be reluctant to participate in the international law-making procedure if the system was too demanding, burdensome or inequitable for them; little might be achieved on global matters in this case. In this respect, for ECOWAS, declaratory guidance is thus likely to be of great assistance in the national formulation of policies and laws for regulating ASM, as it offers flexibility while still providing some form of guidance and direction, particularly for emerging economies. It is useful as it emanates from the international level and thus serves to meet global challenges (particularly environmental ones) while it also acknowledges that national action is required.

The 1972 Stockholm Declaration on the Human Environment (Stockholm Declaration)[4] and the 1992 Rio Declaration on Environment and Development (Rio Declaration),[5] to which we shall return shortly, provide examples of useful environmental soft law. The 1948 Universal Declaration of Human Rights (UDHR)[6] is an example of a soft law human rights declaration. It outlines the basic rights that every human being should be guaranteed. In the context of ASM, relevant rights of the UDHR include Article 23, the right to work (and in just and favourable conditions), to join trade unions and to have social security; Article 25, the right to a standard of living adequate for the health and well-being of self and family; Article 26, the right to education; and Article 28, the right 'to a social and international order in which the rights and freedoms set forth in the Declaration can be fully realized'. These rights inform the scope of advancement needed in the ASM sector.

There are also other human rights agreements mentioned in this chapter that constitute hard law but which have flexible provisions. Some key provisions from the environmental declarations mentioned above and some relevant human rights agreements are examined below, with suggestions on how they can be applied to improve the ASM sector in the context of sustainable development.

Sustainable development

The 1981 African Charter on Human and Peoples' Rights[7] states in Article 24: 'All peoples shall have the right to a general satisfactory environment favourable to their development'. Sound environmental and social regulation could, in theory, not only protect the environment, but also ameliorate negative social conditions that often accompany, contribute to, or are symptomatic of environmental degradation, including poverty. Principle 2 of the 1992 Rio Declaration acknowledges that 'States have, in accordance with the Charter of the United Nations and the principles of international law, the sovereign right to exploit their own resources [but not to harm those of other States] pursuant to their own *environmental* and *developmental* policies', an argument for sustainable development (author's italics and parentheses). If developed and managed sustainably, mining activities can contribute vastly to the local economy, the wealth of individual countries and the livelihoods of many communities. Though there is no firm definition of sustainable development, the one promoted by WCED in 1987, 'development that meets the needs of the present without compromising the ability of future generations to meet their own needs',[8] continues to be an accepted interpretation, provides a blueprint for achieving sustainable development and is sufficient for our purposes.

Central to ASM practices in the context of sustainable development are environmental, economic and social concerns. Reconciling these competing goals is fundamental to the idea or concept of 'sustainable development' (WCED, 1987). Environmental, economic and social goals should be balanced, without gain in one area at the expense of another, in order to advance standards of living in mining communities and to meet their needs and those of future generations.

ASM practices thus need to be regulated in a manner that mitigates potential impacts on the environment, human health and social well-being, as such negative impacts can further exacerbate poverty and other social ills. As Cullet (2003:10) asserts, 'sustainable development implies change in human material activities which lessen the depletion of non-renewable resources and the pollution of the environment'. This does not require that ASM activities stop altogether, but that regulation takes into account other factors such as the need to: maximize the use of resources that are needed to ensure an income stream well into the future (and thus give action to the principle of intra- and inter-generational equity); avoid polluting the environment and protect the health of communities; conserve the surrounding flora and fauna on which communities might rely; and avoid tensions between competing needs and interests.

The concept of sustainable development provides governments and legislators the world over with a general rule of thumb by which to attempt to abide when making policy and regulatory decisions of a social, economic or environmental nature (Sands, 2003: 9). ECOWAS members themselves will determine the precise, practical meaning of sustainable development as it applies to them. This will likely take into account cultural circumstances, employment challenges, geographical circumstances, climatic circumstances, poverty levels, history and social priorities. What is clear is that the improvement of individuals' quality of life is the most important part of the concept of sustainable development, and thus also of any legal and policymaking initiatives undertaken by ECOWAS members.

Sustainable development acknowledges that individuals and communities need to earn a living through the use, or more accurately the sustainable use, of natural resources, since these may be the only available source of income, as is often the case with ASM practices. The concept of sustainable development or use, however, cautions that earning a living should not compromise the environment (Sands, 2003: 252). Nor, ideally, should it give rise to conflict. If resources are used sustainably or for our purposes, more steadily in an organized, regulated manner, environmental harm may be mitigated, conflict may be lessened and poverty may be reduced. Finding an appropriate balance between current social and economic needs and environmental protection goals is not easy.

Although this chapter, to a certain extent, attempts to delineate between environmental law and human rights law, there are inevitable interlinkages between the two areas, as well as an overlap with some issues of significance to the ASM sector. For example, the use of chemicals in ASM can adversely affect the environment, which could result in a breach of the human right to a clean and healthy environment. The interlinkage of issues strengthens our arguments for poverty reduction through the regulation of environmental activities. This could be argued on the basis that the concept of sustainable development provides a bridge across the areas of poverty, ill health, equality, economic needs, social degradation, child labour, security of tenure, land-use conflict, and the like, as it links environmental protection needs with human rights goals.

Here the linkages between the right to the environment, the right to development, other human rights and the need for good governance become visible in the context of ASM practices. Cullet (2003: 10) refers to this interpretation as sustainable human development (though we should not discount here the importance of an eco-centric approach to sustainable development, to support the integrated web of life which indirectly benefits humans). In other words, a number of social, environmental and developmental policies are recognized as having interrelated causes and effects. Development that is sustainable in ASM must then centre on advancing positive environmental and human rights objectives. As illustrated above, the environmental focus of development is that it should be sustainable. How can this be achieved? We can advance sustainable development in ASM communities in several ways. A good starting point for developing some legal and policy recommendations is to refer to existing environmental and human rights agreements that have been advanced at the international level. The following sections explore this proposition.

Achieving poverty reduction in ASM through international environmental law

The Stockholm and Rio Declarations

Certain core Principles[9] from the Stockholm and Rio Declarations (the 'Declarations') can be interpreted here as a means by which to advance sustainable development in ASM. The Declarations provide a useful means of illustrating how national governments can pragmatically apply the principle of sustainable development to the regulation of mining activities. In some West African countries, for example Niger (Alfa, 1999: 3) and Ghana (Hilson, 2001b: 22), ASM practices have been legalized and regulated (Hilson and Potter, 2003: 241) and benefit from some formally organized structure. Such legal or regulatory best practice may offer guidance to other West African countries on how to advance the recommendations presented here. Where there is regulation, however, there may be questions about implementation and enforcement that arise. This section of the chapter raises these concerns, in addition to offering recommendations for those states that have not yet regulated ASM and desire to implement the more general language of public international law.

States agree to attempt to abide by the spirit of international declarations that they are a party to, follow their goals and provide substance to them at the national level. This requires that state parties develop national laws and policies that take into consideration the aims and content of the Principles individually and the goals of the Declarations as a whole, as far as possible. The Declarations may be far-ranging enough to provide ideal templates for development, poverty reduction and environmental protection for ECOWAS, particularly as they also relate to the realization of human rights, the advancement of positive social goals and environmental objectives. Though it is beyond the scope of this chapter to critique the Declarations in their entirety, some Principles of the two Declarations which relate to poverty reduction and relevant environmental and sustainable development objectives, as well as those which impact on human rights, are analyzed in the context of ASM.

Principle 8 of the Stockholm Declaration ('Stockholm') calls on the international community to recognize that 'economic and social development is essential for ensuring a favourable living and working environment for man and for creating conditions on earth that are necessary for the improvement of the quality-of-life'. Here, there is explicit acknowledgement of the need for economic and social development so that individuals might attain a certain quality of life. The Principle calls for states to implement such measures.

Improvement in ASM, likely achievable through effective national regulation and sound enforcement, can go some way towards considerably effecting such circumstances. However, through the reference to creating a 'favourable' environment to 'improve' the quality of life, the Principle also cautions against environmental degradation, resource overexploitation and the negative impacts on human existence.

Principle 5 of the Rio Declaration ('Rio') states, 'all States and all people shall cooperate in the essential task of eradicating poverty as an indispensable requirement for sustainable development, in order to decrease the disparities in standards of living and better meet the needs of the majority of the people of the world'. The Principle provides impetus not only for national action but also for international action on ASM practices and poverty alleviation which could, in part, be achieved through donor aid, capacity-building and technical assistance programmes. It is prudent for ECOWAS to obtain funding as a region, since a commitment to collective action (from the governments of several member countries) may be more persuasive to outside donors than that of a single member. Of crucial importance to the Rio Declaration, though confined to the final provision of the agreement, is the undertaking in Principle 27, that 'States and people shall cooperate in good faith and in a spirit of partnership in the fulfilment of the principles embodied in this Declaration and in the further development of international law in the field of sustainable development'. This is significant for ECOWAS, which, as a region, can work together to achieve environmental protection goals.

Having established that environmental degradation and poverty are interrelated, and the role that sustainable development can play in reversing this, other declaratory Principles offer guidance. Principle 2 of the Stockholm Declaration requires that 'the natural resources of the earth...be safeguarded for the benefit of present and future generations through careful planning or management'. Principle 5 of Stockholm cautions that 'the non-renewable resources of the earth must be employed in such a way as to guard against the danger of their future exhaustion and to ensure that benefits from such employment are shared by all mankind'. In the context of ASM, these Principles remind us that ores are non-renewable but that the benefits of mining should profit all in both environmental management and economic terms if poverty reduction is to be a reality and a long-term objective. They effectively reflect a call for sustainable resource management.

Similar objectives are reaffirmed in Rio Principle 3, which notes: 'the right to development must be fulfilled so as to equitably meet developmental and environmental needs of present and future generations'. Again, here, the concept of intra- and inter-generational equity is reinforced. These Principles arguably require governments to ensure that mining activities do not cause pollution or other destructive practices that will adversely affect species and devastate environmental media for generations unborn or have adverse impacts on present communities.

Practical means of ensuring that mining activities, whether artisanal or small-scale, do not have unacceptable impacts on the environment and natural resources and are sustainable, would be for regulators to require mandatory environmental risk assessment or environmental impact assessment (EIA), to ensure prior approval or licensing of the mine site or activity, and to warrant compliance with certain environmental standards. Practical studies on ASM miners in Ecuador have illustrated that EIA requirements and other forms of environmental assessment can be adapted to fit the social and economic circumstances of communities (Hentschel et al., 2002: 61). In the context of ASM, the focus should be on regulating practices to ensure that livings can be made by the present generation while avoiding destruction of the environment for unborn generations.

Principle 3 of Stockholm calls for the maintenance, restoration and improvement of renewable resources where practicable. In ASM, this requires remediation of land, air and water where some acceptable or inevitable environmental impacts occur. ASM practices should address both environmental protection goals and human needs, and, where practicable, must be regulated.

Related to this, Stockholm Principle 6 announces 'the discharge of toxic substances or of other substances and the release of heat, in such quantities or concentrations as to exceed the capacity of the environment to render them harmless, must be halted in order to ensure that serious or irreversible damage is not inflicted upon ecosystems. The just struggle of the peoples of ill countries against pollution should be supported'. Principle 6 concerns the regulation of the chemicals used in the ASM sector, along with other by-products and environmental impacts of ASM activities. The latter can also be said to touch on the difficulties that ASM communities may have in reconciling earning a living with environmental harm, and the difficulty with obtaining commitments from governments and/or other regulators for improvements in both realms, particularly in terms of entitlement to a clean environment and also participatory, democratic rights or access to justice in environmental matters. Regulation on the use of toxic substances in ASM is clearly called for here, along with accountable, legitimate and safeguarded procedures that allow for redress in instances of environmental abuse or misuse. Projects aimed at sustainable mine management practices for ASM communities make sense, particularly for toxic substances (e.g. heavy metals), the exposure to which can cause harm to humans.

Principle 9 of the Stockholm Declaration is central to the ASM debate: 'Environmental deficiencies generated by the conditions of under-development and natural disasters pose grave problems and can best be remedied by accelerated development through the transfer of substantial quantities of financial and technological assistance as a supplement to the domestic effort of the developing countries and such timely assistance as may be required'. Underdevelopment clearly plays a significant role in environmental degradation, which, in turn, impedes social and economic advancement. Impoverished conditions make ASM an attractive option. It is noted in this Principle that state sovereignty renders governments accountable for their domestic matters, but it is also acknowledged that in some circumstances, governments cannot improve developmental and related circumstances without assistance from the broader international community. Here the Mining Policy Research Initiative (MPRI)[10] has developed useful guidance that states can follow when implementing sustainable, healthy ASM practices, and the Mining, Minerals and Sustainable Development (MMSD)[11] Project has promulgated recommendations on how to maximize the contribution of the ASM sector to sustainable development.

In terms of mined ore and products, Principle 10 of the Stockholm Declaration is of relevance if we are to achieve poverty reduction. It asserts 'for the developing countries, stability of prices and adequate earnings for primary commodities and raw materials are essential to environmental management, since economic factors as well as ecological processes must be taken into account'. Principle 12 of the Rio Declaration is also relevant here. States are required to 'cooperate to promote a supportive and open international economic system that would lead to economic growth and sustainable development in all countries, to better address the problems of environmental degradation'. In terms of the ores mined or even the final product of the ore, some type of formal trading agreement may improve the economies of artisanal and small-scale miners. Depending on the extent of profits, more sustainable mining practices may emerge. Even more preferable would be an ethical, equitable or fair-trade agreement between the miners and purchasers of the ore, with direct profits going to the miners, rather than a middle agent.[12] Perhaps the basis for such an agreement would be a commitment to implement MPRI, MMSD or other such guidance on ASM practices. Such an agreement could go even further and benefit the local communities who work the ore, particularly if it contains gold or diamonds, into tradable materials. The Bolivian Cotapata Gold Mining Co-operative is a success story in this regard (Hentschel et al., 2002: 67).

An increase in trade or even exports would assist in the economic enhancement of ECOWAS and communities therein. If trade was fair, the hope is also that working conditions, profits, wages and lives would improve, along with increased assistance towards more sustainable mining practices by the purchasers of the ore and other organizations that promote and support fair trade. Western consumers of gold may also be persuaded to make a purchase by such an ethical agreement or label; this could be a selling point.

The brief exploration of certain key international environmental law instruments has highlighted their guiding role on the scope of possible, practical changes that could benefit ASM communities through sustainable development, poverty reduction, environmental improvement and citizen empowerment. Crucially, however, the national systems of governance and structures of societies are the levels at which the concept of sustainable development has to be turned into practical action. This is where further work is required. Good governance in ECOWAS is fundamental if the above objectives are to be achieved. Legitimate, accountable organizations at the national level could then be supported by international capacity-building efforts through financial, technological and other aid. The international community is fully aware of the need to provide practical assistance to less developed countries. The following section illustrates how this might be achieved in conjunction with advancing the objectives of international environmental law and human rights law.

The Millennium Development Goals and the World Summit on Sustainable Development

The end of extreme poverty is at hand – within our generation – but only if we grasp the historic opportunity in front of us.

Jeffrey Sachs, 2005, on the Millennium Development Goals

The World Summit on Sustainable Development (WSSD), held in 2002 in Johannesburg, South Africa, resulted in the reaffirmation of the Rio Declaration commitments to sustainable development and pressed forward some practical goals for achieving them. Global dialogue and action towards overcoming some current global problems by 2015, including poverty, environmental degradation, health issues, food and water shortages, and energy crises was advanced. World judges adopted, among other things, the non-binding Johannesburg Principles on the Role of Law and Sustainable Development,[13] emphasizing in Paragraph 3 their 'commitment to the Universal Declaration of Human Rights and the UN Human Rights Conventions...recogni[zing] their close connection with sustainable development and upholding [of] the Rule of Law'.

They and others in the international community reaffirmed their pledges to the 2000 United Nations General Assembly Millennium Declaration[14] and the MDGs of 2000 (contained in the Declaration) to ameliorate social, environmental and rights-based global problems by 2015. These include: halting the spread of HIV/AIDS; reducing poverty; enhancing debt relief; providing more development assistance; increasing access to safe drinking water; providing affordable medicines; increasing access to technologies; improving free trade; cancelling debt; and, crucially for our purposes, integrating the principles of sustainable development into country policies and programmes and reversing the loss of environmental resources. Achieving the MDGs is thus vital if ECOWAS is to see improvements in the ASM sector and interrelated areas of their societies.

The achievement of the MDGs requires considerable international effort and offers great scope for improving the lives and circumstances of ASM communities in ECOWAS. A collaborative international effort to achieve sustainable development and bring about positive environmental and social change through development aid, capacity-building and other collaborative efforts is imperative if changes in ASM communities are to become a reality.[15] The Johannesburg Principles are very much rights-based and acknowledge this point in that: 'the people most affected by environmental degradation are the poor...therefore, there is an urgent need to strengthen the capacity of the poor and their representatives to defend environmental rights, so as to ensure that the weaker sections of society are not prejudiced by environmental degradation and are enabled to enjoy their right to live in a social and physical environment that respects and promotes their dignity'.[16] Law thus plays an important role in facilitating positive change and the fulfilment of rights and in ensuring that such change or rights are not impermanent or superficial: 'The fragile state of the global environment requires the Judiciary as the guardian of the Rule of Law, to...implement and enforce applicable international and national law, which in the field of environment and sustainable development will assist in alleviating poverty.'[17] Once ground rules are agreed upon and set in law, the goals of environmental reparation, poverty reduction and human rights advancement can be built upon firmer foundations. Current legislation provides a route map for international donors and national governments on the steps needed to fulfil the MDGs, as has been demonstrated in the above analysis of the Stockholm and Rio Declarations. The key concerns related to ASM at the intersection of international environmental and human rights law can be examined.

Addressing key ASM concerns through international environmental and human rights law

> Human rights are what reason requires and conscience demands. They are us and we are them. Human rights are rights that any person has as a human being. We are all human beings; we are all deserving of human rights. One cannot be true without the other.
>
>   Kofi Annan, Secretary-General of the United Nations.

As intimated in the discussion thus far, there are overlaps between human rights goals and environmental goals. In simple terms, both aim to improve human existence and the quality of human life. This chapter has examined, to a limited extent, how some key international environmental laws can contribute to this. The chapter now investigates the potential role of international human rights law in addressing some key concerns of ECOWAS ASM communities, particularly environmental and poverty-related issues.

Poverty

ASM frequently takes place illegally or in an unregulated environment (ILO, 1999). The drive to take up such illegal and unregulated activities results from economic hardship. As Hilson (2006b) asserts, 'in West Africa, artisanal mining is predominantly a poverty-driven occupation'. Frequently, ASM activities are an important source of income in an otherwise non-existent employment market (Ayree, 2003a; Grätz, 2003a; Hinton et al., 2003b). A view further supported by the ILO (1999) is that small-scale mining is 'increasingly an activity of considerable economic importance and the only way out of poverty for many people'. Poverty intrinsically contributes to the deterioration of natural resources and the environment (UNEP-UNICEF-WHO, 2002: 20), as people become dependent on natural resources for their livelihoods, food and survival. Poverty, environmental degradation and other physical hazards are often more 'common and inescapable for the poor in densely populated cities, where infectious disease can spread rapidly' (UNEP-UNICEF-WHO, 2002: 24). Poverty also introduces marginalization, which can perpetuate abuse and neglect, either of people and/or the environment. The WCED acknowledged in their 1987 report that 'poverty itself pollutes the environment'.[18]

One way in which to ameliorate poverty is to regulate ASM practices and to link such regulation to the wider objectives of improving living conditions in rural areas, infrastructure and capacity-building. For example, one benefit of regulation is that artisanal and small-scale miners are legally permitted to mine, there may well be greater incentive to administer basic loans through national means or international aid, to facilitate the provision of capital and improve technology. This, in turn, will make environmentally sound practices and standards more attainable, particularly those related to technology needs (and achieving such environmental standards could be a precondition for issuance of a mining licence); this improves health and living standards.

The concept of sustainable development finds a pragmatic basis here. If managed properly, achieving poverty-reduction goals can result in enhanced social conditions, stronger local economies and the attainment of appropriate environmental standards, all prerequisites for sustainable development. However, while there is currently no formally recognized right in international law to sustainable development, international human rights law recognizes a human right to development. If convincingly implemented and enforced, the right to development could empower ASM communities and assist in poverty amelioration and environmental improvement.

Right to development

Notwithstanding the potential for debate as to what exactly constitutes development[19] and the right to it (a debate beyond the scope of this chapter), there follows here an encapsulated perspective of the right to development and its potential validity for improving ASM practices throughout ECOWAS. At the centre of this analysis is the 1986 UN Declaration on the Right to Development[20] (the Declaration), which reaffirms the purpose of the United Nations Charter of achieving international cooperation in solving international problems of an economic, social, cultural and humanitarian nature, and of promoting respect for human rights and fundamental freedoms.[21] In Article 1(1), the Declaration provides that 'the right to development is an inalienable human right by virtue of which every human person and all peoples are entitled to participate in, contribute to, and enjoy economic, social, cultural and political development, in which all human rights and fundamental freedoms can be fully realized'. Article 2(1) further provides that 'the human person is the central subject of development and should be the active participant and beneficiary of the right to development'. This right to development has as its goal the improvement of human life. While strongly anthropocentric in nature, however, there is no reason why a right to development cannot, or should not, include environmentally conscious development.

As French (2005: 2) notes, 'there are mutual linkages between environment and development…they are inseparable in terms of their causes, their dynamism and…their resolution'. Developmental issues are hence central to ASM, and concern both individual and collective rights (i.e. of the miner and of the mining community). Developmental advancement, in whatever shape or form (social, economic, environmental, health, etc), is arguably a prerequisite to the fulfilment of contingent human rights such as the right to life, the right to clean water, the right to a clean environment, the right to work and the right to education. The provisions of the Declaration (along with other related human rights agreements), place obligations on states to facilitate rights and opportunities for development and human advancement. Article 4 of the Declaration provides, in Paragraph 1, that 'States have the duty to take steps, individually and collectively, to formulate international development policies with a view to facilitating the full realization of the right to development'. Paragraph 2 continues: 'Sustained action is required to promote more rapid development of developing countries. As a complement to the efforts of developing countries, effective international co-operation is essential in providing such countries with appropriate means and facilities to foster their comprehensive development'.

Thus, there is a need for good governance at the national level in order for states to implement and fulfil the right to development at the community level. The obligation to advance development is not only on national governments themselves (or collectively as ECOWAS) but also extends to the international community as a whole. This obligation is more convincing when considered in the current context of globalization and global distributive justice. As Steiner and Alston (2000: 1326) observe, the independent expert on the right to development of the United Nations reported to the 1999 UN Commission on Human Rights that '[e]very State which recognized the right to development was obliged to take positive action to assist the citizens of other states in realizing those rights'. It is here that full implementation of the MDGs with considerable international assistance becomes more imperative and has a realistic basis.

However, advancing development is not solely the responsibility of the global community. Article 8 explicitly places some responsibility at the hands of national governments themselves in advancing the right to development: 'States should undertake, at the national level, all necessary measures for the realization of the right to development and shall ensure, *inter alia*, equality of opportunity for all in their access to basic resources, education, health services, food, housing, employment and the fair distribution of income. Effective measures should be undertaken to ensure that women have an active role in the development process. Appropriate economic and social reforms should be carried out with a view to eradicating all social injustices'. Paragraph 2 continues: 'States should encourage popular participation in all spheres as an important factor in development and in the full realization of all human rights'. A minimum goal in this regard should be collective, state-level action towards codifying minimum licensing and formal institutional cooperatives, marketing mechanisms, safety standards and training programmes in ECOWAS.

National governments should consider providing development tools to ASM communities, such as education and access to information; encourage participation in decision-making; and provide opportunities for development, such as employment in safe and environmentally benign conditions. One possible solution would be for the governments of ECOWAS to work together to identify possible developmental options. This may then make the case for international development aid more convincing as the level of accountability increases. Increased and planned development is a means by which to give effect to some of the Principles addressed above and other efforts, so as to gradually achieve environmental improvement and poverty reduction. Some other human rights, environment and development issues are addressed below.

Land-use conflicts, licensing and security of tenure: indigenous and traditional communities and the right to self-determination

Overview

A problem with attaining the right to development relates to land tenure. Access to land is a primary form of social security for ASM communities. Without access to the land on which they live and mine, livelihoods and existence are threatened. Threats to land security commonly occur when large-scale miners are granted legal permission to operate by the state government. As large-scale miners set-up their operations, artisanal and small-scale miners, who often operate illegally (Hilson, 2001b: 18), are asked to leave the area and/or are forcefully evicted, or their land is expropriated (Hilson, 2001b: 19). Frequently, artisanal and small-scale miners have no other form of livelihood or are reluctant to leave land to which they are culturally attached (Hilson, 2001b: 18), where they have invested in construction of mine shafts and basic equipment or where they have built homes. For residents of communities who migrate to land that they have no traditional or cultural link with, perhaps in order to gain compensation in light of new plans to operate a large-scale mine site, the legal claim is more tenuous. Unless occupation or some other form of use is recognized as conferring a right of compensation, there is little room for legal redress. This issue, however, will not be examined in this discussion.[22]

For communities that have traditionally used land for ASM, there are two main arguments. First, illegal ASM practices can give rise to negative environmental and health effects. Second, such practices are necessary for sustainable livelihoods. Hence, these divergences have to be reconciled; some form of use rights recognition in the ASM sector may offer some solutions. Legally demarcating land (and this should not be an excuse to allocate the worst, least valuable, barren areas) and granting land-use rights and land tenure to the ASM community could help ameliorate environmental problems, as certain environmental conditions of use could be stipulated, and subsistence and other social issues could be more formally addressed. The recognition and implementation of human rights standards in relation to assigning land access, rights and tenure can also improve the situation. Such rights include entitlement to life (which can include livelihood); to property; to work; to a clean environment;[23] to prior informed consent; to participate in decision-making (as it applies to the land and community); to equality before the law (in land disputes); to be fully and fairly compensated if requested to leave the land; and to protection from forceful eviction.[24]

As previously noted, artisanal and small-scale miners often have cultural and traditional ties with the land on which they mine; this can give rise to rights in customary law. Thus, we can use a human rights-based argument that centres on self-determination to press for some form of positive change for ASM communities in relation to land rights. Article 1(1) of the 1966 International Covenant on Economic, Social and Cultural Rights[25] recognizes that 'All peoples have the right of self-determination'.[26] By virtue of this right and further to Paragraph 2, 'In no case may a people be deprived of its own means of subsistence'.

Article 5 of the Declaration on the Right to Development requires states to take steps to eliminate violations of the fundamental right of people's self-determination. With a recognized legal right to self-determination, the form of subsistence that prevails in ASM communities could be protected. This would complement any efforts made towards achieving political, economic and social autonomy, and advancement towards poverty reduction, sustainable development and sustainable livelihoods. The right to self-determination also endows communities with responsibility for their land and can go some way towards advancing environmental stewardship. A convincing desire to implement the right to self-determination is needed on the part of governments, as the ASM community cannot fulfil its right to self-determination unilaterally.

Land that has traditionally been held or used by groups of people under some form of traditional tenure (or appropriation), and for which access or utilization might be dependent on acknowledged membership of a group, can give rise to some form of custom. This may, in turn, give rise to the right to self-determination for the community. Such customary law and recognition of the right to self-determination then requires codification into binding law; otherwise, there may not be sufficient legal safeguards when competition for land by other interested parties, such as large-scale companies, arises. Supporting this right, an additional legal measure could be presented, following from the common law of adverse possession, in which ownership or use rights are granted to a user of land for a minimum period of five years of continued possession and use. Such a measure supports the principle that land should be put to productive use where a benefit can be derived from it.

Implementation factors

Advocating a system of rights is one thing, but achieving them in practice is another. The right to self-determination raises the need for some form of community structure and organization. Along with strong regulatory bodies, clear lines of authority need to be established with simple, clear laws as to who has access, access to what and for what purpose, over the land. Competent authorities should be clearly designated, and their roles in regulating ASM and land access be clearly defined. If there are conflicting sources of authority, confusion and deregulation will arise. The legal codification of cooperatives also advances self-determination.

Land tenure developments in West Africa in agriculture offer some examples of best practice that could also assist the region's governments to establish some form of rights-based security for the ASM sector. Some new approaches to land tenure (Lavigne-Delville et al., 2002), which provide some indication of what could be attainable in practice for ASM, include: the identification and mapping of land rights, particularly through rural land plans (used in Côte d'Ivoire, Benin, Guinea, and Burkina Faso); the codification of rules and granting of legal status (undertaken in Niger); the allocation of responsibility for making and managing rules to local structures as decentralized management (undertaken in Madagascar); making land transactions more secure by creating written contracts (used in Guinea); the use of land tenure monitoring systems as a means to formulate new policy (e.g. via *observatoire du foncier* employed in Mali); tenure certificates (used in Côte d'Ivoire); land registers (used in southern Africa and Comores); land commissions at *arrondissement* and village levels (as in Niger); and, significantly, the use of local rule-making, committees and by-laws tested through projects and pilot schemes.

Legal and regulatory frameworks that provide developmental and economic security should not only recognize land claims and user rights, but should also ensure that claims are indefinite or at least predictable over time, protected in the law, and not subject to abuse, impermanency or revocation upon a change of government. In circumstances where communities have land ownership or rights of tenure, there should be robust regulation to ensure that environmental standards are maintained in mining communities, perhaps through licensing. Where there are rights to tenure, loans or other financial assistance should be made available on favourable terms so that livings can be earned and economic potential fulfilled as in the manner aspired to in international human rights law. Some form of regulated worker cooperatives is an option, particularly as this can address other concerns related to poverty, such as illness and education, and offer some form of security (shared financial resources, shared equipment, etc).

Cooperatives might also offer solutions in relation to alternative means of employment through diversification of the local economy (such as through market gardening, craft-making, etc). The Sadiola Mining Co-operative (Mali) presents a best-practice example of how such positive changes can emerge, particularly if assisted through an international agency (Hentschel et al., 2002: 19). Cooperatives also provide a means to formally organize groups that have traditionally emerged in ASM, endow them with a collective community voice and access to decision-making procedures, and assist with financing (of ASM and other activities), while simultaneously providing a means for advancing understanding of the mining laws and other information that a community might struggle to conceptualize, through a leader or some other more formal medium. The Shamva Mining Centre in Zimbabwe illustrates how collective organization can improve the environment through providing local small-scale gold miners with access to mechanized and more efficient minerals processing via equipment hire, education, advice, management and accountability (Simpson, 2001), and the Communities and Small-Scale Mining (CASM) Small Grants Scheme[27] is one avenue for funding such cooperatives.

Accountability is a safety-net that ensures that communities are aware of their rights and the means by which to vocalize these without becoming victims of human rights or environmental abuses. In establishing accountability, guidance and assistance from the global community might be beneficial, in particular from legitimate human rights organizations and perhaps agencies of the UN,[28] especially for capacity-building within systems of governance and ASM communities themselves. This might have an even greater benefit in communities that are reluctant to accept state laws over their own community-based ones. Again, cooperatives can offer a means of attaining accountability and for mobilizing concerns.

Compensation and alternative income sources should be the priority of rights claims if access to lands is not forthcoming, particularly if a challenge based on the law of adverse possession does not provide the desired redress. If land is expropriated for large-scale development, it should be ensured that communities benefit from the consequent changes: more importantly, they should be consulted and participate in accountable, equitable and just decision-making procedures relevant to land use and compensation. Convention 169 concerning Indigenous and Tribal Peoples in Independent Countries, adopted by the General Conference of the ILO,[29] recognizes in Article 7 that: 'The peoples concerned shall have the right to decide their own priorities for the process of development as it affects their lives, beliefs, institutions and spiritual well-being and the lands they occupy or otherwise use, and to exercise control, to the extent possible over their own economic, social and cultural development. In addition they shall participate in the formulation, implementation and evaluation of plans and programmes for national and regional development which may affect them directly'.

Principle 10 of the Rio Declaration is procedural in nature and declares to this effect: 'Environmental issues are best handled with participation of all concerned citizens, at the relevant level. At the national level, each individual shall have appropriate access to information concerning the environment that is held by public authorities, including information on hazardous materials and activities in their communities, and the opportunity to participate in decision-making processes. States shall facilitate and encourage public awareness and participation by making information widely available. Effective access to judicial and administrative proceedings, including redress and remedy, shall be provided'.

Developing land in a sustainable manner and granting communities rights to land resources, whether through regulated ASM or otherwise, is one way of advancing environmental management. For example, if residents of communities are educated on why good environmental practices might benefit them and sustain their livelihoods, culture and community, they will likely become strong environmental custodians and minimize practices that harm not only the environment but also human health. The recognition of communal lands and traditional use rights supported by sustainable development, alternative employment or more highly regulated ASM practices could enhance environmental protection efforts as well as ameliorate poverty. If ASM continues through regulation, competent authorities can suspend mining when it is considered a threat to the environment, and ownership rights can be suspended if communities are in breach of environmental or other standards, though such suspension should be legitimate and not perilous to human existence or a human rights breach.

Women and children in ASM

Women

The right to development explicitly calls for women to have an active role in the development process. It can be argued that women and children will also benefit from stricter regulation in ASM and recognition of environmental and human rights.

Women are frequently involved in ASM, employed to carry out specific tasks (IIED, 2002: 328). For example, the exploitation and selling of gold has traditionally been a female-only activity in the Gaoua region of Burkina Faso (IIED, 2002: 205) and women comprise 75 per cent of the ASM labour force in Guinea (Logan, 2004: 2). However, in general, women are rarely identified as a distinct group of stakeholders in the planning and operation of mine sites (IIED 2002: 205, 212) and their 'compensation typically lags behind that of male mineworkers' (ILO, 2005) as does their access to sufficiently mineralized areas (Logan, 2004: 2). Trusted and efficient means of communication in ASM communities are lacking, a primary reason being that most communication or information-sharing takes place between community leaders, who are generally men.

In terms of sustainable development, Principle 20 of the Rio Declaration acknowledges that 'women have a vital role in environmental management and development. Their full participation is therefore essential to achieve sustainable development'. This Principle could guide the development of national ASM policies. Moreover, if positively implemented, these policies could advance the status of women in ASM communities. Improved access to ASM employment opportunities is important for women for a number of reasons: it provides them with a form of security (financial and other), either through a claim to land or through the sale of mined products; children may benefit from the ability of their mothers to work as may other family members (including the sick or elderly); it decreases their reliance on others (including men), which lowers the risk of abuse, violence and the need for prostitution (IIED, 2002: 205); it creates a sense of self and purpose; and it could contribute to better health and a reduction in other social ills. The health impacts on women, particularly if they are child-bearing, have to be considered. This should be a legitimate area of regulation, as called for under Article 11(1)(f)[30] of the Convention on the Elimination of all forms of Discrimination Against Women (CEDAW).

Convention on the elimination of all forms of discrimination against women

CEDAW[31] defines discrimination in Article 1 as 'distinction, exclusion or restriction made on the basis of sex which has the effect or purpose of impairing or nullifying the recognition, enjoyment or exercise by women, irrespective of their marital status, on a basis of equality of men and women, of human rights and fundamental freedoms in the political, economic, social, cultural, civil or any other field'. By accepting the Convention, members of ECOWAS would commit themselves to undertake a series of measures at the national level to end discrimination against women in all forms, including that experienced in the ASM sector. Such measures would relate to the right to participate in ASM community decision-making, and the right to education, health and employment (whether in mining or alternative occupations, but in healthy and safe conditions). Such measures require tactical implementation, taking into consideration that ASM communities have patriarchal traditions of authority that could result in an adverse backlash on women who assert these measures. The sources of discrimination may be ASM community leaders themselves, and/or an external discriminatory body (such as government or mining companies). State parties would also be bound to take steps to end the sexual exploitation and prostitution of women, particularly in ASM communities.

Of ECOWAS members, only Nigeria and Senegal have ratified CEDAW.[32] This lack of full ratification suggests either an unwillingness (maybe born of cultural differences) on the part of other member states to accept the Convention, or the inability to make its provisions a reality. What is clear is that fundamental to the practical attainment of equality for women under

CEDAW is the need for some form of good governance, financial aid or assistance to ensure that the rights can be implemented. Such implementation could then go some way towards reducing poverty, not only among women, but also among other groups that rely on women and communities as a whole. The empowerment of women in the structures of ASM community leadership is therefore important.

An example of policy being turned into practice is the Southern African Development Community Women in Mining Trust's area-wide commitment to achieving gender equality. This provides an enabling environment for setting targets and achieving substantive change towards greater women's participation in regional mining (IIED, 2002: 210).

Children

The livelihoods of children are also threatened by ASM. Sub-Saharan Africa has approximately 48 million child workers; of this growing pool, almost one child in three (29%) is below the age of 15 (UNICEF, 2004). The Ghana Child Labour Survey (Ghana Statistical Service, 2003) and ILO (2004) cited that the underlying reasons for child labour at the national level were poverty and low family incomes. A lack of meaningful regulation exacerbates this (ILO, 2004: 5). According to ILO figures, approximately 1 million children work in small-scale mining and quarrying around the world, many in some of the worst conditions imaginable, risking dying on the job or sustaining long-term injuries and health problems (ILO, 2004): 'Mining and quarrying are, in virtually all cases, a Worst Form of Child Labour (WFCL) because of the extent and severity of the hazards and risks of injury and disease' (ILO, 2004). A Save the Children 2004 study of ASM in the Sahel region of Burkina Faso identified boys as young as 7 years old working in crudely dug shafts and galleries up to 80 metres deep. Girls break rocks and wash out the gold. For this arduous work, they earn around 50 pence per day.

United Nations Convention on the Rights of the Child

In order to address child labour, the international community has promulgated several legal agreements that attempt to eliminate or regulate child labour (noting that not all child labour or employment is negative or a worst form). These are applicable to the ASM sector and form objectives that members of ECOWAS should strive to implement. All members of ECOWAS have acceded to or ratified the 1989 United Nations Convention on the Rights of the Child (UNCRC),[33] and accept that a child is a human being below the age of 18 years unless stipulated otherwise in national legislation.[34] States pledge under Article 32(1) to recognize the right of the child to be protected from economic exploitation and performing work likely to be hazardous, which interferes with education or is harmful to a child's health, physical, mental, spiritual, moral or social development.

The UNCRC does not directly regulate child labour per se but attempts to legitimize safe and healthy child working practices. If elements of ASM practices were not hazardous or harmful to a child, and the child in question was of legal working age, they would be more acceptable. However, this is to an extent a culturally relative claim as necessity, poverty, hunger and other social issues prevalent in ASM communities as well as cultural and traditional norms may influence what is acceptable. The regulation of child labour in ASM might be more effective when the social circumstances are conducive to full legal implementation and enforcement of the UNCRC and other legal standards, policies and guidance on best practice. Full implementation of Article 32(1) provisions requires state parties to 'take legislative, administrative, social and educational measures' to provide a minimum age of employment, regulate employment hours (particularly so that a child can attend school), regulate employment conditions, and provide appropriate sanctions and penalties as a means of enforcement (Article 32(2)). Frankly, medium-term transformation of the sector to phase out child labour is probably a key requirement. Dialogue between parents, community leaders, mine operators, local competent authorities and international organizations supported by educational initiatives would be a good starting point, along the advocacy lines developed by Save the Children and their local partner in Burkina Faso, APRODEB.[35]

International Labour Organization Conventions

In terms of ASM and child labour, several other conventions should be briefly mentioned. All members of ECOWAS are members of the ILO, though not all have ratified key ILO Conventions.[36] ILO Convention 138 (1973)[37] on the Minimum Age for Admission to Employment requires ratified states to effectively abolish child labour (Article 1) and sets a universal minimum age for employment at 15 (Article 2(3))(or 14 in countries 'whose economy and educational facilities are insufficiently developed' (Article 2(4))). It also aims to protect the 'health, safety or morals of young persons' and recommends age 18 or 16 as the minimum, depending on the type of work and cultural working practices (Article 3). Although it appears, however, that minimum age 18 rather than 14 is advocated for ASM practices, weak monitoring could make this unenforceable in some circumstances. ILO Convention 182 (1999)[38] on WFCL calls for the immediate elimination as a matter of urgency of the 'work which, by its nature or the circumstances in which it is carried out, is likely to harm the health, safety or morals of children' (Article 3(d)). Article 4, however, requires that these types of work be defined by the national legislators (Article 6). This could prove problematic, as this becomes a discretionary provision that hinges on other difficult and related social issues, such as poverty.

ILO Recommendation 190 on WFCL assists states party to Convention 182 in determining which worst forms of child labour are to be eliminated through national 'programmes of action' along the lines of those discussed herein. Article 4(1), however, leaves the determination of employment that will harm the health, safety or morals of the child to the discretion of the member country and employers therein,[39] though the considerations highlighted by Save the Children (2003) for implementing Convention 182 might provide a useful starting point.

If progress has been slow or apparently nonexistent in addressing child labour in ECOWAS ASM communities, this is because child labour is an immensely complex issue, linked to many other cultural and social factors that need to be simultaneously addressed, including poverty. The international community is, however, active in this area. The focus of the World Day Against Child Labour, 12 June 2005, was on children in mining and quarrying, and aimed to raise awareness of the need to remove the more than 1 million children engaged in this activity, and many international organizations, including UNICEF, the World Bank,[40] the ILO[41] and Save the Children, run programmes to this effect. It is hoped that reform in this sphere will be prioritized, but it very much rests upon the resolution of other problem areas outlined in this chapter.

Current ASM regulation and practice in ECOWAS: an overview

Generally, ASM is underregulated. This is due in part to there being no universally accepted definition of 'artisanal and small-scale mining'. Such definition is currently the responsibility of national regulators themselves. As reported by the ILO (1999), several countries have specific small-scale mining legislation in place, some of which is being revised to better account for the unprecedented increase in ASM activities. Several other countries have incorporated, or are incorporating, provisions for small-scale mining in their mining legislation. Such regulation would make economic sense and contribute to 'sustainable, profitable entrepreneurial activity that can provide significant employment in rural areas' (ILO, 1999). Where ASM regulations do exist, however, they are often breached. For example, Hilson and Potter (2003: 240) report that in Ghana, where small-scale mining was legalized in 1989, the vast majority of operators continue to be unregistered.

There are numerous reasons behind the widespread illegality in the industry. The ILO (1999) cites practical reasons such as a shortage of land resources due to mass demarcation of prospecting and exploration concessions to large multinational companies, a view supported by Hilson and Potter (2003: 259), as well as the complexity of laws. Additional reasons for non-compliance relate to the symptoms behind the breach. It may well be that a lack of education, lack of information about the legal requirements in force, lack of information relating to the policy behind the law (say, for environmental protection purposes), or the sheer immediate need for income, results in the bypassing of regulations. Related to this is the difficulty associated with raising the capital needed for mechanization and improved efficiency, which may well be legally mandated requirements. This problem can lead to low productivity, low revenues and environmental challenges. Consequently, miners may be inclined to ignore health, safety and environmental measures outright (ILO, 1999). In the majority of cases, ASM regulations are not only designed to control the exploitation of natural resources, but also exist to ensure workers' safety and health and even contribute to poverty reduction.

ASM has, over the centuries, been a significant source of income for rural and impoverished individuals in Africa (Hilson, 2002b). More recently, the industry has made an important contribution to mineral wealth and foreign-exchange earnings. This is not to discount, however, the severe environmental price that has been paid, including chronic soil degradation, chemical contamination and air pollution. Nevertheless, if managed wisely, formal regulation and thus legitimization of the ASM sector may greatly improve the circumstances of many ECOWAS communities.

Additional implementation factors

This chapter cannot comment on the numerous potential next steps, but some further suggestions in a legal context are offered.[42] Effective ratification and implementation of international law is hugely important if poverty reduction, human rights fulfilment and sustainable development in ASM are to be realized. The agreements addressed above offer legitimate scope for change and improvement if they are taken seriously. We have determined that the achievement of sustainable development is not restricted to national efforts alone. A fundamental objective of international environmental law is to protect the planet as a whole through national and concerted international efforts, including accounting for global inequalities.

The application of the principle of 'common but differentiated obligations', reaffirmed in Principle 7 of the Rio Declaration, attempts to acknowledge that some states have contributed more to global environmental harm than others (generally accepted to be industrialized countries). This Principle thus also recognizes that some states are in more of a position than others to redress the balance, even though the environmental burden affects the planet collectively. Principle 6 of Rio thus calls for 'the special needs' of developing countries to 'be given special priority'. Cooperation through multilateral or bilateral arrangements (particularly through technical assistance projects) or other appropriate means is essential to prevent, reduce and eliminate the adverse environmental effects resulting from activities conducted in all spheres, in such a way that due account is taken of the sovereignty and interests of all states.

Principle 24 of the Stockholm Declaration reaffirms the role of the international community, noting that 'international matters concerning the protection and improvement of the environment should be handled in a cooperative spirit by all countries, big and small, on an equal footing'. The international community recently acknowledged this further through the promulgation of the MDGs, an attempt to move from rhetoric into action. The 2002 Yaoundé Vision Statement[43] outlines recommendations for governments, development partners, international stakeholders, national level stakeholders, NGOs and private-sector parties to plan immediate and future steps to 'contribute to sustainably reduce poverty and improve livelihoods in African [ASM] communities by the year 2015 in line with the MDGs'. Development and enforcement of a clear system of human property rights (including user rights) at the national level is also needed.

Hence, convincing efforts at the national level supported by the international community to give substance to international environmental and human rights law could earnestly improve the situation in ASM communities. What is not needed is law-making at the national level that offers only political tokenism. Okorodudu-Fubara (1998) commented that 'Nigeria has an excellent record of being [a] signatory to almost all the [international] environmental protection treaties, a good record of either acceding to or ratifying many of them, and a very poor record of compliance with the customary international treaty obligation requiring Member States to "take appropriate legal (legislative) measures at the national level" to implement the policy/objective of the treaty'. Effective legislation bolstered by robust implementation and enforcement mechanisms at the national level is thus fundamental if law is to prove a useful tool in facilitating poverty reduction and enhancing social and environmental conditions. Designated competent authorities at national, regional and local levels should be established, with clear mandates for administering the law and being held accountable in doing this legitimately and effectively. Financial, technical and other capacity-building assistance from the international community (public and private donors) can strongly assist members of ECOWAS in defining and achieving such objectives and for moving the ASM sector forward.

International awareness (particularly through non-governmental organizations, NGOs) is fundamental to obtaining accountability among members of ECOWAS and for exerting pressure to ensure good governance, particularly where international aid is provided. Where there is corruption or bad governance at any level, the UN in particular, as well as individual donor countries or organizations, might consider developing systems of technical assistance based on direct aid, technology transfer and preferential trade arrangements with ASM communities. Further means of supporting members of ECOWAS in addressing ASM concerns could occur on the basis of conditional debt relief (i.e. on condition that a country demonstrates greater effort at the national level to improve education standards or environmental standards in ASM communities, the national debt could be reduced or written off if the national government supports initiatives to assist ASM).

NGOs (particularly established international ones) or an ombudsman can play a useful oversight and monitoring role, ensuring that laws are implemented and complied with and that financial and other aid, technical assistance, technology transfer and training are administered effectively in ASM communities. NGOs and other actors can also serve a useful role in working with ASM communities directly in building capacity through education (for example, providing knowledge on basic rights), advising on how to invest in new basic technology and assisting in health-care provision (particularly related to HIV/AIDS reduction), while helping them organize their own communities, laws and finances. Successful advancement of environmental protection goals, human rights, sustainable development and poverty reduction requires that certain preconditions to civil society and democracy be in place. If ASM communities are to benefit effectively from improved regulation, conditions and procedures by which they can express their concerns and demand that human and environmental rights goals are implemented need also to be in place at the regulatory level. ASM communities should be afforded the opportunity to participate in decision-making that may affect their mining livelihoods or communities in general and should have access to information and justice in both an environmental and human rights context, in a manner similar to that advocated under the UN Economic Commission for Europe (ECE) Aarhus Convention and its 'three pillars'.[44] Such procedural rights can also serve as a mechanism to ensure that laws are effectively implemented and administered.

In terms of further examples of cooperation in ECOWAS, the government of Benin entered into a long-term partnership agreement in September 2002, a Strategic Alliance for Sustainable Development (a South–South cooperation) between Benin, Bhutan and Costa Rica (the partner countries of the Bilateral Sustainable Development Agreement) (UNDESA, 2004). The partnership is encouraging in that it is an arrangement purely between developing countries, aside from an external, overseeing body, the Royal Tropical Institute (Dutch), which has a coordinating role, as the government of the Netherlands under the auspices of the existing Sustainable Development Agreement (SDA) provides the funding necessary for this initiative. The focus of the partnership is to 'shar[e] knowledge and experiences to pursue sustainable development among the partner countries; exchange programmes to learn and appreciate each others' approaches towards sustainable development; and [achieve] enhanced participation of civil society organizations in the decision-making process for sustainable development'. The aim is to ensure that existing national institutions will develop innovative projects with various agencies and funding bodies in order to advance national sustainable development goals. As developing countries are best placed to understand the sustainable development needs of their own countries, it is hoped that the outcomes of the long-term partnership will be constructive and effective. Donor aid is a significant step towards actually achieving sustainable development goals at the grassroots, and is a resource that ECOWAS should aim to enhance through properly structured programmes.

An example of another partnership or initiative of the type that can benefit ECOWAS in advancing its sustainable development objectives in ASM is illustrated through the International Union for the Conservation of Nature and Natural Resources (IUCN, but now known as the World Conservation Union) Environmental Law Programme Capacity-building for Sustainable Development Initiative, of January 2003. Of the members of ECOWAS, Benin, Burkina Faso, Côte d'Ivoire, the Gambia, Guinea, Guinea-Bissau, Mali, Niger and Senegal are member states of IUCN; several NGOs based in ECOWAS are also members (IUCN Members Directory, 2004). The main objective of the partnership is 'For every country to have the capacity to actively participate in the international policy debate, to implement what is agreed through coordinated policies, laws and institutions that respect the rule of law and to ensure effective compliance with environmental laws' (UNDESA, 2004). The plight of the ASM sector would serve as a perfect case study in this regard. Partner institutions working with IUCN and providing funding include, for example, the Food and Agriculture Organization (FAO), UNEP and the World Bank.

Conclusion

This chapter has explored the role of international law in ASM, with special emphasis on ECOWAS. It is apparent that strong national regulation to ensure the sustainable development of the sector is needed but in a manner that ensures that local communities and individual miners are protected, and in such a way to preserve their livelihoods, without a national 'sell-out' to large-scale multinational mining ventures (unless ASM operators would be in an improved position), and without breaching human rights. The emphasis is on gradual improvement, and this is achievable if realistic and tangible goals, policies and programmes are well structured and implemented. There is little doubt that ECOWAS would benefit from a well-developed programme of international assistance, but it is equally important to note that the implementation and enforcement of relevant legislation at the national level is crucial to the advancement of ASM communities in civil society.

The further emergence of civil society is, however, often at the mercy of corruption, conflict, lack of administrative infrastructure and financial hardship; this may well continue to impede the development of strong and enforceable laws. The problem then becomes somewhat circular. Perhaps concerted international action has a convincing role in assisting in laying national foundations towards the environmental and human rights objectives expressed here. Change does not only relate to governance or the creation of new laws, but also to the adjustment of cultural practices and traditions, a willingness to take guidance from others and the confidence to move forward. Progress is most definitely within reach and the fulfilment of the MDGs, an imperative for both the wider international community and ASM communities, is a step in the right direction.

Part II

Country case studies: Francophone West Africa

CHAPTER 8
Introduction

Gavin M. Hilson

Unlike Anglophone West Africa, Francophone West Africa has not received significant attention in mining development circles. This is not to say that the industry is insignificant in this group of countries. In fact, French West Africa has a lengthy and eventful mining history: as African historians will agree, the development of the kingdoms of Ghana (700–1100), Mali (800–1550) and Songhay (1300–1600) was fuelled by locally mined gold and to a lesser degree, salt.[1]

Yet, surprisingly, it is only recently that mining-sector development in Francophone West Africa has become a policy and research focus, initiated to a large degree by the World Bank's sudden mineral interests in Mali and Burkina Faso, as well as those of the mining giant AngloGold Ashanti in Mali. Geologically, Francophone West Africa had long been an enigma, because commissioned groups failed repeatedly to pinpoint economic deposits. Moreover, it is well known that the Birimian volcano-sedimentary belt, West Africa's mineral lifeblood, thins noticeably in Burkina Faso and Côte d'Ivoire, providing fewer economic opportunities for mining. As one Ghanaian government officer explained during a personal interview, 'over there [in Burkina], you can only mine for gold in a narrow strip of say 10, 20, 30 or 40 kilometres, whereas here in Ghana, you can dig for gold in one quarter of the country, so get your shovel'. This geological situation, combined with unfavourable mineral policies, certainly hindered mining development in many French West African countries, particularly Guinea, Mali and Burkina Faso.

The recently discovered world-class gold deposits at Sadiola, Morila and Yatela (Mali), however, has certainly changed things. These discoveries were made possible by the overhaul of the country's Mining Code; there is now talk that Mali could become Africa's second-largest gold producer behind South Africa. Moreover, and as previously explained, the Bank's growing presence in the region has also had an impact. The organization has orchestrated the implementation of the US$22.5 million Burkina Faso Mining Sector Capacity Building and Environmental Management Project, the aim of which is to promote private investment in mining, establish capacity in the country for environmental management, and strengthen regulations and institutions.

Naturally, these, and other ongoing, efforts have put ASM under the microscope. Indeed, the ASM regularization challenges implicit with

Anglophone West Africa's more abundant mineral resources are monumental; but this does not mean that the formalization of operations in French West African countries such as Mali and Burkina Faso is itself a simple exercise. Certainly, if the sector is to be restructured and improved so that it functions in a fashion where it is alleviating poverty and benefiting the wider populace, appropriate technologies, policies and support services must be implemented. In order to do so, more information is needed about the ASM populations themselves, an issue which the authors in this section help to address, reflecting upon their personal experiences in the field.

The first chapter of this section, by Dialla Konate, introduces some of the contentions now surrounding ASM in Mali, a topic of growing importance in the country given the recent expansion of large-scale mining, driven largely by AngloGold Ashanti. The focus of Chapters 10 and 11 is ASM in Burkina Faso. First, Eric Jaques, Blaise Zida, Mario Billa, Catherine Greffié and Jean-François Thomassin provide a detailed overview of the sector, examining, among other things, its role in alleviating poverty, environmental impacts and legal issues. The authors draw heavily upon findings from research conducted between 2001 and 2003 as part of an ASM project in Burkina sponsored by the French Geological Survey (BRGM). The second chapter on Burkina, by Sabine Luning, examines the characteristics of indigenous artisanal gold mining populations. After describing the evolution of the country's mining policies and permitting systems, the author presents a much needed anthropological view on ASM community dynamics in a case study of the province of Sanmatenga ('land of gold'). The work sheds light on the various roles of the local actors and hierarchies. The final chapter of this section, by Tilo Grätz, provides a grassroots perspective on gold mining in northwest Benin, where it has proved to be an important source of employment. The author focuses on the country's artisanal gold boom of the 1990s, and examines its impact on immigration and culture.

CHAPTER 9
Artisanal and small-scale mining in Mali: an overview

Dialla Konate

In Mali, the ASM sector is plagued with a number of problems, some of which are being tackled jointly by government policymakers through administration, as well as by private mine operators through social and professional groups. The aim of this chapter, however, is to go beyond conventional analysis and to address some of the wider challenges facing the industry, specifically:

- How, in the absence of suitable technical support and financial resources, can Mali's ASM populations be organized?
- Which mechanisms are available for addressing these challenges?

This chapter builds upon issues originally raised by Keita (2001) as part of the seminal MMSD Project.

A brief overview of ASM

Background

Since the conclusion of the Governmental Seminar on Mining Policy in 1998, Mali's mining administration has strived to design and implement an appropriate legal framework for ASM. Today, the industry employs an estimated 300,000 people (some 5% of Africa's ASM operators are in Mali), although the country has had a flourishing ASM sector for more than seven centuries. Both the ancient Ghanaian and Malian empires achieved considerable power during the medieval period, their rapid growth fuelled by widespread ASM. The pilgrimage of Mansa Kankou Moussa[1] marked the climax of such glory for the Malian empire, which, at the time, epitomized the strong trading ties forged with Arab populations inhabiting the Gulf Region to the east.

Through the Authority of Liptako-Gourma (ALG),[2] the governments of Mali, Niger and Burkina Faso worked to develop a set of definitions for ASM. Standardized definitions were agreed upon by representatives of these Francophone countries during a regional seminar held in Niamey, 5–8 November 1990. Unlike the mining activities being carried out in the majority of Anglophone African countries (e.g. Ghana, South Africa, Botswana and Zimbabwe), locations of modernized technology, mechanized practices and a strong multinational presence, the mining environments of Mali, Niger and Burkina Faso, at the time, were comparatively deteriorated economically, characterized by low levels of equipment and finances. It was therefore agreed that the definitions would be distinctly different from those adopted in Anglophone Africa to better reflect the underdeveloped nature of the sector as a whole.

Representatives of each of the three countries agreed upon the following:
- Artisanal mining comprises all activities that encompass the extraction of economic mineral resources through rudimentary means and prior to the evaluation of ore deposits.
- Small-scale mining comprises all activities that are semi-permanent, and owned by operators with fixed assets but who employ state-of-the-art technology during extraction and processing. Small-scale mine operators generally carry out feasibility studies in order to determine the economic profitability of a selected deposit.

Many experts working in Francophone Sahelian countries, however, consider ASM to be a series of informal, semi-mechanized and semi-industrialized mining operations that do not require large equipment, heavy investment and the application of sophisticated technologies. In ALG, policymakers interpret ASM to include activities operated by miners who use rudimentary tools and equipment, and who have limited access to capital. Operators run these businesses on an individual, familial or associative basis.

Although Burkina, Niger and Mali have collectively embodied these definitions in national legislation, it was recommended that each should integrate additional characteristics relevant to their own country.

Artisanal mining

The government of Mali interprets artisanal mining as operations engaged in the extraction and beneficiation of mineral commodities sourced from primary and secondary deposits, outcrops or sub-outcrops, using manual methods and traditional processes. This type of mining is divided further, as follows:
- Traditional mining operations using artisanal processes to recover gold and diamonds contained in alluvial and eluvial materials, which stem from primary or secondary deposits in the form of outcrops or sub-outcrops. These activities are generally carried out at the village level.
- Semi-mechanized mining activities that are more organized than traditional mining operations, and which feature manual and mechanized winches; membrane-based pumps; and compressors, electrical-powered hammers, mills, concentrators and other small implements.

Small-scale or 'small mining'

These are operations that are semi-permanent; feature semi-industrial or industrial processes; have a high capacity period; do not exceed a certain quantity of saleable commodities (ore, concentrate or metal), the level of which is predefined per individual commodity and by order of the minister in charge of mines; and are run by individuals in possession of limited or fixed assets. In the case of gold extraction, an operation is considered 'small-scale' if its daily throughput of ore does not exceed 150 tonnes.

Social and cultural significance of ASM

As already explained, Mali is a country that has long been known for its artisanal gold mining. Research reveals that traditional mining activity has been carried out on a recognizable scale here and in adjacent countries since the Middle Ages, with artefacts dating back to the thirteenth century, according to the Tarikh El-Sudan[3] (Timbuktu Ancient Library Manuals) and several other contemporary works in indigenous and European geological institutions. Today, traditional mining activity represents the main source of wealth in Mali's principal mining provinces. The gold used in women's jewellery (spanning all ethnic groups across the country),[4] for example, almost exclusively originates from resident artisanal mines. Since the mid-1990s, however, gold output from

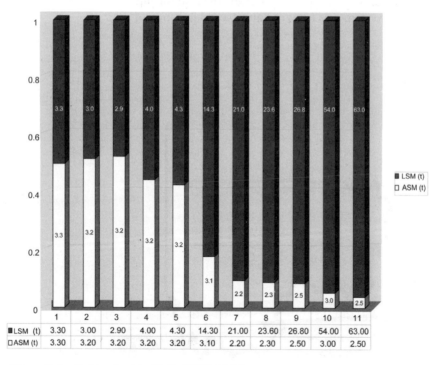

	1	2	3	4	5	6	7	8	9	10	11
■LSM (t)	3.30	3.00	2.90	4.00	4.30	14.30	21.00	23.60	26.80	54.00	63.00
□ASM (t)	3.30	3.20	3.20	3.20	3.20	3.10	2.20	2.30	2.50	3.00	2.50

Figure 9.1 Gold output in Mali, 1992–2002
Note: LSM = large-scale mining.
Source: Statistics from National Directorate of Geology and Mines.

artisanal mines has dwindled relative to that of industrial-scale activity (Figure 9.1), a relatively new phenomenon in Mali. Despite the wide variety of minerals available in Mali, resident ASM activity is typically centred on construction materials, precious and semi-precious metals, and gemstones, although in recent years, gold extraction and processing has become the predominant focal point. Mali possesses several proven gold deposits: its greenstone and Birimian formations cover about 80,000 km² of the country's territory. Several other important minerals are also within these formations, including diamonds, iron ores, manganese, bauxite, phosphates and limestone.

The country's major gold deposits, the preferred targets for artisanal and small-scale miners, are diverse in nature, composition and shape. It is important to note, however, that the most accessible deposits are eluvial and alluvial, with quartz lodes and veinlets rich in gold. Each type of ore has a corresponding array of grades, potential reserve indication and technical constraints as far as extraction and processing is concerned, which ultimately influence local mining activity.

The richest gold deposits occur within the Birimian settings, and are geographically distributed within the following three mining provinces:

- western area (Kéniéba Gold fields);
- southern sites (Yanfolila and Bagoe river sides); and
- southwestern area (sites of Kangaba and Banancoro).

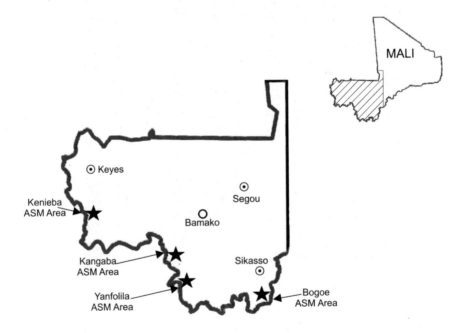

Figure 9.2 Location of major ASM regions in Mali
Source: National Directorate of Geology and Mines.

The gold fields of Kéniéba in western Mali are referred to locally as the Bambouck Mining Province, and feature a variety of minerals that occur within volcanic sediment formations of the Birimian settings alongside mineralized quartz lodes, veins and veinlets. This type of ore, which is generally oxidized, is typically sought after: gold content can be as high as 50 grams per tonne (g/t). The ore encountered in Kéniéba province, however, is often difficult to extract because of dewatering challenges.

The gold fields of Yanfolila in southern Mali feature several important geological formations. These include lode structures with native gold mineralization associated with quartz lodes or dioritic dome, and eluvial and alluvial deposits, which have given rise to several artisanal mine sites such as Kodieran and Kalako. In the Bagoe gold fields, also located in Southern Mali, three types of mineralization have attracted artisanal and small-scale miners, although overall, such activities are less practised here than in the other three provinces. In Bagoe, gold is found in deposits associated with volcanic sediments; alluvial formations, which are sometimes extracted by dredging areas alongside the Bagoe River; and eluvial formations. Finally, in the Kangaba and Banancoro gold fields in southwestern Mali, gold-rich shear zone formations and alluvial deposits are widespread, and have attracted numerous artisanal and small-scale miners over the years. Figure 9.2 provides an overview of Mali's important gold deposits.

As previously explained, gold washing, which has been practised for centuries, remains the chief occupation for over 200,000 Malians, of whom nearly 50 per cent are women. At any given time, however, the number of registered miners rarely rises above 40 per cent (Keita, 2001).

Strategic plans and perspectives

To date, one UN-funded project, the Project for the Promotion of Traditional Mining and Environmental Protection (PAMPE) (1998), and significant World Bank funds have been committed to developing Mali's ASM sector. Under the PAMPE project, 38 ASM sites were identified, as well as 12 economic groups (GIEs).[5] This work complemented the geological surveys carried out by the Department of Mines and Geology in 1997, the aim of which was to determine the mineral potential of five areas earmarked for small-scale mining (Keita, 2001). A World Bank project is currently being carried out in cooperation with the government. It aims to identify possible sources of economic growth, and in particular, ways in which to promote the efficient expansion of the ASM sector.

There has been some activity from professional organizations and local group initiatives in the country's three main artisanal gold-mining provinces of Kéniéba, Kangaba and Yanfolila. Aside from GIEs, other professional organizations such as female local development groups are assisting individuals who have been granted mineral rights – specifically, artisanal mining claims delineated under Article 57 of the Mining Code. Although any commercially registered company outside Mali is eligible to apply for a large-scale mining licence, permits for artisanal mining are awarded exclusively to Malian citizens or citizens from countries which have reciprocal agreements with the government of Mali. The granting and renewal procedures of licences for artisanal mine operations are specified under the Implementation Decree. Among such claims are gold washing corridors, which are reserved for traditional gold washing and governed by a joint order of both the minister in charge of mines and the minister in charge of territorial collectivities. The reserved areas are made known to the public; no mineral rights can be granted over them unless an application is submitted through the local authority. However, traditional gold washing is tolerated in areas free of mineral claims or inside the boundaries of a mineral claim, provided that there has been prior and written agreement from the holders of such rights.

Institutional framework for ASM

As Keita (2001) explains, in Mali, the mining sector is regulated by the Ministry of Mines, Energy and Water Resources. The National Directorate for Geology and Mines (DNGM) is in charge of policy and research issues, undertaking a wide range of cartographic and mineral prospecting activities. The Programme for Mineral Resources and Development (PDRM) and PAMPE, both of which were set up by UNDP, provide, respectively, services on geological and mining research and ASM.

All domestic gold processing and trading is governed by the order no. 99-32 /P-RM, passed 19 August 1999. The important mineral rights awarded for ASM include the following:

- Licence for exploration, issued by the Director of Mines, who makes a decision upon the area demarcated. These are valid for three months and renewable only once. They provide a pre-emptive right to its holder when applying for longer-standing mineral rights such as a research title/license for prospecting; they cannot be issued in an area covered by another mining title.
- Research title/licence for prospecting grants its holder, within the limits of the boundaries of a claim and to an indefinite depth, full rights for prospecting for minerals comprising the group for which the licence is issued. It is valid for three years and can be renewed only once.
- Small-scale mining development licence entitles a holder to operate a small-scale mine and provides mechanized gold washing claims within a demarcated area. As stipulated in Article 47 of the Mining Code, in order to mine legally on a small scale in Mali, 'a licence for operating a small scale mine' must be obtained. It is typically issued to holders of research/ exploration licences who have demonstrated that a deposit can be developed.

Although fairly rudimentary, there are environmental provisions in place for ASM. Specifically, according to Article 121 of the Mining Code, the holder of a small-scale mining licence is bound to provide annually, to the administration in charge of mines and in accordance with Article 72, a report summarizing environmental impacts, strategies for rehabilitating mining activities and approaches to be taken throughout to ensure that the site is safe.

Since its establishment in 1994, the National Association of Mine Operators in Mali (UNOMIN) has worked diligently to analyze the country's mining laws passed hitherto for the mining and petroleum sectors. These include the 1999 Mining Code as well as the 2004 Petroleum Code for Exploration and Exploitation of Petroleum Resources in Mali. The association has also carried out several field meetings throughout the country to inform, organize and train local miners, with the aim of alleviating poverty at ASM sites. It is important to note that the government, through the Ministry of Mines, Energy and Water Resources, has promoted these and related actions, as is evident from the efforts of the PAMPE project.

Recommendations for improvement

Reflecting upon the handful of efforts undertaken to regularize and improve ASM in Mali, Keita (2001: 22) notes that 'links between traditional mining activities and local social and economic opportunities were not taken into account'. The fact remains that the sector, though potentially vibrant economically, is in dire need of support. Perhaps more so than surrounding countries, there is a need to determine the exploitability of ores, specifically, their quantity and quality. This is a necessary first task, and can be accomplished through extensive library research, a review of recent exploration works and additional site-specific geological analysis. Local geologists, supported by either government-funded R&D bodies or indigenous mining consultancies, are best suited to carry out this work. Once the knowledge of local geology has been improved, the government can move to initiate programmes which emphasize the introduction of efficient and environmental-friendly beneficiation tools and processes. Inappropriate beneficiation equipment was widely distributed during the 1980s, when a liberalized mining sector attracted significant foreign direct investment; important ASM regions such as Kéniéba and Kangaba continue to feature inappropriate processing facilities. Given the impoverished nature of Mali's regulatory institutions and limited indigenous expertise, this task should be assigned to bilateral or multilateral organizations, which are clearly in a superior position to identify and develop further suitable processing tools and techniques for local beneficiation.

Recently, several local and regional financial institutions have expressed interests in developing further Mali's mining sector. Notable examples include the Union Economique et Monétaire Ouest Africaine (UEMOA, the region's trade organization),[6] the Arab Development Bank, the European Investment Bank and International Finance Corporation. The latter has provided funds to a number of large mining companies, including AngloGold Ashanti and SOMISY, which, respectively, operate the Sadiola and Syama mines. Local banking institutions such as Banque de Développement du Mali (BDM, or Mali

Development Bank) or Bank of Africa-Mali have also expressed an interest in financing the expansion of local mining activities.

The majority of these organizations, however, continue to be reluctant about dispensing funds for local ASM development, and for good reason: the fact remains that, unlike in neighbouring countries such as Ghana and Burkina Faso, comparatively little is known about resident ASM activity, particularly its anthropological characteristics. The inability to mobilize funding for support continues to hamper development of the sector in a number of key areas, particularly the following.

1. Training of ASM operators. Funds are needed urgently to implement training programmes for local miners, tools makers, technical agents and mining administration representatives, people who are clearly more in tune with the ASM operational environment. For example, most ASM sites feature several tool-making shops that can be made more productive and functional with more efficient sharpening devices, while nearby restaurant and bar owners can be trained in more efficient accounting techniques and shown how to keep records of their consumers.

2. Problems related to ASM equipment selection. Funds are also needed to design and implement appropriate technologies at sites. In doing so, the character of local deposits, production demand and the dynamics of local markets must be taken into account. There is merit in replicating the efforts of the World Bank in Burkina, where local equipment design and production has been emphasized.

Although funds sourced from local finance institutions could be a key to facilitating improvement in each of these areas, most will continue to be reluctant to free up funds for such purposes until more detailed information is made available on the sociocultural characteristics of indigenous ASM operations. More specifically, as many financial institutions have set criteria for the release of their funds, there must be comprehensive written explanations of the potentiality of a mining venture accompanying the submission of a financial request. It is therefore imperative for ASM project promoters in dire need of funding to develop well-articulated feasibility study plans and reports, which detail, among other things, ore characteristics, proposed extraction techniques and the technical issues discussed above.

With Mali braced to become Africa's second-largest gold producer through large-scale mine development, it is imperative that research is carried out on the ground to improve knowledge of the experiences, struggles and needs of the country's ASM communities. The rapid expansion of large-scale development is particularly worrying, although AngloGold Ashanti appears to be taking a more accommodating stance towards indigenous operators than that witnessed in most corners of sub-Saharan Africa. Nevertheless, if the sector expands as rapidly as projected, and there continue to be significant deficiencies in information on ASM, Mali could become like Ghana, where, as discussed in Chapter 6, government officers are struggling to solve disputes between large-scale mines and indigenous operators over land resources.

CHAPTER 10

Artisanal and small-scale gold mines in Burkina Faso: today and tomorrow

Eric Jaques, Blaise Zida, Mario Billa,
Catherine Greffié and Jean-François
Thomassin

Between 2001 and 2003, BRGM carried out, in close collaboration with BUMIGEB,[1] several studies on ASM in Burkina Faso. These studies fell within a BRGM scientific programme of technical and socioeconomic analysis, together with modelling of ASM activities in sub-Saharan Africa. The work aimed to identify the problems, expectations and specific needs of the various actors at all levels of the ASM sector, and to a lesser extent, of connected economic sectors, as well as to evaluate the pressures of such activity on people, the environment and existing resources.

The project mobilized a multidisciplinary field team for a period of four months. The team was comprised of geologists specializing in ASM, ore-deposits specialists, experts in ore beneficiation and sociologists. In all, 60 artisanal gold mine sites were investigated, five reference sites were analyzed and 1,300 persons were interviewed (about 1,000 hours of individual surveys). The classified and structured data were then entered into the Artisanat Minier database. This chapter is partly based on a previous publication by Jaques et al. (2005).

ASM: a blurred boundary

The generic term 'artisanal and small-scale mining' includes all mining operations that occur on a subindustrial scale. The maximum production capacity of such operations is commonly fixed at 150–200 tonnes of ore/day (and 500–1,000 tonnes/day for industrial rocks and minerals, or IRM). The ASM sector covers a wide spectrum of operations, from artisanal mines to small mines. Each of these end-members has its own problems and distinct stakes in terms of sustainable development, even if the boundary between them can be blurred. The following characteristics will be adopted for distinction (Jaques, 2001):
- A small mine is an extractive enterprise of the SME type, administratively recognized and carrying out planned exploitation of a small but explored deposit, with minimal fixed installations and mechanized equipment.

- An artisanal mine is generally an informal operation, exploiting an un-known resource in an unplanned manner, featuring mostly manual methods and rudimentary tools (a hunting-gathering type approach).

The notion of artisanal mining is thus indirectly related to scale. In Burkina Faso, the production capacity of a large artisanal mining operation, mobilizing 2,000–3,000 miners and labourers, seldom exceeds 30–35 tonnes/day of ore. In West Africa, apart from a few English-speaking countries with well-established mining traditions such as Ghana, small mines are very rare.

Gold production by artisanal means

Industrial gold production in Burkina Faso ceased in 1999, following the closure of the Poura and Essakane mines.[2] Today, gold production occurs on an artisanal scale, but such production has declined severely and continuously since 1998: the CBMP[3] estimates that production regressed from about 1 tonne per year in 1998 to less than 250 kg per year in 2002. This trend, though partly due to the increasingly scarce resources available to artisans, is likely a result of the new, more liberal, Mining Code, promulgated in October 1997. Since implementing the code, which opened mining to the private sector, the number of persons involved in mining and marketing has multiplied, rendering such activities more opaque and strengthening informal channels.

Apart from a few historical gold districts in the southwestern Poura region and Lobi (Figure 10.1), artisanal gold mining is a relatively recent phenomenon in Burkina. It began in the 1980s in the Sahel area of the country (Gangaol region), following several dramatic droughts. Today, over 220 artisanal gold mining sites are known in the country, about 100 of which are regularly active. Each year, 5–10 new sites are opened, and 90,000–140,000 people, 30–40 per cent women, are involved in the sector during the dry months between November and May, agricultural activities permitting. It is estimated that artisanal gold mining provides a livelihood to at least 650,000 persons in Burkina Faso, or one in 20 inhabitants.

The Sahel provinces of the north and centre-north, in particular those of Yatenga, Oudalan, Soum and Bam, long the largest gold-producing territories, continue to house the majority of the country's artisanal gold miners. Most are Mossi, the national ethnic majority, who largely practise Islam.

A highly mobile frontline of activity

The increasing rarity and depletion of known and accessible resources, the dearth of new discoveries and the freezing of the best areas by mining companies have, since the late 1990s, forced many artisanal gold miners to abandon the traditional gold-producing areas of the Sahel and migrate to new 'unexplored' ground in the south. The pioneering front of artisanal gold-mining has thus steadily shifted southward by about 50 km per year. This movement has occurred along two main axes, one southwest and another southeast (Figure 10.1); artisanal miners have gradually 'colonized' the entire country.

The shift of artisanal gold mining to the more humid regions of the south, particularly the cotton-growing areas of the southwest, has caused numerous problems, including land-use and water-use conflicts between the mining and agropastoral communities forced to share the same space. This rapid evolution of phenomena requires a flexible approach: artisanal gold mining is a dynamic and transient activity, a proper understanding of which can only be obtained by regular and unflagging observation.

A variety of resources

Birimian volcano-sedimentary rocks cover about 75,000 km² of Burkina Faso, or close to 27 per cent of its territory. As is the case elsewhere in West Africa, these rocks host a large number of gold deposits. In Burkina, almost 250 gold occurrences have been inventoried in the Birimian belts. Most of these are, or have been, exploited in an artisanal manner. Artisanal gold mining in Burkina Faso is marked by a diversity of targets, which include disseminated gold, stockworks, veins, quartzitic or lateritic eluvium, laterite and alluvium. Each deposit type has its own range of grades and potential reserves, and presents unique technical constraints that condition the artisan's interest.

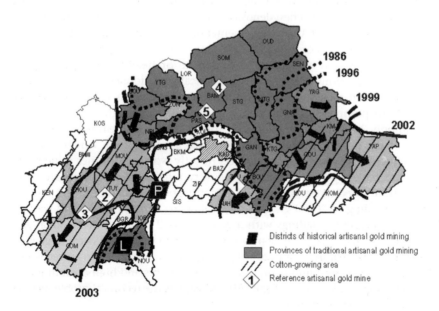

Figure 10.1   Main stages in the migration of the artisanal gold mining frontline in Burkina Faso

Artisanal miners will seek, by preference, shear-zone type targets (disseminated or quartzitic stockwork mineralization), which are fairly typical in the northern reaches of the country. Oxidized, rich (>50 g/t gold) and easy to mine without the use of explosives, such ore can be worked locally underground without pumping to depths of close to 100 metres. Although very attractive, few such targets have been discovered in recent years. Artisanal miners have thus increasingly turned to the larger veins that are much more typical of the newer gold districts of the south; these structures are generally less rich (5–30 g/t gold), minimally oxidized and therefore difficult to mine without explosives. In addition, the southern areas are located in the humid zone, which poses more pressing water-pumping challenges. Motor pumps are needed to lower a water table that, even in the dry season, occurs at a depth of 10–15 metres.

Artisanal mining: a selective process

Today, many artisanal gold miners in Burkina work underground quartz veins; however, because of the major technical constraints mentioned above, this work can be arduous, requiring substantial material and human inputs. Motor pumps and cereal mills, as well as explosives, are increasingly being used at newer underground sites.

Despite the heightened adoption of mechanized equipment, artisanal mining remains a highly selective process in Burkina, with operators generally preferring to work the richest deposits. Due to insufficient pumping technology, high-grade ore (>50 g/t Au) in the cementation zone is often untapped, submerged below several metres of water.

Where there are shortages of dynamite or heavy mining tools, well mineralized portions of large veins are typically abandoned in favour of more accessible wall rock structures and fracture zones. For a standard operation unable to pump water from depths below 30 metres, the cut-off grade is commonly 20–30 g/t gold. After hand-sorting (cobbing) the run-of-mine at the edge of the pit, the poorest ore is discarded as waste, from which gold may subsequently be recovered by villagers (mostly women) or other miners. Our analyses have established that the recovery rates from processing are better than the 40 per cent estimated in the literature, but are still only 60–65 per cent. An ore grading of 20–30 g/t gold will, following three grinding and washing cycles, still produce tailings with a grade of 8–12 g/t gold; the residual gold content was remarkably constant from one site to the next. Where large gold-bearing veins are mined, only 20–40 per cent of potential reserves are recovered. In such cases, basic equipment, technical constraints and high operating costs prevent high gold recovery. Figure 10.2 illustrates the technical problems faced by Burkina's artisanal miners.

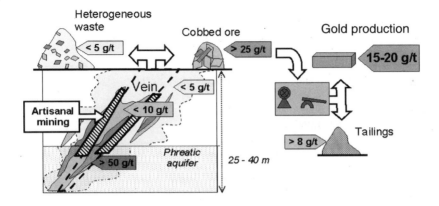

Figure 10.2 Distribution of gold grades at a typical artisanal gold vein mine in Burkina Faso

Artisanal mining: a highly structured and job-creation activity

Burkina's artisanal mines are commonly overpopulated, but striking in terms of their teeming and abundant character. Some operations, such as Bouda (Passoré province) in 1991 or Mogrenore (Boulgou province) in 1998 hosted up to 40,000 individuals during the paroxysmal phase of their gold rushes. Such abundant labour, while outwardly excessive, is necessary because of the low level of material means deployed. The activity is thus characterized by very low productivity, but provides considerable employment opportunities.

- The actual extraction zones of mines generally contain 30–40 per cent of the active population on-site (not counting shops). This is the preserve of men, women and children being theoretically absent; however, young boys of less than 15 years old can occasionally be seen hauling ore that had been mined and sorted at the bottom of a pit.
- The ore-processing areas and grinding shops, which can be located several kilometres from operations if there is insufficient water supply at the mine site, host the remaining 60–70 per cent of the working population. These include occasional labourers from local villages, and others who travel vast distances (as far as 100 km) to take up employment. Here, the majority at work are generally women and children.

However, in the cotton-growing southwest of Burkina, with its majority population of Christian Mandé people, the new artisanal gold-mining sites are disliked and lack local manpower. Mechanized grinding of the ore with cereal mills has gradually replaced manual crushing, a laborious task traditionally performed by the women of the surrounding villages (Table 10.1).

The main artisanal gold mining sites in Burkina have surprisingly well-defined structures and exhibit high degrees of organization, which might resemble a small mine if sufficient material means were deployed. The CBMP,

Table 10.1 The selected reference sites (April 2002 data)

Reference site	Discovery year	Legal owner	Rush dynamics phase	No. workers	Itinerant workers (%)	Seasonal workers (%)	Women (%)	Children (%)
Nagrigré	2002	State (CBMP)	Rush: paroxysm	1,550	68	67	24	2
Bouéré	2001	State (CBMP)	Rush: sta-bilization	1,115	91	49	5	1
Kyin	1999	Private entrep-reneur	Rush: decline	980	84	60	12	4
Algo	1994	Private entrep-reneur	Post-rush: reorgani-zation	1,720	25	73	45	13
Karente-nga	1986	Private entrep-reneur	Post-rush: invest-ment	1,050	13	84	65	22

which, at a very early stage, was given a mandate by the government to help regularize activities, has been chiefly responsible for facilitating improved organization of the country's artisanal mine sites, guidance that has proved indispensable because of the size of operations and the complex exploitation methods adopted. Sites feature well-defined workshops, where everybody carries out a specific task using specific equipment. Certain tasks are set aside for the elderly (such as watchmen), women (manual grinding or winnowing), young boys (crushing, and transport of ore and water) and girls (picking and sorting in the waste heaps). The automatic character of these acts enables the reliable estimation of productivity for each task. Such productivity varies between shifts of 200 kg and 500 kg of ore/man/day, and is less than 50 kg of ore/man/day where manual crushing is involved. Each task has its own fixed price that varies minimally from site to site. Among the miners in the extraction zone, it is common to share the ore and thus the risk. This is performed according to precise rules that are accepted beforehand by all members of the team (apparently a standard feature shared by most artisanal gold miners in Africa). In the processing areas, however, it is common to pay labourers in cash for each task. With knowledge of the average productivity and payments per task, the average cost for certain services per ton of ore processed can be determined (Table 10.2).

Our analysis of activities and productivity has enabled us to establish the following order-of-magnitude figures:

- A minimum of 50 artisans is needed to produce 1 tonne of ore/day; and
- A minimum of 2.5 artisans is needed to produce 1 g of gold/day.

Table 10.2 Productivity and cost per tonne of some services carried out in the processing areas

Task	Average productivity (kg/h/j)	Average cost of service (CFAFr/ tonne)	Average cost of service (€/tonne)
Crushing	200	6,000	9.2
Grinding	42	22,000	33.5
Sluice washing	300	7,500	11.5
Winnowing	375	2300	3.5
Mill grinding	400	25,000	38.2

Production costs and revenues of artisanal miners

Based upon our field enquiries, the production cost for the owner of a gold-mining pit can be broken down as follows: 2 per cent for land rent of the plot (annual licence fee to be paid to the customary owner or site administrator); 8 per cent for the purchase of small equipment (such as tools, rope, pulleys, etc); 20 per cent for the purchase of consumables (supports, wood, water, dynamite, diesel, mercury, animals for ritual sacrifices, etc); and 70 per cent for the cost of subcontracting transport, crushing, washing and winnowing. The total amount of such expenses can easily double with the even occasional rental of motorized equipment, such as pumps, generators, compressors or jackhammers.

The production cost C_O can therefore be calculated using the following formula:

$$C_O = \Sigma F_{AM} + \Sigma F_{LM} + \Sigma F_{CS} + (\Sigma \Delta Min \times T \times T_{RC} \times P_{Au}) + \Sigma F_{ST} F_{AM}:$$

$F_{AM}:$ Purchase of small equipment (CFAFr)
$F_{LM}:$ Mechanized equipment rental (CFAFr)
$F_{CS}:$ Consumables (CFAFr)
$\Delta Min:$ Part of ore given to a subcontractor (t)
$T:$ Average ore grade (g/t gold)
$T_{RC}:$ Gold recovery rate (%))
$P_{AU}:$ Gold purchasing price paid by collector (CFA/g Au)
$F_{ST}:$ Subcontracting costs (CFAFr)

As an example, we estimated the average production cost per ton of ore at Alga[1] (April 2002 data) to be:

$$C_O/t \; _{Alga} = 0.49 \; t \; ore + CFAFr51,500$$

To reach the precarious financial equilibrium under such conditions, the minimum ore grade must be:

- 35.5 g/t gold if the produced gold is sold at the official market price of CFAFr4,500/g; and

- 27.5 g/t gold if the produced gold is sold through parallel channels paying up to CFAFr6,000/g.

As ore grades at Alga are commonly 20–60 g/t gold, it is obvious that, in order to be in a position to pay for his operation, the artisanal miner must sell most of his production to a network of clandestine buyers, who assure him 30 per cent more revenue.

Only after enough ore has been extracted to cover all production costs will the earnings be shared among miners. Half of the remaining ore is owed to the pit owner, and the other half is distributed in equal parts among the various labourers, who may include the watchmen of the pit and the processing shed. It is common for a shift boss to receive some extra ore as a bonus, which is taken from the pit owner's share. A miner's revenue can therefore be calculated as follows:

$$R_M = [(Ot \times Gr \times \text{Rec} \times P_{Au}) \times \Delta C - C_0]/2 \times Nt$$

Ot: Ore tonnage produced by the team (t)
Gr: Average ore grade (g/t gold)
Rec: Gold recovery rate (%)
P_{Au}:   Gold purchasing price paid by collector (CFAFr/g Au)
ΔC: Unofficial mark-up of the collector (%)
Nt: Number of team members (h)

The collector's markup is governed by strict rules, varying only slightly between sites. It corresponds to the difference between the real weight and the weight announced by the collector using traditional assay scales. The collector's profit margin varies by agreement from 17 per cent to 25 per cent of the real weight according to the used conventional commercial unit: mostly matchsticks (brin) or old CFAFr coins. On the reference site of Alga, to gain € 1/day (CFAFr655/d), a miner must process ore with a grade of 43 or 32 g/t gold, depending upon the marketing channel he wants to use. The pit owner, that is, the boss, will receive between four and 10 times more, depending upon the size of his permanent team.

Essentially, to make his operation pay, an artisanal miner in Burkina generally is forced to mine only rich ore (>25 g/t gold); and take advantage of the conditions offered by unofficial channels.

The increasing importance of informal channels

The fraudulent part of gold production which, as mentioned above, seems to have steadily grown since more liberal mining laws entered into force, can be selectively measured. It can be fairly easily evaluated at a given site using well-defined criteria. Specifically, such fraud can be calculated based upon the exact count of the staff in each workshop, from an average productivity calculation for each task, and from gold assays of ore and waste for the various processing steps. The crushing and grinding shops, the usual bottlenecks in ore processing, are well suited to this type of approach. Such fraud can then be calculated using the following formula:

$$F = PrD/PrR = PrD/[(Rt\tau_1 \times Ef\tau_1 \times T_1 \times T_{RC1}) + \ldots \ldots + (Rtt_N \times Eft_N \times T_N \times T_{RCN})]$$

F: Fraudulent part of production (%)
PrD: Declared gold production (g/d)
PrR: Real gold production (g/d)
$Rt\tau_1 \ldots Rt\tau_N$: Average productivity for a task of processing cycles 1… to N (t/h/d)
$Ef\tau_1 \ldots Ef\tau_N$: Manpower for a task of processing cycles 1… to N (h)
$T_1 \ldots T_N$: Grades of ore or waste at the start of processing cycles 1… to N (g/t gold)
$T_{RC1} \ldots T_{RCN}$: Gold-recovery rate for processing cycles 1 to N (%)

Our studies on five reference sites show that the official purchasing channels (CBMP or private) rarely collect more than 20 per cent of the gold produced at a site. In 2002, because of insufficient human or material means, the CBMP estimated to be incapable of recovering more than 3–5 per cent of production in some districts, such as Bagassi (near Boromo) and Kampti in Lobi. Based on these data, the fraudulent part of gold production in Burkina Faso is estimated to be in the range of 90 per cent. For official production declared at 250 kg/year, real production would thus be 2–2.5 tonnes/year. These clandestine gold sales represent a loss of earnings of about CFAFr100 million/year (€150,000/year). The full loss of income, including all taxes, for the state probably exceeds CFAFr1 billion/year (€1.5 million/year).

Experience has shown that the systematic control of gold-producing sites is an expensive and not always efficient proposition for the authorities. To be effective, it should be accompanied by a reduction in the difference between official and unofficial gold prices. This reduction in the markups of middlemen (officially appointed collectors) should then be largely compensated by an increase in the volume of transactions.

Major social and microeconomic impacts of artisanal mining

A few figures will suffice for making a concrete evaluation of the local economic and social impacts of artisanal gold mining in Burkina Faso. For instance, each day at Alga (based upon April 2002 figures):

- 17 tons of ore are mined and processed to produce 420 g of raw gold;
- 1750 miners and labourers work for an average salary of CFAFr1,225/day (€ 1.85/day), including 700 women who work for an average salary of CFAFr640/ day (€0.98/day); and
- CFAFr2 million (€3,055) is distributed in a radius of about 40 km around the site, or about CFAFr25/day/inhabitant (total population).

By simply extrapolating the probable gold production figures of the country (i.e. 2–2.5 tonnes of gold/year), it is not unreasonable to assume that, in past years, during each season of artisanal gold mining in the Burkina countryside, close to CFAFr10 billion (€15 million) is injected into the local economy, in addition to regular agricultural income. In rural areas, an average of 64 per cent of the total wealth generated by artisanal gold mining is directly redistributed to local pit-side producers. Gold is thus a relatively 'fair' (in the sense of 'fair trade') commodity for artisans when compared with gemstones. This is partly explained by the moderate operating costs and markups of commercial channels (collectors and purchasing centres).

A rush of opportunistic shopkeepers generally follows close upon the heels of gold miners. At larger sites, these merchants construct stalls, intent on capturing the artisan's money, selling cold beer, video shows, escort girls, watches and cassette players. In 2002, at Nagrigré (the first rush in Zoundwéogo province), only three months after the discovery of the vein, almost 500 – mostly regional – shopkeepers were servicing the 2,000 artisanal gold miners operating at the site, or one shopkeeper for every four producers. At the same time, the rest of Gomboussougou province had a severe shortage of basic services, such as blacksmiths, millers, cooks, butchers and transporters.

The water trade, especially in the Sahel zone, remains the monopoly of the village that accepts to supply the miners with wells or boreholes. This trade, though an inexhaustible source of user conflicts with farmers, is a wellspring of substantial profits. The village of Boulonga (1,500 inhabitants) which, during the dry season, supplies about 50 m³/day of water to the neighbouring site of Alga at a cost of CFAFr3,750/m³, receives daily in exchange CFAFr150,000–200,000 (up to €305), or more than CFAFr100/day/inhabitant.

With the exception of some pit owners, however, most artisanal gold miners have neither the culture nor the financial capacity to accumulate sizeable capital. Their meagre earnings of about CFAFr800–1,000/day (€1.20–1.55/day) are mostly spent on-site to cover daily essentials, such as food, water, lodging, transport and health services, the costs of which are generally prohibitive in artisanal gold mining regions. Most itinerant gold miners, whether local or foreign, have trouble saving enough to help the family that stays behind in the village. Most of the wealth created locally by gold mining activities never leaves the province (Figure 10.3).

Improved monitoring of environmental impacts

In Burkina Faso, artisanal gold mining has caused a number of ecological problems. Miners typically abandon sites, leaving them defaced and exposed to agents of erosion; through their intensive activity, render farm land infertile; damage forests;[4] lower groundwater tables through excessive pumping (with non-recycled pumping water); and release harmful contaminants, one of the most serious of which is acid from electric batteries.[5] A cause of many of the industry's more pressing environmental problems is excessive use of chemicals on-site, especially mercury. As explained in Chapter 5, this element, legally forbidden and not even a decade ago virtually unknown by the artisanal gold miners in the country, is today found at almost all such sites in Burkina.

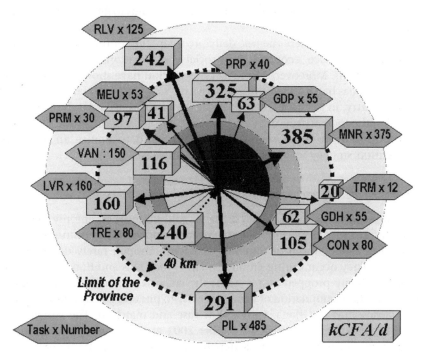

Figure 10.3   Reference site of Alga: distribution of income (CFAFr/day) in terms of tasks and distance between mine site and the original village

PRP: *pit owner;* GDP: *pit watchman;* MNR: *miner;* TRM: *ore transporter;* GDH: *shed watchman;* CON: *crusher;* PIL: *grinder;* TRE: *water transporter;* LVR: *sluice washer;* VAN: *winnower;* PRM: *mill owner;* MEU: *miller;* RLV: *rewasher.*

It is estimated that in producing each gram of gold, 0.5–1 g of mercury is used for amalgamating (gold) concentrates. Nationwide, 500–750 kg mercury[6] are used annually in the sector: 15–20 g 'balls' of mercury, which mainly originate from neighbouring Ghana, are sold by collectors for CFAFr500–1,000 (€0.75– 1.50). Given the climatic conditions of the country, most of the mercury will vaporize; the risk of water contamination, therefore, is minimal. As part of the PRECAGEME[7] project, eight water samples from the major Essakane site (Sahel province of Oudalan) were analyzed (Zunino and Ki, 2001). No trace of mercury was detected (<0.2 mg/l for a standard of <1 mg/l).

However, miners and collectors not in possession of suitable protective equipment expose themselves to toxic mercury through direct contact with the 'ball' during amalgamation and when roasting the amalgam. At the time this research was carried out, none of the sites visited had well-defined areas for these operations. Retorts had never been introduced, nor had officials trained artisanal miners in closed-circuit distillation and the recovery of used mercury. Under PRECAGEME, Burkina's first mercury awareness campaigns have been organized, with demonstrations and the use of visual aids to illustrate the harmful effects of mercury.

In Burkina Faso, where the true daily preoccupation of the rural population is simply subsistence, economic and social considerations override environmental concerns. Moreover, 20 years of observation have shown that artisanal gold mining has had relatively little negative impact on the natural environment of the country; in any case, no irreparable damage has occurred. Nevertheless, in view of the industry's recent developments, it now seems urgent to study and address potential environmental problems, and to devise an efficient intervention strategy for minimizing future impacts.

Addressing health and safety issues

The work carried out at Burkina's artisanal gold mines is commonly high-risk and very arduous, especially for the women and children omnipresent in processing areas. Mortal or disabling accidents, though rarely declared, are common. They occur during ground collapse, rock falls and flooding, and are caused by badly propped-up pit walls, the collapse of small pillars, irregular pumping, the accumulation of waste too close to pits and poorly controlled use of explosives (as in Ghana, with a slow fuse and matches). The last disaster given media coverage was in November 2001 at Guéguéré (Ioba province), where a pile of waste slid into a trench, officially burying 35 miners. Other more long-term hazards are linked to operating and ore-processing conditions. Inadvertent exposure to rock dust, as well as vapours from chemical products such as mercury and nitric acid,[8] can have disastrous consequences such as severe neurological or lung impairment. Less severe hazards include fumes escaping from mills, noise and vibrations. Women, sometimes pregnant, and their small children are particularly susceptible.

During a rush, living conditions for the entire mining community can severely deteriorate. Individuals are commonly cut off from all educational or health structures, residing in a temporary camp that rapidly becomes overpopulated and unhygienic, and where promiscuity is extreme. Malnutrition, precarious housing, a lack of drinking water and the absence of sufficient sanitary installations all favour the development of epidemics. In 1998, the Mogrenore site (Tiba district, Boulgou province) became a vector for cholera, which spread to Ouagadougou (Thomassin and Toux, 1999). In 2002, living conditions at Nagrigré (Zoundweogo Province) made the authorities fear a similar outbreak. To this must be added the fact that children do not attend school (they start participating in artisanal gold mining work at a very young age), and the excessive consumption of alcohol and drugs (Nigerian 'Blue-Blue' or C14 amphetamines) together with prostitution cause criminality and AIDS.

Devising an appropriate development policy

These economic and social stakes make the selection of a development policy challenging. Would it be better to provide direct assistance to traditional artisanal miners, or should the government foster the emergence of small enterprises to disseminate extension?

The contribution of artisanal mining to sustainable development is quite variable. Moreover, the approach of providing support to a community commonly conflicts with approaches taken to deliver support to small mines. An additional problem is that budget restrictions often force triage: the support-of-communities approach entails the risk of extremely selective humanitarian assistance, while the small-mine-support approach not uncommonly results in a few opportunistic persons profiting from the development-aid funds which, in the case of the former, are at least more equitably distributed (Jaques et al., 2003).

Regardless of the approach taken, it is imperative that the resulting actions are of suitable duration (i.e. at least four or five years), and emphasize a participative approach that addresses all key concerns, including social, cultural, technical, economic, financial and environmental. Joint action for strengthening the institutional services and organizations in charge of the sector are of paramount importance.

At this stage, however, it can be said that:

* assistance targeted at tens of thousands of Burkina's artisans must emphasize immediate action, coupled with long-term prevention and educational measures; and
* any assistance for small-mine entrepreneurs in Burkina, addressing at most 100 individuals, should emphasize the provision of short-to-medium-term support, and formal on-the-job training.

Why small-scale enterprises?

Many multilateral development agencies view small private enterprises as important driving forces behind regional economic development in developing countries. Such small, flexible and adaptable enterprises provide innumerable economic opportunities. Moreover, the semi-industrial sector can serve as a platform for the design, application and distribution of innovative processes, and can foster technological dynamism and increased productivity through creating new and better-qualified job opportunities. In the case of the mining sector, small enterprises valorize an intermediate resource that is left aside by artisanal miners and big industry alike. They also help to facilitate formalization of the sector, helping it gain more credibility in the eyes of funding organizations.

Providing direct support to a small enterprise can have rapid and palpable results. Another advantage is that a small miner who respects social and environmental constraints can encourage better working practices among fellow artisans.

Why the need for slow and well-considered mechanization?

Vigilance is obviously required: an all-economic solution should not be to the detriment of social redistribution. The emergence of a network of small mines should not upset the existing fragile equilibrium, which, as mentioned above, permits at least a slight distribution of wealth to a large number of people. It is essential that jobs are not roughly eliminated, thus depriving entire communities of a substantial portion of their incomes. A change in the scale of the activity, if necessary, must be gradual, and if possible, should sustain alternative activities in parallel.

Under actual conditions in Burkina, the introduction of a crusher-grinder unit with a capacity of 1 tonne ore/hour would make approximately 425 local labourers redundant, including 350 women (Figure 10.4). Each takes home €1.20 or the equivalent of €510 for the group in a country where half of the population subsists on less than €0.40 per day (UN, 2003).

Today, the golden rule in Burkina Faso is to introduce a non-competition clause between artisanal mining and small mines. These two activities should strive to complement each other, thus preventing resource conflicts. To do so, the small entrepreneurs must resolutely turn towards resources that are technically inaccessible to artisanal miners. Their priority should be to tackle abandoned artisanal sites for the processing of:

- mine waste and tailings (i.e. anthropic deposits, grading 3–12 g/t gold); and
- residual low-grade ore left unmined (<25 g/t gold).

It is estimated that several million tonnes of waste and tailings could be reprocessed in the country. Such low-grade (1–3 g/t gold for 'waste' and 6–12 g/t

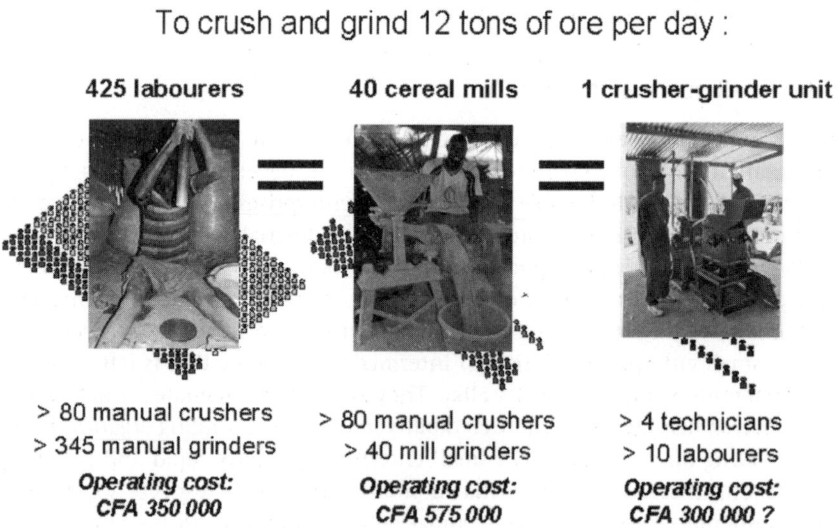

To crush and grind 12 tons of ore per day :

425 labourers   **40 cereal mills**   **1 crusher-grinder unit**

> 80 manual crushers   > 80 manual crushers   > 4 technicians
> 345 manual grinders   > 40 mill grinders   > 10 labourers

Operating cost: *Operating cost:*   *Operating cost:*
CFA 350 000   *CFA 575 000*   *CFA 300 000 ?*

Figure 10.4 Example of job losses through the introduction of new technology

gold for tailings) manmade material represents a substantial potential resource that has been minimally exploited thus far.

An emerging network of small-scale mining entrepreneurs

Today, an increasing number of local entrepreneurs are attempting to develop their own small mining operations in Burkina Faso. In early 2003, almost 50 such entrepreneurs were known. Many are exploration and mining professionals made redundant when the gold price declined in the late 1990s. Most work, or attempt to work, under the rather precarious and not-so-very-reassuring artisanal exploitation authorization framework. Recently, many have established organized associations; the first such group, the National Corporation of Small-Mine Artisans and Operators (CONAPEM), was formed in 2003. Remarkably, these entrepreneurs never extract their own ore. A lack of means generally restricts them to the following tasks:

- reorganizing active artisanal gold mines to better control and collect production; and
- using cyanide to reprocess tailings or other waste from artisanal gold mining (heap or, more rarely, vat-leaching).

Among such artisanal cyanidation operations, the best example of the entrepreneur's ingenuity for reconciling technical nature and reduced cost is the small 'garden plot' (Figure 10.5). These easily organized plots use original leaching processes that obviate all need for mechanization, although in the process of achieving such extreme cost reduction, safety issues are seriously overlooked. As such, these operations have provoked legitimate worries among authorities. In late 2002, two units of this type were operational in the east of the country. A third had just been closed by DEMPEC[9] because of poor adherence to safety issues.

Until now, such units have solely reprocessed artisanal gold mine tailings, using discontinuous descending percolation for the cyanidation of residual gold. Each cyanidation cycle lasts between three and five weeks. The operating mode is as follows.

1. Tailings are transported by cart or wheelbarrow to the processing site, where they are deposited into small depressions made watertight with tarpaulins or plastic bags.
2. The tailings are regularly sprinkled by hand with a cyanide solution in galvanized-iron watering cans.
3. The gold is complexed on zinc at the base of the tailings heap; the cementation cell consists of an emptied truck battery and cyanide solution is recovered in a barrel.
4. The cement is dissolved in sulphuric acid; the auriferous concentrate is then purified with nitric acid to obtain *doré*.
5. The depressions are emptied by shovel; the non-neutralized cyanide waste is then transported by wheelbarrow to an unprotected storage area.

Figure 10.5   Cyanidation 'garden plot'

In late 2002, the largest cyanidation setup of this type employed 12 permanent salaried staff, and produced 350 g/month of gold from 160 t of tailings; the gold recovery rate was approximately 70 per cent. Information provided by the operator, compared with the results of on-site analysis of the process (Thomassin, 2003), shows that this type of operation can only be profitable when making use of certain informal commercial channels. Clandestine merchants sell cyanide at a cost of CFAFr1,000/kg (compared with the official market rate of CFAFr2,600/kg) and buy the produced gold at the rate of CFAFr6,000–6,500/g (CFAFr4,500/g on the official market). These conditions help limit operating costs, here estimated at CFAFr16,000/t, thus reducing the minimum gold grade in the final tailings, which drops to around 4 g/t gold.

Artisanal miner: the sole legal title available for small-scale mining entrepreneurs

Burkina's authorities are keen on developing the country's mining sector, as evidenced by the new Mining Code of 1995 and its application decrees of 1997. Certain texts specifically cover the ASM sector, making a distinction between 'small' and 'artisanal' mines.

At present, however, the category 'artisanal miner' is the only legal option available to small entrepreneurs seeking to profit quickly: unlike a prospective small miner, an artisanal miner is not obliged to obtain an exploration or mining licence. The only requirement is that an Authorization for Artisanal Exploitation is secured, which is issued by the Directorate General of Mines, Geology and Quarries (DGMGC) following consultation with the concerned local authorities.

It covers all commodities and deposit types, with the exception of old mine-waste dumps and industrial minerals. Reserved for nationals, it can cover an area of up to 100 ha and is granted for an initial period of two years, with the option of indefinite renewal. Its holder is given priority to obtain a mining licence in the event that a substantial deposit is discovered.

This authorization, however, has a number of constraints. It does not have the value of a mining licence and thus cannot be ceded or used as a financial guarantee for obtaining a bank loan; nor does it stop the superposition of an exploration licence by someone else, which may result in its suppression (no financial compensation rules are defined). This means that, as soon as his project becomes profitable, the entrepreneur must attempt to safeguard his perimeter by requesting a small-mine exploration licence.

In early 2003, 38 valid artisanal exploitation authorizations had been delivered in Burkina Faso, 13 of which were attributed to CBMP alone; several new requests were in the pipeline. At the same time, only one small-mine exploitation licence had been granted (see Table 10.3 for fees breakdown).

Problems facing the small-scale mining entrepreneur

A lack of knowledge of resources is one of the main problems facing the small-scale mining entrepreneur in Burkina Faso. Here, as elsewhere, most exploration work is carried out by the industrial sector. For small and artisanal miners, only the visible part of the iceberg can be assessed.

The problem is that detailed mineral exploration represents a capital investment beyond the financial reach of such local entrepreneurs. Respecting the classic exploration/reserves ratio of 1/100, a budget of about CFAFr30 million (€45,000) is required for comprehensive gold exploration, but who will provide such funding? The old catch-22, or vicious circle, once again appears. The only hope is to obtain exploration credits from funding organizations or potential investors, through well-targeted and sustained promotion.

Though exploration costs are generally high, budgets can be appreciably reduced through systematic use of low-cost exploration methods and tools.

Table 10.3   Mining-related fees for the ASM sector in Burkina Faso, as of 1 January 2003

	Authorization for artisanal exploitation	Small-mine exploration licence	Small-mine exploitation licence
Initial granting (CFAFr)	400	1,000,000	1,000,000
Renewal (CFAFr)	400	1,500,000	2,000,000
Transfer (CFAFr)	400	2,000,000	2,000,000
Surface tax (CFAFr/km²/year)	30	2,500–7,500	100,000

These include trenching, artisanal pits,[10] soil geophysics (electrical) and short destructive boreholes (Table 10.4).

In addition, small entrepreneurs are commonly faced with other, more or less related, difficulties, including the following.

- Legal and administrative difficulties: minimal access to updated mining records, encountering problems when attempting to obtain exploitation licences in attractive areas and having considerable difficulty safeguarding exploitation licences beyond the legal two-year period (indispensable condition for a carefree investment).
- Technical difficulties: minimal access to expert and consulting services, experiencing great difficulty obtaining suitable equipment at a reasonable cost (locally manufactured if possible) and challenged by demands to produce certain legal documents (e.g. an environmental-impact study).
- Accounting difficulties: ensuring appropriate management of the project.
- Commercial difficulties: selling extracted product at an acceptable price.
- Financial difficulties: producing a suitable financial plan.

Proposal for action

Coherent development policies for small mines emphasize simultaneous observation and control of activities, and the delivery of direct hands-on assistance to operators. It is imperative to dissociate these two areas (i.e. the stick and the carrot) in order to attain maximum credibility and confidence among miners. Each of these actions should be the responsibility of a distinct and well-defined organization with clear prerogatives.

Assistance for small miners could be coordinated and/or centralized within a light and mobile structure of the Support Group for Small Miners type. This structure, consisting of a multidisciplinary team with knowledge of all aspects of small mining (legislation, techniques, accounting, funding, etc), should play the role of promoter, mediator, consultant and expert, proposing quality assistance to the entrepreneur during all stages of his project (Figure 10.6).

Pilot centres for experimentation and specialized technical demonstration, particularly for ore beneficiation, should be a part of this structure. Such centres, which are currently in great demand, would have the objective of promoting innovative processes that facilitate increased profitability, and which respect

Table 10.4 Comparative cost of exploration workings, including sampling at 1-metre intervals and gold analyses (based on BUMIGEB costs, 2003)

Type of working	Cost (CFAFr/metre)
Trench	4
Artisanal pit	16.2
Destructive borehole	20.7
Cored borehole	28

safety, health and environmental constraints. They could also serve as a setting for the organization of regular field centres, which would train not only entrepreneurs but also government agents involved in the artisanal and small mine sector. Moreover, a pilot centre that uses cyanide for processing waste and tailings should be set up as soon as possible.

In partnership with representatives from concerned state organizations and services (DEMPEC, BUMIGEB, CBMP and institutional project teams) and possibly NGOs or specialized local organizations, the support group could also organize specific continuing awareness and education programmes for the artisanal mining community which cover, among other things, workplace safety, child labour and HIV/AIDS. At the same time, with the help of local mediators and popularizers, artisans could be encouraged to formalize their activities, for instance, through cooperative organizations.

Conclusion

Initial technical, social and economic analysis must be considered as an inevitable preliminary step for delivering any slightly ambitious operational assistance to the ASM sector. It helps to identify the complex problems affecting this sector, providing not only a sound understanding of the environment in which intervention will take place, but also guaranteeing the participation spirit that is indispensable for local appropriation. The present analysis of artisanal and small mine activity in Burkina Faso has revealed the following.

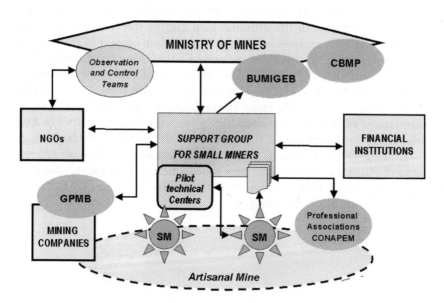

Figure 10.6   Proposal for delivering assistance to artisanal and small mines in Burkina Faso

1. Artisanal and small mine activity has significant microeconomic and social impacts. It is possible to redistribute some of its wealth to large numbers of people; it creates jobs in rural areas, injecting substantial wealth that complements the often insufficient farming incomes. Thus, even though it generates but little revenue for the government's coffers and is associated with poor health and safety conditions, artisanal and small mines as a whole indubitably remain positive enterprises for the country.

2. In recent years, artisanal gold mining has experienced a true mutation. Due in particular to a resource that is becoming increasingly rare and inaccessible in the traditional ASM regions of the Sahel, artisans have progressively migrated to unexplored regions in the south, where they now work new targets in a new environment. Here, they are not only confronted by more severe technical constraints, but there is also a dearth of local manpower at sites. These new conditions have gradually forced artisanal miners to seek greater levels of professionalism and mechanization.

3. This evolution seems favourable for a more radical change of scale in ASM operations. However, such change must be smooth and not upset the equilibrium of the existing system. Despite the efforts made by authorities to promote mining enterprises in recent years, the requisite conditions for facilitating the emergence of a network of small mines in Burkina Faso are not yet in place. Such efforts must continue and be amplified in order to fill the obvious gap in exploration results, safeguard the legal framework for entrepreneurs and convince investors that small mines can be an honourable and profitable activity.

In collaboration with BUMIGEB, BRGM has produced a detailed and quantified evaluation of the artisanal gold mining sector in Burkina Faso; undertaken rigorous analyses of options for providing support to small mines; and, more generally, has identified measures for improving the contribution of ASM to national development. We have provided qualitative and quantitative arguments which justify why development aid to ASM should be a national priority. Even though today many of the bilateral and multilateral funding organizations are beginning to come to grips with the true importance of ASM, national authorities often lack sufficient information, supported by data, on this growing sector of industry. Once crucial data are obtained, an efficient means of clarifying artisanal mining's contribution to national development would be to include important information in the national Poverty Reduction Strategy Paper (PRSP) of Burkina Faso.

CHAPTER 11

Artisanal gold mining in Burkina Faso: permits, poverty and perceptions of the poor in Sanmatenga, the 'land of gold'

Sabine Luning

In Burkina Faso, gold mining is a poverty-driven activity. The sector has expanded rapidly since the country's droughts of the 1980s, which impaired the traditional rural economy; during this period, many people began to mine gold to obtain supplementary sources of income.

According to Gueye (2001), between 100,000 and 200,000 artisanal miners are, at present, actively involved in gold mining in Burkina, dispersed at more than 200 sites across the country. The estimated value of gold produced by non-industrial means since 1986 is placed at US$95 million (CFAFr50,000 million). These figures, however, only include the gold purchased by the CBMP (Gueye, 2001).[1] Today, gold production is seen as a means for reducing poverty in Burkina Faso, which, since 1997, has had HIPC status.

Country officials have repeatedly been involved in negotiations with the World Bank and the IMF in an effort to relieve national debts. Since the early 1990s, structural adjustment programmes (SAPs) have largely shaped Burkina Faso's agendas for financial reorganization. Structural adjustment refers to the set of free-market economic policy reforms imposed on developing countries as a condition for receipt of loans. To ensure a continued inflow of funds, HIPCs have to adhere to conditions mandated by the IMF and World Bank.[2] As is the case in most African countries, in Burkina, SAP measures aim to roll back the state through the privatization of public sectors and encourage the spread of NGOs (Nugent, 2004). The gold-mining sector has been targeted, since gold is, next to cotton, the country's chief export. In the view of the World Bank, improvement in terms of the trade balance hinges upon the developments achieved in this sector. Burkina has therefore received support to liberalize gold mining, and its opening up to local, as well as foreign, investors.

This chapter explores the dynamics of Burkina Faso's artisanal gold-mining sector, and examines the degree to which national policies reflect the interests and needs of subsistence mine operators. The chapter begins by describing the evolution of the country's mining policies, explaining how the present permit system has come about. In the second section of the chapter, a case study of a mine site in the province of Sanmatenga ('land of gold') is presented, which highlights the relations between large corporations and artisanal miners.

Two issues in particular are targeted. The first concerns the interconnections between different players on the ground. In Burkina, liberalization has given rise to a new structure of mining titles and rights governing the purchasing and selling of gold. How has this influenced community dynamics at particular sites? Using findings from fieldwork and secondary analysis, the chapter explains how permit-holders and local people secure access to work at mine sites. The second issue addressed is the ideological debate on poverty. A vast literature on the World Bank and development agencies is concerned with how to define, identify and structurally combat poverty through liberalization. Chapter 3, which examined the poverty–ASM nexus, argued that subsistence miners are trapped in a vicious cycle of poverty; liberalization does not seem to lead to poverty relief. This chapter contributes further to discussions on the ASM-poverty debate by investigating operational dynamics in Burkina Faso, and examining the ways in which gold-mining activities are linked to impoverishment and the 'quest for wealth'.

Policy development in the Burkinabé mining sector

Only certain regions in the present national territory of Burkina Faso have a long history of mining activity. According to Kiétéga (1983), Burkina's first artisanal mining activities took place during the 14th and 15th centuries in Mouhoun (formerly Volta-Noire). Today, Mouhoun houses the country's only industrial mining plant at Poura near Gaoua, referred to locally as Lobi-Dagara country.[3]

French colonial interests in mining in this region were limited. In the 1920s, the colonial administration demarcated zones reserved for indigenous artisanal mining. A small group of companies, which included the Mining Company of Upper Volta and the Equatorial Mining Company, undertook gold exploration in Gaoua at the time, but abandoned their activities during the 1932 economic crisis. After World War II, the French renewed their interests with the aim of exploiting gold in Poura on an industrial scale. Between 1960 and 1991, no further legislative amendments were made relating to the mining industry. The only relevant decree passed concerned land tenure reorganization. This law (zatu no. AN VIII-0039 bis/FP/PRES) stipulates that the land and what lies beneath are the property of state; there are specific laws, however, in place to regulate sites and quarries, depending on the nature and location of activities (Gueye, 2001: 12).

The rights to land and mining became an important issue during the regime of Thomas Sankara, who seized power following a military coup d'état in 1983. During the four years of his regime, he fought foreign domination as well as internal traditional hierarchies. His policies, which were orientated towards land rights and mining, made a clear statement: the state was the sole owner of the land and its resources. Sankara's efforts were touted as a strategy to combat feudalism; however, following these legislative changes, all existing customary rights to land were no longer recognized. At the time, this caused growing unrest among farmers, although the new laws could never be applied realistically. Potential loss of agricultural lands continues to be a major concern of farmers in Burkina, particular in zones where artisanal gold mining can be carried out. The law still stipulates that all lands belong to the state, even though an implicit tolerance towards existing land rights is expected (Lavigne-Delville, 1998).

During his tenure as ruler, Sankara not only wanted to regulate the methods by which gold was mined, but also made considerable effort to control the gold market:

> When the practice of artisanal mining began to increase in the mid eighties...there was no Mining Code in Burkina Faso. In 1986 the state increased regulations and structures to monitor the industry. The Burkinabé Precious Metals Counter (CBMP) was created and it was bestowed with the sole monopoly over collecting, processing and marketing precious metals produced by artisanal, industrial and semi-industrial mining...It employed technicians to purchase gold from artisanal sites and granted authorization cards which permitted local buyers to purchase gold that could be resold to holders of gold marketing cards. CBMP had several local buyers who resold gold to the Counter. [Gueye 2001a: 18–19]

Under Sankara, the state claimed a monopoly on both gold production and marketing; however, the situation has changed drastically over the last 15 years, a period in which there has been progressive liberalization and reduced direct state involvement in all levels of the gold-mining sector.

Contemporary liberalization and legislation: different permits and players

In 1987, Sankara was assassinated during another coup d'état, which brought Blaise Compaore to power. The reasons for this were manifold but also economic: Compaore clearly favoured fewer restrictions on trade, as well as reduced tax burdens for entrepreneurs (Ettema and Gielen, 1992). Compaore has been in power ever since, and was first 'democratically' elected as president in 1992. His regime is characterized by the gradual move to a multiparty democracy, and is based on liberal economic policies (Otayek, 1992). Since 1997, Burkina has retained its HIPC status, and therefore qualifies for loans from the International Development Association (IDA) as part of the so-called Poverty Reduction Support Operation. To qualify for these loans, it was decided that Burkina must fulfil optimistic expectations for gold export, as stipulated in the Debt Sustainability Analysis (DSA): an average growth of 10 per cent a year in volume terms was considered feasible in light of renewed interest by foreign mining firms.

In 2002, the IMF and IDA indicated in their HIPC document that the developments in the gold sector had not enabled Burkina Faso to repay its external debt. A variety of exogenous factors, including changes in the gold price and the closure of the industrial Poura mine, offset the revenues generated by increased mine production (IMF and IDA, 2002: 53). The report nevertheless praised the country's sound macroeconomic and adjustment policies, which aimed to improve the national financial situation; their implementation, as well as increased privatization, were preconditions to obtaining loans in the first place. An initial step taken towards privatization was the introduction of the Mining Code in 1997, along with a new system of mining titles capable of accommodating private players with different capacity and equipment. Since the end of the 1990s, all corporations have had some involvement in artisanal mining due to failures in the industrial mining sector: currently, both multinationals and national companies are all engaged in small-scale mining, having secured the necessary permits.

In Burkina, there exists both an authorization for artisanal mining (*autorisation d'exploitation*) and a permit for small-scale mining (*permis d'exploitation*). The latter facilitates access to mortgages from banks, and grants holders the legal right to sell and export extracted gold; titles are renewable and transferable. Permit-holders are also required to adhere to strict rules on the openness of exploitation results, environmental issues and working conditions on-site. Mining titles are open to foreigners and Burkinabé. By law, however, only Burkinabé can be issued artisanal mining authorizations. These permit a holder to prospect and exploit minerals in a demarcated area within which no deposits have been identified, and the application of heavy machinery is prohibited. If a deposit is discovered, an application must be made for a small-scale mining permit. The title is not transferable, does not guarantee access to bank loans and does not permit a holder to export gold. At the same time, it lacks many of the (social and environmental) obligations associated with small-scale mining permits.

A research permit is awarded for a demarcated plot of 250 km^2, and authorizes its holder to extract minerals at the surface and underground within the boundaries of the permitted zone according to conditions stipulated in the Mining Code. If mineral deposits are found in the research zone, an application for a mining permit should follow. If necessary, this mining permit can overlap with the boundaries of several research permits belonging to the same holder.

Security of tenure and system flexibility are needed if gold extraction is to be increased in Burkina Faso. Security of tenure helps secure investor confidence (placing limits on permit transfer inhibits speculative buying and the selling of permits outright) and facilitates long-term investment (continuous investment in the sector will only occur if guaranteed tenure is granted to a specific plot for an extended period). There is also need for flexibility in the mine permitting processes; this requires ensuring that there are connections between permits and providing incentives to stimulate interaction between permit holders. In Burkina, holders of research permits are required to report annually on research findings, are expected to spend a minimum amount of money per square kilometre; and during the second renewal, must reduce the surface area of their plot by 25 per cent. Any deposit that is discovered must be reported to the government, and can only be worked if the request to transfer the right of research to a mining permit is granted. Once a mining title is obtained, the holder is required to begin extraction activities within two years.

The rules and regulations in place for mining and prospecting give preferential treatment to holders of exploitation permits. This Mining Code does serve to promote the transfer of authorizations to permits; furthermore, if at any point, both types of rights exist for the same plot of land, the permit prevails over the authorization (although the authorization holder is entitled to compensation). The laws encourage both holders of research permits and exploitation authorizations to put forward applications for mining permits.

As explained previously, in the 1980s, the state had a monopoly on mining, and gold purchasing and selling rights. The IDA provided the government of Burkina Faso with a loan for restructuring BUMIGEB and eliminating the monopoly of the state mining company, CBMP, on gold exports. Presently, there are two ways to obtain rights to buy and sell gold. The first is a licence to trade and export in gold, and the second is connected to the system of mining permits.

The government promotes its liberal climate to companies that wish to trade in gold originating from Burkina. Through the internet, private investors are informed about the opportunities available for purchasing and selling gold countrywide:

> Burkina Faso produces and sells gold; the sector is open to the private sector; however private individuals who sell gold must be authorized by the Government on the basis of standard procedures applicable to all those who so request. The list of authorized companies is regularly updated and available through the Ministry of Mines, Quarries and Energy and on this website (http://www.burkinaembassy-usa.org/).

The CBMP is responsible for authorizing and controlling gold exports. It has handed out permits to other counters and has nominated intermediaries authorized to buy gold on mining sites on their behalf.

The differences and interrelations between research and mining rights have social implications for the different parties involved. The case study that follows examines relations between multinationals and Burkinabé enterprises working in the same stretches of the province of Sanmatenga. The coexistence of these groups is determined largely by the success with which research and mining permits are exchanged. Staff at some of the companies at Sanmatenga interact regularly with miner-farmers who themselves are not in possession of permits. They have, however, been granted conditional access to areas of permit-holders: miner-farmers are required to sell their gold to the permit-holders.

For the purposes of this discussion, the authorization to buy and sell gold as part of securing mining titles is most relevant. A mining permit authorizes a holder to own, retain and transport extracted minerals and/or crude mineral-aggregated ore to storage or processing areas, and to market these products inside or outside the country (Gueye, 2001: 14).

Gold mining in Sanmatenga: a case study

This section of the chapter is devoted to assessing critically how the liberalization of the gold-mining sector in Burkina has affected local community dynamics. To explore this thesis, the province of Sanmatenga was selected for investigation. The region can best be introduced with the help of maps developed using donor funding from the EU. The EU supports SYSMIN projects for ACP countries (African, Caribbean and Pacific Group of States) with mining potential. Since 1993, Burkina Faso has received a steady influx of SYSMIN funds, initially for the rehabilitation of the industrial mine at Poura, and from 1999, for developing its programme of geological cartography, 7ACP BK 074. The Bureau de Recherches Géologiques et Minières (BRGM) was responsible for the research, which resulted in maps of scales from 1/1,000,000 to 1/200,000.

Since the site of this research is located in the province of Sanmatenga, its geological and mining characteristics are described on the geological map of Kaya, ND-30-XI, published in 2003. The site is situated in the Arc de Goren, of which Liliga-Goren is again a part. The book that accompanies the map describes the sector Liliga-Goren:

> This zone...called 'Goren' comprises many artisanal mining sites of differ- ent nature, globally organized in a NNE-SSW direction...The mining sites around the village of Goren are relatively large; the exploitation of elluvial mineralizations cover the flanks of saprolitisized slopes and the different ridges...At Liliga the gold sites of the 'Sondo placer' seem to correspond with the uncovering of primary mineralization. [SYSMIN, 2003: 63][4]

The specific mining site described in this article is referred to as Liliga-Goren. Here, the size of artisanal mining activity is limited; the spatial dimension of the site does not exceed 1 km^2; at any given time, the number of people working on-site does not exceed 300; pits are worked by small groups, or individuals without a rigid division of labour; crushing activities are carried out with rudimentary work tools; the site is situated in close proximity to agricultural fields; and arrangements for the incorporation of artisanal mining activity have been a subject of considerable debate. In terms of its scope and work organization, Liliga-Goren differs significantly from the Karengatenga site described in Chapter 10.

Of the limited literature produced on ASM in Burkina, Katja Werthmann's work stands out. She has provided extensive coverage of the country's large artisanal mines both in film (Kirscht and Werthmann, 2003) and writing (Werthmann, 2000a, 2000b, 2003a). Werthmann's work examines the complex social phenomena at work at such sites, and the drivers behind activities, which have attracted opportunistic individuals from all corners of ECOWAS. In Werthmann's most recent work (Werthmann, 2003b), the issue of mine safety is examined, specifically, people's perceptions of mine accidents. As is the case in most developing countries, in Burkina, gold mining is characterized by haphazard working conditions and transgressive social behaviour. Miners also attribute the dangers in mining activities to occult practices. In Burkina, gold is generally considered to be challenging to extract. This aspect has to be taken into account, but can easily lead to an inaccurate picture of the sector overall. On the whole, the ASM sector is a topic in development that is poorly understood, which policymakers associate with being chaotic and transgressive, dominated by mistrust and dangers of all sorts. Recent research has helped dispel such myths, and has revealed that contrary to its anarchic perception, the activities carried out in artisanal mining regions exhibit a recognizable degree of organization, that work is often carried out under strict supervision, and that operation is intimately linked to group trust (Keita, 2001; Grätz, 2004). These points are reinforced in Chapter 3.

The ways in which artisanal mine sites are organized and policed are diverse, and therefore deserve careful study. At Liliga-Goren, order has not been achieved through employee agreements or by exercising vigilante group power. Rather, organization at the site is determined largely by collaboration between legally authorized companies on the one hand, and influential local people on the other: the former bring into play their permits and the rights attached to them, while the latter build their influence on occult ideas about gold and who can or cannot handle it. The working arrangements on this site result from the combination of these two types of claims and arguments.

The research reported in the discussion that follows combines anthropological field data from the province of Sanmatenga with data from the internet and maps. Initially, formal maps and dossiers were consulted to determine the key geological features of the region and identify important mining groups. A map with mining titles, published in January 2005 by BUMIGEB, shows that Liliga-Goren is part of the Bissa permit, which covers an area of 43 km² and is in the possession of the Burkinabé Company GEP-MINES. A research permit covering an area of 249 km² has also been awarded to GEP-MINES for the adjacent Zandkom region (see Figure 11.1 for an illustrative overview of Burkina's mining titles as of January 2005).

Recently, the Canadian multinational Jilbey Gold forged an agreement with GEP-MINES to acquire, in the coming years, a 90 per cent interest in the Bissa and Zandkom projects. These plots are situated at the centre of the company's existing Bissa holding; combined, these three permits cover an area of approximately 800 km². Between 1993 and 2001, some US$9 million was used to explore for gold on these adjacent concessions.

As of January 2005, Jilbey had nine research permits in Burkina, covering a combined area of 2,000 km², five of which are adjacent to the Bissa and Zandkom area (Namtenga 250 km², Tosse 250 km², Gargo 250 km², Raka 107 km² and Tema 186 km²). In this part of the province, Sanmatenga Jilbey has chosen to focus on research in large permitted concession areas, while simultaneously sponsoring local partners in possession of mining permits to carry out exploration activity. Jilbey also works with High River Gold Mines, another Canadian multinational, which possesses exploration licenses at Bissa/Kindo, Taparko and Hounde, covering a combined area of 5,500 km². Even though Jilbey is an important permit-holder at Bissa, only employees from GEP-MINES interact with local miner-farmers. Two GEP-MINES employees are permanently posted in the field, foremost to supervise the purchasing of gold from individual miner-farmers. The company does not, however, play any role in organizing the work of artisanal miners at the site.

In Liliga-Goren, the search for gold on a commercial scale commenced in the mid-1980s; several gold rushes have since occurred. At the beginning of the rainy season in June–July 2004, a frantic gold search commenced following the first rainfalls, which washed away topsoil and uncovered mineralized sediments. Many men and women from resident and adjacent villages immediately began searching for gold. During this season of the gold rush, villagers debated the following three converging issues:

- Should one work the fields or look for gold?
- How can access to the gold area be regulated?
- How can the sale of gold found at the site be arranged?

Throughout much of ECOWAS, ASM is an activity taken up by subsistence people to complement incomes earned in agriculture. Mining is often carried out over a particular period of time (i.e. a season), after which, people resume their agricultural activities. In the case of Liliga-Goren, the situation was more complex, requiring individuals to make quick decisions regarding their

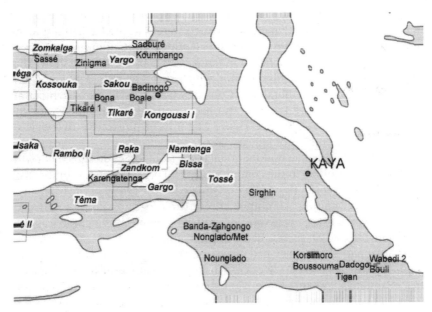

Figure 11.1   Mining titles in Burkina Faso

occupation: the possibility of a gold rush meant there was opportunity for significant income earning. Individuals were faced with deciding whether or not to focus their efforts solely upon finding gold, ignore the temptation and continue to work agricultural fields, or to combine these tasks during the course of the rainy season. This decision, however, had moral implications. The choice not to sow at all – which at least 100 villagers opted for – was considered by many to be morally wrong. Generating income from selling gold or from cultivating crops is perceived as two different exercises. The latter is seen as a more sustainable practice, providing annual yields, whereas the former is viewed more as a short-term stopgap venture, which results in temporary accumulation of wealth. Those who took up mining as an occupation and abandoned farm work entirely did not, of course, hold this view. Nevertheless, the very idea that the search for gold can only lead to shortlived wealth was expressed repeatedly by many villagers.

Another issue concerns land rights. According to the maps and the files of BUMIGEB, the distribution of mining titles appears to be clear; on the ground, however, the situation is far more complicated. At Liliga-Goren, gold was initially discovered in the middle of an agricultural zone, on fields under traditional ownership. The challenge, therefore, was how to take into account these rights, and override them so that gold mining could expand. This issue was handled by a man referred to as 'Mahama', who resides in the village, is in his forties, and has extensive experience in gold mining both inside and outside Burkina. His authority on land issues was based on a combination of different factors, including his prestige as an extraordinary miner, his position as a strong local person with family ties, and his status as close collaborator with GEP-MINES. Mahama managed to negotiate the expansion of the gold site, arranging for the sale of farmland to be used for excavation purposes. Many disapproved of his actions because again, the issue was morally loaded. Some people in the village who opposed mining altogether would sarcastically remark: 'Look what gold does to us. Now we are even selling our lands'. The intention was to convey the disapproval shared by many villagers over miners and Mahama's actions in particular. Others maintained, however, that farmland had not been sold; owners have only been given compensation for the loss of the year's harvest.

The agricultural fields that became available were immediately reallocated to mining villagers and outsiders. Mahama set out to demarcate squares of land, within which pits were dug. Per workplace, CFAFr4,000–5,000 (US$7.50– 10) was paid. It was explained during the course of fieldwork that financial transactions for land acquisition should not be interpreted as the selling of places. What men – as only men were involved in these transactions – paid for was not access to the plot, but rather their freedom: these payments assured individuals that they would not be sent away, would not be robbed and would be safely protected by Mahama. The money simply bought them this protection.

It became clear that Mahama had a reputation for fearlessness, a man one should not tempt or aggravate. His perceived invincibility, therefore, guaranteed people's safety and the protection of property on-site. Anyone who violated a rule would be dealt with swiftly and ruthlessly. Among villagers, Mahama is generally known for his violent inclinations as well as his generosity. With generous gestures, he emphasizes his status as the wealthiest villager at Liliga-Goren. His behaviour is excessive in different respects, which, together with his charisma, makes him an ideal candidate for policing the site.

The third issue for which working arrangements had to be established was gold purchasing. Staff at GEP-MINES explained during personal interviews that different mining companies are active in this region: some are preoccupied with prospecting, while others are more involved on the purchasing side. GEP-MINES functions primarily as a buyer of gold, serving as a *comptoir*. Here again, Mahama plays a major role, acting as an intermediary for GEP-MINES. All miners are obliged to sell him their gold, which, in turn, he sells to the *comptoir* (GEP-MINES) at a standard price of CFAFr36,000 per unit (about US$70).[5]

It was noted that illegal buyers potentially offer higher prices of as high as CFAFr45,000 (US$86) per unit of gold, although legal and clandestine buying often go hand in hand. Mahama himself was suspected of *mélange*: for every 4 kg of gold produced, he would purchase 3 kg at CFAFr36,000 per unit for legal resale to GEP-MINES. He would also buy 1 kg at a higher price for sale through illegal channels at a higher price as well. Moreover, whenever he is offered gold for sale, Mahama subtracts a certain amount from the price for services rendered to the miner. These services constitute a type of insurance, assuring the gold miner that the money he earned will not be stolen. At Liliga-Goren, only Mahama – or men working for him – were, at the time of fieldwork, operating openly as gold buyers. Mahama provides kinsmen and friends with money to purchase gold at different sites within the permit zone of GEP-MINES. Little is known about the relationship between the intermediate buyers for GEP-MINES and other buyers in possession of a licence to trade in gold (CBMP and other gold-buying companies). This is clearly a subject in need of further research. At Liliga-Goren, however, the exploitation permit awarded to GEP-MINES has provided it with a monopoly on gold purchasing in the permit area.

There were strong indications at the time of the research that daily earnings for miner-farmers were in the range of CFAFr4,000–5,000 (US$7.50–10).

Oral history of the mine sites at Liliga-Goren

The first gold rushes at Liliga-Goren occurred in the 1980s during Sankara's tenure as president. During interviews, miner-farmers reflected upon the excessive state control of mining and gold marketing that had occurred at the time. Initially, it was forbidden to seek gold altogether, which forced villagers to search for minerals after dark. After making a move to permit gold mining, the state attempted to regulate extractive and marketing activities. Representatives of the government at the time, the Comité de Défense de la Révolution (CDR), as well as policemen, were present on the sites. Individuals were required to purchase a ticket costing CFAFr200 (US$0.40) per day to work on mine sites. A state cashier would arrive daily from the provincial capital of Kaya to purchase gold, issuing payments in the range of CFAFr2,300 (US$4.40)/g (at present CFAFR6,000 or US$11.50) and travelling under police protection.

Villagers remained ignorant about the market value of gold until one of the men working for the *comptoir* explained to the community that 'half a matchstick of gold values more than a human life'. This remark had two effects. First, it indicated that the price the state paid was less than the real value of gold. Second, and more importantly, it taught miners about the importance of policing the gold site; anyone caught stealing as much as the value of half a matchstick of gold ran the risk of being killed. This story was one of Mahama's favourites: it had taught him the lesson of how to protect the site from theft and other misconduct.

During a personal interview, Mahama elaborated extensively on his prominent role when gold was first found at Liliga-Goren. His stories show that in Burkina, gold is seen as a thing of Earth that can only be obtained if ritual practices are respected (Werthmann, 2003a). In the mid-1980s, Mahama explained, shortly after his return from Côte d'Ivoire, youths discovered gold on a hill nearby the village. They wanted to take it home but could not bring it into their houses. At the doorstep, the gold 'fell to the ground and disappeared'. Mahama advised them to invite the earthpriest to make the necessary sacrifices, which would ensure that the gold could be properly appropriated. This precipitated the gold boom in which Mahama actively participated; he was searching for gold while maintaining peace at Liliga-Goren. Since the mid-1980s, gold has been discovered at different places around the village, giving rise to four separate gold rushes and initiating an influx of opportunistic transient groups. Mahama declared having earned some CFAFr30 million (US$60,000) to date. His dominant role at this gold site seems uncontested, and was confirmed by other miners.

Mahama's role in policing the site was linked to the personal qualities that allowed him to facilitate the appropriation of gold. Not everyone is capable of taking gold into possession. This quality is not simply a function of command over labour power and possession of technical knowledge. Rather, a person must be well-connected to the real owners of gold, particular bush spirits, the so-called *djinns*. Mahama is very well connected to these beings; some people even indicated that his birth was facilitated by *djinns*. Such a connection does, however, have its downside: people who are closely associated with *djinns* do not have the temperate character of 'normal' people. They behave excessively in most respects; they act too generously, too violently, and take too many risks. Mahama's life is filled with excessive events, including fights, road accidents and mixing with unsavoury individuals. Stories of Mahama are told and retold on and off gold sites.

In the mid-1990s, South African scientists came to Liliga-Goren to undertake geological research. It was told that at the time, people lacked knowledge about these strangers. Where had they come from, what were their aims, and what were their land rights in relation to those of the locals? Even today, with the continued presence of GEP-MINES, working relationships with outsiders are not clearcut for many locals. Villagers are well aware that their land rights, when it comes to gold, are in the hands of the state. Foreign groups provide payments to the state to explore or mine particular sites and not to local landowners. Most people do not contest this since the spinoffs are sufficiently interesting: unofficial compensations for land will be made, research provides jobs, strangers are in need of services (house construction, water fetching, etc) that bring in additional money, and gold itself is currency. Nevertheless, more information on the partners the villagers interact with and the formal aspects of their permits in land and gold buying could improve the social situation on the site. Gold rushes at this site are unpredictable and haphazard events, involving strangers who come and go. Information about permits given out and foreign investors is now available on the internet, but the locals most directly affected do not normally have access to these data.

After the gold rush

The rainy season in late 2004 was disastrous. Local debates over mining and farming proved futile: those who had been working the land were, for the most part, unable to harvest. The individuals who had discovered gold had at least earned some income, which, in many cases, would prove to be sufficient to purchase sorghum during the periods of food scarcity that lay ahead.

The response to the bad agricultural season was immediate: the locations at Liliga-Goren where gold could be extracted became very congested. Local people and outsiders from the north – among them many Fulbe[6] – worked desperately to compensate for lost incomes from the poor agricultural season. The social constituencies at the mine sites changed after the rainy season: a diminished local male workforce, greater participation from local women and children, and a higher concentration of men from elsewhere. Foreigners did not have to pay to gain access because in most locations gold reserves had been nearly exhausted. In response to enquiries about the results of extraction efforts, replies were mostly negative: 'Nothing found, nothing gained, but we will pursue, what else are we to do?'

Clearly, the local social situation had become increasingly tense over the year; some people had been successful in finding gold, which caused jealousy and envy occasionally manifested as outbursts and verbal disagreements. The poor harvest increased local disparities in wealth. The daily availability of alcohol on the market of the gold site did not help the social situation. Even the people who had benefited from gold sales earlier in the year appeared to suffer from a post-rush-depression. Gold mining certainly served as a band-aid solution to the poor harvest, but could it provide long-term benefits to the miner-farmers of Burkina?

Some of Mahama's family members clearly benefited from the gold rush: during field visits in August 2004, many claimed to be affluent. During follow-up visits in December, however, it became evident that much of the money earned from gold mining had been spent. The elder brother of Mahama claimed that gold made them suffer. He described the calamities that had occurred with his close kin due to gold discoveries. Two of his children had found substantial amounts of gold at the beginning of the rainy season. This had frightened the elder brother, who in reaction had given all sorts of alms to prevent calamity. Despite this, his mother had fallen ill and is now partly paralyzed. She had first been taken to the local dispensary, and eventually to the hospital in Kaya. Later, his wife and he, himself, had fallen ill. In due course, all of the money gained from gold had been spent on medical bills. Everyone is now recovering slowly, but there are now insufficient funds remaining to purchase supplementary sorghum. He was grateful that at least the alms had prevented death in the family.

Rapid wealth accumulation and subsequent rapid loss of earnings are recurrent throughout the ASM sector. In Burkina, gold mining has not brought lasting wealth: rather, the money earned from gold mining is said to lack *barka* ('blessing' in Arabic). The revenues accrued are unlikely to deliver long-term benefits. By the time this particular gold rush ended, Mahama had moved on. On occasion, he comes back to the village to relax, but his work has now taken him north to Bam province. On a mine site near Sabce, he now engages in activities very similar to the ones described. Again, he is working in a permit zone of GEP-MINES.

Conclusion

This chapter has examined policies governing the gold-mining sector in Burkina Faso, and has assessed critically the impacts of the country's new mine permitting system. A case study of Liliga-Goren was used to illustrate how this system affects parties and transactions on the ground. The chapter also contributes to the growing literature on ASM and poverty, providing a bottom-up perspective of the poor themselves. In Burkina, as in many other parts of the developing world, people will turn to gold mining with the hope of accumulating wealth quickly. If they do not find it, or if the wealth found does not last, the local discourse in Burkina offers an entire repertoire of explanations. Gold creates a wealth that is usually lost faster than it has been gained. Unlike money made through agriculture or cattle-keeping, money earned by mining does not seem to provide a consistent inflow of revenue on which people can build a sustainable future.

CHAPTER 12

Artisanal gold mining in northern Benin: a sociocultural perspective

Tilo Grätz

The aim of this chapter is to provide a general account of ASM[1] in northern Benin.[2] The discussion focuses primarily upon the social aspects of the region's activities.[3]

When compared with operations in other West African countries, such as Burkina Faso, Mali and Ghana, ASM in Benin is a rather marginal economic field both in terms of its importance to the national economy and its role in the mining sector (Ministère de l'Energie, des Mines et de l'Hydraulique/République du Bénin, 1992). Presently, it is confined to one region of the northwest: the southern portion of the Atakora Mountains, near to the district capital of Natitingou (Figure 12.1). At its peak in the 1990s, there were approximately 5,000 people involved in ASM in Benin, but the industry has since diminished considerably, and today is comprised of only around 500 people. Some work on the basis of fragile agreements with official title-holders and the state, although the majority work as informal miners.

The artisanal gold boom of the 1990s triggered considerable changes in northwestern Benin. New economic circuits evolved, and rapid immigration into villages adjacent to mining areas induced dramatic social and cultural transformations.

A brief history of gold production in Benin

The gold-mining region in Benin is situated in the northwestern region of the country, in the Atakora Mountains, south of the district capital of Natitingou and along the Perma River in the vicinity of the villages of Kwatena and Tchantangou. The region is inhabited by Waaba (majority language: Waama*)* and Betammaribe (language: Ditammari), various Fulbe herdsmen and numerous immigrants. Dendi is the *lingua franca* spoken in this region. The main crops harvested include millet, sorghum, yams, rice and cotton.

Gold mining has occurred in this region[4] since the colonial period (when it was called Dahomey). Between 1939 and 1945, an alluvial mining scheme was established in the Atakora Mountains (Vincent, 1962) along the riverbanks close to the village of Kwatena (known locally as Kouekari). At the time, alluvial

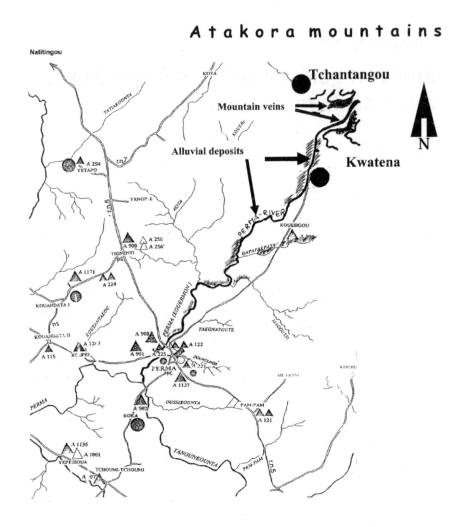

Figure 12.1 Main gold fields in Benin

gold-mining activities were characterized by forced labour, haphazard conditions (causing many deaths), inexperience and hazardous modes of organization. In January 1942, the mining scheme was handed over to the private enterprise, the Société des Mines du Dahomey-Niger (SMDN), which continued to be dominated by forced labour and exploitation driven by the coercive means of the colonial state under martial law.[5] After 1945, exploitation of deposits decreased, and between 1947 and 1956, SMDN abandoned its major projects in response to depressed demand. In 1956, however, the site was ceded to the private French entrepreneur Garnier, who resumed exploitation work, albeit at a low level. During the 1950s, increased private engagements occurred in the mining sector of Dahomey: special licences (*permis de prospection*) were promoted heavily by the colonial administration.[6] In the 1960s and 1970s, several gold exploratory missions were initiated by the state (OBEMINES), with assistance from international donors and experts. In the mid-1980s, deposits were abandoned but remained the property of the state.

Small-scale mining[7] had not been carried out in Dahomey before 1992, after which time, migrants from Togo and Ghana began exploiting alluvial as well as reef deposits south of Natitingou. A gold boom soon followed, inciting further immigration of labour migrants from the region and abroad. Gold miners profited initially from weak government control, which enabled them to mine deposits using simple implements, including pans, sluice boxes, chisels and sledge-hammers. On a number of occasions, government authorities expelled miners and confiscated their equipment, money and gold. Following a series of negotiations and expulsions, alluvial mining was partly permitted, in particular, the working of reef deposits.

Immigrant miners reside within villages situated in close proximity to mining areas, where they either rent houses or construct dwellings of their own. This situation differs from typical West African mine sites, where migrants generally establish a separate camp comprised of tents, straw huts and shelters.

Technical aspects of gold production and organization of labour

In Benin, gold miners work alongside rivers and mountain slopes, where they exploit, respectively, alluvial sediments (placer mining) and elluvial deposits, and undertake reef or lode (mining) activity. Placer mining involves use of hoes and shovels, the extraction of gold-aggregated sediment from ore, and washing/panning using sluices and pans. Occasionally, people use motor-pumps as well as simple pans at the same site, depending on the financial assets of the teams or entrepreneurs.

During reef-mining activity (which dominates large parts of the Atakora site), miners use pickaxes, chisels and sledgehammers to extract gold in mountain shafts, usually alongside one or two colleagues (Figure 12.2). In mountainous regions, mining is much more strenuous and hazardous (especially deep beneath the surface), but usually yields sediments containing higher concentrations of gold. The lode-mining process involves the following: the extraction of gold-bearing rocks in galleries or pits, the pounding and milling of gold ore (performed mainly by women), and washing/panning to separate gold dust.[8]

Miners have developed an intricate system of labour organization, which features hierarchies, shift work and allowances. The main actors in the mining fields include:

- patrons or *chefs d'équipe*;
- assistants or secretaries;
- workers;

Figure 12.2 Chiselling of gold ore in mountain shafts near Kwatena

- assistants;
- guards;
- women and children pounding and milling (refers to reef mining); and
- gold traders.

These categories could, of course, be refined according to criteria such as social and ethnic origin, age and gender. Generally, miners work in small teams headed by a team chief, who, in most cases, is the owner of a shaft or pit.[9] The teams are mixed in terms of the ethnic and regional origins of the workers, who are hired on the basis of their individual abilities and levels of perseverance. The owner may work with trusted organizers and/or participate himself in various phases of the gold extraction process. In any case, owners are small-scale entrepreneurs who invest in equipment and maintain workforces; they generally retain half of the gold yield.[10] Smaller deposits – especially alluvial deposits (i.e. placer gold) – are often worked by small teams who share more or less equally the yields. Some small-scale investors run several shafts and sponsor teams.[11] However, in each case, because of the uncertainty of yield, there is the risk that the entrepreneur receives only part of his/her investment back.

The size of each team varies. In some cases, they are very small, especially in alluvial mining regions. In other situations, workforces can be large, comprised of as many as 20 workers; this is generally the case with reef mining, where subteams work in shifts. In all cases, the degree of formalization of teams and the level of organization of work are low.

The internal property regimes contrast local norms and state laws, creating a particular plural legal situation that does not necessarily lead to conflict. Accessibility to gold deposits and the rules of exploitation are linked to modes of simple appropriation by anteriority (first coming), either by force, negotiation and/or compensation, or the mentioned patronal mode of labour organization that marks the small entrepreneurial activities and which places mining chiefs at the forefront of decision-making and arbitration processes. The typical property regime is characterized by the following:

- The 'right of first discovery' to exploit a shaft, provided that the person is able to meet basic investment needs (equipment, workers, rituals, etc).
- Being tied to actual exploitation and participation of workers, paying of tolls, and respecting and sharing rules.
- Options to lease a shaft, and to obtain shares.
- The possibility to work in turn and to divide shafts according to prosperous veins.

As previously noted, the owner of a mine may exploit or lease a deposit. Often, owners must make payments to local landlords, ritual authorities or common funds of mineworkers.

Generally, the rights of exploitation of shafts and pits are attributed to the person who first discovered and exploited them, assuming he or she has the technical and financial means to do so. In the event that this person does not possess these means (nor does so partially), he/she may forge a contractual agreement with a small-scale entrepreneur or patron who, in turn, engages in exploitation in exchange for shares in the yield or the payment of one-off or recurring compensation. Sharing in this context results in the allocation of yields according to responsibility; as head of the team, the investor receives the largest share (50% in most cases). The remaining shares are divided according to individual work and skill contributions. Provided that the venture is successful, there is always a minimum guaranteed share, regardless of illness or accident, although it can still vary according to an individual's work ethic.

The shaft-owner operates as a small-scale investor, and, at the same time (with all rights and duties), is expected to serve as team leader (*chef d'équipe*). In case the owner is unable (or unwilling) to oversee and manage extraction works on-site, he/she may hire a miner as a trusted organizer (*secrétaire*). Thus, the actual participation of a chief in the exploration and extraction work may be very different, ranging from active permanent engagement of his/her own labour force to the hiring of agents and specialists for each task. The *patron* usually acquires tools, rents motor pumps, and provides food and medical attention to workers when necessary (which he/she may deduct later when it comes time to distribute profits). The shaft owner (*patron, chef de parcelle, chef de trou*) acquires informal user rights to exploit the shaft or plot. However, he/she may lose these rights if the shaft is let to others for an extended period of time (with or without compensation, rent, shares, etc). The same also applies when the shaft is abandoned, even if it later proves to be very prosperous when exploited by successors. This has been a widespread cause of dispute, which is generally settled in favour of the most recent user, but who nevertheless may be asked to pay a stipulated amount of compensation to the initial explorer. These are temporal user rights because these entitlements have to be renewed by permanent actual engagement on the mine site. But there may be a need to sell the claim in the event that an owner no longer has the means to exploit it, wants to leave the mining area permanently, or rents out a shaft during a leave of absence. The terms of a contract may either include finite payments or shares in raw products (gold containing ore).[12] A second type of user rights applies to the shafts that are relatively large, prosperous and difficult to exploit by only one team or which had been discovered by several teams in unison. In such a situation, teams work in turn; it is common for one or more teams to work for a week to 10 days before others are permitted to enter the shaft. The initial team then engages in processing work and rests while waiting for a new period of exploitation to commence.

All territorial rights for exploitation (in terms of limits between shafts or zones of exploitation)[13] are debated and divided among shaft-owners. This procedure can hardly be regarded as a means for defining permanent personal property because it is, as mentioned above, closely linked to actual usage of the shafts. Delimitation disputes are therefore settled within the group of shaft-owners. Overall, quarrels between single shaft-owners are more frequent than conflicts between groups of shaft-owners from different villages. The latter generally occurs when larger, prosperous shafts are discovered, in which case, the shaft is divided into sections, and a decision is made regarding the timing of exploitation of gold veins.

The arrangements between what are generally diversified ethnic work teams as well as immigrant gold miners and local inhabitants are forged in an informal manner, mainly on the basis of unwritten oral rules, contracts and agreements. Associations of miners only partly formalized their rules and proceedings when the federal committee was at its peak in terms of numbers. The most important tasks for the secretary were to construct a record of formally recognized cooperatives (which rarely represented the totality of the active corporate groups) and write letters to the state administration.

Gold is sold on-site in small quantities to petty traders. As is the case in Burkina Faso (Chapter 11), local weighing scales, as well as simple gold weights such as one-CFAFr coins and matchsticks, are used to determine the selling value. The majority of local petty traders work as agents for master merchants, and comprise a large informal and international trading network (Grätz, 2000; Grätz, 2004). Most gold traders also serve as moneylenders who, by providing timely loans, pressure miners into selling them their gold. Notwithstanding this obligation, traders are an important element in the system, linking the guild-like production of gold to the national market. Miners tend to sell their gold immediately because of their constant need for cash flow, which, in turn, fuels the proliferation of the trade altogether.

Rules and norms in mining teams

Generally, the hierarchies in small-scale mining teams are dynamic. Typically, conflicts occur between mining chiefs, who engage in disputes over the boundaries of their mines, the possibilities for expanding operations, and the theft of yields. A number of quarrels also occur between workers and chiefs over production shares, betrayal and the appropriate use of equipment. Usually, conflicts are settled by an association comprised of mining chiefs. As a rule, gold miners try to avoid appealing to any courts outside their group. Only in very few instances are problems presented to local village heads, and there are even fewer cases involving reporting to governmental authorities. The state has only recently been able to intervene in such matters.

Despite these divergent interests, norms of reciprocity and equity commonly exist between miners. Most notably, risk-sharing is a common practice between small pit-owners and miners, as well as between miners and gold traders.[14] In many cases, a miner will receive an appropriate share if he/she has been absent for some time due to illness or a family affair; conversely, a portion may be reduced if he/she has been judged to be lazy or unreliable. Moral obligations include a fair and equal division of hard work and the acceptance of sanctions, but this also requires accepting different tasks according to a person's level of experience, expertise and physical capacity. Apart from these informal rules, there are more concrete institutions that help to guarantee equitable benefits for all parties and oversee redistribution. For example, mining entrepreneurs, team leaders or successful traders are required to contribute to fundraising (French *cotisations, caisses*) during times of need (e.g. to pay medical costs for injured persons, financing rituals[15] and festivities, and bribing state agents).

The number of miners operating in Benin decreases considerably during the peak periods of the agricultural season, and increases in the dry season.[16] The size and composition of the mining population may also change during festivities and religious ceremonies. The composition of many rural communities dependent on mining is influenced by the location of operations and resident miners' experience: many individuals rarely return to their home villages, opting to engage more permanently and exclusively in gold mining over a longer period of time and, when necessary, moving to new areas to mine and/or explore for mineral resources.

The relationships of gold miners to local farmers and state authorities

The described informal user rights in gold mining are generally opposed to the local land rights of the adjacent communities, above all that of farmers, who consider themselves as first-comers (autochthones) and legitimate overseers of all land, and frequently demand compensation.[17] The nature of the relationships between immigrant miners and locals, nevertheless, has changed over time. At the beginning of the gold boom, there were confrontations, with permanent stress resulting in violent clashes between both sides. Various working arrangements were made, including the payment of compensation and fees for rituals. Many local inhabitants are also contemplating a move to the gold-mining profession. Local miners and immigrants have agreed upon a number of resource-sharing arrangements. Specifically, they have cooperatively worked productive shafts, divided up alluvial zones and contributed to fundraisers.

The bargaining position of locals is also weakened by the fact that all mining areas belong to the state. Local land rights, therefore, cannot officially be claimed, and are subject to individual negotiations.

An important element contributing to the growing integration of immigrants into the local communities is the fact that most of the latter rent houses with locals instead of securing their own quarters. Intermarriages have become more common in the process.

There is considerable divergence between the official state law and the local practices described in the relations between gold miners and the state, which is particularly significant in terms of access to resources, the organization of labour and the legitimacy of small investors. As a consequence, conflicts often emerge between gold miners and state authorities. Generally, the governmental authorities in Benin (above all, the Direction des Mines in Cotonou and its regional branch in Natitingou) regard mining rights as the sole domain of the central state, that is, that mining resources are national property, and are therefore subject to be managed and allocated exclusively by the state. This principle is embodied in the official legal framework of the country's national mining law (Code Minier).

Towards the beginning of the gold boom, gold miners in northern Benin simply ignored official laws, disregarding, among other things, official demands to formalize licensing for exploration and exploitation purposes, commercial registration, tax payments and locational work restrictions. Initially, state officials opted not to intervene at all. Eventually, however, several missions were staged to expel miners. The cohort of the *gendarmerie* initially deployed at the site were corrupted and granted entitlement to engage in additional mining, although once these forces were withdrawn, many miners simply returned to productive gold regions. A series of negotiations have since been made, which aim to organize gold miners into cooperatives and oversee the selling of mined gold to the state.

Towards the end of 2001, effort was again made by the state to remove miners outright because many did not accept the conditions set out for them, in particular, the requirement to sell gold to state agents (offering lower prices than informal traders) and to satisfy the demands of the medium-sized Anglo-American enterprise ORACLE,[18] the executives of which signed a contract granting the company exclusive mining rights to a large territory encompassing artisanal regions. Gold mining has since been confined to certain alluvial deposits, as many reef miners and foreigners were expelled from the country's gold-mining region.

The miners were officially organized for a short period (1999–2000) into a federal council that has since changed its function, members and attitudes completely. Its members today merely conduct administrative work, and are not being accepted by miners. In northern Benin, the state has no local trading board but works with ORACLE, which employs gold-buying agents. The illegal gold trade has declined but still exists in places where clandestine gold traders offer high prices.

Markets and sociocultural change

As already explained, major social and economic changes have occurred in mining regions, including a rapid establishment of new markets, an influx of shop-owners and service providers, an increased circulation of money, and the spontaneous development of infrastructure and services. A number of informal traders, barkeepers and prostitutes are also found in small-scale mining regions. In a short period of time, both the small villages of Kwatena and Tchantangou became large settlements; new settler communities have also been established in surrounding areas.

Worldwide, young artisanal miners have a habit of spending large portions of their earnings on alcohol, ostentatious gambling, clothes, video-cinemas, women and entertainment.[19] In Benin, there is clearly a mutual obligation to entertain one another. As is the case in many grassroots settings worldwide,[20] miners typically develop a particular lifestyle and strong self-awareness (Grätz, 2003b). Miners in Benin were observed to engage in excessive drinking, smoking, food consumption, dressing and partying, together with visits to bars and video-cinemas. Some of the young miners spend their money as fast as they earn it. Without ignoring the disastrous effects of such practices, this could be also interpreted as part of the normal moral and cultural standards of the mining community.[21]

The present situation

It is difficult to provide a concise summary of the present state of ASM in northern Benin because of its constantly shifting character. This is primarily due to the rate at which new deposits are being discovered, and the rate at which local miners are re-engaging in exploitation works both in mountain lodes and alluvial settings. Where deposits are rapidly exhausted or cease to be exploitable by simple artisanal means, miners are obliged to engage in other economic activities or to leave regions altogether. Finally, the functionality of the industry is very much dependent upon the amount of state intervention – namely, authorities' tolerance of informal activities and their stance toward protecting the rights of private-sector investors.

ASM will certainly continue, although perhaps to a lesser extent, to be carried out by a regional labour force. Moreover, it is likely that alluvial mining will continue to be a side business for many local inhabitants, particularly during the dry season. However, much depends upon the position taken by ORACLE, which currently has alluvial operations in Kwatena. With the assistance of state agents, on-site staff work to retain artisanal miners on most of their concessions. As pressures from local inhabitants grew, the enterprise was obliged to cede a lease on parts of the Perma River to several formalized mining groups, which are comprised of both local people and immigrants, and use basic equipment (motor pumps and iron washing boxes). This organization notwithstanding, the politics of gold pricing continues to be the chief issue of debate for artisanal miners – informal and formal. Specifically, the price offered by the enterprise is usually less than that provided on the informal gold market, and miners' demands for a better share are consistently ignored.

The authorities actively supported the agreements forged between the state, ORACLE and organized miners in July 2001. It executed a number of supervisory missions as well as engaged in the repeated expulsion of informal miners and illegal gold traders. However, at the same time, state authorities as well as local inhabitants are largely disappointed by the fact that the enterprise has created very few jobs, constantly demands ample state protection and refuses to accept improved arrangements with artisanal miners. The representatives of the enterprise are frustrated because of the yields, which have been lower than expected (and promised by the mining ministry) and the high informal costs (port authorities, etc) they face, especially in cases where they are forced to deploy imported technical equipment. Taking into account some of Benin's macroeconomic elements, as well as unstable gold prices and the political situation in West Africa overall, it is difficult to predict whether or not the company will renew its contracts and expand operations into new areas such as the mountain lodes, or simply retreat to other countries.

Government authorities seem to be in favour of foreign or national investors who are capable of managing artisanal miners. Previous attempts to directly promote artisanal groups have been abandoned because of negligence on the part of miners to organize themselves into recognized cooperatives, pay taxes and sell gold to licensed traders. Presently, tensions seem to be rife between all parties, which makes the future of ASM in Benin very unpredictable.

Part III

Country case studies: Anglophone West Africa

CHAPTER 13
Introduction

Gavin M. Hilson

In 1991, civil war erupted in Sierra Leone. Years of local and regional backlash culminated in a violent, 11-year struggle for control of the country's diamond mines, which would claim the lives of more than 50,000 people. In March 1991, the Revolutionary United Front (RUF), under the leadership of Foday Sankoh, launched its first campaign in Sierra Leone. With the backing of the Liberian warlord and eventual president, Charles Taylor, the RUF initially targeted the rich alluvial diamond fields of Kono District and Tongo Field. Throughout the war, Taylor served as a 'mentor, trainer, banker and weapons supplier for the...collection of dissidents, bandits and mercenaries who called themselves the Revolutionary United Front'[1] (Gberie, 2002: 2). Taylor's motive behind sponsoring the RUF was to destabilize Sierra Leone, which, at the time, served as a rear base for the West African peacekeeping force working to prevent him from seizing Monrovia, Liberia's capital. He armed RUF rebels in exchange for Sierra Leone's diamond riches.

At the convening meeting of the Diamond Development Initiative (DDI),[2] the aim of which was to 'to launch the DDI into concrete action around the political, social and economic challenges facing the artisanal diamond mining sector in Africa', a presenter commented on how at a recent conference in Sierra Leone, a member of the audience stood, with tears in his eyes and said: 'we [Sierra Leoneans] are cursed by diamonds.' Indeed, before the outbreak of war, corruption and mismanagement in the diamond sector was one of the main reasons why, according to the UN, Sierra Leone was the poorest country in the world. The six military coups that followed independence in 1961 had caused state structures to deteriorate. This, in combination with the civil war that had broken out in neighbouring Liberia in 1991, opened corridors for arms, drugs and ammunitions trafficking, and facilitated violent regional crime. A lengthy campaign concerning 'blood diamonds', however, has been instrumental in informing the wider global community about the atrocities of Sierra Leone's diamond-driven civil war; precipitated the rise of a series of voluntary agreements – particularly the Kimberley Process – which today collectively aim to eliminate global exports of diamonds originating from conflict zones; and sparked numerous other campaigns to pressure donor agencies and Western governments to provide support to Sierra Leone and other African countries where diamonds are fuelling civil violence.

Sierra Leonean authorities now face the onerous challenge of regularizing diamond-mining regions, which continue to be rife with illegal activities being carried out by thousands of impoverished citizens. As civil war is now less of a concern and Charles Taylor, who is currently on trial for his war crimes, is supposedly no longer interfering in local politics, naturally, the dynamics of Sierra Leone's diamond-mining sector have changed. The complications which plague the sector today can be broadly placed into the general categories of problems now recognized by experts to be intimately associated with ASM worldwide. These include poverty, technological impotency, child labour and corruption. Recognizing that these problems are perhaps more severe in Sierra Leone than in most sub-Saharan African countries, participants of the DDI conference in Accra were quick to underscore the importance of rapidly improving understanding of conditions on the ground, and using this knowledge to inform policy. Notably, during one breakout session, Ian Smillie of Partnership Africa Canada stressed the importance of targeting corrupt buyers, whom he described as being a 'huge destabilizing force', and promoting economic diversification, combating poverty and improving health. There was consensus among the session's participants that acute shortages of data in the sector have impeded work aimed at achieving improvements in these areas. It was against this background that another participant pointed out that there 'needs to be systematic assessment at the community level'. This, the participant explained, could be achieved by undertaking comprehensive *ex ante* Poverty Social Impact Assessments (PSIAs), which, by 'putting people at the centre', facilitate the compilation of information on community dynamics 'that would feed into policy'.

In the first two chapters of this section, Chapters 14 and 15, Victor Davies and Estelle Levin make significant progress towards this end, examining a number of important community issues in the diamond-mining sector of postwar Sierra Leone. Such information is needed in what will undoubtedly be a costly, lengthy and laborious reconstruction effort in the country; most significantly, such baseline data are needed to identify appropriate avenues for donor funds, and bring the many recommendations of the DDI to fruition. Victor Davies brings the reader up to speed with the important issues surrounding blood diamonds in Sierra Leone. In addition to describing how diamonds have fuelled civil violence in the country, he examines the characteristics of indigenous artisanal diamond mining today and its link to poverty. Estelle Levin's work reported in Chapter 15 provides a more detailed account of the dynamics of artisanal diamond mining in Sierra Leone. Drawing upon research conducted in 2004, the author provides a descriptive analysis of the political economy of contemporary artisanal diamond production in Kono, one of the country's chief diamond-mining districts.

The following four chapters focus upon artisanal mining in Ghana, the location of the largest and most ambitious SAP implemented in sub-Saharan Africa to date. The restructuring of the mining sector has featured prominently in this; state-owned mineral assets have been privatized and small-scale gold mining has been legalized. With considerable World Bank and UN funds having been devoted to strengthening regulatory capacity in the mining sector and formalizing ASM, Ghana has become an important location for industry research and support in recent years: mercury contamination projects and associated pollution studies, credit schemes, livelihoods research and reclamation efforts. What has been ignored amid the manic rush to implement ASM projects in the country, however, is the importance of studying target communities. In fact, the ASM regularization experience in Ghana offers valuable lessons on how *not* to implement industry support schemes; credit programmes for operators, technological support efforts and attempts to license miners have all been minimally effective in practice because of a failure to study ASM populations beforehand. The four chapters on Ghana help bridge this gap, reporting important information on indigenous ASM communities that could go a long way towards strengthening industry policy and support initiatives. The first two chapters focus on artisanal diamond mining in the country, which is confined to Akwatia and adjacent localities. Kaakpema Yelpaala and Saleem Ali in Chapter 16 examine the important health issues in Ghana's diamond-mining sector, underscoring the importance of tackling the diseases (malaria, HIV/AIDS, etc) now rampant in Akwatia. In Chapter 17, Frank K. Nyame and S.K.A. Danso look at in detail the social dynamics of Akwatia, the challenges of regularizing indigenous artisanal diamond miners and the relations these operators have forged with the resident large-scale diamond operator, Ghana Consolidated Diamonds (GCD).

Chapters 18 and 19, on Ghana, focus on relations between artisanal (and generally illegal) operators and large-scale miners. Chapter 18, by Anthony Aubynn, provides insight on the approach taken by managers at Abosso Goldfields (AGL) towards resident illegal miners at its Damang site. The case of Abosso is particularly interesting because the company's leaders deliberately developed a plan of coexistence with ASM: most large-scale miners operating in Ghana are confrontational when it comes to controlling illegal mining. Chapter 19, by Gavin M. Hilson and Natalia Yakovleva, provides an illustration of this, examining the dynamics of the conflict between Bogoso Goldfields (BGL) and indigenous illegal operators in Prestea. In addition to analyzing the ramifications of the company's hostile attitude towards illegal mining, the authors propose workable solutions for resolving the impasse.

Chapter 20, by Miriam Lawal, provides an overview of ASM in Nigeria. The author's analysis of tourmaline mining in the village of Akutayi and granite mining in Malali and Mpape is timely, given the recent US$120 million World Bank loan awarded to the Nigerian government for institutional strengthening and developing the country's solid minerals sector.

CHAPTER 14
Diamonds, poverty and war in Sierra Leone

Victor A. B. Davies

This chapter examines the interactions between diamonds and artisanal mining on the one hand, and poverty and civil conflict in Sierra Leone on the other. The effects of artisanal diamond mining comprise only part of the wider socioeconomic consequences of diamonds, which have strongly dictated Sierra Leone's destiny over the past 50 years. Official production peaked in the late 1960s and early 1970s, accounting for 60 per cent of foreign-exchange earnings and 20 per cent of GDP and averaging US$250 million annually in 1995 dollars. However, despite its rich deposits of diamonds and other mineral resources, Sierra Leone remains one of the poorest countries in the world, with over 80 per cent of the population living below the poverty line in 1990.

The 1991–2001 civil war worsened matters; indeed, diamonds have not always brought good news. It appears that labour movement to diamond-mining areas has been particularly detrimental to agriculture. Moreover, the collapse of the formal diamond sector in the 1970s helped to criminalize and informalize economic activity more generally, leading to loss of government control over the economy, declining fiscal revenues and, ultimately, state collapse. 'Blood diamonds' came to play a major role in the ensuing civil war, financing the rebellion and inducing the participation of pro-government troops to prolong it. Diamonds continue to pose a security threat in the post-conflict period, with many former combatants returning to diamond-mining areas. Concerns about the socioeconomic consequences of diamond mining remain widespread.

Analytical framework

The analytical framework presented in this section of the chapter articulates possible links between diamonds, poverty and civil conflict. As indicated in Figure 14.1, diamonds can influence poverty directly and also indirectly through the civil conflict and non-conflict nexus. The latter, in turn, can be economy-wide: macroeconomy or governance; or sectoral, agriculture and manufacturing.

In terms of a direct link, artisanal diamond-mining provides income for a significant proportion of the labour force in a number of countries. But diamond mining can impact negatively on income by inducing risk behaviour that could result in lower average incomes for the diggers and the economy as a whole.

Oomes and Vocke (2003) suggest that returns for alluvial diamond miners in Africa are often lower than in other sectors of the economy. Natural resources can also affect health and education. Goreux (2001) points out that living in an insecure environment where illicit drugs and sex workers are available, young male diamond miners are particularly exposed to the risk of sexually transmitted diseases (STDs), especially HIV/AIDS. Gylfason (2001) shows that three different measures of education, reflecting education inputs, outcomes and participation, are all inversely related to natural resource abundance. Poor natural resource endowment places a premium upon the efficient use of scarce resources, which promotes market discipline, investment, and human/social capital (Auty, 2001).

In terms of the non-conflict economy-wide nexus, at the macroeconomic level, diamonds could provide substantial fiscal revenues and foreign exchange for poverty reduction. Natural resources, however, influence the choice of

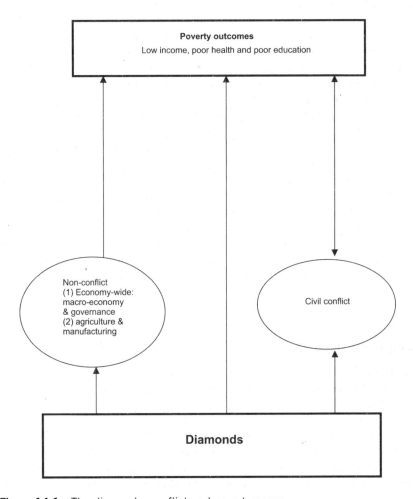

Figure 14.1 The diamonds, conflict and poverty nexus

political leadership, much to the detriment of the population: they inhibit good governance, providing rulers with an alternative source of revenues, thereby reducing the incentive to pursue the implementation of sound economic policies and efficient institutions needed to generate large fiscal revenues. Indeed, resource-rich countries can subsist from their natural resource wealth over extended periods, even with poor economic policies in place (Gylfason, 2001). Since natural resource rents are concentrated and easily appropriable (especially with diamonds), government officials in such countries are tempted into socially damaging rent-seeking rather than pro-growth activities (Sachs and Warner, 2001). Rent-seeking, in turn, breeds corruption in business and government, thereby distorting resource allocation and reducing both economic efficiency and social equity (Gylfason, 2001). Thus, it is argued, rather than a developmental state, a predatory state is very likely to emerge, such as Mobuto's Zaire.

Diamond digging provides an alternative occupation with potentially major implications for food production, manufactured output and prices. Natural resources could crowd out entrepreneurial activity or innovation if wages in the natural resource sector increase high enough to encourage potential innovators and entrepreneurs to work in the resource sector (Sachs and Warner, 2001). Torvik (2002) suggests that a greater amount of natural resources increases the number of entrepreneurs engaged in rent-seeking and reduces the number of running productive firms. By extension, natural resources could attract investment from other sectors with productivity spillover, such as agriculture and manufacturing.

Some authors argue that resource-abundant countries tend to be high-price economies and, perhaps as a consequence, miss out on export-led growth. Auty (2001) also argues that fewer opportunities for primary production induce diversification into competitive manufacturing. Diamonds and natural resources more generally could trigger the onset of Dutch disease, the harmful effects of a natural resource boom on other sectors of the economy, notably agriculture and manufacturing. This can occur when the natural resource boom increases the demand for resources used in agriculture or manufacturing, diverting resources from these sectors. Moreover, a natural resource boom can raise the general price levels, leading to real exchange-rate appreciation, thereby reducing other exports such as agricultural produce (Corden, 1984). The consequences of a natural resource boom are also often negative, as the boom may trigger or exacerbate the above problems. In addition, Tornell and Lane (1999) present a theoretical model of a voracity effect: positive terms of trade shock generate a more than proportionate increase in fiscal redistribution and reduce growth.

In terms of the civil-conflict nexus, Collier and Hoeffler (2004) argue that natural resource abundance increases the risk of civil war by providing a source of finance for rebellion. Natural resource abundance could by itself provide a greed motive for rebellion or merely finance a civil war driven by non-economic factors. The authors also show that poor growth increases the risk of civil conflict. It may be argued that this provides another conduit through which natural resources can increase the risk of civil war by lowering growth. Collier et al. (2003) also argue that communities living in resource-rich regions are more likely to support a secessionist attempt so as to keep the wealth for themselves; secessionist attempts or distributional fights over natural resources are more likely to occur if natural resource management in particular or economic management as a whole is not transparent.

From the above analysis, it is hardly surprising that pessimism about natural resources is a recurring theme in the development literature. It is expressed in the natural resource curse thesis articulated by Gelb (1988), Auty (1993), Lewis (1984, 1989) and others, which suggests that rather than promoting development, natural resource wealth poses a host of developmental problems. Some studies provide empirical (econometric) evidence showing that economies with abundant natural resources have tended to grow less rapidly than economies scarce in natural resources (Sachs and Warner, 1995; Sala-i-Martin, 1997).

Diamonds and poverty

This section examines the links between diamonds and poverty in Sierra Leone through channels other than civil conflict. It begins by providing an overview of the history and nature of artisanal diamond mining.

History and nature of artisanal diamond mining in Sierra Leone

Diamonds were first discovered in Sierra Leone in 1930 in the eastern Kono district. The Sierra Leone Selection Trust (SLST) began the commercial exploitation of diamonds in the mid-1930s, establishing a mining and exploitation monopoly. In 1960, Sierra Leone accounted for one-third of the world diamond output, a share which has since declined to some 2 per cent of the value of global diamond exports (Smillie et al., 2000: 18).

Intensive artisanal mining dates back to the early 1950s, when crop failure enticed a number of farmers to turn to illicit mining in SLST's concession areas. This marked the beginning of the country's diamond rush: between 1952 and 1956, the number of illicit miners increased from 5,000 to an estimated 50,000–75,000 (Van der Laan, 1965). To restore law and order and capture revenues, the colonial administration introduced the Alluvial Diamond Mining Scheme in 1956. Under this scheme, the size of SLST concession areas was reduced to accommodate artisanal mining activities; the move effectively brought the SLST monopoly to an end.

The Alluvial Diamond Mining Scheme did not, however, put an end to the illicit encroachment of artisanal miners in SLST concession areas. By the late 1960s, SLST had stopped prospecting altogether because information on the discovery of new diamond fields was leaking to illegal, unregistered operators. In 1971, the government acquired a 51 per cent interest in SLST, and renamed it the National Diamond Mining Company (NDMC). Over time, political interference and illicit mining stymied NDMC, leading to its liquidation in the early 1990s.

Illegal diamond mining continues to be widespread throughout Sierra Leone for two reasons. First, deposits are dispersed over 19,943 km^2 (about a quarter of the country's total area), although only 1 per cent of this is diamond-bearing soil. Secondly, alluvial diamond deposits (originating from kimberlite pipes) can be mined using simple implements such as picks and shovels. The deposits occur along the paths and banks of ancient and contemporary watercourses, having been transported vast distances and widely dispersed over time. The artisanal mining activities deployed to extract these deposits are undertaken by gangs of 30–50 diggers. Holes as deep as 10 metres are dug into the earth, and soil is collected in large piles, which are subsequently washed and sieved for diamonds. The dry season – November to April/May – is the traditional mining season in Sierra Leone, although activities may take place during the rainy season (May/June to October) with the application of appropriate equipment such as water pumps. Recently, kimberlite deposits were discovered in Kono District (see Chapter 15); these require the use of sophisticated mining equipment for extraction. A major concession for these deposits was awarded to Branch Energy, a subsidiary of Toronto-based DiamondWorks. Branch Energy began production in November 2003.

Sierra Leone's official diamond exports peaked during the late 1960s and early 1970s. Production averaged US$250 million (1995 dollars), accounted for 20 per cent of GDP and contributed 60 per cent of foreign exchange earnings (Table 14.1). By the mid-1970s, however, production had sharply declined. Fiscal revenues from diamonds, derived mainly from the corporate sector, amounted to only 3.6 per cent of GDP in 1974. As indicated in Table 14.1, by 1990, just before the war, official exports plummeted to US$15 million (1995 dollars); fiscal revenues accounted for less than 0.2 per cent of GDP. Underlying such poor performance was the collapse of the corporate sector.

Since the collapse of the corporate sector, a liberal access policy has been upheld: in principle, there are no restrictions on the number of sector participants. Mining can be undertaken both by individuals and companies. Before a mining licence is issued, the prospective miner or mining company must first be demarcated a plot of land by the paramount chief, the traditional leader of the community which communally owns the land. A separate mining licence is required for every acre of land allotted, valid for a year. Up to 50 diggers can be employed under a given licence.

Diggers are at the bottom of Sierra Leone's rather complex diamond production and marketing hierarchy. They are financed by artisanal miners known locally as supporters under a tributor (a term for the holder or occupier of a mining location) system that does not involve wage payment. The supporter provides food and other basic necessities for the diggers in the form of a loan, mining equipment-sieves, picks and shovels. The diggers must sell any diamond

Table 14.1 Diamond exports in Sierra Leone, 1960–2004

Year	Total official output ('000 carats)	Smuggled diamonds ('000 carats)	Official exports (US$ million)	Smuggled diamonds (US$ million)	Real official export revenues (constant 1995 US$)	Official diamond exports (% of total exports)
1960–4*	1,613					
1965–9*	1,566		54		241	60
1970–4*	1,793		72		252	61
1975–9*	1,083		71		196	64
1980	666		66		122	30
1981	446		52		87	34
1982	314		52		83	47
1983	402		40		61	34
1984	190		30		43	22
1985	261		28		39	21
1986	354		28		39	19
1987	353		13		18	10
1988	24		9		11	8
1989	127		22		28	16
1990	90	241	13		15	9
1991	250	284	32		36	22
1992	313	518	31		34	21
1993	156	188	20		21	17
1994	221	305	30		31	26
1995	214	241	22		22	52
1996	270	296	28	58	27	60
1997	104	699	8	71	7	44
1998	9	761	2	58	2	27
1999	9		1.5	69	1	24
2000	77		10		9	77
2001	223		26		22	90
2002	352		42		36	86
2003	500		75			81

*Yearly average.
Sources: Total official exports: 'Sierra Leone: Recent Economic Trends', IMF, 1972 and other years; World Bank, 1994; Smillie, Gberie and Hazleton, 2000. Official diamond export value: World Bank, 1994, 2002a, 2002b; IMF *Balance of Payments Yearbook* various issues.

finds to their supporter, who determines the price and deducts all expenditures. The artisanal miner, in turn, usually has a supporter, a diamond dealer, who can legally buy but not export diamonds. Some diamond dealers are financed by other dealers, who have buying agents. Moyers (2003) identifies unlicensed brokers, '[a] rag-tag-appearing group...who work with smugglers or dealers to sell the winnings', as a recent addition to the chain. Dealers sell the diamonds to exporters. Officially, two or more persons are allowed to share an export licence.

Certain policy measures favourable to Sierra Leoneans have been adopted. For example, artisanal mining licences can only be obtained by Sierra Leoneans. Moreover, until only recently, the export licence fee was US$5,000 for Sierra Leoneans and US$30,000 for foreigners, although widespread corruption has vitiated these measures. Many foreigners have obtained Sierra Leonean citizenship through bribery, circumventing the export licence fee differential. Consequently, a uniform licence fee of US$30,000 is now charged. Furthermore, many Sierra Leoneans lack the capital to finance diamond-mining operations, and therefore serve as surrogates for foreigners.

The Lebanese are the biggest diamond exporters and dealers. Moyers (2003) reports that in 1993, out of a total of 100 licensed dealers in Kono District, 92 were of Lebanese origin. The remaining eight were 'gravely undercapitalized' indigenous Sierra Leoneans. The Lebanese have a strong first-mover advantage, having dominated Sierra Leone's business sector and established a strong presence in the diamond sector even before independence in 1961. The colonial authorities favoured the Lebanese over the Creoles, descendants of freed slaves who resettled in Sierra Leone from 1776 to the early 19th century, whom the Lebanese eventually displaced in the business sector. Strong social capital (a high degree of trust and cohesiveness), finance and external contacts are the principal assets of the Lebanese. Moreover, politicians appear to be more comfortable with tolerating Lebanese affluence and business dominance: because of their foreign origin, they are not seen as a political threat.

There are reports of Lebanese competition-inhibiting behaviour. In the 1980s, the Israelis, led by Nir Gouaz, began making inroads into the diamond industry, offering higher prices to local miners. Gouaz was expelled on allegations of fake currency charges, apparently instigated by Lebanese rivals (Gberie, 2002). It is common knowledge that once a Lebanese dealer offers a price for a diamond, the seller is unlikely to receive the same or higher price from any other dealer. Generally, if the seller does not agree on a quoted price, the Lebanese dealer passes information along to colleagues about the diamond, after which all other Lebanese dealers offer lower prices. When the seller eventually brings the diamond back to the original Lebanese dealer, the latter will almost certainly offer a reduced price, knowing that the seller is unable to sell the diamond elsewhere.

The non-conflict link

Economy-wide effects: the macro-economy

Before 1980, diamonds made substantial contributions to tax revenues and foreign exchange earnings in Sierra Leone. Total taxes – income tax, surtax and diamond industry profits tax – paid by the NDMC (the nationalized SLST) amounted to 70 per cent of net profits; the government received an additional 51 per cent of the balance in dividends. As Table 14.1 indicates, between 1965 and 1979, diamonds accounted for at least 60 per cent of Sierra Leone's official exports.

But diamonds have helped to promote black market activity that has undermined government control of the economy. In the 1980s, exchange/ price controls and exchange-rate overvaluation engendered a lucrative underground trade involving the smuggling of diamonds to purchase scarce essential imports, the sale of which on the black market financed purchases of diamonds for further smuggling. At times, the black market premium exceeded 300 per cent. Consequently, the tax base depleted, with total tax revenues as a proportion of GDP falling from 17 per cent in 1971–9 to 7 per cent in 1983–90. Burgeoning black markets and a collapsing tax base eroded government control of the economy. The state gradually collapsed, precipitating civil war in 1991.

Economy-wide effects: governance

Diamonds have also played a key role in Sierra Leonean politics, influencing politicians, voters and election outcomes, and undermining the state. Diamonds aided the opposition All People's Congress (APC) victory in the 1967 general elections. Siaka Stevens, the APC leader, promised greater scope for artisanal mining. Diamonds, he argued, represented 'the little man's only hope for wealth' (Smillie et al., 2000: 41).

Illicit mining exploded when the APC came into office in 1968. Furthermore, Stevens allegedly deliberately sabotaged the corporate SLST. Notably, in November 1969, the SLST monthly diamond haul was stolen at gunpoint at an airport in Freetown, the national capital. It was widely believed that Jamil Sahid Mohamed, a mixed-race African-Lebanese, who happened to be Stevens's *protégé*, was behind the diamond theft with Stevens' backing (Smillie et al., 2000). Mohamed's rival was deported for the theft. Further down the line in 1993, the head of state under the military National Provisional Ruling Council (NPRC), 1992–6, mysteriously disappeared from Sierra Leone for some two weeks. A journalist was arrested after reprinting a report from a foreign newspaper that the disappearance was in connection with the sale of diamonds in Belgium. Today, many politicians continue to be involved in the diamond trade. In 2001, a government minister was caught smuggling diamonds. He angrily explained that a more senior figure in the government was also involved in diamond mining.

Sierra Leone's diamonds have also attracted organized crime. As already noted, an Israeli foray into the sector began in the mid-1980s. Mostly linked to international criminal groups, Israeli operators also used Sierra Leone to bust sanctions against South Africa, passing off South African diamonds as Sierra Leone diamonds, and trafficking arms to South Africa through Sierra Leone (Reno, 1998). The economic decline of the 1980s facilitated the emergence of these criminal networks. Rejected by conventional donors, President Momoh accepted offers of financial aid from some of these private operators in exchange for diamond-mining concessions.

The debt bondage, lottery and resource-depletion effects

The tributor system for artisanal mining produces two labour-pauperizing effects, which a report by the United States Agency for International Development (USAID 2001: 5) vividly captures:

> Alluvial diamonds are found by diggers, who manually, or with rudimentary equipment, sift through soil and sand, digging up holes up to 30 feet in depth, in areas where they think it is most likely to find stones…Most diggers are the poorest of the poor, doing body breaking work with no certainty of finding any stones, but with the illusion of uncovering a large stone that will provide wealth for life; not a common result for diggers…Because of a requirement to pay a land use fee, the diggers are generally financed by 'dealers'. Dealers are business people who manage groups of diggers by advancing them food, tools and basic household goods, which they deduct from the proceeds of sales of the stones the diggers turn over to them. Over time, poverty has conspired with ignorance to create a system of virtual servitude. A new observer to the scene can hardly imagine how such exploitation can still exist in the 21st century.

The first labour-pauperizing effect is the debt bondage effect or the virtual servitude mentioned in the above quote: diggers must sell any diamond finds to their supporter, who determines the value and deducts all expenditures. Unsurprisingly, supporters usually undervalue diamonds and inflate expenditures. Thus, supporters tend to declare low profits when it comes to sharing diamond winnings. This induces diggers to sell their winnings secretly to others at a discount, fuelling smuggling. Diggers are constrained by the lack of finance, external marketing contacts and technical knowledge. Moyers (2003: 6) makes the following assessment of the tributor system: 'this appears to represent a system of debt bondage, which is monitored worldwide by the UN Commission on Human Rights and is classified by that organization as a contemporary form of slavery'.

The second is a lottery effect. Impoverished diggers take the risk of a smaller income in diamond digging relative to agriculture with the hope of securing a life-changing diamond find. The World Bank (2002a) places lower and upper bounds for returns per head on diamond digging for 2001 at US$130–380 (1995 dollars). Annual agriculture value-added per worker in constant 1995 dollars exceeded US$700 throughout 1982–90 and US$360 throughout 1991–2001 (World Development Indicators, 2003).

The resource-depletion effect exacerbates the above two effects: more and more diggers are finding fewer and fewer diamonds. In the early 1960s, fewer than 30,000 diggers (less than 3% of the labour force) produced an official output of over 1.1 million carats of diamonds a year. If smuggled output is added, the figure would be much higher (data are not available). Before the war, over 100,000 diggers (more than 7% of the labour force) produced less than 400,000 carats (official plus smuggled). The number of diamond diggers was estimated to be more than 100,000 in 2004 (Sierra Leone Government, 2004). A vicious circle, therefore, appears to be at work: resource depletion and state failure increase the general level of poverty. The poorer the peasants who supply diamond-digging labour become, the more they resort to diamond digging in order to escape poverty. They become even poorer, however, through the debt bondage, lottery and resource-depletion effects.

Agriculture

In Sierra Leone, migration and increased participation in diamond mining have adversely affected agriculture, which, during the prewar years, engaged 70–80 per cent of the labour force and accounted for 35–45 per cent of GDP. The diamond rush witnessed large-scale migration from rice farms to diamond-mining areas, causing a marked decline in rice production. Between 1953 and 1957, the number of illicit diggers grew from 5,000 to 70,000; by the end of the 1950s, Sierra Leone, once a net marginal exporter of rice, had become a large net importer. Rice imports accounted for over 60 per cent of the value of total imports during the period 1955–9. A high dependence on rice imports has persisted over the years.

There was also a marked decline in other agricultural exports during the diamond rush period. Export of palm kernels, which diamonds replaced as the leading export produce during the 1950s, fell from over 75,000 tonnes a year in 1951 and 1952 to less than 60,000 tonnes annually during 1955–60. The volume of total agricultural exports decreased from about 90,000 tonnes a year during the period 1950–2 to an average of less than 70,000 tonnes a year in 1955–60. The corresponding fall in the value of agricultural exports largely offset the rise in diamond exports during the diamond rush. Thus, the trade balance moved from a surplus of £1.9 million in 1951 to a deficit of about £10 million a year during 1956–7, the peak of the diamond rush. After adjusting for diamond smuggling, the trade balance was in surplus for 1956 but incurred a deficit of £400,000 in 1957.

The rate of extraction of diamonds has an upper limit, which can be calculated using a certain number of diggers, say X. From society's standpoint, any diamond-digging labour beyond X is excessive, with zero social marginal product (zero additional diamond output for society). However, the opportunity cost (or social cost) given by the foregone agricultural output is almost certainly positive: less than 10 per cent of arable land is actually under cultivation at any point in time. Additional agricultural labour would therefore increase total output, but potential diggers may have a private incentive to switch to diamond digging because they have roughly equal chances of finding diamonds as the existing diggers. For them, the expected return (the private benefit) is positive. Thus, beyond X, the expected private return is positive while the social return is zero and the social cost is positive.

Other problems

Other problems associated with diamond mining include child labour and environmental damage. Partnership Africa Canada and the Network Movement for Justice and Development (2004) note that hundreds, probably thousands, of children are employed at almost every stage of diamond mining in Sierra Leone. The authors cite a 2002 World Vision study, which surveyed 500 child miners in Kono District: 'some children were doing well in school but had to abandon their educational pursuits to follow their peers who transiently became rich and admirable'.

Diamond mining also has significant environmental impacts in Sierra Leone. Partnership Africa Canada and the Network Movement for Justice and Development (2004) note that 'huge pits are left exposed, streams and rivers are muddied and polluted, rocks are sometimes blasted by dynamite, and large tracts of land are cleared and left barren'. The government's mining policy does seek to address environmental problems but enforcement has been weak.

Diamonds and the civil war

The civil war began in the southeastern regions in 1991, triggered by rebels fighting for Charles Taylor in neighbouring Liberia, which borders southeastern Sierra Leone. The underlying causes were a patrimonial system of asset-stripping and the allocation of access rights to diamond resources and rents from market distortions that occurred during the rule of All People's Congress (1968–92). These factors were baneful to economic growth and undermined the government, precipitating state collapse. External instigation was catalytic: the RUF leader, Foday Sankoh, and others, were trained in Libya (Abdullah, 1998). The rebellion grew, with people in the disaffected southeastern regions initially voluntarily enlisting. The RUF had about 20,000 combatants and pro-government forces of over 25,000, in addition to ECOMOG (West African pro-government intervention force) and civil defence militias.

Diamonds helped to sustain the rebellion by financing it and producing a war-prolonging congruence of interests among protagonists (Davies, 2000). Initially, some of the weapons used by the RUF were captured or bought from the Sierra Leone army or ECOMOG. However, organized criminal groups later became instrumental in the supply of arms when Charles Taylor, the RUF's 'godfather', was elected president of Liberia. Taylor was at the epicentre of an arms-for-diamonds trade (Davies and Fofana, 2002). The Sierra Leone blood diamonds were part of a larger network of illicit diamond exports to Europe disguised as emanating from neighbouring Liberia, Guinea, the Gambia and other African countries, to evade taxation, launder money or circumvent UN sanctions on conflict diamonds.

Estimates of RUF diamond revenues vary widely at US$25–125 million a year from 1997 when the RUF controlled much of the diamond-producing regions. De Beers estimates that the value of conflict diamonds from Sierra Leone was US$70 million in 1999 (USAID, 2001). Diamonds also caused a similar congruence of interests among the belligerents who sometimes mined peaceably side by side, attacking civilians to keep them off (Davies and Fofana, 2002). Thus, the war did not significantly disrupt the mining of diamonds.

Sierra Leone's diamonds have also been linked to international terrorism. Following the 11 September 2001 terrorist attacks in the US, it was alleged that al-Qaeda bought millions of dollars of Sierra Leone diamonds to increase asset mobility and facilitate asset concealment in anticipation of tighter financial controls (Douglas, 2001).

Peace was achieved in 2001, aided by a UN embargo on arms to, and diamonds from, Liberia, forcing President Taylor to reduce his arms-for-diamonds support for the rebel movement. The initial framework for peace was the power-sharing Lomé Peace Accord signed by the government and the RUF in July 1999, under which Sankoh enjoyed the diplomatic status of vice-president and was appointed chairman of the Commission for the Management of Strategic Resources, National Reconstruction and Development, *de facto* minister of natural resources.

The disarmament and demobilization of 71,000 ex-combatants was completed in January 2002. It is believed that a significant proportion were not actual combatants but entered the programme for the benefits. Some ex-combatants from both sides were absorbed into the army, which is presently being restructured with British assistance. The government has also launched a National Reconstruction, Resettlement and Rehabilitation Programme. The government and the UN have set up a special court to try people guilty of committing war crimes since 30 November 1996, the date the abortive Abidjan Peace Accord was signed. A Truth and Reconciliation Commission was established as part of a healing process. The commission's recommendations included a call for Libya to pay war reparations to Sierra Leone for its support for the rebels.

The post-conflict era

The propensity for diamonds to fuel civil war in Sierra Leone and elsewhere in Africa has raised interest among donors and civil society. A number of groups are now working to facilitate the improved management of diamond resources to help preserve peace and promote sustainable development. The following are among initiatives that have been launched.

International efforts

A UN diamond certificate of origin scheme was launched in October 2000 to certify that diamond exports from Sierra Leone did not originate from rebel-held areas. Official diamond exports increased from US$1.5 million in 1999 (prior to the launch of the scheme) to US$10 million in October–December 2000 (during the initial months following implementation of the scheme). At the end of the war, the scheme gave way to the Kimberley Process, a voluntary pact launched by the government of South Africa in 2000. The Kimberley Process is

> a joint government, international diamond industry and civil society initiative to stem the flow of conflict diamonds – rough diamonds that are used by rebel movements to finance wars against legitimate governments...in countries such as Angola, the Democratic Republic of Congo and Sierra Leone...The Kimberley Process is composed of 45 Participants, including the European Community...The Participants account for approximately 99.8% of the global production of rough diamonds. [Kimberley Process, 2006]

Under the Kimberley Process Certification Scheme (KPCS), launched in January 2003, participants:
(a)   ensure that each export or import of rough diamonds is accompanied by a Kimberley Process Certificate;
(b)   commit to trading with other participants who have met the minimum requirements of the Certification Scheme;
(c)   designate an importing and exporting authority;
(d)   amend or enact appropriate laws or regulations to implement and enforce the certification scheme; and
(e)   collect and maintain relevant production, import and export data.

The Republic of Congo was expelled from the scheme in 2004 'for exporting diamonds at a rate 100 times greater than its estimated production', but it has since been reinstated (Kimberley Process, 2006).

In Sierra Leone, the certificate of origin is issued through the Government Gold and Diamond Office (GGDO). This is what happens (Williams et al., 2002: 63–4). First, all rough diamonds are sealed in a transparent security bag by a GGDO official; the bag includes a fully visible certificate of origin that has a unique export registration number, with details of total carat weight and total export value (in US dollars) of the rough shipment; the certificate is signed by the GGDO manager, the Minister of Mineral Resources, the governor of the Bank of Sierra Leone and the Customs and Excise authority; and the shipment data (registration number, total carat weight and total export value) are recorded in the GGDO computer system with pictures of the diamond parcels. These are transmitted electronically to the relevant importing country authorities.

The Kimberley Process is credited with facilitating a sharp rise in Sierra Leone's diamond exports, which increased from US$1.5 million in 1999, to US$75 million by 2003, and exceeded US$100 million in January–September 2004. Thus, although conceived for blood or conflict diamonds, the Kimberley Process is proving useful in Sierra Leone's post-conflict context. However, some industry observers believe that as much as half of the country's diamonds are still smuggled (Partnership Africa Canada and Network Movement for Justice and Development, 2004): requirements to pay an exporter's licence fee of US$30,000 a year, a 3 per cent export tax, and additional 'taxes' through bribes have discouraged legal operation.

Critics such as Amnesty International concede that the Kimberley Process is an important step towards dealing with the problem of conflict diamonds, but until the diamond trade is subject to mandatory, impartial monitoring, there is no guarantee that all conflict diamonds will be identified and removed from the market. Others contend that the Kimberley Process leaves the diamond industry, including retailers, free to monitor itself. In answer to the question 'How do I know I am not buying a conflict diamond?', the official Kimberley Process website offers the following telling advice:

> Always buy from a reputable retailer. Don't be afraid to ask questions like: were the stones traded under the auspices of the Kimberley Process?…Your retailer should be able to answer these questions for you. The most important tip to guard against purchasing a conflict diamond is use your intuition. Do not be afraid to shop around. If something arouses your suspicion move on to another retailer. Unless you are satisfied with the answers and service provided, do not make your purchase.

Domestic efforts

A number of domestic initiatives have been undertaken by government and civil society. First, there have been some changes made to artisanal diamond mining policy, although current market access policy is liberal and not much different from prewar policy. The government imposes a 3 per cent tax on diamond exports and to encourage official exports, the annual export tax has been reduced to 2.5 per cent for exports of US$10 million or more. The tax is administered by the GGDO and is allocated in percentage points as follows: GGDO, 0.75; mines monitoring, 0.25; government treasury, 0.75; independent valuer, 0.50; and community development, 0.75. Mines monitoring refers to the division of the Ministry of Mineral Resources responsible for monitoring the diamond-mining areas. The independent valuer refers to the services of a diamond valuer who values diamond exports independently of GGDO as part of the domestic arrangements for the Kimberly Process Certification Scheme. The 0.75 per cent points of the tax allocated to community development is paid to a Diamond Area Community Development Fund for the benefit of the diamond-producing community. The extent to which the diamond-producing community actually benefits from the tax depends very much on the personal integrity of the paramount chief, the traditional ruler. Gberie (2002) reports that in 2001, 'much of the money was mismanaged or embezzled. The funds were disbursed to Paramount Chiefs, who, displaced by the war, had little attachment to their people. Few used the money for the benefit of their chiefdoms'.

The 3 per cent export tax is unlikely to generate large fiscal revenues. Official diamond exports reached a record high of US$100 million for January–September 2004, yielding export taxes of only US$3 million or less (some exporters export US$10 million in goods and pay 2.5 per cent); of this amount, only US$750,000 was channelled to the national treasury. The revenues collected through licence fees are unlikely to exceed US$2 million, given the number of licensed miners, dealers and exporters. Thus, export taxes and licence fees in 2004 likely amounted to US$5 million, of which less than US$3 million went to the treasury. Given the informality and non-transparency of the production and marketing mechanisms for artisanal mining, and the widespread level of corruption, it is unlikely that much additional fiscal revenue is collected downstream from income taxes. The low fiscal revenues reflect a key disadvantage of liberal access to alluvial diamond deposits. Any attempt to increase export taxes would only increase the incentive to smuggle.

The Peace Diamond Alliance (PDA) was launched in December 2002. It groups local and international NGOs, diamond buyers, mining companies and government officials. Its purpose is to provide training and credit to diggers by eliminating the need for middlemen, therefore increasing returns. It runs valuation training programmes to enable its members to better understand the market and diamond valuation. According to its website, it has already established 20 mining cooperatives 'capable of mining and exporting their own production'. It continues: 'If successful, the lessons learned in the target areas of Kono District and Tongo Fields can be transferred to other diamond-iferous regions, both in Sierra Leone and other countries rich in alluvial diamonds' (Peace Diamond Alliance, 2005). The Peace Diamond Alliance is funded by USAID and managed by the Washington-based consulting firm, Management Systems International.

The Campaign for Just Mining was launched by the Network Movement for Justice and Development in January 2000. It advocates accountability, transparency and social responsibility within the mining sector (Partnership Africa Canada and Network Movement for Justice and Development, 2004). The campaign has established task forces in each of the four regions of Sierra Leone to monitor developments in the mining sector. The task force members are broad civil society organizations. The campaign was instrumental in establishing the Diamond Area Community Development Fund, and ensuring that community development committees were established and trained to manage the fund (Partnership Africa Canada and Network Movement for Justice and Development, 2004).

USAID is considering re-establishing, in collaboration with the government, a formal credit delivery mechanism for small-scale diamond miners in Kono district. The scheme was first launched in 1960 but by about 1970, it was 'corrupted to the point that operations were terminated' (Moyers, 2003). The idea behind the scheme is that if diggers have access to credit to conduct their own mining, they would be free to sell their winnings to the highest bidder, raising their income and reducing the incentive to smuggle. However, the sustainability of such a venture is doubtful. First, while contract enforcement is generally problematic in Sierra Leone, it would be much worse in the chaotic diamond sector, impeding loan recovery. Moreover, as diamond digging is a lottery, unlucky miners who genuinely intend to repay their loans would simply be unable to do so. Lastly, although interventions seeking to improve the livelihoods of marginalized diggers and other stakeholders appear well-intentioned, they could have the unintended consequence of attracting labour from agriculture with positive marginal product to diamond digging where, as discussed earlier, the marginal product of labour is close to zero.

Conclusions

Diamonds and artisanal diamond mining have played a primordial role in the socioeconomic and political life of Sierra Leone. The country's alluvial diamonds have generated substantial foreign exchange and income but at the same time have had a corrupting political influence, and artisanal diamond mining appears to have been particularly costly to agriculture; worse still, the diamonds sustained the country's 1991–2001 civil war. Sound management of diamond resources is therefore crucial for peace and economic development in the post-conflict era. The Kimberley Process, a key international initiative, has helped to increase Sierra Leone's official diamond exports. It could be improved by subjecting it to mandatory impartial monitoring. Domestic interventions targeting diggers and other marginalized stakeholders appear well intentioned. They could indeed reduce poverty for some of the target beneficiaries. However, large divergences between private and social benefits, and private and social costs, could produce undesirable and unintended consequences in certain cases, namely, reduced agricultural output as labour is diverted from agriculture to diamond mining. This drawback reflects the complexity of the diamonds problem facing Sierra Leone today. It also highlights the need for a more comprehensive approach that places diamonds in the wider context of the country's overall development process.

CHAPTER 15

Reflections on the political economy of artisanal diamond mining in Kono District, Sierra Leone

Estelle Levin

Between 1991 and 2002, the diamonds of Sierra Leone were implicated in a particularly brutal war, which involved the commitment of horrific acts against civilians by all factions (Human Rights Watch, 1998). By trading diamonds, the various factions were able to acquire the arms and resources necessary to perpetuate the conflict. Public attention to the diamond-fuelled wars in Sierra Leone, Angola and the Democratic Republic of Congo led to the implementation of the Kimberley Process Certification Scheme (KPCS), an international effort aimed at minimizing trade in conflict or blood diamonds.[1] Today, the KPCS involves 45 countries, which comprise 99.8 per cent of the world's US$7 billion annual global diamond trade (Kimberley Process, 2006; Smillie et al., 2000). Since the conflicts in Angola and Sierra Leone have subsided, the Kimberley Process has given rise to the DDI, which, based on the success of the KPCS in Sierra Leone and Democratic Republic of Congo, aims to go a step further to make diamonds work for development as well as peace (DDI, 2005). The DDI requires adjustments in the practices by which diamonds are produced, traded and exported. An understanding of the structures, relations, procedures and priorities of those who engage in production and marketing is vital if the DDI is to make progress, as it will assist formalization and certification through the formulation of appropriate policy and regulatory frameworks and monitoring systems. This chapter contributes to this understanding, specifically in relation to the political economy of artisanal diamond mining in Koidu, Kono District, Sierra Leone.

Although there is kimberlite mining in Sierra Leone, eluvial and alluvial[2] deposits provide the greatest hope of the big find shared by the country's 200,000 artisanal miners (Pratt, 2003). Alluvial diamonds are found in swamps and the gravels of river channels, flood-plains and terraces (Hall, 1968). The distribution of diamonds is concentrated in the south and east of the country, covering an area of about 20,000 km². In this area, only 207 km² (~1 per cent) of the ground is diamondiferous. The most important alluvial fields are those of Kono, Tongo and the Sewa Valley, which are serviced by the towns of Koidu, Kenema and Bo, respectively (Hall, 1968).

The research reported in this chapter was conducted at the beginning of the rainy season (June–August) of 2004 in the northern, western and central chiefdoms in Kono District (Figure 15.1). The research was funded by USAID and the Social Science and Humanities Research Council (SSHRC) of Canada, and conducted in partnership with Helen Temple, a development consultant.[3] Assistance with data collection was provided by Ansumana Babar Turay, who acted as chief research assistant and interpreter, as well as Andrew Abdulai, Michael Conteh, Mahmoud Fieka and Ibrahim Sebba. The purpose of the research was to evaluate USAID's Diamond Sector Reform Programme, which, in November 2004, was renamed the Integrated Diamond Management and Policy Programme, based on a livelihood analysis of artisanal diamond mining in Kono District and an assessment of the causal links between the political economy of diamond production, marketing and war. The research encompassed 62 interviews with diggers, miners and divers; 25 interviews with government officials, local NGOs, social issues experts, industry experts, businessmen, dealers, exporters and family members of diggers; two focus groups (one with a mining and agricultural cooperative, and another with members of the PDA); and three workshops (with miners and mining families). This chapter draws upon the analysis of these interviews, focus groups and workshops throughout.

The chapter provides a descriptive analysis of the political economy of contemporary artisanal diamond production in Kono. Specifically, it examines those actors who perform standard roles in production and the procedures, routines and relations that structure their activities and relationships. It describes how diamonds are mined and considers who is involved, how the various actors manage the risks and opportunities which frame their business decisions and what terms of exchange frame the passage of a diamond from one pair of hands to another. A short, historical contextualization of the alluvial diamond industry in Sierra Leone helps to frame contemporary practices.

An overview of diamond mining in Kono

In 1930, the first diamond to be identified as such in Sierra Leone was discovered in the Gbobora Stream near the village of Fotingaia, when the country was still under British colonial rule (Hall, 1968). The Consolidated African Selection Trust (CAST), a subsidiary of De Beers, began prospecting the area in March 1931. Mining commenced in 1932 and Kono – especially the Koidu locality – was recognized to contain rich deposits of alluvial diamonds (Hall, 1968). As explained in the previous chapter, in 1934, the SLST was formed as a subsidiary of CAST. The colonial government granted SLST a 99-year monopoly on prospecting and mining diamonds in the entire country in return for a 27.5 per cent tax on net profits, with a view that the establishment of such a monopoly would provide the legal means to control informal indigenous mining (Hall, 1968; Reno, 1995). Diamond exports rose from zero in 1931 to

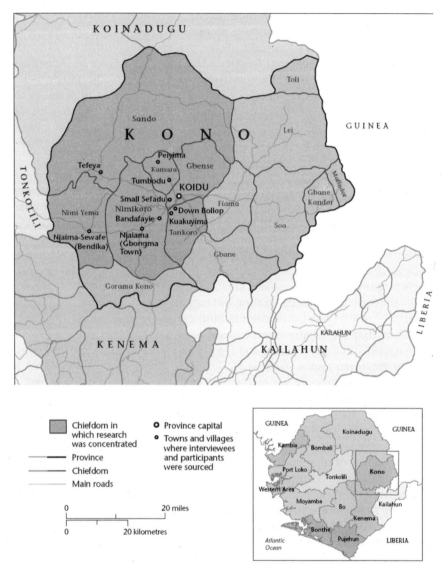

Figure 15.1   Kono District showing the chiefdoms and mining sites where research was conducted[4]

56 per cent of total exports in 1936, bringing the colony from a trade deficit to a consistent surplus up until the start of World War II (Reno, 1995: 48).

In many parts of the world, people turn to artisanal mining to cope with idiosyncratic risk events, including crop failure and post-conflict livelihood recovery. As soon as the first diamonds were discovered in Sierra Leone, a few bad harvests prompted people to start mining (Fairburn, 1965; Greenhalgh, 1985). Sierra Leoneans were joined by Guineans in the pits. The policy of SLST to protect their resource – and the colonial government their revenues – led to efforts to minimize indigenous mining. The government passed laws in 1936 prohibiting even the possession of diamonds (Reno, 1995). In 1945, SLST established a Diamond Protection Force, which was supplemented by the stationing of a detachment of the Sierra Leonean Police Force in Yengema in 1952.[5] In addition to these attempts to enforce the law directly, both SLST and the government adopted strategies of indirect rule by trying to persuade the local chiefs to serve their interests; but although SLST paid the chiefs to withhold settler rights, the chiefs accepted rent from 'strangers' (i.e. non-Konos) in exchange for protection and 'consideration' for access to land for mining (Reno, 1995; Greenhalgh, 1985: 165).[6] Likewise, the Native Authority Scheme, set up in 1937, was supposed to curtail the chiefs' interests in illicit mining and marketing by giving them a higher stake in local government. The chiefs were granted greater responsibilities over local government, traditional customary benefits were transformed into salaries for administrators and local hut taxes were increased by 25 per cent. Rather than strengthening any ties of loyalty between the local and colonial authorities, however, chiefs' and local officials' increased legal incomes enabled them to further their personal agendas, including the expansion of their diamond interests (Reno, 1995).

By the early 1950s, illegal dealing and digging were interpreted by indigenes as acts of resistance against colonial and corporate domination. It became apparent that the suppression of illegal activities was impossible and so in January 1955, the government and SLST began talks. In that year, there was a riot in Freetown and a strike at SLST, which subsequently surrendered its country-wide monopoly but maintained exclusive access in defined areas of Yengema and Tongo, and received £1.57 million in compensation from the government (Hall, 1968; Greenhalgh, 1985). By the time the Alluvial Diamond Mining Scheme (ADMS) was implemented in February 1956, some 60,000 diggers were operating in Kono (Greenhalgh, 1985). Under the ADMS, all mining and marketing of diamonds was to be conducted by licensed individuals and native firms only. Within a few months, thousands of mining licences were granted and nearly all mining activities had been legalized (Greenhalgh, 1985). Though the scheme successfully decriminalized production, it did not significantly appease some Konos (embodied in the Kono Progressive Movement), who were aware that they had been granted access to marginally-productive lands (Reno, 1995; Minikin, 1971, cited in Zack-Williams, 1995). More unrest in 1957–8 led to the beginning of contract mining in the SLST zone in 1959, whereby the company subleased plots for six-month periods, and offered equipment hire and diamond valuation services for a fee (Zack-Williams, 1995: 138; Greenhalgh, 1985: 167). This allowed some legitimate access to the SLST resource – albeit the less accessible plots for industrial extraction within the company's lease (Hall, 1968) – but also increased the feasibility of illegal activities therein.

In 1961, Sierra Leone gained its independence. The artisanal mining industry continued to be conducted mostly legally in the 1960s until the inauguration of Stevens' APC government in 1968. In the same year, Hall reported (1968: 7):

The picture now...is one of stability and predominately legitimate operations. Alluvial diamond mining has become an established and accepted feature of the economy of the country, and provides a living for about 25,000 miners, now mostly Sierra Leoneans. Smuggling is no longer a serious problem, and the miners now receive a reasonable proportion of the export value of their diamonds.

Within only a few years of his statement, however, the rules of the game had changed and the legal gains of the previous decade had been lost.

Kono was important politically, as its diamonds provided a large proportion of government revenue (Reno, 1995). During the first few years of Stevens's regime, political turbulence and local challenges by wealthy chiefs and their privileged clients threatened his authority in Kono. The APC took measures to disempower potential political rivals by centralizing government, manipulating local elections and discriminating against indigenous elites and Sierra Leone Peoples Party (SLPP) supporters in favour of the politically ostracized[7] Lebanese community. The APC patrons attempted to cut off their clients' sources of independent wealth and increase their dependency on Freetown for the protection of their interests. The chiefs' established revenue streams were severed when the government stopped paying them the local development funds and when SLST was effectively nationalized following the formation of the National Diamond Mining Company (NDMC) in 1971. Through the realignment and reconstitution of the patronage networks, Stevens harnessed the control of diamond revenues and established greater political security, if not popular support, for his government in Kono (Reno, 1995). The APC's diamond policies and elitist politics made it clear that, in contrast to their pre-election pretensions, power to the people was certainly not their intention (Reno, 1995: 107–8).

During the early 1970s, the government-owned Gold and Diamond Office (GGDO), which purchased all alluvially produced stones, had begun to discriminate against indigenous miners and pay higher prices to Lebanese dealers. The undervaluation of purchased stones gave miners an incentive to sell their diamonds outside official channels. Smuggling increased, and those mine managers and supporters who did sell their stones to the GGDO transferred the costs down the chain, paying diggers less, which, in turn, encouraged diggers to seek their profits independently. Illicit mining soon became the norm once again (Zack-Williams, 1995: 179–80).

Moreover, large plots of land for small-scale mining were rezoned for cooperative mining, which effectively increased APC clients' access to diamonds at the expense of the ordinary miner, who could not afford the increasingly prohibitive expense of mining legally. At the same time, the government toughened its position on illegal digging, instituting a paramilitary Internal Security Unit in 1975, whose purpose was to suppress diamond poaching. Finding themselves in a lose-or-lose position, diggers and miners had little choice but to slot themselves into the patronage networks by aligning with

APC-affiliated operations, or to maintain independence by protecting their illicit activities using violence.

In the 1970s, state bureaucracy had shifted definitively from serving the interests of the Sierra Leonean nation to maintaining the authority and wealth of those who had access to its assets. The colonial Native Authority Scheme of the 1930s had normalized the utilization of state resources and the exercise of political authority for personal gain (Reno, 1995). By the 1970s, the political economy of the diamond industry and the culture of government were firmly characterized by patrimonialism, 'big-man politics' and kleptocracy (Jackson and Rosberg, 1982; Bayart, 1993; Reno, 1995, 1998; Richards, 1996). The diamond industry provided substantial state revenues, and was crucial in the attraction of foreign investors, aid and loans from the IFIs. Corrupt bureaucrats and politicians used these investments and revenues as political and economic weapons to disempower competing 'big-men' in order to satisfy their personal ambitions and patrimonial obligations (Reno, 1995, 1998; Pugh and Cooper, 2004). By the 1980s, the state had all but failed due to shrinking aid budgets; declining revenues from legal diamond mining and other formal economic activities; the incapacitation of ordinary state functions; and economic homogenization around informal diamond production and marketing (Reno, 1995; Archibald and Richards, 2002). Social development was removed from the political agenda and society became increasingly disenfranchised from the state. The citizenry came to depend even more on patrimony and patronage for support and security. With money increasingly at the centre of political influence, the economy became grafted to political ends as the market replaced the ballot box as the site of political contestation. By the time Stevens handed over formal power to Joseph Momoh in 1985, his personal fortune amounted to US$500 million (Reno, 1998), while only 60,000 of the country's 3.5 million people were in paid employment (Abdullah, 1998). During Stevens's regime, the poor got poorer and more people became impoverished. Yet, the option of electing an alternative simply did not exist. The APC had created a *de facto* single-party state by 1973 and *de jure* single-party state by 1978, and violently suppressed any political opposition (Reno, 1995; Abdullah, 1998; Adebajo, 2002; Kandeh, 2002). By the time the war began in 1991, the APC had headed the country for 23 years. In this climate of intensifying insecurity, patrimonial dependency, escalating violence, political alienation and economic decline, some people came to believe that war was the only option for effecting change (Abdullah, 1998). With the state ruined, the availability of easily accessible diamonds soon depleted, and with regional support for resistance to the established regime present from Colonel Muammar Gaddafi of Libya and Charles Taylor of Liberia, war was not only desirable but possible (Reno, 1995; Richards, 1996; Bangura, 1997; Abdullah, 1998; Alao, 1999; Kandeh, 2002; Pugh and Cooper, 2004). Thus, on 23 March 1991, the war, which would kill 75,000, maim 10,000 and displace almost half of Sierra Leone's 4.5 million people, began.

A political economy of contemporary artisanal diamond production

Artisanal mining is defined as 'all non mechanised, low output extraction of minerals carried out by individuals and small groups, frequently on intermittent [*sic*] basis, and employing essentially traditional manual techniques' (Keili, 2003). In the third workshop held in Koidu, participants agreed that the standard arrangement for artisanal diamond production in Kono is one in which the mining costs are covered by a supporter who is in business with a licensed miner. Both parties employ mines managers (foremen) to protect their interests at the mine. The diamonds are then sold to a dealer or his agent with the assistance of a coaxer, before being sold to an exporter in a similar fashion. Figure 15.2 illustrates the typical legal artisanal diamond supply chain, from production to export.

There are many variations of the actors and relations in this chain. For example, the supporter may also be a dealer who sells directly to an exporter or may even be an exporter himself;[8] the licence-holder may be financially independent and support his/her own operations; or the miner might be unlicensed himself but be affiliated with a licence-holder to provide legal security for his operations.[9] The illegal chain is very similar to Figure 15.3; it differs only in so far as there is no licence-holder involved in production, though

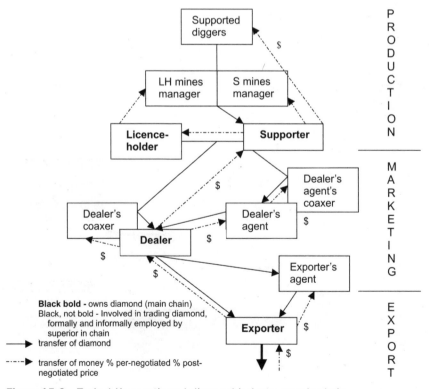

Figure 15.2 Typical Kono artisanal diamond industry supply chain

licence-holders are known to launder illicit diamonds (see Figure 15.3). The other possible combinations described above may still apply. In addition, there may be a landowner (e.g. a farmer) who is compensated with a share of the proceeds for allowing mining to be conducted on his/her land.

Besides those directly involved in the production and marketing of diamonds, there are other people who benefit from the trade. Some are presented in Figures 15.2 and 15.3. The latter also illustrates some of the economic spinoffs the diamond industry generates in Koidu. Diamond mining produces livelihood options outside the industry and makes other existing ones (e.g. food trading) more viable by increasing demand for its product. The other industries that rely on the artisanal diamond industry include mining services (tool making, mending, selling and rentals, mechanics, petrol traders, etc), commerce (rice sellers, supermarkets, electronic shops and stalls selling consumables such as sunglasses, watches and cassettes) and general services (construction, prostitution, restaurants, bars and night-clubs).

Productivity

Diamonds were once so abundant in Kono that people are said to have been able to pick them up off the streets after a rainstorm or find them under their houses in Koidu. According to local opinion, there is decreasing productivity from artisanal activity in the traditional mining areas of Gbense, Nimi Yema, Tankoro and Nimikoro. Miners are forced to work deeper gravels to yield satisfactory returns. Going deeper, however, involves greater risk and

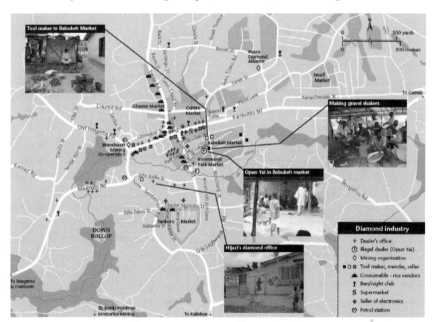

Figure 15.3 The diamond economy in Koidu

investment. In time, mining in Kono's traditional mining chiefdoms will be increasingly consolidated into small-scale, mechanized operations, as artisanal mining becomes decreasingly viable. Smaller, poorer players will eventually be squeezed from the market, although some may persist by overkicking[10] or taking up other artisanal activities. But mining is apparently on the increase in the eastern provinces and elsewhere in Sierra Leone; people are flocking to exploit these 'virgin' (and largely unregulated) soils, where diamonds are more accessible.

This changing geography of opportunity and risk in the industry is further complicated by the incomplete and outdated knowledge of diamond deposits in the country. The diamond reserve in Sierra Leone is very much imagined, as there has been no widespread prospecting since Hall led the Geological Survey in mapping the country's reserves in the 1960s (Hall, 1968). Today, rather than scientific prospecting, the payability of ground is ascertained more by experience; knowledge of the geography of historical, local mining; the presence of indicator minerals; and instinct and guesswork. The displacement of people indigenous to Kono during the war has weakened the value of even indigenous knowledge, as most returnees are unaware of exactly where the armed factions concentrated their mining. People know productivity is declining but they do not know where.

Mining techniques, tools and technologies

Alluvial mining requires exposing, extracting and washing diamond-bearing gravel. This gravel is found on riverbeds, in swamps and under lateritic overburden in terraces and alluvial flats (Fairbairn, 1965; Hall, 1968). The mining procedure represented below as standard was developed by local miners. The procedure is the same for illegal mining, except that Step 3 would be omitted and possibly replaced by something like 'ensure protection in cases of harassment by authorities or other parties'. The procedure is as follows:

1. Raise funds to get licence (and perhaps for the rest of your operations).
2. Identify the land you wish to mine.
3. Get a licence.
4. Find a supporter (if necessary).
5. Arrange logistics (i.e. employ and house diggers, and buy tools).

Small-scale	*Artisanal*
6. Bulldozing (caterpillar)	Brush land (machetes)
7. Bulldozing (caterpillar)	Stripping (removing the mud – shovels)
8. Excavate gravel (caterpillar with diff. parts)	Extract gravel (manually – shovels)
9. Wash gravel (the plant, the rocker)	Wash gravel (the rocker, shakers)

10. Restart 6–9 in different part of plot or pack up tools and leave land to government.

Typically, the distinction between small-scale and artisanal mining is not precise, as miners use small-scale equipment in their artisanal operations whenever it is possible or desirable. For example, at Step 9, when they are washing the gravel, miners may invest in the plant to reduce the risk of theft, while having had all the gravel extracted manually.

In artisanal mining, diggers use machetes to 'brush' the ground (i.e. to remove the overgrowth), shovels to 'strip' it (i.e. to remove the overburden) and to extract the gravel, and picks to break up any boulders or rocks which get in their way. Manual brushing, stripping and extraction can take between two and three months (presuming 50 diggers are at work), whereas with the use of a bulldozer, it takes about a week. To rent and fuel a bulldozer for six days can cost US$8,200–10,000, whereas to get diggers to do the same work would cost on average US$7,900.[11] During extraction, a water pump may be necessary if the rains have begun or if groundwater is high. Sometimes, the youngest member of the gang has the job of water-boy and so removes the excess water with a bucket.

Once the gravel has been extracted, it is stockpiled for washing or is washed contemporaneously. It may be washed where it is found or be transported elsewhere, usually in a rice sack on someone's head, if there is no immediate water source. Washing is performed using a shaker, the rocker and/or the plant. The rocker and plant require water pumps. The plant requires a small generator and has the advantages that no further washing is required; it makes it more difficult for people to steal diamonds; and it produces a higher yield of diamonds than traditional artisanal washing methods. When operations use the rocker and shaker, women are sometimes employed to sift the smallest grains to find the smallest stones – the 'number 10s' – and any gold dust which might be present.

Licensing procedure and access to land

The number of artisanal mining licences issued in Kono has vastly increased since licensing began after the war (see Table 15.1). The licensing procedure usually takes about two weeks 'because there is some go and come, go and come, go and come', as the following summary outlines.

1. Apply to the town chief by letter or in person (to get and complete the application forms).[12]
2. Chief recommends application to the Chiefdom Mining Committee (CMC).
3. CMC approves application.
4. Miner pays surface fees and chiefdom development fund fees to CMC.
5. Miner goes to the Ministry of Mineral Resources (MMR) mines warden with CMC receipt to apply for government approval.
6. Miner and warden go to allocated site to demarcate the boundaries.[13]
7. A plan is drawn of the site.
8. The plan is taken to the town and paramount chiefs for signature.
9. The mines engineer signs the plan.

Table 15.1 Number of mining licences issued in Kono, December 2001–
August 2004

Date	No. licences issued
Dec 2001	0
June 2002	87
Dec 2002	457
June 2003	952
August 2004	>1,500[14]

10. The miner pays the government fees.
11. The miner is licensed.

This procedure is intended to be simple enough to encourage people to apply for licences. However, the actual cost of a licence remains uncertain: although the government has established and publicized that a mining licence should cost no more than Le410,000 to acquire, people still pay more because of the various 'handshakes' they must give to expedite the process, or to maintain or generate good favour with the authorities. In one case, a female licence-holder paid Le710,000 for her licence, which was cheaper than others would have to have paid, in her view, because she was married to a town chief.

These costs make it exceedingly challenging for people to acquire a licence. Those who have the advantage when applying for licences are men, people native to the village, people from Kono, people with money, local people who do not already have access to mining land and people who are close to the chiefs or some other person involved in the process. According to the chairwoman of the district council, if diamonds are to work for peace and prosperity, then 'people should have access to land (and) there should be no discrimination as to who gets what'. There is still discrimination in who gets access to land and on what terms. This is of concern if social injustice and unequal access to opportunity is accepted as a cause of the war (Peters and Richards, 1998; Archibald and Richards, 2002; Abdullah, 2004). Furthermore, this discrimination and the unpredictability of costs may discourage some from licensing their site.

The mining calendar and implications of seasonality

Mining activities are planned around the coming of the rains and how precipitation affects the costs of mining. Investors undertake more mining during the dry season because of the associated hazards and costs, which Table 15.2 outlines. Some mining does occur in the rainy season, but principally where there is black mud, where the gravel has already been extracted and removed to a drier location, or where water levels do not threaten to wash gravel away or cover it completely (e.g. in river bed mining). The seasonality of mining costs and activities has implications for how people use opportunities in mining as part of their livelihoods.[15]

Table 15.2 Variations in mining costs between the wet and dry seasons

	Dry season (mid-September to mid-May)	Rainy season (end-May to early-September)	Why the costs change in the rainy season
Labour supply villages	↑	↓	— Seasonal labourers return to
Labour costs	↓	↑	— Food costs increase — Work is more arduous — Increased sickness rate — Shelter more easily damaged
Crime rates	↓	↑	— Unemployed engage in theft — Migrants who cannot afford to return to their villages engage in theft
Food costs[16]	↓	↑	— Supply shortages (low stocks, bad roads, etc) — Diggers eat more (cold, harder work, etc)
Fuel costs	↓	↑	— Supply shortages: bad roads and increased demand (use of water pumps and machines to wash the gravel) — Work is more arduous
Shelter costs	↓	↑	— Bad weather makes good shelter more important (to reduce health costs) — Shelter more vulnerable to damage
Equipment costs	↓	↑	— Increased demand for water pumps and machines to wash the gravel

Risks and dilemmas facing miners in planning their operations

Table 15.3 was produced by miners in the third Kono workshop. It demonstrates what mining actually entails and so emphasizes the method and complexity of artisanal diamond mining as a livelihood option and its entrepreneurial nature.

These risks provide an indication of the dilemmas miners face when planning their operations. By far the biggest risk is theft: the selection of supporters and dealers is therefore based on friends' recommendations on who is most trustworthy and fair. They look for the same traits in their diggers and mines managers, as well as loyalty and industriousness. For this reason, some miners prefer to employ particular tribes who they associate with being loyal, hard-

Table 15.3 Risks miners must consider when planning their operations

Dilemma	Risks	
How to get money (support)	No support, no mining	
	Trustworthiness	risk of going into an arrangement with a dishonest supporter
How many people to engage	Price changes	risk of underestimating the cost of support per person, e.g. vulnerability to seasonal changes in costs (see Table 15.2)
	Overemployment	according to what work is possible at each stage; it is expensive if workers are idle
	Underemployment	increases the duration of mining
Where shall I mine (what kind of mining)?	Occurrence of boulders or 'ballop' (mud) in the overburden	increases costs or can be impassable – their existence is generally unpredictable
	Productivity	risk of low yield
	Water level	places with higher water level are more expensive to mine; risk of water level rising with the rains
		lack of water means gravel must be transported to a washing pit
Which tools and machines should I use? (what kind of mining?)	Poor quality	if the machines are badly manufactured or not maintained there is a risk they might blow up or not work so well
	Poor judgement	use of wrong machines or too few machines, or delays in hiring machines, can prolong the work
Where shall I house my workers?	Location	proximity affects transport
	Quality	affects health
How much food to give each day?	Over-feeding	causes laziness
How to keep my workers healthy?	Contagious diseases	
Duration of the work	Uncertainty	if the work takes too long it costs more
	Bad weather	can make the work last longer
Who do I sell to?	Duping	risk that the person you sell to will cheat you of a fair price or switch stones on you
	Theft	risk that buyer will steal it
	Smuggling	risk that buyer will smuggle the stone
	Criminals	risk of selling to an unlicensed buyer
How much to sell for?	Ignorance	risk of not knowing the value of your diamond
Financial security	Theft	risk that other members of the production team have a criminal attitude or are disloyal

(Contd. 15.3)

(Cont'd. 15.3)

Physical security harm	*Violence*	exposure to people who might want to you
Who to employ?	*Risk of criminal or violent dispositions* *Risk of disloyalty*	
Which contract terms to use	*Winnings*	Choice of winnings allocation system depends on the expected productivity of the mine and the knowledge and wishes of partners and employees
	Allocation systems	
Who handles the diamonds?	*Risk of theft*	

working and experienced. Others will employ family or people of the same tribe as themselves.[17] Trust is clearly one of the most important assets in a diamond-production relationship, albeit something very hard to come by.

Roles and responsibilities in the industry

The role someone takes in diamond production differs according to his/her knowledge, ability, contacts and investment capacity. In some positions, tribe and gender also determine participation (Levin, 2005). The arrangements forged depend on the degree of trust and dependency between business partners.

The divers (riverbed mining only)

Divers extract the gravel from the riverbed. They usually spend about three hours underwater. Diving is the most dangerous form of gravel extraction and divers are very vulnerable to poor health. Blindness, deafness and chills are common, as is poisoning and pulmonary damage owing to the level of diesel fumes and carbon monoxide they inhale. Because of this greater risk, divers can earn substantially more than other gang members. For example, one diver reported working for an enormous monthly wage of Le1,000,000[18] although he was not entitled to any of the profits accrued from the sale of the diamonds found. Another earned three cups of rice and Le2,000 a day, had his health needs attended to and received a share of all winnings. In his gang, the divers got three times as much of the winnings per person as the washers.

The diggers

Diggers include all people employed by miners to carry out hard labour (stripping, extraction and gravel washing). Occasionally, diggers work alone or in pairs, and undertake all three tasks if the location requires it. Otherwise, diggers who work alone tend to engage in overkicking. In a mining gang, the diggers will sometimes have specialized functions, determined by their skill levels or the extent to which the financier trusts them.[19]

Of all the actors in the supply chain, the diggers are the most vulnerable in terms of overall poverty. They are at the greatest risk of poor health, physical violence and economic exploitation; they also receive minimal and usually uncertain benefits. In the digger category, the exposure to risk and resiliency is further dictated by one's position in the hierarchy of the gang, which determines one's role, participation in decision-making, and entitlement to winnings.

At the top is the gang leader, who reconciles internal disputes and disciplines diggers who break the gang's code of conduct. Gang leaders usually negotiate with the licence-holder on behalf of the gang in the post-negotiated pricing system. They also allocate tasks and the winnings within the gang. Usually, the gang leader will receive a tip (gratuity) from the other diggers in recognition of his authority. In between are the ordinary diggers, and at the bottom are the youngest members of the gangs, who carry out basic chores such as fetching food and water, or else are assigned the tedious job of water-boy.[20] As one digger explained during a personal interview: 'The elder ones, normally their pride doesn't allow them to do certain work. They feel they are too big to do such work. So...the young one in the group can be sent to do anything and he will not refuse because elders are telling him and he will respect the elders to do that'.

The youngest are generally given smaller shares of winnings. It is this type of bias which some believe fuelled the war (Peters and Richards, 1998, Archibald and Richards, 2002).

Permanently employed labour

Some diggers are employed for the entire mining season. If the miner is pleased with their work, he/she might support them over the rainy season (even when there is no mining to be done) in order to retain their services for the following mining season. Diggers supported by a licensed miner will typically work 7.5 hours a day, six days a week, although during gravel extraction and washing, they may work continuously, day and night, in order to get their winnings as soon as possible, as well as to reduce the risk of theft.

Independent labour – gado gangs and overkickers

Gado is illegal mining conducted by an unsupported gang of diggers who share their winnings equally among themselves. They generally receive less formal support than permanently employed labourers, which gives them greater flexibility once they do find a diamond as their obligation to their supporter is minimal. They are often free to sell to whomever they please at whatever price.

Gado gangs and other individual diggers will sometimes seek contract work with licence-holders (called *jagaja*). In return, they may be paid in cash and food for the day or they will do *kongoma* (see below). One female overkicker admitted during an interview that other diggers had even offered her their labour in exchange for sexual acts or a meal at the end of the day.

Overkickers wash the tailings that have already been washed. The only tools they require are shakers, buckets, and perhaps picks and shovels. Overkicking occurs on the plots of legal mining operations to ensure that nothing is overlooked; it is also carried out illegally wherever gravel is easily accessed. It is often pursued seasonally by diggers who have been involved in riverbed mining during the dry season and so are without work in the rainy season. Sometimes, they do overkicking on behalf of their previous supporter or they operate independently. Its significance lies in it being a very common livelihood among the very vulnerable.

Both *gado* and overkicking are tactics that improve a digger's chances of obtaining winnings. In overkicking, the digger spends most of his time washing without having to do three months of stripping and extraction beforehand. In *gado*, diggers do not have a boss with whom they have to share their winnings. In most cases, however, they are without the benefit (or restrictions) of daily support, although in some cases, *gado* gangs and overkickers are provided occasional support by their customers, a previous supporter, a village elder or a wealthier member of the gang (such as one with a family farm).

Gado and overkicking can only be legal if the individual or gang conducts activities on a licensed plot and sells the diamonds to the licence-holder. It is considered illegal when it occurs on unlicensed land or when diamonds are sold to anyone but the licence-holder. In fact, the majority of people mining illegally do *gado* or overkicking. Reducing illegal mining, therefore, requires more consideration of the role these types of miners have in increasing people's security by assessing the particular benefits and disadvantages they bring compared with more formalized or structured alternatives. It may prove problematic to persuade those doing *gado* or overkicking to cease their illegal activities if they prefer the independence it brings them, or if it is the only mining option available to them (i.e. in cases where, for whatever reason, they are not welcome in a legal operation). This raises the question of what else can be done to encourage overkickers and *gado* gangs to mine legally. One solution may be the designation of certain areas for mining, which would provide these people with a legal option; it would also protect them from harassment from officials. This type of land-use designation could be a zoning process.

Watchers and security guards

Theft of gravel or equipment is very common. Miners employ watchers to prevent theft; in the majority of cases, watchers are only necessary once extraction and washing have begun. Often, the watcher is a trusted relative. One miner interviewed employed a security guard to secure his gravel, paying him Le100,000 and a bag of rice (equivalent to Le60,000) a month. In one diving operation investigated, the supporter employed guards to protect fuel and diving equipment. In most cases, however, diggers do the watching themselves. They may take turns, sharing the responsibility, or else the whole gang will spend the night at the site because, as one miner put it, 'if you send one person, the gangs that come to wash the gravel at night will hurt the person so for that the group goes'. During extraction and washing, therefore, the gang may live permanently at the pit, which puts them at a greater risk of contracting malaria.

The miner

The miner manages production. He/she may also finance the operations and be the licence-holder, although this is not always the case. Thus, the miner may be the gang leader (illegal operations), the mines manager or foreman (the licence-holder's or supporter's representative at the mine), or the licence-holder himself (a miner in possession of a licence).

The mines manager, also called the foreman, is usually employed by the supporter or licence-holder to represent them at the pit and to manage operations on their behalf. He supervises, directs and organizes activities. In some situations, he will be the one to buy the diamonds from the diggers on behalf of the licence-holder or supporter. He also acts as the supervisor when the gravel is being washed. Mines managers never own the diamonds; they are paid a percentage of the licence-holder's or supporter's share of the diamond sales.[21] There is usually a good degree of trust between the foreman and his boss. Often, licence-holders employ family members (husband, brother, son or nephew) as their foreman.

Occasionally, a licence-holder allows another miner to mine a portion of his/her land for a pre-negotiated share of the gravel or winnings as rent. This arrangement enables a licence-holder to exploit his/her plot at a greater rate than he/she is capable given available capital and/or the desire to mine independently (i.e. without a supporter). Subleasing reduces the licence-holder's capital investment, while enabling him/her to maximize exploitation of the land, which he/she may be unable to mine within the year. It is a way of maximizing returns and spreading risk and bringing benefits to both the licence-holder and the tenant miner.

The licence-holder

According to the law, licence-holders must be Sierra Leonean. They may also perform the roles of financier and mines manager. When this is the case, a mines manager is not necessary, provided that the licence-holder is prepared to manage the mine full-time. In some situations, the licence-holder performs no other role other than that of providing the title to the land. In such situations, he/she may enter a business agreement with a self-supported miner or supporter. In the case of the latter, the licence-holder will employ his/her own miner to manage and supervise the operations and protect his/her interests; the supporter will do the same.

The supporter

By the early 1960s, surface diamond deposits had started to deplete. The requirement to remove greater volumes of overburden to access the diamond-bearing soil increased the costs (and altered the methods) of artisanal diamond production. This encouraged miners to turn to their buyers and local businessmen for financial support. This is how the supporter system was born (Zack-Williams, 1995: 147–54).

Not all mining supporters are dealers, but all established dealers – legal and illegal – are supporters. By providing support, they hope to oblige miners and diggers to bring their diamonds to them for sale. However, there is no guarantee that people will be loyal to the supporter unless the arrangements are formal and prosecutable by law. An exporter explained during an interview that 'it's not a structured relationship, it's a risky relationship. I sometimes wonder the extent to which people are ahead in supporting'.

There are many different types of supporter–client relationships between various actors in the artisanal mining industry. Support may be formal or informal, substantial or piecemeal, or occasional or regular. It may exist between diggers and a financier, miners and a financier, or between diggers themselves. These different arrangements present different risks and obligations between parties, and different potentials for exploitation. A brief exploration of supportive relationships should help elucidate the scope of their diversity.

Some supporters enter into formal arrangements with their clients, with the conditions of their agreement written, witnessed, signed and lodged with the MMR. This type of support is usually substantial and intended principally for small-scale mining-related activities, although the supporter may also offer the client relief as and when he/she requires it. This is the system used mostly by Lebanese dealers and international investors to support licensed miners and, by extension, their diggers; it is a business arrangement. One miner explained how his relationship with his supporter works:

> He does all the logistics of the work, all the financing, and then after all the exercise, we go and sit down in his office...and he will calculate his expenditure and my manager will produce his own document and they will do a comparison. After that, we come to business. After the business, he will tell me that this diamond is so-so-so-so-so, and out of that, we will divide it between us. He will get his own 60 per cent and I will also take my own 40 per cent. He'll remove the expenditure before we go into the share.

If the miner has not kept a careful record of expenditures, and if he does not have the skills to value the diamond, the supporter can argue that the cost of the operations exceeded the value of the diamond and give him nothing. This is a very common strategy for cheating miners and diggers, and is the principal route by which miners end up in a state of debt bondage (Moyers, 2003). The same miner explained how this happened with his previous supporter:

> Last year, I got diamonds but I was cheated. The financier told me that all his expenditure was twenty six million Leones and then all the winnings cost twenty two million Leones, so I took him to the Mines office. The Mines engineer interfered in the issue. Later on, he paid my money. From there, the agreement was over.

It can actually happen that the mining expenditures are at a deficit and the diamonds discovered are not likely to bring any gains. In this case, the miner might cheat the supporter:

> You may be in their hold for 30 million Leones to a supporter, you find a stone worth 25. You're not going to be inclined to want to go to that guy because you still owe him five million after you've given him the stone. So what happens is you then go somewhere else, you try and liquidate, get your 25 million and you continue your operation with that 25 million and in the meantime, you say to your supporter, 'Hang on, something good will come'.

This is a risky move for a miner. If a supporter feels a digger or miner has cheated him, he will involve the police and most likely get his way because, as a local politician explained, 'It is the person who has the money who gets their way'.

Similar support arrangements can be entered into for mining operations but without the formality of a written agreement. This type of informal but committed support may be regular or piecemeal according to the supporter's liquidity or the beneficiary's needs. These relationships are based more on trust and good will, or a pre-established sense of reciprocity, for example, among family members. Some diggers provide this type of support to their gang, especially in *gado* gangs. They depend on other personal or household livelihood activities (e.g. farming, petty trading and gold panning) to provide the cash and food to support their gang, or otherwise have a relationship of support with a wealthier person, either on a fully committed or occasional basis.

Lastly, there is the type of support that is irregular and without commitment. This type of arrangement exists mostly between the small-time illegal dealers/local patrons and the most vulnerable diggers, although the Lebanese dealers interviewed admitted offering occasional relief to certain community members. While the obligation therein is small on either side, there is still some expectation that the diggers and miners will bring their winnings to the supporter. Since the commitment is weak, it is common for the diggers to seek support from more than one person. This may lead to problems once a diamond is discovered but it also gives the digger or miner options on to whom to sell the stone.

In summary, the supporter is a type of patron. Supporting mining activities is one of many options for a patron in a society where patronage is both a coping and livelihood strategy and, historically, has been the principal means of social protection and promotion. Supporters serve similar roles in society as the state and the bank does, say, in Europe. People rely on wealthier community members to provide them with welfare relief and investment capital. They are instrumental in the redistribution of wealth and provide the fuel for economic growth. In Sierra Leone, the state and the banks are incapable of providing these services: just as the Western nation-state expects the person receiving welfare to be loyal to the state and meet his/her civic responsibilities, supporters expect the person receiving support to be loyal to them and to meet their responsibilities as a client (after Wood, 2003).

Entitlements and terms of exchange

The discussion that follows examines the terms of exchange that exist between the principal actors in the industry, with special emphasis on the levels of support provided to diggers and how winnings are shared between the various actors.

Regular support

Supporters give miners what they need to extract diamonds, that is, rice, tools, machines and financial support. In turn, miners provide subsistence to the diggers. Generally, the miners or supporters provide diggers with at least some rice (between two and three cups daily) and some money to buy other foodstuffs for making 'soup' (i.e. sauce or stew). This daily cash payment varies geographically: some of the worst-supported diggers interviewed lived in Kamara chiefdom. They received Le500 (c. US$0.20) daily. In other parts, people were paid as much as Le5,000 (c. US$2.00) a day, and provided additional support. The average daily amount received by the diggers interviewed was Le1,900 (c. US$1.20).

Apart from rice and money, diggers may also be supported in their health, shelter, transport and funeral expenses, and even their children's education and family welfare. Supported diggers usually receive enough to tend to their individual needs. Some supporters make allowances for married diggers by providing them with their own room, for example, but it is unusual for a supporter to provide for the daily needs of diggers' families. Diggers depend on other household members to do this. In addition, not all diggers are permanently supported. In the investigations carried out for this research, just over half of those mining illegally did so without support.

Winnings allocation systems

Different allocation systems are used in different relationships and in accordance with the type of mining being conducted. Here, the following two principal relationships of exchange are reviewed: first, within the mining gang; and second, between the gang and the financier. The relationship between the

Table 15.4 Winnings allocation systems

	Legal status		Actors between whom winnings are to be shared				
	Legal	Illegal	Among gado gang	Among em-ployed diggers	Diggers + financ-ier (LH and/or S*)	LH + S	LH + lessee
Wage only	✓	(✓)	✗	✗	✓	✗	
Pre-negotiated % winnings	✓	(✓)		✓	✓	☑	✓
Pre-negotiated % gravel 2 pile							
3 pile (5:5:2)	✗	✓	✓	✗	✓	✗	☑
Bucket system	✓	✓	✗	✗	✓	✗	✓
Post-negotiated price	✓	(✓)	✗	☑	☑	✓	✗
Kongoma	✓	✓		✓	✓	✗	✗
Gado/Kabudu	✗	✓					

(✓) not ordinarily used in this system.
☑ predominant system used to allocate winnings between these actors today.
*LH = licence-holder; S = supporter.
Note: Kabudu means a group of people from many ethnic backgrounds.

financier and the licence-holder has already been considered. From this, an assessment is made of who benefits from the most common arrangements. A typology of the various systems used today is set out as follows.

Wage labour

Diggers are sometimes employed seasonally and paid on a cash only basis (i.e. they get none of the winnings and receive no other benefits such as food and shelter). The amount paid daily is usually Le 5,000. Occasional labour is often paid in this manner as well.

Pre-negotiated percentage of the cash winnings

Before beginning work, the parties agree on the percentage share of the cash received from selling the diamonds. Whatever the quality of diamonds, they split the winnings according to this pre-negotiated percentage. This system is used today between supporters and licensed miners. The usual split is 60:40 or 70:30. This system was common between diggers and the miner during the 1960s. From the miner's perspective, it is the optimum system if the diggers know how to value diamonds. From the digger's perspective, it should be the preferable system if they do not know how to value diamonds.

Pre-negotiations are also made to determine winnings allocations among the diggers, many of whom share winnings equally among themselves. This is usually the case in *gado* gangs. In other gangs, winnings are distributed according to productivity (based on effort and skill) or according to age and position in the hierarchy. The gang leader decides who should get what. Usually, he will also receive a tip from the remaining diggers. Winnings may also be allocated differently according to the value of the gem: equally when the gem is of low value, and unequally when it is of high value, with the gang leader taking a bigger share.

Pre-negotiated percentage of the gravel (pile and bucket systems)

Before beginning work, the parties agree on a percentage share of the gravel. This generally happens when diggers are unsupported or where a miner has subleased a portion of licensed land and pays the licence-holder in gravel rather than winnings. This was the system used by the rebels and government forces during the war because it requires no financial input other than the purchase of tools: half of the gravel was washed for the commander, and the other half was washed and shared among the junior soldiers who carried out the digging. It is a high-risk arrangement because there is no guarantee that a pile contains a diamond and when a colleague finds one, one has no claim to it (unlike in other systems). This system entails the biggest gamble and could appropriately be called the casino system.

The bucket system is practically identical to the pile system. Instead of paying diggers in one big pile out of which the winnings are split among the group (i.e. up to 50 men), the diggers are divided into teams of maybe four, each receiving a bucket of extracted gravel to wash for the boss and a bucket to wash for themselves. If they find any diamonds in their bucket, their team gets to keep the winnings in their entirety; none is shared with the other diggers or the boss. In practice, however, the gang will usually either sell the diamonds to the boss (who can then sell them under his licence) or will sell the diamonds under the boss's licence and give him a tip or commission allowing this.

Kongoma

This system is used when the supporter is no longer able to sponsor the required work, and thus he/she receives no share of the winnings found in the payment gravel. One such scenario might be as follows: it is looking unlikely that all the gravel will be extracted before the rains begin with the number of labourers currently working on the site. The employed diggers or mines manager will call on contract diggers – perhaps a *gado* gang – who will help out with the work and receive a share of the extracted gravel as payment at the end of the day. Another scenario might be that the supporter has no liquidity and can no longer afford to pay his employed diggers. In such cases, diggers may agree to provide labour in exchange for a bucket of gravel. In *kongoma*, the licence-holder and the supporter lose nothing if the gravel proves to be unproductive because they receive free labour.

Post-negotiated price

In this situation, diggers 'sell' their winnings to the mines manager or directly to the licence-holder/supporter team. If the diamond is small, diggers are more likely to receive a fair price because they are well acquainted with the value of smaller stones, and miners are content with sacrificing small amounts of money to keep diggers satisfied. If, however, winnings prove to be scarce, and consequently put the supporter in deficit, then diggers are unlikely to receive any compensation for small finds; this may encourage theft. Diggers are far less likely to know the value of big winnings and often sell winnings for too low a price. A knowledgeable miner can therefore earn a sizeable sum at the expense of ignorant diggers, although, according to at least one miner, this agreement is the best way to 'really satisfy the diggers [as] they get satisfied when you agree on the price, and they know that is what you have to pay them'. Post-negotiated pricing is the most common strategy in Sierra Leone, in combination with a pre-negotiated share: parties agree on percentages and then renegotiate these once winnings are found, according to expenditure and winnings to date.

The various winnings allocation systems are summarized in Table 15.4.

Illegal mining

Illegal mining occurs whenever somebody works land that is unlicensed, or wherever somebody who does not have a claim to the licence mines licensed land. This section of the chapter considers the reasons why people in Sierra Leone mine illegally.

The decision to mine legally is determined by the strength of an individual's protection networks, their ability to finance themselves, what livelihood options are available to them and the relative attractiveness of these options. Legal mining is the optimal choice for someone who can afford to obtain a licence and conduct mining activities without support. Independent legal miners have explicit and enforceable rights, and greater freedom to sell to whomever they please: this reduces the chance of theft and enables them to fetch higher prices locally. For others, the legal option requires entering a supported arrangement in order to obtain a licence and/or to finance production. If the mine is unproductive, the miner might find himself with no earnings at the end of the year, or worse still, in debt. With general productivity falling, the risk of more people going into debt is increasing.

Illegal mining, *gado* and overkicking offer people greater independence and a higher share of winnings. Working for a licence-holder greatly reduces a digger's returns and also binds the digger to his authority. This means less flexibility in selecting which days he mines and the times when he starts and finishes work. For diggers who mine to supplement one another, illegal operations (i.e. *gado* or overkicking) are more feasible than working in a legal gang. One digger interviewed claimed that he mined illegally although his brothers had licensed plots. He indicated that he would rather work independently because if he were to find anything, the money is all his, and also because his brothers, like other licence-holders, do not support their workers satisfactorily in his opinion. He does, however, use his brothers' licences to sell his diamonds and gives them a tip for allowing him to do this. Licence-holders who purchase diamonds directly or who permit selling to a licensed dealer under his/her licence provide illegal diggers with a greater selection of buyer options that extend beyond the network of illegal dealers who propagate illicit activities (they also bring illegally mined stones into legal marketing channels, which limits smuggling).

One miner stated that those who mine illegally either do not have the money to pay for a licence or are related to the authorities and so effectively have indemnity. Four out of 12 interviewees who were related to chiefs in some way mined illegally. This lends some support to one interviewee's claim that 'for other people, like sons of paramount and town chiefs, they exercise their father's authorities to mine without licence. They only look out for mines warden to demarcate lands and from that point, straight away they start to mine'.

If illegal mining is to be properly discouraged, chiefs must be further sensitized and/or suitably reprimanded for facilitating or ignoring illegal mining among family members. If they do not respect their own laws, how can they expect people in an increasingly individualistic society (Archibald and Richards, 2002) to respect them as well?

Illegal mining increases the risk of persecution from the authorities, theft or duping. Without money to pay bribes or for the protection of a 'big-man', such activity becomes a risky business. For some people, however, mining illegally is no option: they cannot afford the licence or are excluded from participating in a legal gang either productively or at all because of their gender or age. But where people have strong social contacts, illegal mining is a logical choice because it offers greater profitability and independence. Illegal mining is the secure person's preferable option and the poor person's fate. As the government proceeds to develop its capacity to eliminate illegal mining, these different motivations need to be taken into consideration to ensure that the powerful do not continue to bear indemnity, and that the vulnerable are not further marginalized.

Monitoring and disciplining the industry

The Kimberley Process requires that artisanal diamond mining activities are better monitored. In Sierra Leone, the government bodies currently involved in monitoring diamond marketing and exports include the MMR, the police, the GGDO, and Customs and Excise. The ability of these state authorities to

Table 15.5: Profit-making and corrupt gains in the industry

	Profit-making Total rankings	Profit-making Overall rank	Corrupt gains Total rankings	Corrupt gains Overall rank
Exporters	81	10	80	10
Dealers	78	9	78	9
Supporters	72	8	62	8
Mines monitors	52	7	56	7
Paramount chiefs	47	6	38	3
Freetown (national) politicians	42	5	49	5
Police	34	4	54	6
Section chiefs	30	3	19	2
Local politicians	28	2	39	4
Town chiefs	26	1	15	1

perform their duties is vastly inhibited by extremely restricted resources, a paucity of competent middle management and pervasive corruption. All were accused of corruption over the course of the interviewing carried out for this research, with workshop participants individually ranking the relative profit-making potential and corrupt gains of a variety of people in the industry.

These findings indicate that people have the most faith in their chiefs to not be corrupt and suggest an overall distrust in government officials and industry actors. Table 15.5 and Figure 15.4 provide an overview of the groups of people who benefit directly from the artisanal diamond supply chain in Sierra Leone, including those who are not supposed to.

The underpayment and inadequate provision of resources to officials perpetuates, rather than prevents, smuggling, illegal mining and illicit dealing. Police officers continue to use their monopoly on violence and cursory justice to extort bribes in order to allow diamonds to enter illegal channels.[22] Mines wardens continue to take bribes to turn a blind eye and misreport events.[23] Mines wardens typically ask miners for the cost of their transport in coming to the mining site to settle a dispute or to demarcate boundaries. Miners noted that mines wardens have expectations based on historic privileges that come with the job, and that it is likely that officials will be corrupt when they are dealing with diamonds because 'with diamonds [*inaudible*] everybody thinks you just get rich overnight. You don't expect be a poor man when you're in the diamond industry. So no matter how much money somebody gives to you, you just consider it small money compared to what he gets in the diamonds'.

In order to encourage industry officials to be less corrupt, workshop participants suggested that a structure be put in place that provides them with incentives to do their job appropriately, the premise being that the more illegal activities they prevent and the more legal activities they encourage, the more benefits they should receive on their jobs (e.g. motorbikes) and individually (e.g. cash or rice bonuses). One miner suggested that rotating the wardens

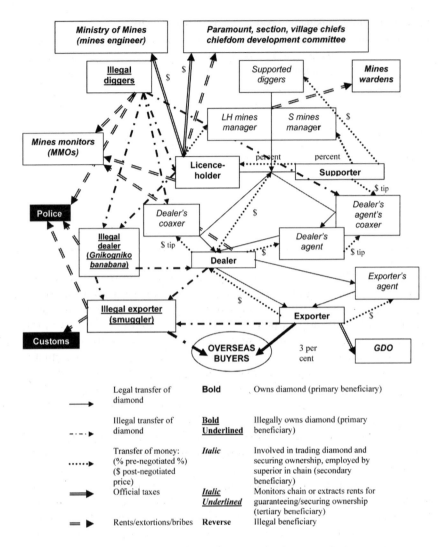

Figure 15.4 Primary, secondary and tertiary beneficiaries in the artisanal diamond supply chain

between places would make it harder for them to extort tips because they would have less knowledge of winnings. Another suggested the opposite. He believed monitors should be local to the mining communities as then they would have a greater loyalty and accountability to the community, and a personal stake in increasing the community's revenues through the Diamond Area Community Development Fund by encouraging legal mining and marketing.[24]

A member of the MMR indicated that the relationship between the ministry and the police is very poor because the latter have their own division concerned with mining-related crime, and do not coordinate their efforts with the former.

This is a waste of resources and leads to incomplete knowledge on either side. Furthermore, a source who acted as an arbitrator in disputes between dealers, miners and diggers claimed that he prefers not to call the police in such instances, as the police will tend to intervene on the side of whoever can pay the most, be it cash or a sheet of zinc, regardless of whose rights have been violated. Although efforts have been made by partner governments and multilateral institutions such as DFID, USAID and the Extractive Industries Transparency Initiative to reduce corruption, further assistance is needed to enable the police and other officials to exercise their authority appropriately, act in the interest of the law, and protect the rights of all Sierra Leoneans. As soon as the justice system is amended and once the political will is instilled, real progress can be made in bringing to account officials who abuse their positions in all branches of national and local government.

An opportunity for countering corruption among state officials lies in making explicit the importance of effective legal enforcement in preventing smuggling as a strategy of avoiding war in the future for the sake of whichever community they most identify with. While most interviewees identified most strongly with their respective tribe, there is also a nascent nationalism sparked by the war, which could be exploited to encourage officials to perform their roles responsibly. In his article on the imbrications between oil and community in Nigeria, Watts (2004: 211) notes that 'Nation-building...rests in its modern form on a sort of calculation, integration, and state and bureaucratic rationality which the logic of rent-seeking, petro-corruption, ethnic spoils and state multiplication works to systematically undermine'. Could the nurturing of a sense of community, be it based on nation or chiefdom, be used to undermine the allure of corruption in the surveillance and disciplining of the diamond complex? One mines monitoring officer said that this is exactly what is happening in Kono. According to the officer, the training and logistical support provided by USAID's Diamond Sector Reform Programme has encouraged monitors to be 'more nationalistic in their approach to the job' and, because of this, 'the monitoring (has) improved'.

Conclusion

This overview of artisanal diamond mining in Kono District, Sierra Leone, has been largely descriptive. This conclusion considers the implications of some of these findings for development practitioners who are seeking to make diamonds work for peace and prosperity, not poverty and war, in line with the objectives of the Kimberley Process and the DDI.

First, declining productivity is making artisanal mining decreasingly viable in traditional mining areas. This calls for attention to be given to the likely impacts of this transition on the chiefdoms suffering decline and those experiencing growth in artisanal mining. This will help these chiefdoms, and the people who live and work there, to adjust to the changing livelihood and revenue-earning opportunities, and the externalities which arise with these socio-environmental changes.

Second, corruption is still pervasive in the licensing procedure, with chiefs and officials continuing to accept 'handshakes' (bribes). Access to land is also inequitable, with people being discriminated against in the licensing procedure based on their identity (gender, tribe, age, relationship with the community, etc), wealth (ability to give 'handshakes') and social capital (position in the networks of patrimony and patriarchy which continue today). This discrimination denies certain people opportunities in the industry, and is likely to generate grievances in the new political economy, which is supposed to offer fairer opportunities for everyone.

Third, miners are businesspeople. Their operations are not erratic and simplistic, but require skill and a good sense for business. Mining is conducted with an entrepreneurial rather than casino mentality, as is commonly commented. Furthermore, diggers require skilling in order to carry out their jobs productively. This challenges the view that mining is an unskilled occupation and one to be discouraged, which was an opinion expressed by several elite interviewees. This prejudice may unhelpfully impede efforts to transform the image of diamonds into a force for prosperity and not war because it discourages donors from investing in improving productivity (for example, through provision of training in business skills).

Fourth, this analysis challenges the assumption that the supporter-miner relationship is necessarily one based on exploitation in which the miner will often find himself in a position of debt bondage. Importantly, this research reveals that the supporter–miner relationship is more than just a business strategy in the majority of cases; it is also a livelihood strategy, which enables vulnerable people to cope with idiosyncratic risk events by establishing social relations with a more powerful community member who will provide relief when required. Only those individuals willing to de-emphasize relief and dependency in favour of higher returns and greater independence are likely to participate in schemes designed to formalize the industry. Unless something else is devised with the explicit intention of incorporating the more vulnerable into the legal system, then those who are unable or unwilling to mine formally are likely to continue to mine illegally. Legalizing land for *gado* and overkicking activities would create a legal option – and reduce risks of persecution – for such people. In short, vulnerable people find that supported mining brings (at least a sense of) security.

Lastly, artisanal diamond mining in Kono has a variety of modes of production, which present different challenges to the formalization of activities. Indeed, people's motivations for mining illegally extend beyond the fulcrum of relative profitability to considerations of possibility (some people are just not welcome at legal operations) and flexibility (some people do not wish to mine full-time but on an occasional basis, in combination with their other, principal livelihood). The people most likely to mine illegally are those who have some immunity (e.g. they are protected by 'big-men' such as chiefs), those who seek flexibility (e.g. Konos who wish to combine overkicking, say, with their farming or tailoring), those who seek independence (e.g. they wish to have a greater share of the winnings but find it hard to get a licence or to be included in licensed operations, such as women), and those who have limited alternatives for coping with their extreme vulnerability (e.g. war widows). It may be of great utility for practitioners and researchers to move past common assumptions on the reasons why people mine illegally (or rather, why they do not mine legally), on what the tradeoffs are in choosing between legal and illegal mining, and what, therefore, these diggers' and miners' priorities are.

CHAPTER 16

Perspectives on diamond mining and public health in Akwatia, Ghana

Kaakpema Yelpaala and Saleem H. Ali

This chapter examines public health challenges in Akwatia, Ghana's largest diamond-production town. Environmental health issues related to mining have received an increasing amount of attention in recent years (Pyatt and Grattan, 2001; Donoghue, 2004; Ross and Murray, 2004), in particular the health burden of mercury when used in small-scale gold mining (Eisler, 2003), as well as the rise in the incidence of HIV/AIDS in mining communities (Elias and Taylor, 2001). Studies have shown that mercury used during the amalgamation process in gold-mining has a detrimental impact upon the health of miners and the communities situated in close proximity to sites (van Straaten, 2000a; Ogola, Mitullah and Omulo, 2002). But diamond mining does not involve intensive chemical processes and hence has been neglected as a public health concern. Although the health impacts of diamond mining in Akwatia are not linked to environmental contamination, there are some important public health questions related to access to health care, health status and health promotion that this chapter addresses.

Methodology

Data for this chapter were collected via a combination of bibliographic research carried out in the US and Ghana, and field research in Akwatia. Fieldwork for the research project spanned from July to August 2003. Both qualitative and quantitative research techniques were employed to collect data on the mining industry in Ghana, mining practices in Akwatia, mining-related sickness and information from the major diamond-mining company operating in Akwatia. This process included structured interviews with miners, mining officials, government officials and local community members. Interviews were recorded as text immediately after being conducted. Recording devices were not used during interviews, given the sensitivity of the topic to the region and the possibility of getting erroneous or misleading feedback from respondents.

Diamond mining in Ghana: an overview

The mining sector has made noteworthy contributions to foreign-exchange earnings and GDP in Ghana. The industry contributes approximately 40 per cent of national gross foreign-exchange earnings and accounts for 5.6 per cent of GDP. In 2000, minerals accounted for 38.96 per cent of total export earnings, followed by cocoa (22.51%) and timber (9.03%) (ISSER, 2001). Ghana is the second-largest producer of gold in sub-Saharan Africa, and has experienced a significant increase in national mining productivity over the last two decades. Between 1983 and 1998, the mining industry brought approximately US$4 billion in foreign direct investment to the country (Aryee, 2001). Although large-scale mining contributes a significant proportion of Ghana's national mining product, small-scale mining activities are also significant, and date back more than 2,000 years.[1]

Akwatia is a small town in the Kwaebibibrem District, Ghana (Eastern Region). Diamonds were first discovered along the Birim River in 1919, in an area 30.5 km northwest of Akwatia (GCD, 1999). Over 100 million carats of diamonds have since been recovered at Akwatia. Ghana Consolidated Diamonds (GCD) is the chief producer of diamonds in the town and the country, in possession of a concession area of 480 square kilometres in the Birim diamond field and Kobriso Gold Concession (GCD, 1999). Historically, mining has brought economic benefits to Akwatia, including employment and poverty alleviation.

For many years, GCD's large-scale mine production eclipsed that of artisanal (diamond) mining. There has been a steady decline in national diamond mining production over the past two decades, but small-scale diamond mining product has increased exponentially. Between 1980 and 1989, the artisanal mining sector produced 207,272 carats of diamonds, in comparison with 5,328,054 carats by GCD (GCD, 2003). In contrast, between 1990 and 1999, small-scale diamond mining output rose sharply to 4,637,093 carats, while GCD production declined by about 50 per cent to 2,244,240 carats. In 1980, artisanal mining accounted for less than 1 per cent of total diamond-mining product in Ghana, but by 1989, it accounted for 53 per cent; by 1999, it was the source of approximately 70 per cent of national diamond output. This paralleled a decrease in production by GCD, from 99 per cent of total diamond-mining production in 1980, to 47 per cent in 1989 and 30 per cent in 1999.

The primary driving force behind the increase in artisanal mining activities in Akwatia was GCD's decision to begin selling licences to small-scale miners to mine its concession (Iddirisu and Tsikata, 1998). The move made practical business sense at the time because in 1992, GCD was granted permission to sell diamonds independently of the PMMC, through its own selling company (Tsikata, 1997). The main small-scale mine site in Akwatia is Saltpond, which is located on the GCD premises; prospective miners are required to obtain licences to mine from either the Minerals Commission or the mining company.[2]

Mining, environmental health and economic development

The connections between a healthy environment and healthy productive communities are significant. There is a combination of physical, chemical, biological, political, social, economic and cultural factors that relate to how people experience the environment around them (Corvolán et al., 1999). From an environmental health perspective, these complex interactions mandate that issues are not only addressed in the health sector, but also as broader problems of every segment of society.[3]

The connections between economic development and health are also salient. A cornerstone policy document that addressed health and development in the 1990s was the World Bank 1993 World Development Report entitled *Investing in Health* (World Bank, 1993). In recognition of this important topic in the health sector, the former WHO director-general Gro Harlem Brundtland established the Commission on Macroeconomics and Health (CMH) in January 2000 to assess the interrelationship between health and global economic development.[4]

Attention has been given to the occupational and environmental health impact of mining practices for artisanal and large-scale miners and communities in close proximity. Health and safety risks associated with small-scale and large-scale mining are complex, and depend on the mineral mined, depth of mining and scale of operation (Ahern and Stephens, 2001). Migratory labour at mines in African countries such as South Africa has been identified as a major factor in the spread of HIV/AIDS (Jochelson, Mothibeli and Ledger, 1991; Campbell and Williams, 1999; Campbell, 2000).

Small-scale gold mining, which involves chemical processes to extract gold, and its associated health and environmental impact is a topic that has attracted more attention in recent years. Worldwide, artisanal miners use mercury in the gold amalgamation process, which has been documented to have a negative environmental and health impact in a number of countries, including Brazil, French Guiana, Ghana, the Philippines, Tanzania and Zimbabwe (Malm, 1998; Frery et al., 2001).

Diamond mining and health challenges in Akwatia

Chemical environmental contamination is not a major health issue in Akwatia because diamond mining does not feature chemical processes. However, there are health problems directly and proximately related to mining in Akwatia. Ghana is malaria-endemic; the disease accounts for 43 per cent of total outpatient morbidity in the country, and 38 per cent in the Eastern Region, where Akwatia is located (Ghana Ministry of Health, 2001). Malaria is also the leading cause of outpatient cases at St Dominic's Hospital, the major healthcare provider in Akwatia (St Dominic's Hospital, 2001).[5] The diamond extraction activities carried out by both legal operators on GCD's sites and illegal *galamsey* miners create large pits which fill with water during the rainy season. Stagnant water is a breeding ground for *Anopheles* mosquitoes, the vector of transmission for malaria in African countries.

Standing water from mining activities is a commonly cited problem in both gold and diamond-mining communities in Ghana, and other parts of the world (Clarke, 1998; Dianou and Poda, 1999). In a study on mining in Tarkwa, one of Ghana's largest gold production areas, Akabzaa and Darimani (2001) pointed out that many people in Tarkwa complained that the intensity of both large- and small-scale mining activities increased malaria cases.[6] The Wassa West District, where Tarkwa is located, has the highest prevalence of malaria in the Western Region. Because Ghana is malaria-endemic, it would be unreasonable to claim that malaria cases are related to mining alone; however, mining activities certainly facilitate and increase the spread of the disease. In Akwatia, though it is known that standing water likely increases malaria-related morbidity, according to health officials in the area, there have been no substantial or sustained interventions made by GCD to drain these pits, or to determine cost-effective measures for mitigating malaria-related morbidity.

In an informal interview, a company official explained that unless GCD oversees the filling of pits, no reclamation will take place. Vegetation subsequently grows and covers them; these pits can become death traps, posing a health and safety risk for Akwatia residents. To avert some of the land degradation and accidents related to the described hazards, between 2000 and 2002, GCD pledged over US$75,000 towards filling open pits from its mining activities, using 420,400 m³ of gravel (GCD, 2000).[7] Its report also points out that financial resources are limited, preventing full reclamation of all mined-out areas (GCD, 2000).

Land degradation from illicit mining activities reduces biodiversity, and can subsequently decrease the availability of medicinal plants (Ayitey-Smith, 1989; Barbier, 1989; Biodiversity Support Programme, 1993; Savannah Resources Management Project, 2000). A local herbalist certified by the Traditional Medical Practitioners Association in Ghana (TMPAG) claimed that the mining activities of *galamsey* destroy medicinal plants that are used for treating a variety of ailments, including anaemia, asthma, gonorrhea, measles and typhoid. The healer did indicate that it was still possible to find the herbs but he often had to travel longer distances to obtain plants that were once found near his shop. This illuminates the potential of mining activities to deplete local natural resources that can treat the health problems of people in Akwatia and surrounding areas.

GCD has a hospital, St Dominic's, on the company's grounds to serve the healthcare needs of its company workers, their dependants and the people of Akwatia; however, it is severely underresourced (GCD, 2001). The company takes various measures to minimize occupational and safety hazards, in accordance with Ghana's national policy. In 2000, there were only three fatalities on the company's grounds (GCD, 2001). Historically, GCD has provided drinking water to the residents of Akwatia from a water tower, but in recent years it has not been able to treat the water because of limited financial resources. This has been cited as a major source of waterborne diseases, including diarrhoea, cholera and typhoid. Neither diarrhoeal disease nor typhoid is a significant cause of morbidity at St Dominic's Hospital; they are the 12th and 8th ranking causes of outpatient morbidity at the hospital (St Dominic's Hospital, 2001). Nevertheless, community members and doctors note that this decrease in waterborne diseases is owed chiefly to the increased sales of bottled water in the area. See Table 16.1 for a summary of causes of outpatient morbidity in Ghana.

HIV/AIDS and mining in Akwatia: a looming problem?

A number of seminal studies have shown the interrelationship between migration, sexual networking, social and familial disruption, and the transmission of HIV/AIDS in mining communities (Meekers, 2000). Although the focus of this chapter is not mining and HIV/AIDS, it is important to take note of the issue as it relates to the Akwatia case study. Since HIV first emerged on the scene in Ghana in the mid-1980s, HIV/AIDS cases have risen. According to UNAIDS, at the end of 2003, HIV prevalence for people between the ages of 15–49 was 3.1 per cent (range 1.9–5.0%). In Ghana, HIV/AIDS is a heterosexual epidemic, following the broader trend of HIV transmission in sub-Saharan Africa. Women bear the brunt of the epidemic because of a combination of biological, sociocultural and gender-related factors: two women are infected with HIV/AIDS for every man in Ghana. Some 80 per cent of HIV transmission in the country occurs through heterosexual unprotected sexual intercourse, 15

Table 16.1 Top five causes of outpatient morbidity: national level, Eastern Region, Kwaebibirem District, St Dominic's Hospital (GCD Hospital), 2001*

	Ghana	Eastern Region	Kwaebibirem District	St Dominic's Hospital
1	Malaria	Malaria	Malaria	Malaria
2	Upper respiratory tract infection	Pregnancy and related complications	Diarrhoeal disease	All other diseases*
3	Diarrhoeal disease	Upper respiratory tract infection	All other diseases*	Gynaecological disorder
4	Diseases of skin and ulcer	Gynaecological disorder	Upper respiratory tract infection	Pregnancy and related complications
5	Accidents (fracture and burns)	Accidents (fracture and burns)	Accidents (fracture and burns)	Hypertension

*The District Level Ministry of Health Outpatient Morbidity Tally Sheets do not identify what specific diseases are classified as 'All other diseases'. The same applies for St Dominic's Hospital.

per cent is attributed to perinatal transmission and 5 per cent through blood transfusion (UNAIDS, 2003).

According to health officials in Akwatia, HIV/AIDS is a significant problem. Residents have minimal access to comprehensive prevention, care and treatment services; moreover, little is known about HIV/AIDS in Akwatia as it relates to mining. The incidence of HIV in Akwatia is nearly three times the national prevalence rate, recorded at 8.5 per cent in 2003 (Ghana NACP, 2003). In its 2003 report, the Ghana National AIDS/STI Control Programme (NACP) highlighted the growing HIV incidence at a number of sentinel sites, including mine sites and ports.[8] The NACP reports that at 10 sentinel sites in the country, including Obuasi, Ghana's largest gold-mining site, HIV prevalence in 2002 was 50 per cent higher than in 2000. At a conference on artisanal mining in 2003, Benjamin Aryee, the director of the Minerals Commission in Ghana, emphasized the growing challenges related to HIV/AIDS in Ghana's mining areas (Aryee, 2003b).

Gold-mining companies and the government of Ghana appear to be engaging in positive public–private partnerships to combat HIV/AIDS. For example, Ashanti Goldfields[9] has instituted a programme of distributing condoms with pay packets, and has managed to significantly reduce the number of HIV-infected employees. At the Obuasi mine, which employs more than 7,000 miners, detected HIV cases fell from 262 in 1998 to 62 in 2003 (British Broadcasting Corporation, 2003). In November 2003, Ashanti Goldfields launched its second HIV/AIDS awareness day to sensitive employees and the community at large about HIV/AIDS to make informed choices to prevent the spread of the virus (PANA, 2003). The company has also formed a partnership with the African Medical Relief Foundation (AMREF) to reduce the spread of HIV at all its mines across Africa. However, the prevalence of HIV/AIDS in the diamond-mining sector has not received this degree of attention.

A framework: the need for more robust understanding of the links between environment and health challenges in Akwatia

The DPSEEA framework is commonly used to examine environmental health issues (Briggs, 1999). According to the framework, **D**riving forces such as economic policies and population growth create **P**ressures on the environment, which alter its **S**tate. This altered state of the environment subsequently affects environmental **E**xposures of people within a defined space, which can have negative health **E**ffects. Once this framework has been established, **A**ction can be taken at each level of the framework to mitigate negative health outcomes related to environmental factors. As has been shown, GCD policy changes, as well the evolution of national policy measures for mining, have been the principal driving forces behind increased diamond-mining activity, which has exerted various pressures on the environment, manifested as land degradation in the case of Akwatia. Pressures on the environment alter human interactions with the environment (exposure), in turn, affecting health. Policy intervention is necessary to address each level of this framework.

In Akwatia, as has been seen, there is a need for selecting strong environmental health indicators that can be used to address health issues. Health-related environmental monitoring mandated in mining areas under Ghana's national environmental policy include the monitoring of air, water, noise, emissions and food contamination. There is a need for a study in Akwatia to investigate whether or not the described indicators apply, and how significant the links are between the various components of this DPSEEA framework. This will allow for the determination of the best stage of the framework, and help decide which action(s) should be taken to address health problems related to mining discovered through qualitative investigation.

Conclusion

Mining has positive returns in Akwatia and for Ghana's economy, including foreign exchange, employment and governmental revenue. However, the extent of localized health benefits from operations and revenue accrued from mining activities in Akwatia is questionable. As has been explained in this chapter, there are a number of health problems in Akwatia, some of which have stronger links to mining activities than others. Moreover, services from the GCD hospital are impoverished, and few ancillary health promotion activities and vector control programmes have been implemented by GCD.

The World Health Organization (WHO) defines health as 'a state of complete physical, mental and social well-being and not merely the absence of disease or infirmity'. In the context of sustainable development and the environment, it is important to keep in mind how efforts to bolster the Ghanaian economy and the quality of life of the people may also have detrimental environmental health impacts. If these negative links exist, policymakers and researchers are challenged to find ways of producing sound, convincing data. Much of the information provided has been qualitative in nature, pulled together through field research and informal interviews. This indicates the need for a stronger quantitative analysis of the impact of mining on health in Akwatia in order to produce sound data to justify the implementation of the most cost-effective interventions which will address the region's health problems as they relate to mining activities.

To summarize, achieving good health and living in a healthy environment are justifiable rights of any person, and should be at the centre of any major governmental policies (Sen, 2001). In recognition of this fact, the Ghanaian government recently established a country branch of the Commission on Macroeconomics and Health to begin building the foundations to address this major issue for economic development (Ghana Macroeconomics and Health Initiative, 2002). In the context of Akwatia, a fundamental question arises about economic development and health when a small town can be the source of

US$48 million in diamond-mining revenue, but its people do not have widespread access to clean drinking water or other health-improving interventions. Although GCD should be held accountable for the social needs of Akwatia community members, the government is also accountable. Responsibility to improve health and the quality of life in Akwatia also lies in the remit of the policy and programme planning of local, regional and government officials. Gaining insight into questions of economic development, environmental degradation and health are critical to building sustained and effective interventions to bolster health and the quality of life, while simultaneously improving economic livelihoods.

CHAPTER 17

Socioeconomic, environmental and policy implications of alluvial diamond mining in the Birim diamondiferous field, eastern Ghana

Frank K. Nyame and S. K. A. Danso

Alluvial diamond mining in the Birim diamondiferous field in the Akwatia area, eastern Ghana, was for a very long time carried out by large-scale companies. The Akwatia mine commenced operation in the 1920s. It was initially owned by the Consolidated African Selection Trust (CAST), which operated the mine from pre- to post-independence Ghana until 1982, when the-then government took over ownership and renamed the company Ghana Consolidated Diamonds (GCD). Both CAST and GCD exploited diamond-bearing gravels in valleys and terraces in the drainage basin of the Birim River. During the period, small-scale diamond mining was of very little significance, apart from a few people who practised the trade using rudimentary techniques usually on the outer fringes of the company's vast concession. For nearly three decades, however, small-scale diamond mining has gained prominence, aided by the Small-Scale Gold Mining Law (PNDC Law 218 of 1989), which more or less legalized the sector (Hilson, 2002f; UNECA, 2002a; UNECA, 2002b). Numerous small-scale mine operators currently exploit diamonds in the concession areas of GCD according to a symbiotic arrangement, locally termed the tributor system, in which GCD leases out small plots of land in their concession to small-scale miners (Nyame and Danso, 2004). This chapter not only documents some pertinent socioeconomic and environmental issues resulting from the dynamics of the alluvial diamond-mining activities at Akwatia but also examines their significance in terms of policy in the small-scale mining sector in general.

Akwatia and its environs have served as, and continue to be, the hub of the alluvial diamond-mining industry in Ghana. For a long time diamond mining thrived on a more or less formal and/or regularized system, under which GCD owned and/or acquired vast stretches of land in the Birim drainage basin for exploration and exploitation of alluvial diamonds. Like most mining concerns at their onset, establishment of the large-scale alluvial mine in the early part of the century brought with it many and varied socioeconomic benefits to the area and the national economy as a whole. Provision of infrastructure in the form of roads, health and educational facilities, together with employment opportunities for many people from far and near, directly led to a vibrant local economy, which ultimately resulted in the Akwatia Township. Fuelled by economic prospects and the potential for skills acquisition, there was a continued influx of migrants, both skilled and unskilled. These individuals were mainly seeking jobs at the mine but many found employment in the array of opportunities created by the mine's establishment. Secondary industries in the banking, telecommunications and transportation sectors were also established mainly by private companies to not only service but also actively support the burgeoning diamond industry. Farmers, petty traders and many people also flocked to the area to undertake various economic ventures. All of these activities immensely contributed to a rapid growth in population in the otherwise small villages and towns in the area. The net result was a knockon effect which led to, among other things, a plethora of changes in the social, cultural, economic and political landscape of the area. Following nationalization, however, a combination of factors ushered in a systematic period of downscaling or downsizing of GCD, which, ironically but almost simultaneously, has led to increased small-scale mining activity in the area.

Study area and methods

The dominant tribe in Akwatia is Akan – specifically, Akims – but many people from all over the country have settled in the area as farmers and petty traders, as have several generations of mineworkers and their dependants. The most prominent topographic feature is the Atiwa Range, which is forested and extends for several kilometres. Apart from this major feature, most of the land is low-lying and in some places, extensive marshlands occur. The area is drained by the Birim River, a tributary of the Pra River. The Birim drainage basin comprises many small rivers, most of which have headwaters in the Atiwa Forest. The vegetation is semi-deciduous forest and the Atiwa and Ayaola forest reserves in the west and east, respectively, are the major forest reserves in the area. The population density in the area is estimated at nearly 130 persons per km^2 compared with an average of approximately 110 persons per square kilometre for the Eastern Region. The fairly high population density, presumably resulting from an influx of migrants in search of work at the mine and local farms, exerts tremendous pressure on the natural resource base in the area. Available data indicate roughly 62 per cent of the population is aged between 15 and 64 years, 36 per cent between 0 and 14, and only about 3 per cent above 64 years (Kesse Tagoe and Associates, 2000). Many of the inhabitants engage in subsistence agriculture of food and cash crops, mainly rice, maize, plantain, cocoa and sugarcane. Petty trading of foodstuffs and basic consumer items are undertaken by some individuals, especially women. Artisanal mining is also actively carried out by certain groups, including children and the aged. A very brisk but informal diamond trade goes on at Akwatia, where sellers and buyers of diamonds won mainly from the area meet to transact business.

Data for this study were obtained through several visits to the study area. At the Akwatia mine site, mine officials and workers were interviewed for information on alluvial diamond mining. Field visits were then made to several abandoned and active mining sites, those of GCD and, subsequently, small-scale operations. Interactions with people at various extraction sites, together with observations at sites of interest, produced a wealth of information.

Socioeconomic and environmental factors

Large-scale mining (GCD) compared with small-scale mining

The socioeconomic and environmental factors at play in the Akwatia area may be viewed in the context of the spatial and temporal relationships involving the operations of GCD, a relatively large-scale company, and the numerous resident small-scale miners. The area falls within the Birimian rock formation of Ghana (Figure 17.1), which also hosts numerous gold deposits (Kesse, 1985). The diamond-bearing gravels may have been deposited some hundreds of thousands of years ago from eroded and/or transported rock material, the source of which has not yet been determined. During its tenure, CAST established its head office at Akwatia and undertook massive infrastructural development in the form of buildings, plant and equipment, road networks, schools and hospitals. The company also provided employment for an array of expatriates, as

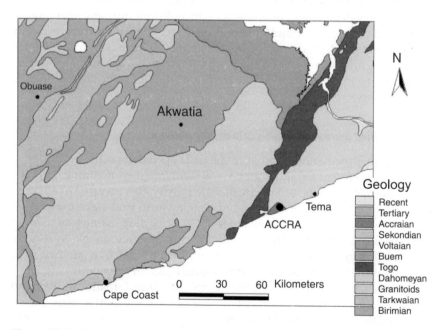

Figure 17.1   Basic geology of Akwatia

well as skilled and unskilled workers both from the area and beyond. Various communities in the concession area experienced growth and/or increases in population, were linked with road networks and were provided with pipe-borne water and electricity. Whereas some communities benefited directly from the mine's operations, others profited from secondary industries that surfaced in the area to service the mine's operations and workers.

It is apparent that up until the late 1980s, the socioeconomic activities in the area were more or less intimately dependent upon the economic perform-ance and health of CAST (and subsequently, GCD), with several people either in the direct employ of these companies or working as direct and indirect dependants of the mine and/or its mineworkers. Many such people acquired skills in various trades. Small-scale mining remained either insignificant in terms of scale of activity or was limited to a small group of people who won diamonds outside or on the fringes of the company's concessions; activities may have also taken place ostensibly to supplement income between farming periods. As the company became starved of enough investment to even re-place obsolete equipment, the extraction of diamonds on a small scale gained prominence to such an extent that GCD managers had no choice but to enter into a marriage of convenience with the numerous operators under the tribu-tor system (Nyame and Danso, 2004). Meanwhile, downsizing of GCD's opera-tions caused, among other things, a massive retrenchment of the workforce, which, in turn, directly resulted in loss of income and livelihoods not only for mineworkers but also their numerous dependants both inside and outside the area. Other important aspects of GCD's economic downtown – as is the case in most resource-dependent communities – included an outward migration of people and skills; collapse and/or relocation of secondary industries, including farming; and the deterioration of infrastructure (Seidman, 1993). The overall impact was most severe among the more vulnerable groups such as the aged, youth and women, most of whom continue to suffer from neglect and ex-treme poverty.

Factors behind increased small-scale mining activity

Not long after the nationalization of the GCD operation (at the beginning of the 1990s), there was a gradual shift in scale and intensity of mining, from the large-scale operations of GCD to small-scale activity; this occurred in response to a lack of investment in capital and equipment to undertake exploration work. Many workers made redundant by GCD, struggling to find jobs to offset the generally high cost of living in mining communities, unable to relocate and resorting to desperate measures to earn a living, decided to put their skills acquired at the mine to use in the area (Figure 17.2). An apparently correlative but inverse relationship between the health of GCD and small-scale diamond mining, therefore, began. Thus downsizing of GCD's activities were, almost concurrently, complemented by intense but illegal small-scale mining activity in various parts of its concessions. This served to attract more people into the

Figure 17.2 Informal diamond miners at work in Akwatia

initially illegal but burgeoning small-scale diamond-mining sector, which may have curbed the outward migration of some redundant mineworkers at the time.

This study has also revealed that small-scale diamond-mining methods are becoming more complicated and capital-intensive. Mechanized equipment, including bulldozers, heavy duty trucks and water pumps, has been introduced, which has facilitated increased production. Interviews carried out with certain small-scale mine operators suggest some sort of pseudo-plant pool is being coordinated by sponsors or financiers who make this equipment readily available on credit. This is generally on an hourly or daily basis, with the proviso that diamonds won are sold to them (i.e. sponsors) or a representative of the sponsor at the site of production, who then markets the diamonds and deducts the cost involved. The socioeconomic implications of such arrangements and similar agreements require careful study.

One important consequence of the intense small-scale mining activity in the area is the reinvigoration of the informal diamond market at Akwatia. Even though this market has had a very long history of existence, it would appear that increased production from small-scale miners has spawned a very brisk diamond market with an increase in both the volume of trade and dealers (sellers and buyers) in the past decade. Gberie (2003) suggested that smuggling of conflict diamonds from other countries in the West African subregion has probably accounted for increased annual volumes of diamonds purchased and exported from Ghana. Nyame and Danso (2004), however, contend the increase could have resulted from increased output from small-scale diamond mining on-site: the brisk diamond market appears to fuel increased small-scale mining activity, as traders from both far and near constantly congregate at Akwatia to trade in diamonds.

Environmental considerations

Various environmental challenges are presented by both the large-scale (GCD) and small-scale diamond mining activities in the area. For a company such as GCD that continues to struggle to cope with using obsolete equipment and even to pay the salaries of the few dedicated staff at post, economic considerations may far outweigh environmental concerns. The usual environmental issues of concern associated with surface mining activities of whatever form (i.e. land degradation, loss of biodiversity and pollution of water bodies) may also be prevalent, except that the company's operations generally do not pose much significant threat to the environment in terms of chemicals usage. Destruction of the physical landscape, however, may be much more prominent.

In the past several years, vast pools of stagnant water have collected in several mined-out pits in the concession area, since the costs involved in reclamation were obviously beyond the company's financial means. Portions of some river courses were also diverted to make way for mining and were never redirected even after mining, creating what could be called artificial lakes. Mining is, of late, being practised in close proximity to rivers and streams, which could have serious effects on the water levels and ultimately, flow regimes and the dynamics of surface and groundwater flow. This could, in addition, increase the sediment load of rivers, especially during flood, and increase the risk of siltation of river courses. With not much use for waste after processing, mountains of gravel have had to be stockpiled near processing plants. On the positive side, pools of stagnant water could be used for small-scale irrigation schemes to enhance the livelihoods of many farmers engaged in subsistence agriculture. Such water bodies could also be used as demonstration outlets to train farmers, for research purposes, or for aquaculture purposes.

Unlike GCD, the activities of small-scale miners have, as indicated above, experienced a surge not only in terms of numbers of participants but also in economic fortunes. Increasing mechanization of the sector via the introduction of more sophisticated extraction equipment, coupled with the infusion of capital by sponsors in the form of loans retrievable by diamonds won, strongly suggests that activity will continue vigorously for some time. The sheer number of participants involved, the depth of overburden (very small ore-to-waste ratio) and lack of reclamation means that small-scale mining renders the environment the worst casualty in terms of impacts to vegetation, land/soil, biodiversity and water resources. Vast quantities of material are often heaped close to excavated pits or along river banks. Even though the diamond-bearing gravel is, at times, transported to processing centres near rivers far from the extraction site, a great deal of processing (to fine sand before diamonds are handpicked) also occurs in pools of water at the place of extraction (Figure 17.3). These activities likely result in land and soil degradation, increase sediment load and attendant siltation in streams and rivers, and increase turbidity levels in water bodies. In a preliminary study, Nyame and Danso (2004) documented various environmental impacts and the contributory factors resulting from the tributor system of small diamond mining in the Akwatia area.

Policy issues

The nature of alluvial diamond extraction (both large- and small-scale) may have important implications in terms of the general policy in Ghana's mining sector. First, it appears that during the entire period of GCD's state-ownership, attempts were not made to put in place plans for effective maintenance and, more importantly, the replacement of plants and equipment with time. This has resulted in a situation where all plants and equipment have outlived their usefulness. The power consumption of even those plants that are still 'alive' is said to be so high and efficiency so low, that the company is better off not using them in all parts of the production process. Second, the inability of government to attract investment to recapitalize the company or to make a firm decision on the company's future has had a profound impact on not only the entire workforce but also the Akwatia area as a whole. The company has been on divestiture for decades, with no firm decision yet on its future. As is often

Figure 17.3 Processing of diamond gravels on site

the case, there seems to be no laid down or clearcut policy on divestiture in the mining law(s). In addition, compensation packages, whenever applicable, are woefully inadequate. Furthermore, uncertainties often surround the procedural arrangements of the divestiture process itself, most of which tend to be shrouded in secrecy. The inordinately long period and the challenges imposed by the decision to put the company on divestiture, coupled with the lack of investment capital from the government, have all culminated in severe socioeconomic strain on the area, a necessary outlet of which has been the upsurge in small-scale mining activity and the decreased influence of GCD.

Third, there is a need to critically assess the tributor system that is being operated in the diamond mining industry at Akwatia. If studied carefully for its merits and demerits, it could serve as a framework or model in which large-scale mining companies (including those with interests in gold) may be encouraged to offload areas in their concessions to small-scale miners. Such an arrangement could have the potential to reduce conflict on resource utilization between companies and communities and small-scale miners, which are now prevalent in the gold-mining industry in Ghana. Also, ways must be found to mitigate the adverse socioeconomic, environmental and health impacts of artisanal and small-scale mining, especially child labour, truancy among schoolchildren, exposure of children to quick money, with its attendant influence on children maturing and entering married life, and HIV/AIDS and other STDs and drug use.

Conclusion

The current study has demonstrated the need for prompt policy action to tackle the various socioeconomic and environmental issues arising from the complex and dynamic relationships in the alluvial diamond-mining industry in Akwatia. Downsizing and a lack of recapitalization of the large-scale alluvial diamond mine, GCD, has led to intense small-scale mining activity, which, in turn, continues to have a significant impact both positively and negatively on local people and the environment. The government may have to accelerate efforts to either divest the company for private ownership or ensure its survival to avert possible consequences. In either case, a study of the tributor system would go a long way towards improving our understanding of conflict resolution in Ghana's mining sector.

CHAPTER 18

'Live and let live': The relationship between artisanal/small-scale and large-scale miners at Abosso Goldfields, Ghana

Anthony Kwesi Aubynn

In recent years, there has been widespread economic and complementary livelihoods analysis of large-scale mining and ASM. Several studies (ILO, 1999; Hilson, 2001b; D'Souza, 2002) have underscored, in particular, the economic importance of both large-scale mining and ASM, how they can contribute to poverty reduction and their environment impacts.

The case of Ghana has been well documented in the literature. Since 1990, Ghana has produced, on average, 1,000,000 oz of gold and 800,000 carats of diamonds per year. Of these output totals, approximately 100,000 oz (about 10% of national production) and 700,000 carats (about 70% of national production) of gold and diamonds, respectively, originate from the country's ASM operations. Large-scale mining provides direct employment to approximately 15,000 Ghanaians, but 100,000–200,000 people are projected to be directly engaged in ASM, of whom an estimated 30 per cent are women. Since 1989, gold and diamond production from the ASM sector has generated over US$400 million.

In recent years, land-use conflicts between Ghana's ASM and large-scale mining parties have escalated, due in large part to diminished prospects for underground mining and the rapid rise of open-pit mining. Today, in the mining regions of the southern portion of the country, most artisanal and small-scale miners operate either on the concessions of large-scale miners or as uncomfortable neighbours competing for the same mineral resources. Although there is a widespread suggestion that the relationship between Ghana's large-scale, and artisanal and small-scale miners has deteriorated under reform, there continues to be minimal information on the current state of affairs. This raises the following question: what is the nature of relations between the country's ASM and large-scale mine operators, and can these parties coexist peacefully and harmoniously?

Surprisingly, this question has not been adequately raised or addressed. In recent years, the issue of relationships between large-scale and ASM operators has exercised many government regulatory agencies in Ghana, including the

Minerals Commission and the Environmental Protection Agency (EPA); industry associations, such as the Ghana Chamber of Mines; and the companies themselves. It is now widely recognized that good relationships between these parties are crucial. However, very little has been done to improve the understanding of the nature of such problems and more importantly, to unravel the causes of the often conflictual consequences of their intercourse. Significantly less has been done to identify policy options for helping to improve relations and reduce conflicts between mine operators. In Ghana, poor policy has been responsible for mutual suspicion, acrimony and a vicious cycle of violent clashes, interspersed by uneasy calm, broken promises and blackmail between the two groups.

Purpose of engagement and data

This chapter examines the relationship between large-scale mining and ASM parties in Ghana, drawing mainly upon the case of Abosso Goldfields (AGL) at Damang in the mining district of Tarkwa, Western Region. The case of AGL is especially attractive because of the company's leadership in deliberately developing a plan of coexistence with ASM. The implications of the current lack of enforcement of the country's mining law with particular reference to 'encroachment' are discussed. The chapter looks in detail at the piecemeal arrangements, devised in the mid-1990s, between AGL and its neighbouring ASM operators, arising out of the latter's encroachment on the former's mining lease area, and the extent to which they have worked.

The central argument is that the absence of clear and enforceable national policies prevents peaceful relations between large-scale mining and ASM parties. The key objective is to underscore the importance of establishing such a policy framework. The AGL experience demonstrates that with an appropriate arrangement, working relationships and partnerships can be established between large-scale mining and ASM, to the mutual benefit of both parties. The AGL experience is worth looking at, as it should address the apparently intractable ASM question in Ghana.

The data presented were collected from local mining documents (obtained from the Minerals Commission, the Mines Department, the Chamber of Mines, etc), corporate reports and previously published studies conducted in this area (Hilson, 2001b; MIME, 2002; D'Souza, 2002; Asante, 2003; Ofei-Aboagye et al., 2004). Media reports and other journal publications also proved to be important sources of background information. Finally, complementary information was obtained through informal interviews with a number of officers employed at large- and small-scale mining operations. The author draws on his own direct experience as a player in negotiating and maintaining arrangements with ASM parties to make sense of the data presented here.

The chapter is organized as follows. The next section examines the situation in Ghana in the 1990s, when large-scale open-pit (surface) mining became widespread; the regulatory environment for mining; and mine operators' perceptions of land ownership rights, disputes over which have fuelled confrontation between resident mining parties. The subsequent sections focus on the Abosso Goldfields experience, and examine the impact of the 'Live and let live' conceptual policy approach introduced by the company. Finally, some conclusions and lessons are drawn.

Prevailing situation and the need for a change in approach

In some countries (e.g. Mali, Niger and Burkina Faso), differentiation is made in law and policy between purely manual artisanal mining, and more mechanized small-scale mining or semi-permanent installations (Hentschel et al., 2002). Such a distinction is of little relevance to Ghana, where the size and mode of operations are almost the same. The terms 'small-scale mining' and 'artisanal mining' are therefore used interchangeably throughout this chapter.

A distinction is, however, made between formally registered operators and illicit *galamsey*.[1] Such a distinction, though artificial and theoretical, is relevant because of its implication for the management of relationships not only between ASM and large-scale mining parties but also between government institutions. Officers at the Minerals Commission and the Precious Minerals and Marketing Corporation (PMMC) estimate that less than 30 per cent of the more than 200,000 ASM operators in the country are duly registered and licensed.

It is against this background that the mining terrain of Ghana in the early 1990s, when large-scale open pit operations began to gain preponderance in the formal mining sector of the country, is examined. It is instructive to describe the complex relationship between land ownership and mineral rights in Ghana, as well as the general perception of local ASM operators towards entitlement to both land and mineral resources. This may help improve the understanding of the defiant posture often associated with illicit *galamsey* operators.

The law, territoriality and ownership

The current legislative framework for mining in Ghana is laid down in the Minerals and Mining Law 1986 (PNDCL 153 (2)), as amended by the Minerals and Mining Amendment Act 1993, Act 475, and modified by the provisions of the Constitution of 1992 (Article 156). By law, mineral deposits in lands (and elsewhere) in their natural state are vested in the president on behalf of, and in trust for, the people of Ghana. Only approximately 20 per cent of Ghana's total land surface is owned by the state. The remaining 80 per cent (under which minerals often occur) are customarily owned by the traditional stools and skins (that is, the chiefs, who 'sit on the stools' and control the land as traditional landowners), who hold such lands in trust for their respective communities. Thus, regardless of who owns the land upon or under which minerals are situated, the exercise of any mineral right requires, by law, a licence to be granted by agents of the state and not the landowner. With regards to the appropriation of rents and revenue accruing from mineral extraction, it was not until 1986, following implementation of the Minerals and Mining Law, that there was a policy in place requiring payment (4% of mineral royalties) to be made to traditional landowners; the state or central government, however, has always held the exclusive right to appropriate lands.

Historically, the motives behind the promulgation of mining laws and regulations in Ghana have been to promote investment in the large-scale mining sector. Until 1989, all ASM was virtually illegal, with mining laws and regulations only minimally addressing the interests of operators in this segment of the economy.[2] In 1989, however, the government passed three key pieces of legislation, which effectively legalized ASM. The first cornerstone piece, the *Small-Scale Gold Mining Law 1989* (PNDCL 218), legalized small-scale gold mining, requiring prospective operators to go through a licensing process. The second piece, the *Mercury Law 1989* (PNDCL 217), was promulgated to allow for the legitimate purchase and use of mercury in gold processing. The final piece, the *Precious Minerals and Marketing Corporation Law 1989* (PNDCL 219) was passed to establish PMMC, which serves as a legitimate sales outlet for the gold and diamonds produced by ASM operators.[3]

In spite of this legislation, which provides an opportunity for miners to regularize and mainstream their operations, more than three-quarters of the ASM population fails to operate within the ambit of the law. The failure of ASM operators to legalize their activities has been largely attributed to the long and cumbersome process of registration.[4] At the two-day National Workshop on Artisanal Mining organized in Accra by Ghana's Centre for Scientific and Industrial Research and the Ministry of the Environment and Science on 29–30 July 2003, participants indicated that the nature of the registration process was a major disincentive for ASM operators to regularize their activities.[5] According to Hilson and Potter (2003), this situation is aggravated by the unavailability of mineralized lands for ASM; many operators, therefore, view the hassle of registration as an exercise in futility.

Violent clashes

During the mid-1990s there was a series of violent confrontations between artisanal miners on the one hand, and large-scale miners and state security forces on the other. The Ghanaian media profiled many of the major clashes, which were characterized by excessive violence and fatalities. In July 1996, for example, a major clash occurred between ASM operators working on the Ashanti Goldfields (AGC) mining lease area and the state security forces at Obuasi, during which an estimated US$10 million in mining equipment was destroyed.[6] Another clash occurred in July 1996 between artisanal miners and a contingent of police on the concession of Barnex in Prestea, some 45 km from Damang. At the same time, Goldfields' operations in Tarkwa were not spared violent clashes amid their preparations to suspend underground operations in favour of the development of surface resources. During one of numerous clashes with encroaching *galamsey* miners, a senior manager of the company was reported to have been brutally assaulted.

Nearly three-quarters of ASM operators interviewed claimed that it was their birthright to mine. As one miner put it:

> This is our own land and we, and not anybody from anywhere, decides how to use it to our benefit. If we can farm on this land, why can't we mine the gold in it?[7]

Responses of this nature resonated during several informal interviews with ASM operators at Damang and Amoanda. From the ASM perspective, the conflictual relationship between indigenous mining groups and large-scale miners is a contest for survival and a fight against the intrusion on what they perceive as their traditional rights to work on the land, whether it is mining or farming. The ASM operators interviewed were mainly local and indigenous people who argued that ownership of the mineral deposits (gold) was their God-given right. They would therefore not compromise their livelihoods on the ground of any statutory laws of the country. But large-scale miners contend that these confrontations are unfortunately necessary to protect their legally exclusive concessions against unlawful encroachment and intrusion. To a certain extent, the confrontations could be interpreted as a contest between traditional rights and legal rights.

Political sensitivity

The control of illicit mining in Ghana has always been a delicate issue, especially since the beginning of constitutional rule in 1993. During the military regime of the Provisional National Defence Council (PNDC) government of the 1980s, it was common to witness police raids on *galamsey* operators in the Wassa West mining district, which occasionally led to the arrest and prosecution of 'culprits'.[8] Controlling illicit mining activities became associated with the use of force and brutality; thus, attempts to enforce legal mining under the new democratic dispensation necessarily were politically sensitive. Evidently, the-then National Democratic Congress (NDC) government did not possess the political will to control ASM operations: the government believed that any attempt to wholeheartedly stop *galamsey* operations without providing acceptable alternative livelihood sources risked putting more people out of jobs, with suicidal political consequences. Needless to say, most of the serious clashes and demonstrations intensified between June and November 1996, when the country was preparing for national elections. The situation seems to be the same under the current New Patriotic Party government (NPP).[9]

Abosso Goldfields and neighbouring ASM

AGL operates an open-pit gold mine with a Carbon-In-Leach (CIL) processing facility near Damang, approximately 29 km north of Tarkwa in the Western

Region of Ghana (Figure 18.1). It was constructed in the late 1980s as a subsidiary of Ranger Minerals, an Australian-based junior mining company, to develop the mineral resources in a 104 km² concession in the Tarkwa and Abosso areas. In February 1990, the company was issued a prospecting licence by the government of Ghana for the above area, and by 1993, had been granted a mining lease of approximately 57 km², extending from Damang in the northwest to the old Abosso mining area towards the southeast.[10]

As with most mining areas in Ghana, AGL's present operation at Damang was preceded by active artisanal mining activities. Available anecdotal evidence suggests that ASM operations in the area provided important geological leads for AGL.[11] Records from PMMC indicate that a small group of ASM operators, consisting of seven cooperatives, was duly registered in accordance with PNDC Law 218 before AGL's prospecting licence was issued in 1990. The mineral cooperatives had licences covering an area of 0.63 km², the last of which expired on 13 November 1996.

A pragmatic shift: the concept of 'Live and let live'

By the mid-1990s, the problem of illicit mining on the concessions of large-scale mining companies had become intractable. Scarcely a week went by without reports of some form of confrontation at one mine operation or another.

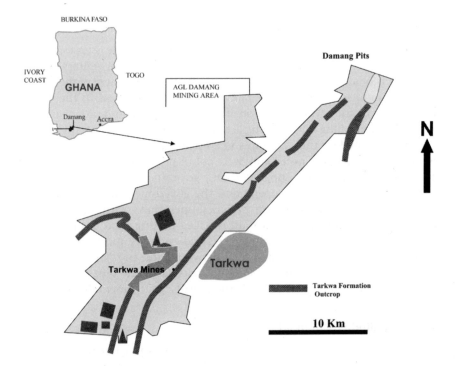

Figure 18.1 Location of AGL's Damang mining area

The resultant economic, social and environmental costs were becoming unbearable. After assessing the nature of the conflicts between ASM and large-scale mining operators in Ghana and elsewhere in the world, AGL officers realized that the company needed to do something different if it was to avoid the same predicaments. The failure of aggressive policies provided a strong case for engineering a paradigm shift towards a more innovative and pragmatic strategy for dealing with problems to ensure that the company operated peacefully, harmoniously and profitably. In line with this need, AGL adopted a more negotiable and compromising approach, which would become encapsulated in the concept of 'Live and let live'. This approach sought to accommodate artisanal miners on AGL's lease area in so far as their operations did not cause operational threats to the company.

According to the management of AGL, the new approach was founded on two key principles. First was the recognition that ASM activities had for a long time been an important activity both socially and economically to the indigenous operators of Damang, Huni-Valley and other surrounding villages. Second, a well-organized and harmonious relationship between artisanal operators would ensure sound and safe mining practices, and also help to eliminate some of the suspicions ASM operators had of government agencies and large-scale mining companies.

Initially, the company adopted a compromised approach by offering to set aside areas for indigenous ASM operators. This gesture met initial difficulties, especially how to confine the operators to their designated areas. Nearly 600 *galamsey* operators intensified their activities and easily encroached on exploration trenches where high-grade gold ores were exposed at drilling sites on the mining concession. Attempts by law enforcement agencies to control the situation often resulted in violent clashes. A typical example was the conflict between *galamsey* and the police at Bompieso, a village close to AGL's concession, in November 1996, which resulted in serious casualties.

Managing the relationship

The new approach required the adoption of a completely new structure and rules. To draw up and agree on the rules that would govern the relationship between AGL officers and ASM operators, a management committee was formed. Efforts were made to ensure that the base of the committee was broad enough to accommodate wide shades of opinion among the stakeholders and to enable open, honest and frank discussions to take place. The committee was comprised of the following groups of people:
- three technical personnel from AGL;
- two artisanal miners, who represented each of the five local communities of Damang, Amoanda, Huni-Valley, Bompieso and Nyamebekyere;
- three district assembly representatives (one from each community);
- chiefs and opinion leaders;
- one district police officer; and

- one officer from the National Bureau of Investigation (BNI).

The committee's task was: to initiate and develop a workable mining policy for AGL and small-scale mining based on the Ghana Mining Regulations' tributor system (LI.665 1970), consistent with the company's new philosophy of accommodation. The committee came up with the following blueprints.

- ASM operators licensed to operate on the concession would operate during the AGL exploration phase. The duration of licences would be for an initial period of two years with the prospect of a further two-year renewal, after which there would be no further renewals.
- In the event that reserves were established by AGL in the area worked by small-scale miners, the government would be notified, and no more small-scale mining licences would be renewed in that area. The company would not be required to compensate small-scale mining licence-holders.
- Holders of small-scale mining licences would not transfer their licences to large-scale mining companies while the AGL prospecting licence remained valid.
- AGL would not be held responsible for any environmental degradation or social disruption caused by ASM operators.
- To help formulate and implement these policies, AGL would appoint and maintain a professional mining engineer to be placed at the disposal of ASM operators.[1]

Ground implementation and trust-building

To ensure the smooth implementation of the new arrangements, the company demarcated an alternative site on an active mining lease area for the short-term relocation of the ASM groups, who were working close to areas earmarked for active mining by the company. Site allocations took cognizance of the proximity to the various groups. For example, ASM operators resident in the Damang area were allocated areas which were closer to the Damang village, while those in Amoanda, Huni-Valley and Bompieso to the north of the operations were awarded areas more northward. To provide some form of permit and authorization for ASM operations and to further control the immigration of artisanal miners from areas outside AGL's catchment communities of Damang Huni-Valley, Amoanda and Bompieso, the indigenous ASM operators from each of the communities were identified and issued photo identity cards (ID cards).

The sudden accommodating attitude of AGL, a large-scale miner, towards ASM operators was a revelation at the time, but ironically raised some doubt in indigenous communities, where people expressed concern about the company's real intentions. For instance, the ID cards generated initial scepticism among local people, who feared that it was a clever ploy by the company to facilitate their arrest for prosecution. There was also concern that openly identifying oneself as a leading *galamsey* operator ran the risk of being blacklisted for future employment in mainstream operations. Some operators also saw it as a ploy to force them to sell their produce to AGL at below-market prices. This confirmed the age-old axiom that trust is a necessary ingredient in any successful human relationship, in this case between ASM and large-scale mining parties.

As a means of building trust and confidence, the company ran a series of educational campaigns and seminars. These sought to underscore the benefit of the new relationship, such as the dissemination of improved safety practices, and to reassure ASM operators of their total ownership and control of operations, including their produce. Crucially, AGL officers informed ASM operators that they were free to sell extracted product to the PMMC gold buyer of their choice.[2]

The operators were also assured that there would be no police harassment, provided that they abided by the mutually agreed rules. The company further demonstrated commitment by providing ASM operators with small inputs such as water pumps, gold pans and mercury retorts. Officers also worked to educate miners on improved technology for better gold recovery.

Impact of 'Live and let live' policy

As previously explained, the overall purpose of the new approach was to ensure mutual peace, safety and environmentally sustainable operations. The ultimate goal was to reduce and eventually remove the ASM operators on AGL's mining lease area.

Profile of indigenous mining population

By December 1996, a total of 740 small-scale miners had registered with AGL (Table 18.1). One year later, the number had dwindled sharply to less than half of this figure (360). A number of factors were responsible for this drastic decline. First, AGL began active recruitment for the commencement of its mine production in early 1997. It appears that AGL and the allied contractors had absorbed a large number of the operators into mainstream mining through the company's local employment programmes.[3] Second, some of the shrewder operators had mobilized sufficient funding to launch their own small-scale

Table 18.1 Details of registered small-scale miners on AGL's concession, December 1996

Community	No. people registered
Damang	120
Huni-Valley	60
Amoanda	120
Bompieso	230
Nyamebekyere	210
Total	740

contracting companies, which provided a host of services to the main company. Finally, most of the non-indigenous operators who failed to secure any gainful employment had returned to their hometowns, particularly during the drought period, which persisted throughout the last quarter of 1996 and the first quarter of 1997, creating a dearth of water for ore processing. This, combined with the global decline in the gold price during the last quarter of 1997, which had adverse effects on the revenue and profitability of artisanal mining overall, prompted many of the operators registered on AGL's concession to entertain employment opportunities elsewhere.

Improved mining and ore-processing methods

In order to ensure that artisanal miners worked safely, achieved high recovery and minimized the environmental effects of their operations, company officials worked diligently to introduce improved methods of mining and ore-processing. It is well known that artisanal mining is a near-surface activity. Operators mine consolidated sandstone and conglomerate bands with shallow overburden using basic implements such as shovels, pickaxes, chisels and hammers. Before AGL's involvement in the ASM project, informal miners in the area scrambled for positions along the strike of the exposed reef under shallow overburden and mined in all directions, creating a vast open stope with no roof support and ventilation channels. Using lanterns fuelled by kerosene, the soot of the lamps created unhealthy working conditions, with increasing levels of carbon dioxide and carbon monoxide.

There were numerous fatalities, generally linked to ground collapse and asphyxiation, and were more pronounced where smuggled explosives were used. With technical assistance from AGL, a room and pillar mining method was introduced for the reef miners. Room and pillar mining is the process whereby rooms are cut into the bed, leaving a series of pillars, or columns, to help support the mine roof and control the flow of air. As mining advances, a grid-like pattern of rooms and pillars is formed. Pillars are left in place in a regular pattern while the rooms are mined out. The move was initially met with resistance, since initial development slowed down production, but seminars were organized for team leaders, who quickly grasped the concept and passed acquired knowledge on to their colleagues in the field.

Occasionally, work on the alluvial surface resulted in fatalities. The alluvial miners tended to undercut the thick overburden; workers often became trapped by overburden collapse. This group of miners received direct field instructions on the risk of undercutting alluvial formations. Here, training centred mainly upon overburden removal: individuals were told, following excavation, to direct sluice box operations into the cavity created, and then spread the barren overburden over the worked-out area. This practice was accepted as a safe and environmentally sound method.

In ore-processing, the traditional practice has been to introduce a high flow of water on sluice boxes filled with ore. The use of high water flow in sluice boxes means that gold nuggets are collected on the blankets, while large quantities of gravels and stones are washed out of the sluice box by the running water. The main problem with this method is that finer-sized gold is also lost, dispensed with the high water flow. Unfortunately, a lower water flow also means more removal of stone by hand on the headboard, and the need to stir the bed to stop it packing down on the sluice box.

Screen headboards and woollen carpets were introduced to replace the traditional wooden sluice box (which featured jute matting) to improve gold-trapping efficiency. Screen headboards were constructed from corrugated roofing sheets, with holes punched through at the base to retain the large oversize stone to allow for small stones and sand, which host gold, to flow over the sluice box (with riffle arrangement). In such a setup, the gravel fed into the screen must be completely soaked with water to ensure all clay and soil lumps are broken up to allow fine materials to pass through the screen. The riffles on the screen headboard act as speed bumps that encourage the settlement of heavy minerals (gold) carried by the passing water current.

The common method of gold recovery in the ASM sector is mercury amalgamation, which has been used in Ghana for over a century; current statutory laws permit its use at the operations of (registered) small-scale mining operators. In order to reduce high levels of environmental contamination resulting from the use of mercury in sluice boxes and reduce exposure, AGL ordered 20 Garret gravity traps, which were distributed freely in the camps. Gravity traps are used to pan the gold concentrate from the sluice box for better recovery of gold nuggets or dust, thus reducing the amount of mercury required for amalgamation. In September 2000, the company, in partnership with the Ghana Association of Artisanal and Small-Scale Miners, the umbrella association for ASM operators, donated eight sets of amalgamated mercury retorts to operators in different catchment communities. The retort not only reduces exposure to toxic mercury but also significantly improves gold recovery.

The successful introduction of such new, albeit simple, technologies requires a change of attitude. Initial resistance by a section of the miners was therefore expected but as time passed, and as others became more acquainted with the introduced methods, they were accepted. For example, at one point, in the minds of some operators, the idea of using gravity traps to pan gold without mercury was totally inconceivable. However, the evidence of improved recovery and decreased exposure to mercury reportedly stimulated a sharp increase in local demand for gravity traps. According to AGL's Small-Scale Mining Supervisor, those who became well vested in the art of panning engaged in concentrate panning for a fee.

Gold production, safety and the environment

Introduction of the abovementioned technology led to improvements in production, safety and environmental management at the ASM operations within the AGL concession (Table 18.2). Company officials placed artisanal

Table 18.2 Gold production under the AGL scheme, 1998

Area	No. of miners	Jan	Feb	Mar	Apr	May	Jun	July	Aug	Sep	Oct	Nov	Dec
Tomento	50	10	8	11	9	8	6	7	12	11	12	13	10
Nyamebekyere	40	6	9	12	8	4	5	7	11	12	12	9	12
Amoanda Alluvials	80	8	6	8	9	5	7	8	13	10	11	11	8
World-Bank	30	10	9	7	8	6	5	8	9	11	14	12	10
Rex North	50	9	10	7	6	2	6	7	10	12	10	8	10
Bompieso Alluvials	35	12	13	9	9	6	7	6	10	11	13	12	17
Bompieso Process Base	25	10	12	11	7	7	7	6	9	10	12	8	12
BCM Old Camp	30	15	13	10	8	6	9	9	11	13	12	12	11
Total	340	80	80	75	64	46	52	58	85	90	96	85	90

gold mine production at 35 oz for the month of January 1997; by August, production had jumped to 368 oz. Production remained consistently high throughout 1998 as well.[4]

Conclusion

This chapter has examined the relationship between illegal ASM operators and their large-scale counterparts in Ghana. Although artisanal gold mining has been carried out in Ghana since time immemorial, the recent increase in open-pit gold mining activity carried out by multinational companies has intensified competition for limited mineralized land resources. The encroachment of ASM operators on concessions demarcated to large-scale mining companies is now a common occurrence; indigenous grassroots operators believe that the acquisition of large tracts of mining lands is an encroachment on their livelihoods. The prevailing legal and traditional interpretation of land-mineral ownership rights, coupled with the lack of political will to enforce laws on illegal encroachment of property, have exacerbated tensions between Ghana's mining parties.

The laws of Ghana allow for the relative exclusivity of right of concession for mining leaseholders, which makes any encroachment for competing activities (i.e. mining) unacceptable. Although it is the duty of the government to ensure the protection of legitimate holders of mining concessions or leases, since the advent of democratic dispensation in Ghana in the early 1990s and regular multiparty elections, ASM operators have created a political niche (which some analysts have described as a form of blackmail) for themselves. This has made successive governments appear unwilling to fully enforce the laws on illicit mining, largely for political purposes: after all, ASM presents major solutions to social problems in the country, providing important sources of employment to a burgeoning group of unemployed youth. The onus for addressing relations between ASM and large-scale mining, therefore, appears to have fallen on the shoulders of companies, which are expected to demonstrate leadership by adopting pragmatic, rather than legal protectionist approaches.

As explained, taking stock of the ineffectiveness of confrontational policy, AGL approached the encroachment problem prevalent on their concessions by adopting a 'Live and let live' strategy: the company permitted artisanal miners to operate on portions of its plot, provided that certain rules were abided by. The move was controversial because the mining laws of Ghana prohibit the mining of gold by unauthorized persons; however, importantly, the move created relatively peacefully conditions, helping to ensure that the activities of the indigenous miners were not impaired. There is consensus among AGL officers that despite potentially compromising its own operations, the company's 'Live and let live' approach was the best policy at the time. As noted, the approach has yielded significant dividends through efficient operations, and more particularly in the area of gold production, safety and environmental management.

The key lesson to be learnt is twofold. First, effective engagement by large-scale mining companies *can* yield mutual dividends. As illustrated here, the case of AGL proves that under the right conditions, ASM and large-scale mining can coexist. This does, however, require adoption of a pragmatic policy, including a commitment to formalizing and improving relationships, and ceding portions of concessions which are only economically viable for ASM. Assistance and capacity-building will pave the way for constructive engagement. It is important to note that the AGL example may not lend itself to ready duplication, as there might be certain peculiarities, such as the number of indigenes or community members directly involved in ASM activity, which have implications for the ability to create internal controls in operations; moreover, such an approach may, in other cases, only provide a temporary respite. Additional problems are likely to arise as the company decides, depending upon the metal price environment, to convert its marginal resources (temporarily ceded to ASM operations) into active mining. The above concerns notwithstanding, the AGL example provides a basis for careful study for possible adaptation.

Second, from the perspective of government, the ASM conundrum could be addressed using a carrot and stick approach. The Ghanaian government must demarcate mineralized areas specifically for ASM. This is an idea which has been discussed regularly in indigenous mining circles in recent years but has yet to materialize; how to concretely achieve this noble idea has been persistently elusive, as available geological data are inadequate. While suggesting that further investigations are required, the comprehensive mobilization of data on existing exploration results from various companies will help the government identify suitable areas for ASM. Going forward, such demarcations may be based on the extent of ore body concentration. Presumably, mineralization of less than a 30-acre (0.12 km²) radius with no complementary adjacent or geographically contiguous mineralization may not be viable for large-scale mining operations. Furthermore, the factors presently inhibiting ASM operators from formalizing operations need to be removed. Measures have to be put in place to ensure that registration is straightforward, and less cumbersome and time-consuming for prospective miners. Other incentivization mechanisms, including special rewards (i.e. paying higher rates for gold produced) for ASM operators who can demonstrate adoption of good practices, could serve as bait for encouraging informal operators to enter the legal bracket.

It is, however, the responsibility of the government to fully enforce the laws on encroachment on mining concessions, and apprehend and prosecute offenders in accordance with the laws of the country.

CHAPTER 19

Strained relations: a critical assessment of the mining conflict in Prestea, Ghana

Gavin M. Hilson and Natalia Yakovleva

This chapter examines the dynamics of the ongoing conflict in Prestea, Ghana, where indigenous artisanal *galamsey* mining groups are operating illegally on a large-scale mining concession awarded to Bogoso Gold (BGL). Despite being issued firm orders by the authorities to abandon their activities, *galamsey* leaders maintain that they are working areas of the concession that are of little interest to the company; they further counter that there are few alternative sources of local employment, which is why they are mining in the first place. Tensions reached a peak in June 2005, when, during a public demonstration against BGL's operations, the army opened fire on the crowd, wounding seven locals.

Although the Ghanaian government is working diligently to set aside plots to relocate illegal mining parties and develop alternative livelihood projects, its efforts have been far from encouraging: aside from a series of overlooked logistical problems, the gold content of the areas targeted for relocation has yet to be determined, and the alternative livelihood projects being developed are proving to be highly inappropriate. In addition to analyzing the dynamics of the impasse at Prestea, this chapter further critiques these conflict resolution measures, and outlines more robust measures for resolving ongoing disputes. The analysis uses findings from interviews conducted with government officials, BGL officers, representatives from local NGOs and *galamsey* between May and September 2005.

Description of the conflict zone

For over 100 years, Prestea,[1] which is located in southwestern Ghana approximately 200 km west of the country's capital, Accra, has been an important location for industrial-scale gold mining. To date more than 11 million oz of gold have been produced in Prestea and the adjacent Bogoso locality. During the past two decades, however, these concessions have changed ownership several times; the resulting changes (Table 19.1) have caused considerable confusion in host communities and have gone a long way toward fuelling the current conflict at Prestea.

Table 19.1 Chronology of major events in Prestea, 1870s–2005

Year	Events
1873	Mining, primarily underground, starts at Prestea. At the time, the Prestea concession comprised a number of different licences secured by several independent mining companies.
1965	All companies operating in the current Prestea concession were amalgamated by the post-independence Government of Ghana into Prestea Goldfields under the State Gold Mining Corporation (SGMC). Prestea Goldfields begins working both surface and underground gold deposits.
1986	The Minerals and Mining Law (PNDCL 153) is passed, which vests all minerals in the state.
13 October 1994	A mining lease agreement is forged between JCI Barnex and the government covering an area of 129.05 km² of the Prestea concession (providing both surface and underground rights).
13 September 1995	A project development agreement is signed between the government, SGMC and PGL on the one hand, and JCI Barnex on the other.
20 May 1996	The 'main agreement' is signed, empowering JCI Barnex to assume full management of the existing Prestea underground operation.
September 1998	JCI Barnex closes down the underground mine at Prestea.
December 1998	Prestea Gold Resources (PGR) is formed by ex-employees of the underground mine, and is granted a permit by the government to operate the underground mine.
June 2001	Golden Star Resources, through its 90%-owned subsidiary BGL, acquires the Prestea concession.
June 2001	The Government of Ghana grants BGL a lease for surface rights down to a depth of 200 metres. It furthermore grants PGR the rights to mine underground below this level. BGL acquires the Prestea mining lease for a period of 30 years, which covers surface and mining rights.
February 2002	Action is taken by the workforce of PGR to secure delayed salary payment from the company. PGR ceases operation of the Prestea underground mine after incurring a series of financial losses.
March 2002	The Prestea Underground Joint Venture is formed between BGL, SGMC, the Ghana Mine Workers Union, the Ghanaian Government and PGR to manage Prestea's underground operation. It is agreed that BGL manages the venture.
1 December 2004	BGL acquires 90% of the interest in the Prestea underground mine (the remaining 10% is acquired by the Government of Ghana).
March–May 2005	The Government of Ghana announces its relocation plans for illegal miners operating in the Western Region.
June 2005	Public demonstration against BGL's operations, resulting in casualties.

In 2001, Golden Star Resources (GSR), a Canadian-listed and Colorado-based mining company, acquired 90% of BGL, which owns the 145 km² Bogoso concession; the surface mining rights (to a depth of 200 metres) of the adjoining 129 km² Prestea property; a joint-venture interest in the Prestea underground mine; and a number of contiguous properties to the west and north of Bogoso, known respectively as Akropong and Dunkwa (Figure 19.1). For economic reasons, however, the underground operation in Prestea, long a staple source of employment in the town, was not reopened by GSR, prompting thousands of locals and migrant labourers to continue mining the deposit as unregistered *galamsey*. Despite working in areas where the company is not operating and appears to have little intention of working, the government has repeatedly called for all illegal artisanal gold miners operating in Prestea to abandon their activities. Tensions have been exacerbated by GSR management's reluctance to relinquish unused portions of its concession – the underground deposit in particular – as well as their refusal to honour a resettlement package negotiated by its predecessor.

Perspectives on the impasse at Prestea

Each stakeholder group presents valid arguments concerning their position on the conflict. The managers of GSR charge that they have exclusive rights to land, having secured concessions through legal channels by obtaining the

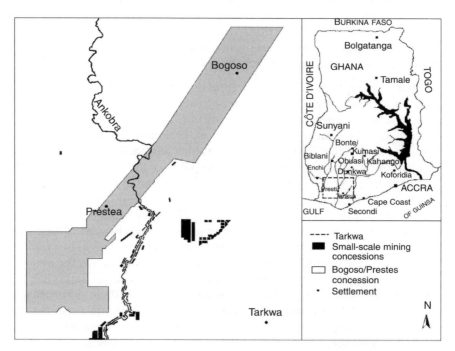

Figure 19.1 Golden Star Resources' (BGL) concessions, Western Region, Ghana

requisite permits; artisanal *galamsey* claim that they have indigenous ties to land, have obtained permission to work on the company's concessions and that recent policy changes are inappropriate because they had previously operated undisturbed; and the government argues that as an authority, it – and it alone – is responsible for mining policy in the country, which includes decisions on where people can operate. Analysis of each viewpoint is essential if appropriate conflict resolution mechanisms are to be identified. Drawing upon these findings, this section summarizes stakeholders' perspectives on the conflict.

The government and BGL

Since legalizing small-scale gold mining in 1989, the government of Ghana has adopted a confrontational policy towards illegal mining. In the case of Prestea, a deadline (31 March 2005)[2] was set for all *galamsey* miners to vacate the BGL concession. The official press statement issued by the Chief Director of the Ministry of Lands, Forestry and Mines and reproduced in the 31 May 2005 issue of the *Daily Graphic* reads: 'For the past two years, illegal miners have invaded this concession, making it difficult for the company to carry out its planned programmes'. Understandably, and as clarified by one official, the government does not want to be seen as endorsing illegal mining activity:

> The *galamsey* mandate is one of an illegal operator, operating on somebody's concession. So if you go there to advise the person, then it means that you are glorifying illegality and that is dangerous. Because if you are going there where the *galamsey* people are operating and say out of circumstances you are injured, you can even be imprisoned for that.

Despite the press statement indicating that the 'government decided that to show a "Human Face" to the exercise', with few exceptions, the standard approach taken to deal with illegal mining in Ghana is force, that is, to solicit the services of the army and security forces. Generally, government officials see *galamsey* as a threat to wider society (Palmer and Sackey, 2004), and have made a concerted effort to inform the wider public of the 'menacing' nature of illegal mining.[3] As one government official put it: 'But at times the guys are, you know, with violence, it is not that you go, flag...and say "I am a regulator, I have come [so] you have to leave the place". They may lynch you!'

Despite the obvious passivity of Prestean *galamsey*, there is agreement among the majority of officials that illegal miners are violent and should be avoided at all costs. Another official argued that 'they [*galamsey*] are mostly the wanted criminals and escaped convicts of our society who are fleeing the authorities to make money and are [therefore] dangerous'. Although there is consensus worldwide that ASM is 'typically practised in the poorest and most remote rural areas by a largely itinerant, poorly educated populace, men, and women with few employment alternatives' (MMSD, 2002b), few of the officers consulted conceded this to be the case in Prestea, despite the wealth of evidence pointing towards poverty and a lack of alternative employment being the principal driving forces of local *galamsey* activities.

BGL management has yet to enter into any sort of negotiation or direct dialogue with the *galamsey* miners operating on its concession. As one company official explained, 'As far as we are concerned, we don't even recognize them [*galamsey*] because we see them as people robbing our property...and I see them as any other armed robber'. Company executives firmly believe that the illegal mining problem is the responsibility of the government, and that the onus of initiating dialogue with encroachers should not fall on BGL managers. The government, however, also appears adamantly opposed to engaging in any dialogue with *galamsey*. This was reinforced by one officer, who explained that extending assistance to such illegal mining groups would be 'just like an armed robber breaking through someone's window, and you go there and basically give him a push'.

The fixed positions of the government and BGL notwithstanding, it is imperative that the deadlock is broken before it becomes an unmanageable situation. Fortunately, there is another – albeit a minority – group of individuals in the government who are more sympathetic towards illegal mining. Most of these have moved from field posts to take up more senior positions in Accra, and are thus more familiar with the situation on the ground. The group recognizes that there are wider economic issues propelling illegal mining activity nationwide:

> The unemployment situation has also become worse. In fact, in Ghana it is estimated that about 200,000 young men leave the secondary school every year and you have less than 10% or at most, 20% going to the universities and polytechnics and all of that and the rest have nothing to do, you see. So, every year you have say about 100,000 coming into the [*galamsey*] system; it creates a lot of problems. That's why you see that even the ages are now far younger. In the *galamsey* groups, the ages are now far younger than they used to be. At the early stages, it was the people who had returned from the mines who were actually coming into the *galamsey*, but now many people are getting in there...we don't have mass employment factories where you can put these people. [Senior government official]

It is crucial that these officers take the lead and establish contact with *galamsey* heads, and facilitate dialogue between Presteans and BGL officers. If left in the hands of other inflexible government officers, public agitation towards *galamsey* operators will mount, and problems with illegal mining will continue unresolved. Foremost of these will be the impasse at Prestea.

The galamsey*: a silent, marginalized voice?*

Indigenous *galamsey* appear willing to engage in peaceful dialogue with BGL and the authorities. However, attempts made to initiate communication by representatives of Prestea's *galamsey* camps, particularly Number Four Bungalow and 'I Trust My Legs',[4] have rarely materialized into meaningful consultation. It is important to clarify that despite BGL officers' assertion that *galamsey* 'still think that that right (mining) belongs to them [and that they] don't even understand what is law', communities do, in fact, recognize that they are mining illegally. As one senior officer at Number Four Bungalow explained, 'What we are doing here, we normally don't have a relationship, they [BGL] don't come to we, we don't go to them, because our mining, our jobs here are not legalized'. Illegal miners have simply not been pressured by BGL staff to vacate the Prestea concession because the company has little intention of working the idle underground operation. It is the recent antagonistic approach taken by the government towards illegal mining that has prompted many Presteans to initiate dialogue with BGL staff, with the hope that the company will relinquish unused portions of its concession so that locals can register as small-scale miners and have the security of tenure they so desperately seek.

The broken promises made by BGL about community development have been the main source of community opposition to the mine. As a condition for its acquisition of the Bogoso and Prestea concessions, BGL was required to conduct a feasibility study on the underground operation, which, at one time, employed at least 3,000 locals. When a decision was made not to recommence the project on economic grounds, redundant labourers called for BGL to relinquish portions of the concession. The imperativeness of this move was explained at length by a *galamsey* leader at the Bondaye camp:

> You know, you were saying something about something like illegal, just imagine the water level so we are fighting the BGL, you have taken the whole land, so give us some bread, so that we need the men...so that we can get some small job...There's no job in the country and then the BGL people have taken the whole land so what the community is saying is 'give us some place', so that we can [work], we need to.

Following meetings with Prestean *galamsey* in January 2003, BGL staff drafted a circular[5] which reiterated the company's commitment to 'continue with the exploration of the underground mine to determine the economics of the mine' and most significantly, stressed that 'BGL, in conjunction with government, shall assist in identification of a site for registered small scale miners to carry out legalized mining activities'. Letters were subsequently written and signed by company officials, permitting miners to operate on their concession.[6] These agreements, however, have provided communities with little protection, as government officials claim that signed letters are not legally binding.

An assessment of proposed solutions

As a means of resolving ongoing conflicts in Prestea, government officials and BGL staff have proposed to develop sustainable (alternative) livelihood projects and relocate *galamsey*. Analysis of these initiatives, however, suggests that policy is being driven from the top down, with insufficient consideration of conditions on the ground.

Sustainable livelihoods

Sustainable Livelihoods (SL) approaches were initially conceptualized to improve the understanding of, and support livelihoods in, rural areas. It is argued that, by using the SL approach, policymakers are able to identify options for change, as well as their likely impact on rural populations (Ngugi and Nyariki, 2005). In the case of ASM communities, there is a need to identify appropriate alternative livelihoods which, on their own, will be sustainable once surface deposits are exhausted.

The implementation of SL projects has been identified as a possible means for alleviating the conflict in Prestea/Bogoso. However, of the projects that have been implemented in Ghana to date, including those in Prestea and adjacent areas, the majority have had minimal impact because they have failed to address key community concerns: projects have generally been conceived based upon short episodes of fieldwork carried out in more established ASM regions, as opposed to more remote areas in greater need of market diversification. One key ASM stakeholder referred to these poorly-designed initiatives as 'fashionable projects':

> There are some fashionable projects. I call them 'fashionable things'...A few years ago, they trained people to do batik and soap making, and...there are things that if you look at them very carefully, they are not viable. If some-one in Bogoso or some village in Damang is doing batik, what is the quality of batik you will make? How many people will come to Ghana to buy it? So at the end of the day, he will know how to make the batik but he will never apply it. It will come in the newspaper that some people have trained some women to do batik...to me, I think it's more for the newspapers but it must be studied and done in a way that will be viable and people will want to stick to it. I don't believe in the normal alternative livelihoods the govern-ment talks.

Communications with miners in Prestea corroborate such claims over 'fashionable projects'. A *galamsey* head at 'I Trust My Legs', for example, explained that:

> We are ready to do other skills...They [BGL and the government] brought in a livelihood project but they were asking us to do grasscutter rearing, snail rearing...We are endowed with snails...I will take you to the back here, and I will count about 100 snails. I don't even eat them. Here, I don't even eat them. You have to go into Kumasi...you will find about 1,000 snails dodging and then moving around. We don't even eat them. Who's going to buy? It would mean that I would have to take these snails to Kumasi. Who is going to help me and take them into Kumasi?

It was furthermore noted that startup funding allegedly being provided by BGL for silkworm cultivation, another 'fashionable project', is insufficient because it can take up to one year before profits are earned; this is hardly an appropriate livelihood option for impoverished groups.

Personnel consulted at BGL did not appear cognizant of who, in fact, comprises Prestea's *galamsey* camps. In communications with workers at the Number Four Bungalow camp, it was explained that, contrary to claims made by BGL officers that 'they [the *galamsey*] are all illiterates...almost all of them are illiterates', there is an abundance of trained and skilled individuals working as illegal artisanal miners in Prestea:

> They [the *galamsey*] have transported their skills because some are blast men and blast men with certificates, [and] we have, how do you call it...drillers, we have the drillers...We have machine drivers, we have machine men and what do you call it, carpenters. What I say is, when you talk of machine drivers, when we dig the rock we teach him to be the machine driver. The ones who put the timber, we teach him to be one of the timber men, and...the ones who work in the haulage...they are the shaft-men, the shaft-men, see that the haulage-way is always safety. These are some of the skills... [Senior *galamsey* leader, Number Four Bungalow]

Why has local SL work not taken advantage of these skills to design and implement more appropriate initiatives? As one key stakeholder put it, for reskilling exercises to be successful in the ASM sector, 'we must prove that moving them will get them at least what they are getting as *galamsey*'. There is little evidence, however, that the alternative livelihood projects being implemented in the BGL catchment area, the majority of which have been developed without extensive analysis of local community dynamics, are capable of doing so.

Relocation

Wherever feasible, large-scale miners have sought to uproot, relocate and compensate communities situated within the boundaries of their concessions, although agreements have commonly proven to be unsustainable, causing a series of long-term problems. Management of large-scale mining companies, working in tandem with governments, tend to overlook community needs, failing to devote considerable time to liaise with, and study the dynamics of, relocated groups. Specifically, these questions are not being adequately addressed:

- Is the infrastructure in the relocated locality appropriate for incoming parties?
- Are there income-earning opportunities in these settings?
- What is the breadth of skill in relocated groups?

It appears that a similar approach is being taken in Prestea.

In March 2005, the acting chief director of the Ministry of Lands, Forestry and Mines announced that the Ghanaian government was working to identify alternative locations for Prestean *galamsey* to form cooperatives and register operations. These included Japa in the Western Region; Adjumadium, also in the Western Region; and Winneba in the Central Region. It was later argued in a CNN Matthews press release, that 'having made these areas available, it is high time all illegal miners working on Golden Star's Concession took advantage of the opportunity created and vacated Bogoso Limited concessions by May 31 2005'.[7] It was added that 'these three identified areas can host nearly 600 cooperatives or groups of at least 10 members each'.

The credibility of these claims, however, is open to debate for a number of reasons. First, has the Ghanaian government carried out prospecting in these areas to ascertain their mineral content?[8] Although some US$1.88 million was pledged under the World Bank Mining Sector Environmental Project to prospect and demarcate areas appropriate for small-scale mining, and to make geological information available to prospective operators (World Bank, 1995), the initiative failed because of financial mismanagement and a series of logistical factors. The Ghanaian government continues to overlook the importance of prospecting, failing to produce detailed geochemical maps with areas earmarked for ASM: there is little chance that miners will relocate to areas where mineral content has not been determined. This is a major concern, particularly in the case of Winneba, where it is well known that the country's gold belts thin considerably. A telling sign of Winneba's questionable mineral potential is the low concentration of *galamsey*, recognized by government officials as the country's mineral pathfinders and the most knowledgeable gold prospectors.[9] One key actor in the sector expressed concern over a government move to relocate Prestea-based miners to Winneba:

> If they [the *galamsey*] can be assured that there is gold there, then they will probably move. But why didn't they go there in the first place? If they were sure of gold being there, why didn't they go there?...Why, if the government has a place where it can be legal and no one will harass you, have they not rushed there? So we have to ask those questions.

The highly mineralized Japa is another challenge entirely: with an estimated 300 *galamsey* camps currently situated in the earmarked region, where does the government intend to relocate Prestea-based operators? Locals confirmed during visits to Japa some two months after the minister's announcement that government officers had yet to visit the location. Moreover, if followed through, the move promises to cause conflict. The *galamsey* consulted in both Japa and Prestea indicated that an influx of non-native artisanal miners would intensify competition for limited gold resources, netting individuals less profits. At least one stakeholder consulted was cognizant of this:

> I am sceptical...whether the Japa people would be prepared to accept foreigners coming to mine there. I don't know what has been done to get that in place, I don't know. I have a feeling that people will be very protective of their territories, so if people from let's say, Tarkwa have been asked by the government to go to Winneba or Japa, the people in Winneba and Japa who

probably are *galamsey* themselves might say 'look we are not entertaining them there'.

Moreover, a local (registered) small-scale miner is in the process of organizing *galamsey* equipment owners in Japa into a cooperative to put them in an improved position to obtain a small-scale mining licence and hence legitimize their operations. The problem, however, is that the very lands where the government plans to relocate Prestea-based *galamsey* are being targeted for the licence.

Second, such a rapid relocation exercise overlooks local economic needs. In spite of claims made by government officers of 'once a miner, always a miner', certain operators expressed reluctance to relocate not because of an obsession with mining, but because they recognize that an inevitable outcome of such mass migration is the economic collapse of local towns. As one miner explained:

> When we get to Japa...what we earn we will spend it at Japa, so we talk about the impacts to the community then the community cannot survive at Prestea...Because we talk of the impact on the community...This work we are doing, what we get from here, we want to spend the money in Prestea, and that based on that, it also boosts the morale of the community.

Another miner at Number Four Bungalow echoed these words, explaining that 'in 2001 [when we came], since this time, it is this activity that is bringing the money to the community [of Prestea], so the decision to go to Japa or Winneba, fine [but] it is not good, though'. Another important microeconomic issue that must be taken into account by the government is investment: several Prestea-based miners are being sponsored by local chiefs and buyers, and have invested heavily in equipment.

Finally, the government appears to have overlooked several logistical issues in its proposal that the local media have also failed to emphasize. For example, in a recent article published in the *Ghanaian Chronicle*, it was suggested that operators at Number Four Bungalow were resistant toward the idea of relocation, reporting: 'we are settlers on Prestea and we think that this is something good. We want government to make it [*galamsey*] legal, there should be a second look at moving us from here' (*Ghanaian Chronicle*, 2005b). The basic logistical issues raised by targeted mining populations over the plots designated for resettlement, however, were not outlined. The first concerns distance. On the prospect of moving to Winneba, a mine leader at the Ecomog *galamsey* camp argued: 'It's too far for us...we have got this work and we are doing it...we are [therefore] not willing to go...if they think the place is good, they should give it to other investors to also go there'. A *galamsey* leader at Number Four Bungalow was also outspoken on the idea:

> The impact? Let us consider the people working here were leaving for Japa. It's a small village, so if we move from here many kilometres, that means we have to find transport, find homes there. In fact, it is a big problem...The whole community of Prestea, you have to be real, we have to move from

here 700 km move away from here? Look at the one in the Western Region in Japa? How?...There is no place that the government has put aside for this in Japa or Winneba.

It appears that the government has overlooked these issues and that it has not yet fully conceptualized the sheer scale of the proposed undertaking. As one miner in Bondaye explained, during the operation of the underground mine, 'the workers were many...we were three thousand workers, so three thousand multiplied by your family means [almost] ten thousand'. It is estimated that during the dry season, 4,000 individuals work at Number Four Bungalow camp alone.

It was against the background of these concerns that a gang leader at 'I Trust My Legs' summed up the challenge of implementing the proposed relocation plan:

> If you want to go there to go and [get] ore, you will have to go and move us, and where will we get the finance to go to that place? And looking at the population here, as of now, we have not less than 10,000 *galamsey* operators here. To move 10,000 people from here even to Japa, where are we going to get the finance? Where are we going to get this accommodation? What are we going to eat and do there? Have you seen if the environment is good enough for us there? How are you going to get education for 2,000 children?

To avoid further complications, greater attention must be paid to such detail.

Possible ways forward

At the plenary forum on ASM in Yaoundé, Cameroon, 19–22 November 2002, it was emphasized that 'the economic viability of the [ASM] sector, with the ultimate goal of sustained poverty reduction, depended on a drastic change in the official perception of – and attitude towards – the ASM sector' (Labonne, 2003: 134). This certainly applies to Prestea: in Ghana, policymakers and mining company officials alike exhibit a poor understanding of the social dynamics of ASM. In particular, BGL managers and certain government officers have failed to recognize that the sector is poverty-driven, and that the alleviation of the illegal mining problem hinges upon appropriate intervention taken by governments and companies in the areas of reskilling, job creation and sustainable livelihoods. As explained above, job redundancies followed BGL's closure of its underground operation; an acute shortage of local employment opportunities has since forced thousands of skilled and semi-skilled workers to take up work as *galamsey*. While the recommendations prescribed in the discussion that follows could go a long way towards ameliorating the current conflict at Prestea, their implementation and effectiveness are contingent upon policymakers and company officials first recognizing the magnitude of the unemployment problem, and fully committing resources toward improving community development.

Barry's (1996: 5) point that a participatory approach is the key to resolving ongoing disputes between artisanal and large-scale miners certainly applies to the present analysis. In the case of Prestea, given BGL's fixed position on the impasse, the government must take the lead by initiating dialogue with the community because, based upon interviews with certain *galamsey*, trust in the government has deteriorated. The dispatching of officers to sites to communicate with mine leaders and foremen would go a long way towards repairing strained relations. Once some confidence is recaptured, and *galamsey* are sufficiently empowered to participate in decision-making processes, the government must pressure BGL officers to participate in discussions, with the aim of developing a sustainable working agreement. The importance of this process is framed in the seminal Mining, Minerals and Sustainable Development report (2002a 208), *Breaking New Ground*:

> If mining operations are to help communities work towards sustainable development, the communities need to be able to participate effectively in the decision-making process for establishing and running the operations, in order to avoid or minimize potential problems. Moreover, the relationships between the community and other actors, including the company and government, need to be ones of collaboration, trust and respect... Furthermore, the benefits need to be shared equitably within communities and sustained after the life of the mine.

Perhaps the most telling evidence that dialogue could yield positive results in Prestea is the initiative taken by Goldfields SA in its nearby catchment communities in Damang. Here, it has established the Damang Mine Community Consultation Committee, which regularly meets chiefs, the 'queen mothers', assembly members, the area council, youth leaders, and business and educational experts from other catchment communities. The company has also established the Goldfields Foundation Trust Fund,[10] the funds from which are used, following extensive consultation with communities, to finance and develop local infrastructure. Most importantly, as explained in Chapter 18, officers at Damang are on good terms with local *galamsey*: an informal arrangement has been established, whereby *galamsey* are permitted to operate provided that they abandon their work if the company expresses an interest in working their plots. The majority of initiatives that have been taken by Goldfields at Damang could be readily replicated at Prestea.

Second, there must be a concerted effort made by both BGL and the government to identify and develop more sustainable alternative livelihoods for *galamsey*. As explained earlier, the series of 'fashionable' projects pursued in recent years will have limited effectiveness over the long term because most were conceived without sufficient analysis of local population dynamics and market characteristics. The benefits of using community participation as a means of identifying appropriate alternative livelihoods projects – in this case, for ASM – are highlighted in the following passage by Fraser et al. (2006: 115):

The first benefit is pragmatic: since it is impossible to ensure that indicators chosen by 'development experts' will be relevant to local situations, local input is necessary to make sure indicators accurately measure what is locally important. Regular community input should also ensure indicators evolve over time as circumstances change...and help allow projects to continue after funding stops. The second reason is that preliminary research shows local engagement may help build community capacity to address future problems.

Taking into account the above analysis, there are two initiatives which show considerable promise for alleviating poverty in Prestea and reducing illegal mining. The first involves the farming of tilapia, the cichlid fish species comprising the genus *Tilapia* native to Africa. In Ghana, tilapia has long been a staple food, featuring prominently in an assortment of local dishes, including *Red Red*, *Banku* and *Fufu*. Given the market for fish, tilapia aquaculture is certainly a livelihood option worthy of further investigation, particularly in mining regions. In Ghana, officers at Goldfields SA have already established fish ponds at its Damang site with some success. As one of its on-site personnel indicated during a personal interview:

Here [at Damang] we have fish ponds systems [as] tilapia is a delicacy in Ghana. Yesterday, I bought one in Tarkwa – thirty thousand [cedis for a] small one. I tell you, for [a] small one, I paid thirty thousand [cedis]. You have so many water bodies around...We are looking at coming out with bigger ponds to give them.

With a flourishing tilapia market in Tarkwa-Prestea, BGL could readily integrate a fish pond scheme into the company's Alternative Livelihood Programme.

A second promising alternative livelihood is cocoa farming, which is already widely practised in the region. As one stakeholder explained, 'The land here is very suitable for cocoa and palm oil...that is two major cash crops that they have'. The potential value of cocoa farming in Prestea was revealed during a discussion with a representative from a local NGO on crop compensation:

If you take a cocoa tree, the average life span of the cocoa tree is 50 years...Now, there is a scientific proof that an average cocoa tree can produce for every year a minimum a half a bag – let's say half a bag of cocoa. Now...Let's say you have maybe 3–4 hectares...if you have 3 hectares...a hectare takes on average 1,000 trees.

There is the challenge, as one company officer put it, of how to 'convince a person who takes or gets a million in a week into a livelihood like cocoa or oil palm that will take him three years before he gets a penny'. The key, however, is education: *galamsey* must be made aware of the long-term sustainability of the exercise, that managing a flourishing cocoa patch is certainly a more viable, and less hazardous, occupation than 'hit-and-miss' artisanal gold mining. To ease the transition, the government can partner rural banks to provide sufficient startup capital and continuous support for activities until farms develop.

Finally, the government must pressure BGL to relinquish unused portions of its concession, particularly the abandoned underground mine in Prestea where the Number Four Bungalow Camp is currently based. During an interview with a BGL officer, there were calls for *galamsey* to recognize the law and the rights of the company:

> Once the government sold the rights, the concession rights to this company, it becomes the property of the company. So it's like, you rented a house, and the landlord says this part you rented, I will take my money but I will still sleep in the house. That is what is happening in Prestea, because like I said, they are illiterates, so they don't regard laws or regulations.

What the officer failed to make reference to was the amount of land that has been demarcated to the company, and, more importantly, the amount of land on the concession that has gone unused. As explained by Aubynn (1997), this is a problem throughout the entire Western Region, one-third of which is currently under concession to large-scale mining companies; the situation is most problematic in Wassa West, where 60 per cent of lands are under concession. A representative of a local NGO clarified the issue further during a personal interview:

> No mining company in this country operates beyond 30% of their concession. Some are operating at a low of 13% of their concession. It's like the whole of this table, 13 is only [points at the piece of A4 paper] you know, this big part, and all of this is protected [points at the entire table], you know. The mine has mine life of let's say 30 years...so all this site [pointing at the table] is idle, you can't find there, you can't do *galamsey* there. So I think, they actually need to begin to offload portions of their concessions for the small-scale miners.

The attempts made by the government to offload the problem, while commendable, are flawed. As explained previously, if carried through, the prospecting and demarcation exercises being entertained promise to bring additional complications. Moreover, with the low numbers of qualified staff and minimal resources on hand, it could take years to prospect and demarcate areas suitable for mining. The most logical move, therefore, would be for the government to pressure BGL to free unused areas of its concession; in fact, BGL should be taking the lead in this area, given the obviousness of the move as a solution to the lingering illegal mining problem that its officers openly complain about.

In summary, these recommendations, which are rooted in a bottom-up approach, would go a long way towards ameliorating the impasse at Prestea. However, until certain government officials and BGL officers concede that the illegal mining problem in the region is owed largely to mass unemployment, and initiate dialogue with local *galamsey* leaders, the problem will intensify, with the possibility of becoming an unmanageable crisis.

CHAPTER 20

Addressing the environmental challenges of artisanal and small-scale mining in Nigeria

Miriam Anike Lawal

If properly harnessed, mining could become one of Nigeria's most vibrant industrial sectors. Since the mid-1960s, the Nigerian economy has been dominated by oil.[1] Prior to the oil boom of the 1970s, coal and tin were the solid minerals that enjoyed significant exploitation, ranking high as foreign-exchange earners in the country (Dikko, 2001). Production of both tapered off toward the end of the 1970s, however, as attention shifted almost exclusively to oil (Raufu, 2004).[2] By the late 1980s, over-reliance on oil production was identified as the underlying cause of Nigeria's economic decline.[3] Diversification of the country's economy was therefore sought to break this dependence; one of the strategies identified was development of the solid minerals sector.[4]

Focusing on the planned diversification, the federal government established the (federal) Ministry of Solid Minerals in 1995, publishing soon afterward its Solid Minerals Policy (1998). In 1999, a new minerals and mining decree was enacted, replacing national mining laws that had been in existence since 1946.[5] Moreover, in July 2002, a presidential committee on the development of solid minerals was constituted to draft a seven-year action plan for the development of the sector.

Despite these institutional developments, most mining (apart from coal and tin) in Nigeria occurs on an artisanal and small scale.[6] In an impoverished economy with high unemployment,[7] mining on this scale has its attractions. Its principal attribute is its low barriers to entry in terms of capital, skills and infrastructure (Masialeti, 2004). The easily generated employment produces income, savings and investment, which, in turn, further the cause for local development.

Artisanal mining in Nigeria is largely unregulated, informal and illegal. This has several negative effects, not the least of which are hazardous environmental practices, wastage of resources, and poor social, health and safety conditions. This face of artisanal mining – dirty, destructive and illegal – has brought it into conflict with environmentalists and generally given it a bad name.[8]

Given the severe financial and technological constraints in Nigeria, there is little doubt that artisanal mining will continue to play a major role in the foreseeable future (Dikko, 2001). The challenge of realistic policy will be how best to eliminate (or at least mitigate) the adverse environmental effects of artisanal mining without destroying its potential as a significant contributor to economic growth. This chapter looks at these issues, and makes recommendations for addressing some of the industry's thornier environmental and social problems.

ASM in context

What is ASM?

There is no universally accepted definition of artisanal or small-scale mining. The two terms are often used interchangeably but do not necessarily mean the same thing (Bugnosen, 2003).[9] Kambani (2003) adopts a useful structural approach, breaking down the concept of 'small-scale mining' into three levels. The first and lowest level is artisanal mining (or micro-scale mining). This features the most rudimentary operations and tools, and is completely informal. The level of investment is low and because of their simplicity, operations can be readily started and dismantled. Artisanal mine sites can grow rapidly because migrant miners are easily mobilized and tend to flock to areas of new finds.

The second is the traditional level of small-scale mining. It features both licensed and unlicensed activities, and may be semi-mechanized or non-mechanized. Basic management structures tend to be visible here, and hired labour is more the norm than the exception.

The highest level consists of licensed operations, which essentially function within the boundaries of the law. They generally feature formal management structures and equipment that tends to be highly mechanized (Masialeti and Kinabo, 2003).

All three levels of Kambani's hierarchical table are evident in Nigeria's small-scale mining sector. At a typical mine site in Akutayi, two licensed companies are responsible for development, with a combination of artisanal and semi-mechanized means used to mine tourmaline. Advanced small-scale operations are the highest form observed in Nigeria, and occur, for example, in granite-rich regions in Abuja.

Artisanal mining and the poverty cycle

ASM is often characterized as 'poverty-driven'. Nöetstaller (1996) argues that both informal miners and government are 'caught in negative circles of cause and effect' (Labonne, 2003).[10] The use of rudimentary methods and tools leads to low productivity and low income, thereby preventing the accumulation of capital for investment. A lack of capital, in turn, confines miners to crude methods and inefficient processes. Gyan-Baffour (2004) emphasizes that while mining can be a major source of poverty reduction, it can also be a cause of the increased poverty witnessed in mining areas.[11]

On the government side, mining and environmental authorities usually lack the resources to enforce existing regulations. This results in illegal mining, poor environmental standards and a loss of potential revenues. Without revenues, the inability of government to perform its regulatory functions diminishes, giving leeway to the growth of unregulated and unsafe artisanal mining activities.[12]

Nöetstaller and Gyan-Baffour's circles of poverty and negativity apply in Nigeria. Over 57 types of solid minerals exist in the country, almost all of which are mined predominantly, if not exclusively, on a small scale and by artisanal means.[13] Unsurprisingly, mining in Nigeria barely yields 1 per cent of its estimated potential in revenue terms.[14] Despite the existence of mining laws purporting to regulate all aspects of mining operations, enforcement is weak, which perpetuates illegal artisanal mining.

Most artisanal and small-scale miners do not hold mining titles or leases, are not creditworthy and engage in crude mining practices detrimental to the environment. These miners rely mostly on manual labour and rudimentary tools to mine gemstones, gold and industrial minerals.[15] Coal, tin and bitumen are still mined mainly by large-scale and 'advanced' small-scale operators.

Artisanal mining occurs throughout the country but there is a notorious concentration of such operations in the middle-belt and north-central regions, where geological formations favour the occurrence of a wide variety of valuable solid minerals in commercial quantities. The sites vary in size and character. Some are active and others dormant. Some are easily accessible, situated adjacent to highways or in builtup areas, while others are located in remote hinterlands.[16]

Environmental degradation is the most visible negative aspect of ASM activities. Mine abandonment, acid mine drainage, soil degradation and erosion, deforestation, pollution and siltation of rivers and streams are some notable examples of problems. Health issues include occupational diseases, the absence of safety gear for workers and perilous mine structures. Visits to two typical mine sites – one granite, the other tourmaline – bear out environmentalists' worst fears.

Case study no. 1: mining tourmaline at Akutayi village

Of surrealism and tourmaline

Save for the blazing mid-morning sun that gives it a decidedly earthly feel, the artisanal mine site at Akutayi would probably fit comfortably in the lunar landscape. Mine pits resembling mini-craters pockmark the site. There are approximately 25 pits at Akutayi, and during the mining season, each is worked by scores of miners from about 7 am until 6 pm. Each pit is about 18 metres deep and 1 metre wide, and produces yields 30–40 25 kg bags of tourmaline daily.[17]

The dwellings surrounding the mine site are mainly thatched mud huts. There is no pipe-borne water or electricity, and the main sources of energy are firewood and kerosene. There are no tarred roads; only dusty footpaths and tracks. Transportation is by foot or on rickety bicycles. Sanitation is poor and latrines are holes dug in the ground or, more commonly, shrubs at the edges of the mine site. The one stream that passes through Akutayi is used for all purposes: drinking, cooking, washing, irrigation and sluicing.

Mining at Akutayi is a seasonal activity, taking place mainly during the dry season.[18] In the closed season, farming takes over as the main subsistence activity in the area. The land is farmed for root crops, grain and sugarcane. There is no shifting cultivation and it is not hard to conceive of the depletion of nutrients in the soil.

The nearest town to Akutayi is Sarkin Pawa, which is approximately 3 km away. It is also dominated by thatched structures but with a sprinkling of cement buildings. It has schools, houses of worship, small shops and a police station. There is limited electricity and pipe-borne water. There is a river running through the town, which provides fish during the rainy season.

Undermining the physical and social environment

During peak mining periods, when thousands (miners, hawkers, tent-makers, etc) congregate in Akutayi, there are several detrimental social and environmental patterns. There is bush burning to clear lands for dwellings. Timber is felled to provide firewood and wedging for housing structures as well as for support in mining pits. Wood is also used to make wooden pegs used to hold down tents that can be rented by merchants or other interested parties. Clay and sand are extracted to construct storage structures and earthenware with scarcely any thought given to remediation and repair.

Carbon emissions from the burning of wood for fuel pose a major hazard. Being the predominant source of fuel for combustion, several trees are cut down daily; no saplings are planted in their place. Land is also cleared for houses to be built. This clearing enhances erosion and desertification, as the town is situated in the middle-belt of Nigeria, and does not experience substantial rainfall throughout the year (Figure 20.1). In addition, the clearing of land devastates the natural vegetation. Bush burning, apart from contributing to air pollution, upsets the balance of the ecosystem by driving out bush animals, degrading topsoil and endangering subterranean life.

The mining activity itself is a cause of more specific environmental problems. Mine pits are ugly gashes in the topography; there is little likelihood of rehabilitation. Excavated topsoil and mineral waste are carried by rainwater. Some traces of quartz and mineral have been dispersed up to 2 km from the mine site. This has deceived artisanal prospectors into clearing and digging up further field in the hope of finding more minerals. These holes are abandoned when there are no finds, paving the way for further erosion (Figure 20.2).

When the mine site is inactive, it accumulates stagnant water at its base, a veritable breeding ground for tropical mosquitoes, and therefore malaria, as well as waterborne diseases. This somewhat toxic water (alongside stone waste)

Figure 20.1   Deserted settlers camp by the mine adjacent to burned land and vegetation

is then pumped once mining resumes, and is absorbed in fields used to cultivate food crops.[19]

Miners' health

There is no gainsaying the fact that the conditions at the Akutayi mine are harsh. Here, artisanal miners are driven by poverty to work in poor conditions, as mining provides a slightly higher income than other subsistence work. Miners generally avoid spending their hard-earned wages on health care, a problem compounded by their limited education and ignorance of the risks they are exposed to. Where health problems manifest themselves, recourse is normally to self-help or engage in traditional medicinal practices of dubious value.

The mineworkers at Akutayi are exposed daily to the elements without any form of protective gear. They are subjected to incessant noise, dust, extreme heat, rain, physical strain and contaminated water. The continuous digging in bent-over positions may lead to muscular and skeletal disorders over the long term. To make matters worse, the blend of poor nutrition and backbreaking labour can only work to reduce their resistance to disease.

The ubiquitous pools of water around the mine site also make the community susceptible to high levels of malaria as well as diarrhoea, which is a natural consequence of ingesting water from contaminated water sources. Cholera is also difficult to contain if there is an outbreak. The perennial inhalation of

Figure 20.2 Several mining pits clustered together at Akutayi

dust and sand particles by miners exposes them to the risk of respiratory disorders and lung diseases.

Locals indicate that there is a high prevalence of STDs (and possibly, HIV/AIDS) in the mining community. Like many artisanal mine sites, the nomadic nature of the workers encourages promiscuity. There was no evidence at Akutayi that sexual protection was a high priority among men and women.

It is not only social diseases that the miners need protection against. The mine pits themselves hardly epitomize the best standards of health and safety. Wooden wedges, sticks and sand bags are used to provide rudimentary support for mine pits. Mine collapse is said to be a regular occurrence.[20]

Despite the huge numbers of miners involved during the high season, there is no first-aid centre at the mine site; in fact, there is a complete lack of healthcare facilities at Akutayi itself. Although Sarkin Pawa fares marginally better, there is no indication that there is any monitoring of the health problems that arise as a result of mining in the area.

Case study no. 2: granite mining at Malali and Mpape

Tale of two sites

Unlike Akutayi, which is remote and relatively difficult to access, the Malali granite quarry is in Kaduna, the capital city of Kaduna state and one of the largest towns in the north of Nigeria. Malali is a residential district, and the quarry is surrounded by middle-class homes, some with private garden patches.

The work in the quarry is manual and carried out by dozens of freelance artisans under the auspices of a quarry union.[21] Dynamite is used to blast the rock, after which chisels, hand drills, wedges and other rudimentary tools are used to break up the loose boulders. It takes about four days for one miner to break up enough rock to fill one lorry.[22] The miners sit in the open, in the rain or under the sun, chiselling away. They work for roughly nine hours a day, starting at 7 am, and take occasional breaks to smoke cigarettes or cool off with cold drinks sold by itinerant hawkers. A few marketers loiter around the quarry, prospecting for sales.

The operations at Malali are micro-scale, but the granite quarries at Mpape, a district of Abuja, tend to be more advanced small-scale operations. Nationally renowned construction companies run them, and idle machinery testifies to their level of mechanization.[23] Larger machines such as crushers are used to reduce the size of granite stones. Hand tools and explosives are also used.

The quarries dominate the local economy of Mpape. There is a brisk trade in granite, with substantial tonnage being disposed of each day.[24] The size of the town has been growing due to the presence of the quarries and life resembles most small towns in Nigeria, with shops, schools and a few clinics.

Environmental and social impacts

Despite the difference in the scale of operation, there are common environmental hazards at both Malali and Mpape. Quarrying is a noisy, open-cast mining activity. The dynamite explosions and drilling at Malali have their counterpart in the constant grind of mechanical excavators and crushers at Mpape. Dust pollution from blasting is an accompaniment of quarrying, whether by mechanized or manual means. There is little evidence in both areas of any measures being taken to reduce the quarry dust emissions into the atmosphere. A white blanket of dust covers the vegetation near the Mpape quarries, and is visible on the houses nearest the rock face in Malali.

Mpape has additional problems. The excavation sites remain unrehabilitated. There is no reinforcement or drainage on the dirt roads leading to the quarries at Mpape, which contributes to erosion. Some of the quarries are littered with heaps of stone waste and granite rubble, and are lined with black soot, ostensibly from the machinery used. The waste is exposed to the elements and prone to be carried away by rain to wind into nearby streams and farmlands.

There is a large artificial lake at Mpape, which is used for mining activities. The lake also provides water for some local residents during water shortages. Excavation at the quarries also results in localized pits in which stagnant water collects.

The seemingly reckless attitude taken by the operators of the quarry towards environmental protection has not helped matters. At one location, adjacent to a small settlement, erosion had caused part of the road to cave in, exposing miners and local residents to accidents and disasters. In another area, construction had commenced on a bridge over a stream. The project appeared to have been abandoned, resulting in a wide stagnant pool on the side of the stream.

Trees are felled in this area to clear the way for dirt roads to the quarries. As the sites are exhausted and demand grows, the quarrying sites expand. More trees are felled and the area is increasingly being stripped of natural vegetation. Bush burning is also rife, as the miners and settlers require bush animals for food.[25] This burning emits untold quantities of carbon dioxide into the air.

Miners' health

Potential health problems are more pronounced at Malali than Mpape. The workers at Malali wear little or no protective gear. They work in the open, exposing themselves to all types of weather. Inhalation of dust and rock particles is evident and likely results in respiratory problems and general illness over the long term.

There is the danger of direct injury from the hand tools that they use, as well as not so obvious health impacts from overexposure to noise and heat. There is the ever looming danger from the explosives used on the quarry face, and this is made worse by the fact that the site is situated in a residential neighbourhood. Vibrations from blasts pose further health hazards.

There are no first-aid or medical facilities visible at the Malali site.[26] Even at Mpape, despite the use of machinery and some protective clothing and equipment, workers are still exposed to potentially harmful dust and particles (as well as noise and heat), as are the inhabitants of surrounding areas.[27]

Small scale, giant hazard

The environmental problems encountered at Akutayi, Malali and Mpape are typical of ASM in Nigeria. The situation is made more worrisome because the operations at the three sites are licensed. In theory, therefore, they should be subject to monitoring and sanctioning from regulatory authorities. In reality, there is little regulation, and the mining operations are patently run oblivious to environmental protection and appropriate health and safety standards.

The thousands of illegal artisanal and small-scale sites fare even worse, falling as they do even further outside the radar of supervisory agencies. Each site and the operations conducted thereon may be relatively small but the cumulative effect of all the sites is undeniably significant. As has been shown, the adverse environmental impacts have a multiplier propensity and are not confined to the immediate vicinity of the sites. Point source pollutants, for instance, tend to be dispersed rather quickly and ultimately affect areas far beyond the mining districts.

Recourse may be had to the 'Maslow effect' for explaining, in part, why ASM in Nigeria is conducted in such an environmentally inimical manner (Aryee, 2003a). Maslow constructed a hierarchy of needs, which suggested that the most basic needs of man are physiological (food, shelter, clothing, etc).[28] Until such needs are satisfied, higher needs such as safety, love and self-esteem are irrelevant. Nigeria is a poor country, with more than 70 per cent of its population subsisting on less than US$1 per day. Artisanal miners are drawn from the impoverished masses and are consumed by a daily struggle to meet their basic needs. The desperate pursuit of the physiological takes precedence over all other concerns, including caring for the environment. This is only rational according to Maslow's theory.

Apart from leading to the desperado mentality that is antithetical to good environmental practices, poverty also accounts for a high degree of illiteracy among artisanal miners and a consequent lack of awareness of the damage induced. From the point of view of the government, poverty ensures that there are not enough resources, human and material, to enforce or induce environmentally friendly mining.

A solution to the environmental problems of small-scale mining would therefore be to drastically reduce or eliminate poverty in Nigeria. As Bugnosen (2003) points out, developed countries have small-scale mining sectors but these operate in much the same way, environmentally and otherwise, as resident large-scale mining sectors. However, the problems of overall poverty reduction in Nigeria are an integral part of the complex and hydra-headed puzzle of national development.

An environment that is already in grave danger cannot wait for the resolution, in the long term, of the country's economic, social and political problems. Immediate steps must be taken to meet the pressing environmental challenges of ASM. Otherwise, the dirty face of this type of mining will continue to obscure and obstruct its economic potential in Nigeria.

In the main, there are two challenges: one, mitigating or eliminating the negative effects of ASM on the physical environment; and the other, reducing the health and safety risks of ASM. As a statement of general policy, it is easy to assert that meeting these challenges requires improving the legal, regulatory and institutional framework governing ASM. The devil is in the detail.

Inadequacies of law, regulation and institutions

Inadequacy of framework legislation?

The Minerals and Mining Act is the national framework legislation governing the mining of solid minerals in Nigeria. The Act, however, is most notable for the absence of specific definitions of the terms 'artisanal' and 'small-scale' in relation to mining. This is unexplicable given that ASM is the dominant means of extracting solid minerals in Nigeria.

The closest to which the Act gets to a specific definition of small-scale mining is in section 191(2), which defines a small-scale operator as a small- or middle-scale company, which conducts tin mining operations on 'a scale approved by the minister'.[29] This definition is, however, expressly limited to the determination of eligibility for loans from the tin production and development revolving loan fund for 'eligible small mining operators'.[30]

The Act does make some provisions for small-scale mining, even if it does not provide a definition. The minister is required to extend assistance to small-scale mining by organizing and grouping small miners into cooperatives. The minister is further required to promote improved mining techniques for small-scale miners, as well as provide them with basic equipment, technical consultancy and support services.[31]

The only other section where small-scale mining is mentioned is in documents relevant to the Small-Scale Mining Credit Guarantee Scheme Fund.[32] The fund was established to provide loans for small-scale miners, although again, the term 'small scale' is not defined.

By not providing a special regulatory framework for ASM, the Mining and Minerals Act adopts a uniform approach to the regulation of all types of mining. The provisions relating to environmental protection, and health and safety are the same, whether the mine is large, small or artisanal in character. This is a somewhat questionable approach in view of contemporary recognition of the peculiar utility and problems of small-scale mining in developing countries.[33]

The law vests primary responsibility in the minister to ensure the orderly and systematic development of mineral resources in the country.[34] The minister is enjoined to have a coherent programme of exploration of mineral resources that takes environmental factors, among others, into account.[35] The minister is also empowered to protect society and the environment from the adverse effects of unapproved mining practices and operations.[36]

The minister is given specific powers to draft regulations to ensure the safety of mine structures and mine sites. He may also draft regulations to ensure the safety, welfare and health of miners, as well as for the continuation of mining operations in a safe and sanitary manner. Furthermore, the minister may implement regulations for the prevention or control of pollution, and environmental degradation caused by mining operations, including the disposal of poisonous or noxious products. The power to make regulations extends to the construction of roads, grazing of cattle in the mining area and felling of timber for mining operations.[37]

In addition, the minister is empowered to make regulations to 'prescribe any matters to be prescribed' under the Act and for giving full effect to its provisions. There is sufficient leverage given by the wording of the Act for the minister to even provide specific definitions of small-scale and artisanal mining in the regulations.

If such specific regulations were made, they would probably rest the criticism of there being no specificity in the Nigerian legal framework with regard to ASM and attendant environmental problems. However, regulations have not yet been made, and it is often the case in developing countries like Nigeria that primary legislation is more preferable for efficacy, certainty and durability than secondary legislation.

Inadequate law enforcement

Nigeria has mining and environmental laws, even if lacking in certain respects, but there is a lack of adequate enforcement. In the absence of proper coordination between the Solid Minerals Ministry and the Environment Ministry, miners, whether licensed or not, are rarely monitored, and if or when violations are discovered, punishment by way of fines and jail terms prescribed in the Minerals and Mining Act are not executed. The Act does provide for mines inspection authorities at federal and state levels.[38] However, due to corruption and a severe shortage of staff and resources, monitoring is far too inadequate and infrequent to deter environmentally damaging practices.[39]

Lack of coordination between responsible agencies

There are different bodies whose areas of authority bear upon a safe, profitable and sustainable mining sector. These ministries and agencies include those with responsibility for solid minerals, the environment, water resources, trade, education, police, finance and rural development. The Mines Department within the Federal Ministry of Solid Ministry exists to uphold the Minerals and Mining Act, and the Federal Ministry of Environment is charged with overall environmental responsibility in Nigeria. The responsibilities of the different bodies overlap with regard to many environmental issues, resulting in confusion and sometimes contention over which body has responsibility in particular situations. The lack of coordination to protect the environment from mining practices and oversee rehabilitation, monitor practices, ensure compliance and punish offenders has led to a weak enforcement of laws, as variances in enforcement have occurred between the two ministries in particular.

Negligible environmental penalties

The penalties set by the law in the case of violation of environmental protection provisions are low. Miners would rather continue degrading the environment and pay, if caught, the relatively small fines payable. A US$120 fine is negligible to a miner who can sell a single gemstone for ten times that amount. None of the environmental penalties prescribed under the Minerals and Mining Act, including those for timber felling, bush burning and non-rehabilitation of mine sites, is greater than N20,000 (about US$150).[40] Pollution of watercourses attracts a penalty not exceeding N50,000 (US$345, 15 June 2004).[41]

Illegal mining

Illegal mining will persist as long as monitoring and enforcement remain weak and penalties are light. Illegal mining is not subjected to the terms of a lease or licence, and is not regulated or supervised. It is therefore carried out in a reckless manner detrimental to the physical environment, as well as to the health and safety of the miners and the wider community. It has been argued that revocation of licences by the government will, rather than benefit the sector, lead to increased illegal mining activity.

Inadequate funding and lack of modern equipment and technology

Some environmental protection or rehabilitation measures, such as restoration of degraded mine sites, are quite expensive to implement. The lack of access to credit and financing for small-scale miners contributes heavily to their selection of crude mining methods and equipment.

Inadequate infrastructure

Nigeria suffers from a chronic lack of public infrastructure, such as serviceable roads to mining sites and localities; the transportation system is chaotic and unreliable. There are no roads in many of the areas where solid minerals are found. Even when they exist, roads are often in a bad state and in desperate need of repair. The rail network is highly restricted and consists of a slow, narrow-gauge rail line. In rural areas, there is scarcely any electricity or water supply, especially in the remote parts where much of the small-scale mining takes place.

Lack of knowledge and expertise

The shortage of sufficiently skilled and technically knowledgeable manpower in the Nigerian government has also contributed to environmental degradation by mining activities. This has resulted in derisory supervision of mining practices, without much advice or tutoring being passed on to miners.

Overcoming the challenges

World Bank intervention

The federal government of Nigeria is dedicated to developing the ASM sector. With the boost given by the World Bank, the feat should be made simpler in view of its (World Bank) standards for project implementation, monitoring and compliance. The project, the Sustainable Management of Mineral Resources in Nigeria,[42] is partly focused upon formalizing small-scale mining, attending to social and environmental issues, small grants and funding programmes, and training and knowledge dissemination. No less important are the targets set for capacity-building, legal and fiscal reform, and crucially, environmental and social management. The project seeks to increase the government's long-term institutional and technical capacity to manage Nigeria's mineral resources in a sustainable way while establishing a basis for poverty reduction and rural economic renewal through ASM.

The chief components of the World Bank project include assessment and studies, knowledge generation, policy and legal reform, institutional strengthening, ASM, and environmental and social management. Furthermore, the project, which features three stages – the project preparation (2004), its review and approval by the World Bank and Nigerian government (2004) and the project implementation itself (2005–9) – will have its funding shared among the following four core aspects.

- Economic development and livelihood diversification in artisanal and small-scale mining areas – this requires the highest amount of funding at an estimated US$24 million. It includes pilot studies for the formalization of small-scale mining, funding programmes and assisting local entrepreneurs in the production of raw materials for domestic consumption.
- Private sector development – this is budgeted at US$22 million, and directed at the restructuring of state-owned mining enterprises, including the Nigeria Coal Corporation (NCC) and the Nigerian Mining Corporation (NMC), both of which are being privatized. In addition, there is a focus on developing the country's much needed geological infrastructure (geological information being a basis for environmental planning).
- Strengthening governance and transparency in mining – funding is estimated at US$20 million and is aimed at developing legal and fiscal reforms, and environmental and social management.
- Project coordination and management – taking up US$4 million, this aspect is dedicated to overseeing the projects undertaken in terms of finance, funds disbursement, implementation, monitoring, and evaluation of projects and project results.

Recommended amendments to the Minerals and Mining Act

There is a need to amend certain provisions in the legislation on mining and, more specifically, ASM. The omission of provisions for artisanal miners needs reviewing. There is a need to adopt and include a Nigerian definition of artisanal and small-scale mining, while also laying out sufficient prerequisites for titles, leases and licences for artisanal and small-scale mine operators, emphasizing environmental protection requirements.[43] A specific foundation for assistance should also be provided, including an EIA.

In addition, minimum fines, as stipulated in the Decree, should be raised. Although the law does provide for the establishment of mines field police[44] and mines officers, it does not stipulate training requirements. This needs to be amended so that the mines field police and mines officers are adequately trained by the Nigeria Police Force to be able to protect the environment and miners' safety, while ensuring maximum compliance with established laws and regulations.

The Decree should encapsulate more of the environment while maintaining state security, national interests and economic development. Immediate economic development may occur because of natural resources exploitation, but long-term economic development hinges on sustainable exploitation.

Improved coordination between institutions

The mining law clearly sets the duties of the Director of Mines to include consultation with other agencies of government in the reclamation of mines land,[45] and cooperation with federal and state government agencies to minimize the duplication of inspection and administration of minerals and mining.[46] These functions should be rekindled and made to work alongside a proposed restructuring of the Ministry of Solid Minerals, which may result in the ministry having three key departments.[47] The proposed functions of the Mines Engineering and Parastatals Department include regular liaison with the Federal Ministry of Environment for the enforcement (and development) of environmental guidelines on mining activities; monitoring and evaluation of rehabilitation; and utilization of lands, while also coordinating the activities of the ASM project. Although this is crucial to monitoring mining activities and environmental impacts, a sister department needs to be established in the environment ministry with the same baseline objectives. This liaison will see better monitoring and compliance. It may be necessary for the two departments to have regular roundtable discussions, inviting mining and environment technocrats and NGO representatives to share ideas and proffer solutions to problems. These persons should have international exposure with experiences from other mining countries.

Mineral Resources Trust Fund

A Mineral Resources Trust Fund (MRTF) should be set up with a proportion of solid minerals revenues accruing, or a dedicated amount allocated, from the national account towards the development of the sector. Through planned and guided infrastructural development of the sector,[48] construction of access roads to mining areas and provision of water in communities will reduce environmental hazards, such as unregulated land clearing for roads, ensuing erosion and deforestation. The fund should be used to finance the construction of local clinics and schools in these communities.

Mining and environmental literacy and education

At the state level, the government should set up mining education forums, and carry out environmental awareness and training programmes in key as well as potential mining cities. Administration can occur through the Mines Engineering Department,[49] and initially, funding can be sourced from the proposed MRTF or ecological funds allocated to federal states on a monthly basis. Moreover, miners, schools, mining companies and NGOs could be encouraged to make contributions. These can be by way of actual teaching and training, sharing experiences, providing necessary materials, including manuals and pictures, or even by providing a teaching framework. Larger mining companies can contribute by showing commitment to the environment and mining communities[50] through funding learning aids or sponsoring Nigerian students abroad in mining courses. The Federal Ministry of Solid Minerals oversees the Solid Minerals Development Fund,[51] like its counterpart in the petroleum sector,[52] and provides scholarships for Nigerian students to take up specialized mining, geology and environment degrees. Alternatively, the ministry could liaise with the petroleum sector in the interim to include mining students in their programmes, as petroleum is ultimately mined, and as a natural resource, has a number of similarities.

NGO participation

The federal government needs to encourage NGO participation in the mining sector. This is much needed and would be most welcome, since the majority of miners and community members are poor and illiterate. Judging from the experiences in the country's oil communities, NGO, rather than government participation, should be encouraged at the community level: many feel that the government is responsible for resources depletion and land degradation, without compensation for lands mined. Another angle for consideration is that international donor agencies make available resources for NGOs, including research facilities and funding, which can be used for increasing awareness of environmental issues, as well as developing small-scale training programmes for miners.

Integrating small-scale miners into the formal sector

By formalizing ASM, the government would minimize health and social problems, provide increased employment, capture revenues and, importantly, reduce environmental degradation. Formalization could be accomplished through a process of legislative review and inventory taking[53] on the government's part, and through joining mining cooperatives on the miners' part. Under such a scheme, all miners would be registered in registered cooperatives which would then be eligible for small scheme loans, machinery and equipment for rent and purchase at reduced prices. By formalizing ASM[54] through the creation of mining cooperatives, miners should be provided with free access to environmental and case study material, easier loans, basic education on mining as a trade (bookkeeping, marketing, etc), as well as vital technical aid in such areas as impact assessment, prospecting, mine construction, mineral testing, waste management and mine and land rehabilitation. This could be funded from a MRTF or the ecological fund until mining cooperatives are able to generate funds on their own. Through formalization, the Mines Department would be able to keep a tab on all licensed operators in the sector, and hence be able to seek out violators more efficiently. This, of course, must have adequate backing – most crucially, finance.

Mining cooperatives

The federal government has set terms for the formalization of small-scale miners in the sector. First, all ASM operators must form cooperative societies to qualify for mining titles; thereafter, the cooperative society can apply for a mining lease, which may be granted after the payment of requisite fees. All cooperatives will be eligible for loans under the Small Scale Mining Guarantee Scheme Fund, as provided in the Minerals and Mining Decree.[55] These cooperatives will have better access to international aid and technical assistance, and access to local funding from banks or individuals willing to invest in the minerals sector. Tax breaks can be made or import duties can be waived on equipment and tools to encourage small-scale miners to take up less harmful practices and methods (for themselves and the environment). Cooperatives will also be able to sell their minerals and gemstones in organized minerals markets at going world prices, with concessions being granted by the government for using the market. There should be a constant review of cooperative practices and competence by the Ministry of Solid Minerals; cooperatives should be subjected to fines or suspension for substandard practices.

Conclusion

Mining is not sustainable, and must therefore be planned and managed in an appropriate manner. Effective environmental management is one way, a path on which Nigeria seemingly has a long trek. This is mainly due to lack of adequate legislation guarding the environment in terms of mining practices, as well as poor enforcement of what appear to be inadequate laws. A lack of technology and insufficient data pose additional problems. In the case of ASM, the pattern of environmental degradation that is now widespread throughout the sector is being perpetuated by the impoverished state of miners and mining communities, as well as illiteracy and a lack of environmental awareness.

It is hoped that recognition of the economic potential of Nigeria's ASM sector, coupled with the current World Bank mining project, will facilitate improvements on the environmental front. Accomplishing this will require dedication on part of officers, amendments to be made to existing laws, implementation of poverty alleviation schemes, increased environmental awareness among all parties involved and increased financial assistance for operators. These changes constitute the basis of a more formalized industrial sector.

Postscript: progress on the horizon?

To recapitulate, since the early 1990s, when donor agencies began to recognize the importance of formalizing ASM, a number of industry-specific support-related initiatives and programmes have been implemented in sub-Saharan Africa, Asia and Latin America. Primary examples include projects emphasizing regulatory and institutional strengthening, financial support, technological assistance and environmental awareness. These exercises, however, have, for the most part, proved futile, failing both to facilitate marked regularization of the sector and raise the living standards of its predominantly impoverished participants.

Despite possessing limited knowledge of the dynamics of ASM communities, the consultants and so-called experts hired to identify and ameliorate the sector's pressing problems have repeatedly dismissed the importance of involving mining populations in policy-making activities and carrying out preliminary community-orientated research. This has inevitably led to the design and implementation of inappropriate technologies, unsustainable support services and extension, and ineffective policies and regulations, among other things. For years, miners have lacked a mouthpiece to provide feedback on bureaucratic licensing schemes and regulations, poorly designed equipment and unsuitable credit facilities. The Communities and Small-Scale Mining (CASM) Secretariat was established to change this, with the intention of providing the ASM community with the voice it has so desperately needed.

In September 2005, CASM held its Fifth Annual General Meeting and Learning Event in Salvador de Bahia, Brazil. An important prelude to this conference was the organization's donors' meeting in June 2005, the aim of which was to expand the network of organizations involved in ASM, bring the sector further into the mainstream international development agenda, and most significantly, attract additional donor funding. Yet, few individuals working on the ground – including miners and representatives of NGOs lobbying on their behalf – were invited to the meeting; nor were any researchers, who, as mentioned at the outset of this book, are most acquainted with the situation in the field, and therefore in the best position to provide feedback and advice on priority industry needs. If there was concern over grassroots parties and academics sabotaging the donors' meeting, why was a seminar not held specifically for these parties during the months before?[1] This would have undoubtedly provided fresh insight on ASM needs, which, in turn, could have been tabled at the donors' meeting.

Unfortunately, the donors' meeting to a large degree set the stage for Salvador: potentially a valuable educational initiative for the ASM community, the CASM Learning Event also lacked significant grassroots representation. Consequently, what promised to be productive breakout sessions on 'Building Community Capacity through Community-Driven Development' and 'Integrated Rural Development' were, in the end, theoretical exercises. Moreover, the assortment of learning modules, including 'The Feasibility of Environmental Licensing', 'Government Best Practice in ASM' and 'Tools for Communications in ASM' were similarly one-dimensional, featuring primarily inputs from those based in bureaucratic institutions. This was particularly significant for Africa, where ASM is in a most impoverished and rudimentary state: the majority of African attendees were government officials based in city capitals. Despite ample evidence which underscores the ineffectiveness of ASM top-down policy, officers at multilateral and bilateral institutions continue to overlook the importance of undertaking community-orientated research before administering support to the sector's participants; the small group of consultants advising these agencies and entrusted to implement solutions have also failed to understand the need for extensive grassroots intervention. The representation at the meetings in Washington and Salvador are obvious indications.

During recent research in Ghana, one of the country's key ASM stakeholders commented on the donor community's obsession with pursuing 'fashionable projects'. These, the individual explained, are 'idealistic interventions' which lack substance because they have been implemented without careful analysis of target populations beforehand. In support of this argument, reference was made to the recent fixation on promoting sustainable, alternative livelihoods for artisanal and small-scale miners, the majority of which are simply *not* sustainable, having been developed without studying the characteristics of local markets. Key examples include training women miners engaged in batik in villages where there are no markets for products; promoting silkworm farming in artisanal mining communities without providing sufficient startup funding; and encouraging snail rearing where snail consumption is not widespread. To date, hundreds of thousands of dollars have been pledged towards this cause but with limited success because again, the majority of individuals carrying out the work have failed to study local markets and communities.

In the absence of a clearly defined agenda for ASM support, several other 'fashionable projects' have been proposed by influential individuals. One which is in the pipeline, and discussed at length at the CASM Learning Event, is the prospect of promoting the extraction of industrial minerals on an artisanal and small scale. The logic behind such a move, it is argued, is that developing countries could satisfy their own needs for industrial mineral product. Those championing this, however, have overlooked the fact that with few exceptions (e.g. Nigeria), developing countries are already doing so. To justify the expansion of industrial mining on the grounds of domestic consumption, there must be some commitment to developing infrastructure which uses extracted industrial mineral product. Why should greater emphasis be placed on extracting industrial minerals and aggregates if no roads, buildings or sewerage pipes are being built?

Most significantly, and contrary to the views of certain 'experts', how can ASM operators possibly be the foundation of an industrial mineral economy? This assumes, for starters, that poverty-stricken Africans are willing to abandon high-value gold and gemstone extraction activities in favour of high-volume, low-profit sand, salt and phosphate mining. Secondly, how can ASM, which is semi-mechanized in the most advanced of situations, compete alongside a large-scale mining sector extracting the same minerals? Can 40 men with shovels realistically compete with an excavator? Finally, assuming that the aforementioned hurdles can be overcome, in order to encourage individuals to obtain concessions to mine industrial minerals, adequate support systems must be in place. This has not occurred in the small-scale gold- and diamond-mining sector to date, so what reason is there to believe that the same 'experts' can establish and regularize an ASM sector based on industrial minerals? Before pledging millions of dollars towards this cause, donors must shy away from such unsubstantiated claims, and commit to first evaluating the potential for expanding ASM to incorporate an industrial minerals dimension. This requires careful study of local and regional market conditions and, crucially, the actors involved.

On a more positive note, donor agencies' lack of interest in sponsoring community research on, and development of grounded bottom-up policy for, ASM has not deterred certain researchers long committed to making change on the ground. Under the Global Mercury Project, for example, researchers are working in ASM communities in Zimbabwe, the Sudan, Brazil, Laos, the Philippines and Indonesia to develop local solutions to mercury pollution problems. Through extensive interaction with miners, excellent local solutions have been developed, including pipe and kitchen retorts. Plans have also been put forward to construct mobile ore-processing centres and establish AIDS/malaria treatment facilities. In the Guianas, officers at the WWF Guianas are also working with ASM communities to reduce exposure to mercury by conducting educational seminars in the field and implementing an assortment of environmental technologies. At the CASM conference in Salvador, a presentation was made on the Cleangold™ sluice, a simple piece of equipment which enables impoverished miners to triple their recovery of gold. In the words of its inventor: 'Cleangold™ may be the solution [to this impoverishment]…two Universities have taken on board studies of Cleangold™ and have proven its efficiency…It has been researched, tested on the ground in Europe, NA, Suriname, and Africa, and *proven* to work'. The contributors to this book are also committed to implementing local solutions, drawing upon key experiences on the ground. Work of this nature has proved to be the key to strengthening donor agencies' support projects for ASM.

Yet, the individuals who have devoted considerable time to improving understanding of the dynamics of ASM populations and carrying out promising work in the field are finding it increasingly difficult to secure funds to continue their research. In the words of one attendee of the CASM meeting, 'Forget hiring these consultants...I just asked my boss for money, bought some equipment, set it up and demonstrated it, and gave it to the people'. Has this what getting results in the ASM sector has come down to, where those genuinely working to alleviate poverty in communities are forced to avoid donor agencies and their network of advising consultants altogether? The research carried out by the authors of this book, for instance, was independently funded – using mainly funds secured through university outlets and charities – with minimal direct involvement from donor institutions, who continue to favour tendering million-dollar contracts to consultants championing top-down policy.

With ASM becoming more of a focal point in the field of international development, it is high time that multilateral and bilateral agencies revise their policy and research agendas, and begin sponsoring the community-centred work which promises to strengthen industry assistance, environmental management and livelihoods projects. Importantly, CASM must fulfil its commitment to supporting and promoting 'the development of projects and approaches, by individuals, communities and institutions that will directly or indirectly contribute to the reduction of poverty and the construction of more viable livelihoods in communities and rural areas where small-scale mining is a significant activity'[2] by providing impoverished participants in the ASM sector with more of a voice. In the meantime, the contributors to this book and others active on the ground must double their efforts to secure sponsorship from academic outlets and charities.

We must not lose hope: those in the donor community will eventually come to realize that the small group of individuals they have entrusted to facilitate improvements are not doing so, and that researchers working in partnership with the people in affected communities are in the best position to prescribe wholesale changes.

Gavin M. Hilson
September 2005

Notes

1 An Overview

1 In 1996, the World Bank and the International Monetary Fund (IMF) launched the Heavily Indebted Poor Countries (HIPC) Initiative, which established a framework for all creditors to provide debt relief to the world's poorest and most heavily indebted countries. In July 2005, at the G-8 Summit in London, leaders called upon the World Bank, the IMF and the African Development Bank to cancel all debts owed by countries qualifying for irrevocable debt relief under the HIPC Initiative. Nigeria is surprisingly ineligible for debt reduction under the HIPIC programme, although its income levels per head and ratio of debt to GDP are comparable with those included under the Initiative. Nigeria's debt amounts to more than 90 per cent of its GNP, a higher percentage than that of 15 countries on the HIPC list, including Burkina Faso and Senegal. The logic behind its exclusion is that it produces over US$20 billion in annual exports of oil, which, officials at the Bank believe, can be used to service its debts. See http://www.eastwest.be/news-oct-2002/nigeria.html.

5 Mercury: an agent of poverty in West Africa's small-scale gold-mining industry

1 As explained on its website (http://www.unites.uqam.ca/gmf/intranet/gmp/index_gmp.htm), the Global Mercury Project aims to demonstrate ways of overcoming the barriers to adopting pollution prevention measures that limit mercury contamination of international waters from ASM.

2 As Yakubu (2003b) explains, in Ghana, licensed gold buying agents purchase mercury stored in beer bottles from 'mercury importers'. One beer bottle (8.625 kg) costs 900,000 cedis (approximately US$90), and one vial (52.2 g), known locally as *poho*, costs 8000 cedis (approximately US$0.80).

3 To their credit, the Ghanaian government has sponsored a series of radio programmes in the local Twi dialect, in which the toxic impacts of mercury have been discussed extensively. The sparingly few successful ASM support-related initiatives have made extensive use of radio communication (Crispin, 2003; Heemskerk and Oliveira, 2003; Hilson, 2006a).

7 Artisanal and small-scale mining in West Africa: achieving sustainable development through environmental and human rights law

1 Some commentators are promoting arguments for the advancement of a distinct area of sustainable development law. This seems quite a legitimate proposal noting that the distinct areas of environmental law, human rights law, economic law and others all seek to address related issues that are united under the umbrella of sustainable development, such as poverty.

2 The dates on which the individual states of ECOWAS joined the UN are: Benin, 20 Sept 1960; Burkina Faso, 20 Sept 1960; Cape Verde, 16 Sept 1975; Côte d'Ivoire, 20 Sept 1960; Gambia, 21 Sept 1965; Ghana, 8 Mar. 1957; Guinea, 12 Dec. 1958; Guinea-Bissau, 17 Sept 1974; Liberia, 2 Nov. 1945; Mali, 28 Sept 1960; Mauritania, 27 Oct. 1961; Niger, 20 Sept 1960; Nigeria, 7 Oct. 1960; Senegal, 28 Sept 1960; Sierra Leone, 27 Sept 1961; Togo, 20 Sept 1960. From United Nations website, http://www.un.org/Overview/unmember.html, accessed 13 December 2004.

3 The term 'soft law', which originated in international law, tends to refer to quasi-legal instruments that do not have any binding force, or whose binding force is weaker than hard law. Soft law tends to include non-treaty obligations such as declarations, resolutions, guidelines and action plans that cannot really be enforced but that nevertheless arguably contribute to the advancement of international law. Soft law can be contrasted with hard law, which comprises traditional, binding law such as treaties that states are required to enforce and be bound by.

4 The Declaration of the United Nations Conference on the Human Environment, convened at Stockholm 5–16 June 1972 to consider 'the need for a common outlook and for common principles to inspire and guide the peoples of the world in the preservation and enhancement of the human environment'. It comprises 26 Principles.

5 The Rio Declaration on Environment and Development, adopted at the 1992 UNCED. It is an international environmental agreement negotiated between both developed and developing countries and adopted by more than 178 governments in an attempt to balance environmental and developmental goals, and comprises 27 Principles.

6 Adopted by General Assembly Resolution 217 A (III).

7 The Banjul Charter, adopted 27 June 1981.

8 After Gro Harlem Brundtland, Chair of the World Commission on Environment and Development (WCED) (WCED, 1987: 43). See also Second preambular paragraph of UN General Assembly Resolution on the Report of the World Commission on Environment and Development, A/RES/42/187, 96th plenary meeting, 11 December 1987.

9 For our purposes, the term 'Principle', as applied in the Declarations, refers to the individual provisions and the obligations contained therein.

10 A multi-stakeholder mining initiative, created in 1998 by the International Development Research Centre, Canada.

11 MMSD was initiated by the World Business Council for Sustainable Development and supported by the Global Mining Initiative (GMI); it was managed by the International Institute for Environment and Development in London, UK, 2000–2.

12 In some countries. For example, in the early 1990s, the government-owned bank of Tanzania purchased precious minerals from ASM operators as a means to stimulate the ASM industry. See Lawyers' Environmental Action Team Company LEAT), *Complaint Relating to Violations of Fundamental Rights and Duties Arising from Forced Evictions of Artisanal and Small-Scale Miners from Afrika Mashariki Gold Mine, Tarime (submitted to the Tanzania Commission for Human Rights and Good Governance)*, 25 July 2003.

13 Adopted on 20 August 2002, in Johannesburg, South Africa, at the Global Judges Symposium 18–20 August 2002. Available online at: http://www.inece.org/wssd_principles.html or http://www.unep.org/dpdl/symposium/Principles.htm or http://www.unep.org/dpdl/symposium/Documents/RESOULUTION%201-FINAL%2020%20AUGUST.doc.

14 UN General Assembly Millennium Declaration, A/RES/55/2, adopted 18 September 2000 at the 55th session. This Declaration is soft law; as 'the decisions of the Assembly have no legally binding force for governments, they carry the weight of world opinion, as well as the moral authority of the world community'. From *Basic Facts About the United Nations*, DPI/2155 Rev.1 – December 2002 – 40M.

15 The UNDP is the UN's global development network responsible for linking and coordinating global and national efforts to achieve the MDGs.

16 Paragraph 14, Johannesburg Principles on the Role of Law and Sustainable Development 2002.

17 Paragraph 8, Johannesburg Principles on the Role of Law and Sustainable Development 2002.

18 See foonote 5 .

19 For insight into the debate, see Gillespie (2001: 3–6); Steiner and Alston (2000: 1315–34).

20 Adopted by General Assembly resolution 41/128 at the 97th plenary meeting of 4 December 1986.

21 Preamble paragraph 1 of the 1986 Declaration on the Right to Development.

22 See International Institute for Environment and Development (IIED), 2002: Chapter 9.

23 See examples of these human rights norms and standards enunciated in the 1981 African Charter on Human and Peoples' Rights and the 1948 Universal Declaration of Human Rights.

24 See ILO Convention No. 107 (1950), UN Commission for Human Rights Resolution 1993/77 and General Comment No. 4 (1991) of the Economic, Social and Cultural Rights Committee. See also *Social and Economic Rights Action Centre and Center for Economic and Social Rights vs. Nigeria* legal petition to the African Commission on Human and Peoples' Rights and the Commission's findings in Communication 155/96 of violation of Articles

2, 14, 16, 18(1), 21 and 24 of the African Charter on Human and Peoples' Rights by the Federal Republic of Nigeria in respect to the citizens of Ogoniland.

25 Adopted and opened for signature, ratification and accession by General Assembly resolution 2200A (XXI) of 16 December, entry into force 3 January 1976.

26 This right is also enunciated in several other human rights agreements, including Articles 1(1) and (2) of the 1966 International Covenant on Civil and Political Rights and Article 20 of the 1981 African (Banjul) Charter on Human and People's Rights.

27 CASM multi-donor network, launched March 2001. Its mission is 'to reduce poverty by supporting integrated sustainable development of communities affected by or involved in artisanal and small-scale mining in developing countries': see http://www.casmsite.org.

28 Such as UNIDO (of which ECOWAS is a member), UNDP, ILO (of which ECOWAS is a member), and UNEP.

29 Geneva, 27 June 1980. Entered into force 5 September 1991.

30 The right to protection of health and to safety in working conditions, including the safeguarding of the function of reproduction.

31 CEDAW was adopted in 1979 by the UN General Assembly. CEDAW comprises a preamble and 30 Articles. It entered into force on 3 September 1981.

32 Nigeria signed on 8 September and ratified on 22 November 2004, and Senegal signed on 10 December 1999 and ratified 26 May 2000. All other ECOWAS members have signed or acceded to the Convention, other than Cape Verde, Côte d'Ivoire, the Gambia, Mauritania and Togo.

33 The United Nations Convention on the Rights of the Child was adopted and opened for signature, ratification and accession by General Assembly Resolution 44/25 of 20 November 1989. It is ratified by 192 eligible countries, except Somalia and the US.

34 Article 1.

35 *Action pour la Promotion des Droits de l'Enfant au Burkina Faso* (Action for the Promotion of the Rights of the Burkinabe Child).

36 ILO Convention 138 has not been ratified by Cape Verde, Ghana, Guinea-Bissau, Liberia or Sierra Leone.

37 Date of entry into force 19 June 1976.

38 Date of entry into force 10 November 2000 (ratified ECOWAS states: Benin, Burkina Faso, Cape Verde, The Gambia, Ghana, Guinea (Guinea Bissau not yet ratified but ratification approved), Niger, Nigeria, Senegal and Togo).

39 'The types of work referred to under Article 3(d) shall be determined by national laws or regulations or by the competent authority, after consultation with the organizations of employers and workers concerned, taking into consideration relevant international standards, in particular Paragraphs 3 and 4 of the Worst Forms of Child Labour Recommendation,

1999; and Article 4(1) of the ILO Convention on the Worst Forms of Child Labour, 1999 (No. 182).

40 Through their Global Child Labour Programme.

41 Through their International Programme on the Elimination of Child Labour (IPEC).

42 For more comprehensive recommendations, the reader is directed to 'Our common interest', the Report of the Commission for Africa, March 2005, UK: http://www.commissionforafrica.org/english/report/introduction.html English version (but available in other languages), accessed 21 March 2005. The Commission for Africa was launched by the British Prime Minister Tony Blair in February 2004. The aim of the Commission is 'to take a fresh look at Africa's past and present and the international community's role in its development path'.

43 UNECA (2002a).

44 1998 UN Economic Commission for Europe Convention on Access to Information, Public Participation in Decision-Making and Access to Justice in Environmental Matters (the latter comprise the 'three pillars' upon which the Convention is built and depends for its full implementation).

8 Introduction

1 The kingdom of Ghana did not consist of the territory that is present-day Ghana. It extended into present-day Mauritania, Mali and Guinea. The kingdom of Mali extended into Mauritania, Mali, Guinea, Niger and small areas of Burkina Faso, Guinea-Bissau, Côte d'Ivoire, Benin, Sierra Leone and Liberia. The Songhay kingdom extended into all of these, as well as a small area in northwest Nigeria.

9 Artisanal and small-scale mining in Mali: an overview

1 A Muslim sovereign of Mali who made the pilgrimage to Mecca in AD 1324–5.

2 The Authority of Liptako Gourma is a subregional organization that consists of Burkina Faso, Niger and Mali, three Sahelian and landlocked West African countries.

3 Tarikh El-Sudan, a medieval scribe.

4 Malinké/Khassonké, Fulani and Tuareg.

5 GIE stands for 'Economic Interest Group' (abbreviated in French).

6 In English, the West African Monetary and Economic Union.

10 Artisanal and small-scale gold mines in Burkina Faso: today and tomorrow

1 Bureau des Mines et de la Géologie du Burkina Faso.

2 These mines closed because of the collapse of the gold price.

3 Comptoir Burkinabé des Métaux Précieux (Burkinabe Precious Metals Office), the state corporation for management and control of the artisanal sector.

4 Post-rush site reorganized by a cooperative group is typical of artisanal gold mining in north Burkina. Rudimentary mining (no pumping) at a location of large quartz veins extending as deep as 40 metres.

5 At Gueguere (Ioba province), the equivalent of almost 30 ha of forest have been destroyed for shoring up a trench 100 metres in length and 25 metres deep.

6 The Chinese saline electric batteries used by the miners, however, pollute very little.

7 Ghana officially imports about 5 tonnes of mercury each year for the sole needs of artisanal gold miners.

8 Projet institutionnel de renforcement des capacités nationales du secteur minier et de gestion de l'environnement, World Bank-supported institutional project for strengthening national capacities in the mining sector and environmental management.

9 Hot nitric acid is used locally after flotation for the roasting of sulphuric oxides and the liberation of gold from concentrates.

10 Directorate of small-scale mine exploitation, directly attached to the Directorate General of Mines, Geology and Quarries (DGMGC).

11 To dig a pit 30 m depth, four labourers need about two months.

11 Artisanal gold mining in Burkina Faso: permits, poverty and perceptions of the poor in Sanmatenga, the 'land of gold'

1 The Burkinabé Precious Metals Counter (CBMP) was created and bestowed with the sole monopoly over collecting, processing and marketing precious metals produced by artisanal, industrial and semi-industrial mining.

2 SAP measures can differ per country, but generally include: shifts to the production of cash crops or other commodities (like rubber, cotton, coffee, copper, tin, etc) for export; currency devaluation measures which help stimulate the export of domestically produced goods; liberalization of trade and investment and high interest rates to attract foreign investment; and privatization of government-held enterprises.

3 The Lobi-Dagara country is situated in the southwest of Burkina Faso. In colonial times, the term Lobi was used to designate a whole range of groups with different ethnic identities, such as Lobi, Gan, Dagara, Djan and Birifor. Most of these groups were supposed to have egalitarian social structures. In this region, women were assigned the privilege of searching for gold.

4 Ce secteur...dites de 'Goren' renferme de nombreuses exploitations artisanales de nature diverses, globalement organisées suivant une direction NNE-SSW...Les orpaillages du village de Goren sont relativement vastes; l'exploitation des minéralisations éluvionnaires couvre les flancs de relief saprolitisés et les différents talwegs...A Liliga les orpaillages du 'placer de

Sondo' paraissent en fait plutot correspondre au démantelement d'une mineralisation primaire.

5 The weights used in the scales are coins and matchsticks. At the site, one matchstick of gold is valued at CFAFr500 (US$1); an old franc coin (with the weight of 1 g) in gold gives a price of CFAFr6,000 (US$11.50). For northern Benin, Grätz (2004: 151–2) describes a similar system of weighing gold dust in scales, with coins serving as weights. In most cases, traders use one whole CFA franc coin, as well as one CFA coin that has been cut in half or quarters. The author states that the CFA weighs 1.2 g.

6 The Fulbe, also known as Fula, Fulani, Pulaar and Tukolor, are dispersed from Senegal to northern Cameroon, and even the Sudan. The Fulbe consider themselves to be cattle-herders, but today have established sedentary populations across this region. These groups are not exclusively cattle-herders, although cattle remain an important part of their identity.

12 Artisanal gold mining in northern Benin: a sociocultural perspective

1 The term 'artisanal goldmining' is used synonymously with non-mechanized or small-scale mining. Some authors refer to such activity as illegal or informal mining.

2 This account deviates from governmental evaluations and the perspective of many miners.

3 Apart from the work of the French geologists Chermette and Olory (1963), Vincent (1962) and colleagues in the early 1960s, there are few published studies on the geological and environmental aspects of gold mining in Benin. There are, however, unpublished evaluations produced on behalf of BRGM, particularly studies documenting periods of active exploration; but few describe the technological aspects of artisanal mining. There are also some unpublished (internal) reports which discuss the state of small-scale mining in Benin. Few could be accessed to supplement the material presented in this chapter, however.

4 Mineral deposits in the Atakora region were referred to in documents published in 1903 and 1908. The first professional geological missions commissioned to explore Benin's mineral deposits occurred in the 1920s. According to Chermette and Olory (1963), it was the geologist Chetelat who first discovered gold deposits in the Atakora Mountains (in 1927). Other important explorers included R. Pougnet, a geologist at the Central Mining Board in Dakar (Direction Fédérale des Mines et de la Géologie) who worked in Dahomey between 1946 and 1952, and Chermette himself who led the most important geological exploration missions up to 1963.

5 The overall production of SMDN in this period was approximately 900 kg gold. The average content of gold was estimated at 0.6 g/m³.

6   The same policy, which is followed as a guide to issue licences for both prospecting and exploiting deposits – with priority for the entitlement of an exploration company – is used today.

7   Although the mine close to the village of Kwatena was known to the locals because of its partial exploitation during colonial times, there had been no small-scale gold activities carried out, mainly because of the rigid state control of those zones, which were considered to be exclusive property of the state up to the end of the 1980s.

8   Unlike miners in both Ghana and Burkina Faso, miners operating in Benin do not use crushing machines and mercury.

9   For a hard day's work, miners may earn CFAFr1,000–30,000.

10 This system of risk-sharing (Grätz, 2003a) is typical of all mining sites in West Africa, especially in the case of reef mining (Werthmann, 2003c). Such a social contract comprises a kind of trade-off: the more unpredictable the yield, the greater the possible gain for the team chief in situations of success. But a chief must satisfy the basic living requirements of mine labourers, regardless of output.

11 Systems involving sponsors and tributors also dominate artisanal diamond mining in Sierra Leone (Richards, 1996). However, hierarchies in small-scale gold mining seem to be more shallow and flexible: a shaft owner who is unsuccessful may continue working as a simple miner and vice versa.

12 In arrangements similar to tenancy, there are rarely fixed sums but irregularly paid shares (in most cases, in raw products), the amount of which is very much determined by the actual success of the team.

13 The delimitation of zones and claims are marked out (using charcoal, wooden barriers, etc) in the presence of witnesses.

14 The author interprets the mentioned social hierarchies as an accepted part of the rules of the game in the mining field. They are based on shallow patronal relationships and cannot simply be subordinated in terms of exploitation or oppression. A sort of trade-off is observable, namely, the accepting of a bigger share of the profits reserved for the patrons in exchange for a supply of materials and expertise as well as managing capacities. Miners recognize an effective team leader as someone who possesses knowledge of not only where and how to exploit gold veins and to organize the shifts, but also how to work efficiently and how to excavate in ways which prevent injuries and accidents. An experienced team leader commands respect and prestige; miners are more inclined to follow the advice of an experienced team leader. Team leaders must fulfil their responsibilities to ensure that workers stay with them and do not join another team leader for the next extraction cycle. Hierarchies thus provide security for working arrangements. They are flexible enough so that former gold diggers may become team leaders or small entrepreneurs after acquiring experience, esteem and, of course, sufficient capital.

15 In all cases, miners observe and respect more or less voluntary ritual prescriptions, taboos and ceremonies, and contribute to collections for such rituals.

16 In Kwatena, there is a characteristic pattern of small-scale migration, which is simply a way of commuting, especially from the area of Kwatena, exercised by some people on weekly basis, likely because of short travel distances and frequent transport facilities.

17 The fundraising (*cotisation*) organized by representatives of the local population does not only constitute a tax for the exclusive benefit of the locals. This contribution in cash and in kind may be redistributed during festivities but also in forms of communal infrastructure such as schools, medical centres and churches that are principally open to all.

18 They work an easily movable washing and concentrating device, operated by one American expatriate and some Beninese staff.

19 For a similar account on diamond divers, see de Boeck (1998).

20 For a comparative perspective on the lifestyle of gold miners, see Werthmann (2003c).

21 Many local inhabitants offer goods, sell food, water and building materials, and make other valuable contributions during mining booms.

13 Introduction

1 The violent, inhuman tactics of the RUF have been well documented. The rebels carried out brutal sweeps of communities, chopping the arms, legs and noses off suspected government supporters, including women and children. The group amputated the limbs of the victims it did not murder – particularly children – indicating that the reason for doing so was that amputees could not vote or grow crops that might be used to support government troops. In fact, children were used extensively in the campaign: girls served as prostitutes and boys were recruited as soldiers, often forced to murder their parents. It is claimed that officers rubbed cocaine into the open wounds of soldiers in an effort to make them fearless; that guerrillas carved the initials 'RUF' on their chests; and for entertainment, some soldiers would bet on the sex of an unborn baby, then proceed to slice open a woman's womb to determine the winner.

2 October 2005 in Accra, Ghana.

15 Reflections on the political economy of artisanal diamond mining in Kono District, Sierra Leone

1 Blood diamonds is the term coined for those diamonds whose proceeds are used by rebel forces to fund their wars. The term is used interchangeably with 'conflict diamonds' (See also Chapter 14). Branding diamonds in this way gave NGOs currency to exert pressure on the industry and on those governments of countries where diamonds are produced, traded and

marketed as these stakeholders had reason to fear the public boycotting of the commodity in light of the NGOs' blood diamonds campaign.

2. Eluvial deposits are those which have been transported by the lateral or vertical movement of the soil. Alluvial deposits are those which have been transported by the movement of water.

3 Thanks due to Eric Leinberger, cartographer for the Department of Geography at the University of British Columbia, for creating this map.

4 The first official report from this research can be found at http://www.peacediamonds.org and Temple et al. (2005).

5 SLST's private security force was increased from 85 in 1950 to 662 in 1957, then to 1,313 (plus 245 auxiliary police on their payroll) in 1971 (Greenhalgh, 1985).

6 This practice dates back to the protection of itinerant traders in the 19th century.

7 There were constitutional (and popular) prohibitions against the involvement of ethnic non-Africans in politics. This included a 1960 constitutional decree which denied citizenship to those of non-African parentage (Reno, 1995).

8 This was the case for one miner, whose Spanish supporter held an exporting licence. The miner believed that this enabled him to receive a better price for his diamonds compared with others.

9 This happens when the miner is not Sierra Leonean and thus is not permitted to hold a licence, or is not a Kono and therefore finds it difficult to get a licence himself.

10 Overkicking is a common type of mining conducted by people independently or in pairs.

11 Presuming a gang of 50 diggers is doing the work for 2.5 months (10 six-day weeks) at a cost of US$2.64 (Le7,000) per digger per day.

12 In Sandor chiefdom, one cannot make one's application by letter but must go in person.

13 Licensed plots used to be 400 x 400 feet before the war but now the plot size is 210 x 210 feet.

14 Estimate provided by an official at the MMR.

15 Black mud is 'the layer of soil on the gravel that sometimes is removed and put aside and is something you go back to in the rain', as one miner explained in the Structure of the Mining Industry Workshop I, held in July 2004.

16 The price of rice differs by about 15 per cent between the two seasons (Le60,000–70,000).

17 Half of the miners interviewed indicated a preference for employing people of particular tribes, either Temne, Koranko or other Konos.

18 At the time of research, the official exchange rate was US$1:Le2,600. However, the 'street' rate (i.e. the rate which the majority of Sierra Leoneans would receive) was US$1:Le2,800.

19 It is during the washing stage where it is easiest for diggers to steal diamonds.

20 In one case, a woman digger was employed as a waterwoman and cook.

21 One miner reported paying his mines manager 10 per cent of his 40 per cent share of the winnings (i.e. 4 per cent of the overall winnings).

22 Interview with the chairman of the Kono Dealers Association, June 2004.

23 The staff at a South African company who had just begun work in Sandor chiefdom explained their experience with mines wardens who were to be monitoring their activities. In paraphrase, the mines warden told them, 'We don't earn enough money to keep our families, so if you give us something we'll turn a blind eye, and when you find 40 carats, we'll report 0.4 carats'.

24 For more information on the Diamond Area Community Development Fund, see *Search For Common Ground and Talking Drum Studios* (2003).

16 Perspectives on diamond mining and public health in Akwatia, Ghana

1 There is evidence citing gold mining going as far back as the seventh and eighth centuries AD (Hilson, 2001b).

2 In some cases, a person or group or people may obtain a licence to mine a plot of land, and then hire labourers to mine the plot, paying them a percentage of findings.

3 In support of this claim, Corvolán et al. (1999) point out that: 'It is [now] understood that appropriate developments must occur in agriculture, industry, and energy if sustainable health improvements are to be attained. That said, the health sector has an important role as advocate and guide for healthy development'.

4 It was recognized in a report published by the CMH in 2001 that: 'improving the health and longevity of the poor is an end in itself, a fundamental goal of economic development. But it is also a *means* to achieving the other development goals of the United Nations Millennium Development Goals relating to poverty reduction' (WHO, 2001: 3).

5 Malaria accounted for 20 per cent of outpatient cases at St Dominic's Hospital in 2001.

6 In support of this statement, in another report on mining and the environment at the Tarkwa-Abosa-Nsuta mine, Songsore et al. (1994) pointed out that: '[an] important environmentally-related disease [at the Tarkwa-Abosa-Nsuta mine] is malaria, with an increasing incidence because of new surface mines which have led to the creation of stagnant waters which serve as breeding sites for malarial mosquitoes'.

7 In this same time period, through its revegetation plan, GCD planted 140 beds in areas that could be revegetated with 28,000 seedlings, investing just over US$20,000 for this project (GCD, 2000).

8 For example, Tema, Ghana's largest port, has the third-highest HIV/AIDS prevalence in Ghana, at 6.6 per cent. The report suggests that this is connected to truck-drivers who come through the port to transfer goods

to West African countries along the major West African highway, as well as ships that travel in and out of the port. Obuasi, a gold-mining town that is Ghana's largest and most active mine site, has the fifth-highest HIV incidence of sentinel sites in Ghana at 6.0 per cent. In light of findings in other parts of the world, both of these sites are important areas for further research, as they relate to the spread of HIV/AIDS.

9   Now AngloGold-Ashanti, following a merger with Anglo American in 2004.

18 'Live and let live': The relationship between artisanal/small-scale and large-scale miners at Abosso Goldfields, Ghana

1   As previously noted, in Ghana, the entire ASM segment of the mining industry is commonly referred to by the omnibus name of *galamsey,* an adulterated English phrase for 'gather them and sell', which has a very defiant subterfuge attitude towards the law.

2   For instance, colonial mining laws such as the Concessions Ordinance 1890 (CAP 87) and the Gold Mining Protection Ordinance, No. 3 1905, were designed specifically to protect the interests of large-scale mining concessionaires.

3   As a direct sequel to this Act, the PMMC, hitherto the Diamond Marketing Company, was set up by the government to purchase and sell gold and diamonds produced by ASM operators.

4   See Hilson (2001b: 22–3) for a vivid documentation of the regulatory framework, as well as the registration procedures for ASM in Ghana.

5   A similar sentiment was expressed by participants at a validation workshop (August 2004) on research on ASM commissioned by DFID and organized at the Institute of Local Government Studies.

6   AGC is a Ghanaian multinational gold mining company. In 2004, AGC merged with another multinational mining giant, Anglo American, to form AngloGold-Ashanti.

7   An ASM operator who gave his name as 'Taller' during an interview, 12 November 1996.

8   As a high-school graduate, the author personally witnessed some of these police raids, commonly called 'scatter', and heard stories from the victims of such raids. The brutal nature of some of the raids occasionally led to fatalities and other human rights abuses.

9   The 1996 national elections were held in December of that year. During the runup to the 2004 elections, the ruling NPP government was also accused by a section of the media (*The Chronicle* in particular) for failing to address the *galamsey* encroachment problems on the lands demarcated to the Bogoso Mine because of political sensitivity.

10   Ranger Minerals sold its interests in Abosso to Goldfields SA and Iamgold, a Canadian-based exploration and development company.

11 Until the discovery of a bankable deposit in the present Damang area in 1995, the primary interest of Ranger Minerals in Ghana was treatment of the old Abosso tailings.

12 A Ghanaian mining engineer with considerable experience (17 years at underground operations and eight years at various surface mines, both gold and diamond) was employed by AGL.

13 Again, PMMC is a government-appointed agency responsible for the purchase and marketing of gold and other precious minerals from small-scale miners in Ghana.

14 It was the policy of the company to ensure that at least 70 per cent of its unskilled labour requirements were sourced from the local area.

15 The AGL Small Scale Mining Supervisor liaised with accredited gold buying agents for monthly gold purchases from (the company's) small-scale miners, which enabled the company to submit detailed monthly returns to the Minerals Commission and Mines Department.

19 Strained relations: a critical assessment of the mining conflict in Prestea, Ghana

1 According to local tradition, the name 'Prestea' is a corrupted pronunciation of the phrase 'Preston's Well'. In the 1700s, an Englishman known as 'Preston' had constructed a well to aid with the excavation and processing of local surface gold deposits ubiquitous in the area at the time.

2 Following protests, the deadline was changed to 31 May 2005.

3 The former website of the Ghana Chamber of Mines, the representative body of the country's mining sector, described the *galamsey* as a 'menace', as has the Bank of Ghana, which, in its recent publication *Report on the Mining Sector* (Bank of Ghana, 2003), refers to the existence of widespread artisanal gold-mining activity as 'The Menace of "*Galamsey*" Operations'.

4 There are conflicting views on how the 'I Trust My Legs' label came about. According to an article in *Grist Magazine* (Harkinson, 2003), it is a reference made to several of the camp's *galamsey* miners having 'trusted their legs' when successfully fleeing on foot from security forces. In communicating with the local chief, however, it transpired that the 'I Trust My Legs' label has come about because the specific mine labour itself is arduous, involving extensive underground work and therefore requiring considerable 'trust in one's legs'.

5 Circular entitled 'Memorandum of Understanding Between Bogoso Gold Limited and Prestea-Himan-Bondaye Area'.

6 Following a meeting held on 29 January 2003 between the then BGL mine manager, BGL security consultants and Prestea Mining Group executives, it was agreed that the Number Four Bungalow site would be released to the Prestea Mining Group for small-scale mining activities. The details of the agreement were as follows: the site would be operated solely by the people of Prestea, Himan and Bondaye; only 100 pits and 100 people should

be allowed to operate on the site; and ejection of operations from Number Four Bungalow shall be based strictly upon negotiation.

7   'Golden Star Reports on Ghanaian Government Nationwide Action to Stop Illegal Mining', http://www.ccnmatthews.com/news/releases. Controller?action=check4Cookies&actionFor=543716, CNN Matthews, 31 May 2005, accessed 28 September 2005.

8   At the time at which this research was being carried out, the Geological Survey Department was beginning to prospect near Bondaye to identify areas suitable for small-scale mining.

9   It is a well-known fact that prospecting companies in Ghana have used indigenous people, who possess a deep knowledge of local geology, to identify economic deposits.

10   Unlike most mining companies' community trust funds, the amount of funds within which is generally based upon the amount of profit recorded, Gold Fields' fund is independent of earnings. The company puts a fixed percentage of money in its fund for every ounce of gold mined; thus, even in cases where minimal profits have been recorded, the community still benefits from the finances accrued within the fund.

20 Addressing the environmental challenges of artisanal and small-scale mining in Nigeria

1   Oil accounts for 20 per cent of Nigeria's GDP, 95 per cent of foreign-exchange earnings and about 65 per cent of budgetary revenues; information available online at: http://worldfacts.us/Nigeria.htm (accessed 15 March 2004).

2   In the 1970s, Nigeria produced an average of 10,000 tonnes of tin annually. In the 1980s, output fell to 3,000 tonnes and by 1990, it was down to 500 tonnes. Coal production fell from 940,000 tonnes in 1958 to 73,000 tonnes in 1986; information available online at: http://countrystudies.us/nigeria/ 64.htm (accessed 17 January 2004). Declining production was exacerbated in the case of coal by declining world demand and in the case of tin, by exhaustion of high-grade ores.

3   According to the World Bank, poor management, country circumstances (such as pilfering from state coffers) and changing global economics resulted in the decline. See the Project Information Document of the World Bank, presented at the Stakeholder Orientation and Discussion on Sustainable Management of Mineral Resources in Nigeria, Abuja, Nigeria, 30 March 2004. The document is also available online at:
http://www-wds.worldbank.org (accessed 24 May 2004).

4   Solid minerals were identified as potential high-revenue earners.

5   With the adoption of a democratic constitution in Nigeria, from May 1999, all decrees made by previous military governments became designated as Acts. Accordingly, in this chapter, the Minerals and Mining Decree No. 34 of 1999 will simply be called the Minerals and Mining Act.

6   It is estimated that small-scale mining in Africa employs almost 4 million people: ILO Report on Social and Labour Issues in Small-Scale Mines; information available online at: http://www.ilo.org/public/english/ dialogue/sector/techmeet/tmssm99/tmssmr.htm (accessed 12 December 2004). In an interview with the *Thisday* newspaper in 2002, Okwudili Uzoka, the chairman of the House of Representatives' Committee on Solid Minerals, estimated that ASM accounted for 95 per cent of mining activities in Nigeria: available online at: http://www.thisdayonline.com/archive/ 2001/08/index.html (last visited 4 March 2006).

7   A 2001 UNDP survey shows that 70% of Nigerians live below the international poverty line of US$1 a day. See online at: http://www.undp.org.ng/abnga1.htm (accessed 17 January 2004).

8   Shoko argues, whilst making comparisons between alluvial gold panning and land tilling, that agricultural activity actually does more damage to the environment in terms of land degradation and river siltation. He maintains that mining is concentrated in small areas, and is considered less of a lifeline than agriculture and therefore is perceived to be the worse offender.

9   Bugnosen discusses the problems of definition and the approaches adopted by different countries in legislating for the sector. Several countries have avoided specific definitions altogether. Others have adopted categorizations based on number of miners involved, output of mine, size of reserves or organization of the mining enterprise.

10 Nöetstaller (1996) delivered a keynote address at an international roundtable organized by the World Bank in May 1995, in which he discussed the problems of informal and small-scale mining. The proceedings are available online at: http://www-wds.worldbank.org/servlet/ WDS_IBank_Servlet?pcont=details&eid=000009265_3980429111204 (accessed 4 March 2006). Labonne (2003) also refers to this 'negative cycle of cause and effect' in a keynote address at a plenary forum on Artisanal and Small-Scale Mining in Yaoundé, Cameroon, 19–22 November 2002.

11 Gyan-Baffour (2003) notes that for every US$1 generated from artisanal mining, US$3 are generated in other non-mining jobs. He also points out that a large number of miners pursuing limited resources results in low incomes that do not allow miners to progress from primitive mining equipment used. This contributes to further lowering incomes and equally importantly, environmental degradation, which, in turn, affects mining productivity.

12 Nigeria runs a consolidated revenue system in which all revenues of the federation from diverse sources do not accrue to collecting agencies but are consolidated into a federation account. It is therefore arguable that an increase in mining revenues does not necessarily guarantee a proportionate increase in allocations to mining regulation. On the other hand, as has been the case in the oil industry, a substantial increase in official revenues

from mining should motivate more attention being paid to all aspects of the sector, including allocations to enforcement of regulations.

13 Nigeria's solid mineral occurrences can be broken down into five categories, namely (i) metalliferous, (ii) carbonaceous, (iii) non-metallic, (iv) precious and (v) radioactive. This categorization is given by the Federal Ministry of Solid Minerals in Nigeria Mineral Occurrences – See S. 259 2(a), (b), (c), (d) and (e) of the Minerals and Mining Act (MMA). Examples of the minerals according to category include cobalt and tungsten, coal and tarsands, limestone and marble, gold and tourmaline, and uranium, respectively.

14 In 2001, total official revenues from solid minerals was US$89 million. See online at: http://www.nigeriabusinessinfo.com/minerals.htm (accessed 17 March 2002). Potential revenues of US$32 million can be generated annually from alluvial gold, cassiterite and some industrial minerals alone. This is still a conservative estimate. There is insufficient data for gemstones' and other minerals' revenue potential.

15 Gemstones, precious metals and industrial minerals are the near-exclusive preserve of artisanal mining.

16 Nigeria's alluvial deposits are virgin, high-grade and occur near the surface, making them attractive and easily accessible to artisanal miners. This ease of access has contributed to the growth of artisanal mining and its attendant environmental problems – Presidential Committee on Solid Minerals Development, in an unpublished report on 'A Seven Year (2002–2009) Strategic Action Plan for Solid Minerals Development' of November 2002, p. 64, where the report describes Nigeria's mineral setting.

17 Tourmaline is found in at least seven states of Nigeria, including Cross River, Nasarawa and Niger States with the latter two located in the middle belt of Nigeria. It is a hard crystalline borosilicate, sold as gemstone but also used in electrical and optical devices. It manifests in green, blue, pink or black varieties. Each bag of tourmaline from the Akutayi site is predominantly pink and can be sold for as high as N2,000 (US$14) per gram or as low as N2,000 per 25kg bag, depending on grade. Grade is determined by the marketers on inspection.

18 As of May 2004, the mine site at Akutayi had been closed for three months. The two enterprises operating the site were working out modalities for its re-opening. The miners worked on a casual basis, being remunerated by a share of the tourmaline mined. Both the operators and the miners sold their respective shares to roving marketers around the mine site. The marketers then sold on to bigger marketers or end-users in the cities.

19 Locally fabricated pumping machines, belching clouds of noxious fumes, contribute their own quota to harmful emissions into the atmosphere.

20 The locals allege that fatalities have occurred in the past as a result of the caving in of mine walls.

21 Any miner is free to join the quarry provided he pays the required royalty on quantities mined to the union, which, in turn, pays certain sums to the local government council.

22 A truckload of granite, mostly used for construction of pavements, roads and houses, is sold for about N4,500–11,000, depending on the size of granite stones and distance of delivery.

23 The Committee Report notes that no large-scale mining currently exists in Nigeria, only a small-scale mining sector structured into illegal artisanal operations and legal small-scale operations.

24 There are granite quarries in at least 20 out of Nigeria's 36 states. Several are advanced small-scale operations run by construction companies. Apart from use in construction, granite is used as raw material for steel, glass and refractory industries. Nigerian granite is named mainly according to location and colour – Kaduna Pink, Kano Red and Maraba Black.

25 Increased bush burning is attributed to the growth of the district and thus the influx of quarries. Fire wood is a predominant source of energy in rural Nigeria, and the ensuing demand needs to be contained, especially in fast growing localities such as Mpape. Fire wood is sold for additional income by settlers.

26 The location of the Mpape and Malali sites within or near urban concentrations mean that miners have much better access to health facilities and living conditions than at Akutayi. However, many granite quarrying sites in Nigeria are in locations as remote as Akutayi, and it is not inconceivable that conditions there are closer to Akutayi's.

27 Air and noise assessments have been randomly carried out at mine sites and quarries in Nigeria. Results in most cases show that the acceptable levels of noise and air pollution are exceeded. See Committee Report.

28 A synopsis of Maslow's hierachy-of-needs theory is available online at: http://www.ship.edu/~cgboeree/maslow.html (accessed 6 June 2004).

29 See S.191(2) (a) MMA.

30 See preceding footnote.

31 See S. 25 MMA.

32 S. 233(1) MMA.

33 At the international roundtable on small-scale mining organized by the World Bank in 1995, delegates accepted that ideally, all mining should be subjected to the same environmental, health and safety regulations. A more realistic approach, however, would be to create a separate framework of standards for small-scale mining that would be achievable in light of the poverty that drove and attended the sector. Setting unrealistically high standards for artisanal and small-scale miners would be counter-productive in economic and environmental terms. Proceedings of the roundtable are available online at: http://www.worldbank.org/htm/fpd/mining/m3files/art/art1.htm (accessed 3 June 2004).

34 S. 2(a) MMA.

35 S. 2(b) MMA.

36 S. 2(o) MMA.

37 See particularly, S.146(1)(k),(l),(m) and (n) and S. 146(2)(a),(e),(j), (k) and (m).

38 Through Mines Field Police, S. 2(n) and through the Director of Mines Office, S. 101(f).

39 Reasons for the inefficiencies of the Solid Minerals Ministry include an inadequately equipped mines department, low levels of funding and the absence of a government revenue-collection system. See Presidential Committee Report (above).

40 S. 123(2)(a) states that 'a person who is guilty of an offence under subsection (1) of this section is liable on conviction: at the first instance, to a fine not exceeding N15,000 or to imprisonment for a term not exceeding 2 years or to both fine and imprisonment'. S. 127(1) provides for 'a fine not exceeding N20,000 or imprisonment for a term not exceeding 2 years or to both the fine and imprisonment' for convictions for which offences under the Decree which have no penalty.

41 S. 127(3).

42 This is in form of an IDA loan to the tune of US$75 million and an agreed counterfunding by the Nigerian government of US$5 million.

43 It remains a fact that small-scale miners are not entitled to mining titles unless they are members of registered mining cooperatives. The requirement for joining these cooperatives is not set, nor is the minimum size of cooperatives. S. 10(d) of the law requires an applicant for an exclusive prospecting licence, mining lease or mining title to provide a detailed programme of progressive reclamation and rehabilitation of lands so disturbed.

44 S. 254(2).

45 S. 101(g).

46 S. 101 (h).

47 These will be the Mines Inspectorate Department, Mines Engineering and Parastatals Department and Minerals Economics and Promotion Department. Enforcement of the Minerals and Mining Law remains a responsibility of the Mines Department at federal and state levels. See Presidential Committee Report (above).

48 Revenue from the Petroleum Trust Fund in Nigeria was used to build roads and provide drugs for State-owned hospitals at subsidised rates.

49 This is a function for the department after restructuring (all proposed). See Presidential Committee Report (above).

50 Major oil companies in Nigeria show commitment to community development and sustainable development by way of health and water projects, schools and research centres.

51 The legal instrument for the establishment of the fund is yet to be processed. It is not clear if this proposed fund will act as a trust fund for infrastructural development or a development fund for education and training.

52 Petroleum Technology Development Fund. A development fund targeted at training Nigerians in petroleum issues – law, engineering and management – towards the long-term goal of developing a source of Nigerian expertise.

53 Of mines, licensed miners, illegal miners.

54 Success with the formalization of small-scale miners can be seen in Colombia's coal mining sector, where MINERCOL, the state-owned coal company, awards licences to formalized/legal small-scale miners. The company gave small-scale miners two years to legalize operations or face closure. Thereafter, small-scale miners were provided training and technical support, while also receiving free inspections of mines, free emergency services and better access to loans: 'Small scale mining: a social and environmental problem turned into an opportunity for economic development', A. Zamora, paper prepared for the Berlin Roundtable on Mining and the Environment, November 1999. http://www.dundee.ac.uk/cepmlp/journal/html/vol6/article6-6.html (accessed 25 February 2004).

55 S. 233.

Postscript: progress on the horizon?

1   It is worth noting that on 16–17 June 2005, CASM did host The Millennium Development Goals and Small-Scale Mining: A Conference for Forging Partnerships for Action in Washington, DC. Significantly, this conference occurred *after* the donors' meeting and was also dominated by consultants and individuals based in multilateral institutions. An assortment of important regional conferences and learning events have, however, been held in places such as Zimbabwe, Papua New Guinea and the Philippines over the past year or two, but have not received the attention they have deserved.

2   http://www.casmsite.org/about.html.

References

Abdullah, I. (1998) 'Bush path to destruction: the origin and character of the Revolutionary United Front/Sierra Leone', *Journal of Modern African Studies*, **36** (2), pp. 203–34.

Abdullah, I. (2004) 'Beyond greed: memo on the Sierra Leone conflict', paper presented at the Social Science Research Council Program on Global Security and Cooperation, Washington, DC (19–20 April).

Adebajo, A. (2002) *Building Peace in West Africa: Liberia, Sierra Leone, and Guinea-Bissau*, Lynne Rienner, Boulder, CO.

Adepoju, A. (2002) 'Fostering free movement of persons in West Africa: achievements, constraints, and prospects for intraregional migration', *International Migration*, **40** (2), pp. 3–28.

Ahern, M. and Stephens, C. (2001) 'Workers and community health impacts related to mining operations internationally: a rapid review of the literature', Mining, Minerals, and Sustainable Development (MMSD) Project, International Institute for Environment and Development (IIED), London.

Akabzaa, T. and Darimani, A. (2001) 'Impact of mining sector investment in Ghana: a study of the Tarkwa Mining Region', draft report for Structural Adjustment Participatory Review International Network (SAPRIN), Washington, DC.

Akagi, H., Branches, F.J.P., Kinjo, Y., Kashima, Y., Guimaraes, J.R.D., Oliveira, R.B., Haraguchi, K., Pfeiffer, W.C., Takizawa, Y. and Kato, H. (1995) 'Human exposure to mercury due to goldmining in the Tapajos River Basin, Amazon, Brazil – speciation of mercury human hair, blood and urine', *Water, Air and Soil Pollution*, **80** (1–4), pp. 85–94.

Ajayi, J.F.A. and Crowder, M., eds (1987) *History of West Africa*, Vol. 2, 2nd edn, Longman Group, Harlow.

Alao, A. (1999) 'Diamonds are forever…but so also are controversies: diamonds and the actors in Sierra Leone's civil war', *Civil Wars*, **2** (3), pp. 43–64.

Alfa, S. (1999) 'Child labour in small-scale mines in Niger', in N. Jennings, ed., 'Child labour in small-scale mining: examples from Niger, Peru and Philippines' (Jennings Report on Child Labour), Working Paper 137, International Labour Organization, Geneva.

Amankwah, R.K. and Anim-Sackey, C. (2004) 'Promoting co-operation between small- and large-scale mining companies in Ghana', *Mining Magazine* (April), pp. 36–9.

Amegbey, N., Ampong, C.H. and Ndur, S.A. (1994) 'Water pollution from mining in Prestea, Ghana', in *Proceedings presented at Third International Conference on Environmental Issues and Waste Management in Energy and Mineral Production*, Perth, Australia, pp. 179–84.

Andrew, J.S. (2003) 'Potential application of mediation to land use conflicts in small-scale mining', *Journal of Cleaner Production*, **11** (2), pp. 117–30.

Andrews-Speed, P., Zamora, A., Rogers, C.D., Shen, L., Cao, S. and Yang, M. (2002) 'A framework for policy formulation for small-scale mines: the case of coal in China', *Natural Resources Forum*, **26** (1), pp. 45–54.

Appiah, H. (1998) 'Organization of small scale mining activities in Ghana', *Journal of the South African Institute of Mining and Metallurgy*, **98** (7), pp. 307–10.

Appleton, J.D., Williams, T.M., Breward, N., Apostol, A., Miguel, J. and Miranda, C. (1999) 'Mercury contamination associated with artisanal gold mining on the island of Mindanao, the Philippines', *Science of the Total Environment*, **228**, pp. 95–109.

Archibald, S. and Richards, P. (2002) 'Converts to human rights? Popular debate about war and justice in rural central Sierra Leone', *Africa*, **72** (3), pp. 339–67.

Aryee, B.N.A. (2001) 'Ghana's mining sector: its contribution to the national economy', *Resources Policy*, **27** (2), pp. 61–75.

Aryee, B.N.A. (2003a) 'Small-scale mining in Ghana as a sustainable development activity: its development and a review of the contemporary issues and challenge', in G. Hilson, ed., *The Socioeconomic Impacts of Artisanal and Small-Scale Mining in Developing Countries*, A.A. Balkema, Rotterdam, pp. 379–418.

Aryee, B. (2003b) 'Retrospective on the Ghana experience: overview of artisanal mining and its regulation in Ghana', presentation at the 3rd Annual General Meeting of the World Bank Communities and Small-Scale Mining Programme, Elmina, Ghana.

Aryee, B.N.A., Ntibery, B.K. and Atorkui, E. (2003) 'Trends in the small-scale mining of precious minerals in Ghana: a perspective on its environmental impact', *Journal of Cleaner Production*, **11** (2), pp. 131–40.

Aspinall, C. (2001) 'Small-scale mining in Indonesia', Working Paper 79, Mining, Minerals, and Sustainable Development (MMSD) Project, International Institute for Environment and Development (IIED), London.

Asante, G. (2003) 'Socio-economic importance of artisanal mining in Ghana', paper presented at a National Workshop on Artisanal Mining, Its Economic Importance and Effect on the Environment, Accra.

Associates for International Resources and Development (AIRD) (2002) 'The value of gold in the Republic of Mali', SEGIR/GBTI Contract PCE-I-00-98-00016-00, Associates for International Resources and Development (AIRD), Cambridge.

Aubynn, A. (1997) 'Liberalism and economic adjustment in resource frontiers: land-based resource alienation and local responses, a reflection from western Ghana', Working Paper 9/97, IDS, University of Helsinki, Finland.

Auty, R.M. (1993) *Sustaining Development in Mineral Economies: The resource curse thesis*, Routledge, London.

Auty, R.M. (2001) 'The political economy of resource-driven growth', *European Economic Review*, **45**, pp. 839–46.

Ayitey-Smith, E. (1989) *Prospects and Scope of Plant Medicine in Healthcare*, Ghana University Press, Accra.

Babut, M., Sekyi, R., Rambaud, A., Potin-Gautier, M., Tellier, S., Bannerman, W. and Beinhoff, C. (2003) 'Improving the environmental management of small-scale gold mining in Ghana: a case study of Dumasi', *Journal of Cleaner Production*, **11** (2), pp. 215–21.

Bangura, Y. (1997) 'Understanding the political and cultural dynamics of the Sierra Leone war: a critique of Paul Richards's fighting for the rain forest', *Africa Development*, **22** (3/4), pp. 117–48.

Bank of Ghana (2003) 'Report on the Mining Sector', Report 1(3), Bank of Ghana, Ghana.

Bannerman, W., Potin-Gautier, M., Amouroux, D., Tellier, S., Rambaud, A., Babut, M., Adimado, A. and Beinhoff, C. (2003) 'Mercury and arsenic in the gold mining regions of the Ankobra River basin in Ghana', *Journal de Physique*, **107**, pp. 107–10.

Barbier, E. (1989) *Economics, Natural Resource Scarcity and Development: Conventional and Alternative Views*, Earthscan, London.

Barry, M, ed. (1996). 'Regularizing informal mining: a summary of the proceedings of the international roundtable on artisanal mining' organized by the World Bank, 17–19 May 1995, Industry and Energy Department Occasional Paper 6, Washington,, DC.

Barry, M. (1997) 'Addressing social tensions in mining: a framework for greater community consultation and participation', in A.J. Ghose (ed.), *Mining on a Small and Medium Scale: A global perspective*, Intermediate Technology Publications, London, pp. 3–8.

Bayah, J., Iddirisu, Y. and Tinorgah, C. (2003) 'Artisanal and small-scale mining as a tool in rural development: experiences from a World Bank supported project in Burkina Faso', Regional Consultation Workshop for Africa, Maputo, Mozambique.

Bayart, J.F. (1993) *The State in Africa: The politics of the belly*, Longman, London and New York.

Berry, L.B., ed. (1995) *Ghana : A country study*, 3rd edn, Federal Research Division, Library of Congress, Washington, DC.

Biodiversity Support Programme (1993) *African Biodiversity: Foundation for the future*, Professional Printing, Beltsville, MD.

Boers, R. (2003) 'Considerations on small-scale mining', paper presented at the African Workshop of the World Bank Extractive Industries Reviews, Maputo, Mozambique.

Bonzongo J.C., Donkor, A.K. and Nartey, V.K. (2003) 'Environmental impacts of mercury related to artisanal gold mining in Ghana', *Journal de Physique*, 4 (107), pp. 217–20.

Briggs, D. (1999) *Environmental Health Indicators: Frameworks and methodologies*, World Health Organization, Geneva.

British Broadcasting Corporation (BBC) (2003) 'Ghana gold workers paid in condoms', BBC News (19 February).

Bugnosen E.M. (2003) 'Small-scale mining legislation: a general review and an attempt to apply lessons learned', in G. Hilson, ed., *The Socioeconomic Impacts of Artisanal and Small-Scale Mining in Developing Countries*, A.A. Balkema, Rotterdam, pp. 7–23.

Campbell, B. (2003a) 'African mining codes questioned', *Mining Journal* (14 February), pp. 106–9.

Campbell, B. (2003b) 'Factoring in governance is not enough. Mining codes in Africa, policy reform and corporate responsibility', *Minerals and Energy*, 18 (3), pp. 2–13.

Campbell, B., Akabzaa, T. and Butler, P. (2003) 'The challenges of development, mining codes in Africa and corporate responsibility', in E. Bastida, T. Walde and J. Warden, eds, *International and Comparative Mineral Law and Policy Trends and Prospects*, Kluwer Law International, The Hague, pp. 801–22.

Campbell, B. and Clapp, J. (1995) 'Guinea's economic performance under structural adjustment – importance of mining and agriculture', *Journal of Modern African Studies*, 33 (3), pp. 425–49.

Campbell, C. (2000) 'Selling sex in the time of AIDS: the psycho-social context of condom use by sex workers on a southern African mine', *Social Science and Medicine*, 50 (4), pp. 479–94.

Campbell, C. and Williams, B. (1999) 'Beyond the biomedical and behavioral: towards and integrated approach to HIV prevention in the southern African mining industry', *Social Science and Medicine*, 48 (11), pp. 1625–39.

Carnegie, J. (2002) 'Sustainable livelihoods approach and artisanal and small-scale mining', in B. Labonne, ed., *Seminar on Artisanal and Small-Scale Mining in West Africa: Identifying Best Practices and Building the Sustainable Livelihoods of Communities*, Yaoundé, pp. 63–5.

Carney, D.E. (1961) *Government and Economy in British West Africa*, Bookman Associates, New York.

Chakravorty, S.L. (2001) 'Artisanal and small-scale mining in India', Working Paper 78, Mining, Minerals, and Sustainable Development (MMSD) Project, International Institute for Environment and Development (IIED), London.

Chermette, A. and Olory, G. (1963) 'Les Recherches Minières de la République du Dahomey', Département de Mines et Métallurgie, Benin.

Church, R.J.H. (1966) *Some Geographical Aspects of West African Development*, The Camelot Press, London.

Clarke, E. (1998) 'Working and health conditions among small scale miners in rural Ghana', Occupational Health Unit, Ministry of Health, Ghana.

Collier, P., Elliott, V.L., Hegre, H., Hoeffler, A., Reynal-Querol, M. and Sambanis, N. (2003) *Breaking the Conflict Trap: Civil war and development policy*, Oxford University Press, Oxford.

Collier, P. and Hoeffler, A. (2004) 'Greed and grievance in civil war', *Oxford Economic Papers*, **56**, pp. 563–95.

Commission Européenne (2003) *Rapport Annuel Conjoint 2002 sur la Mise en Oeuvre des Actions de Cooperation dans le Cadre des Conventions ACP-UE au Burkina Faso*, Delegation de la Commission Européenne au Burkina Faso, Ouagadougou.

Corden, W.M. (1984) 'Booming sector and Dutch disease economics: survey and consolidation', *Oxford Economic Papers*, **36**, pp. 359–80.

Corvalán, C.F., Kjellstrom, T. and Smith, K.R. (1999) 'Health, environment, and sustainable development: identifying links and indicators to promote action', *Epidemiology*, **10** (5), pp. 656–60.

Crisp, B.F. and Kelly, M.J. (1999) 'The socioeconomic impacts of structural adjustment', *International Studies Quarterly*, **43**, pp. 533–52.

Crispin, G. (2003) 'Environmental management in small scale mining in PNG', *Journal of Cleaner Production*, **11** (2), pp. 175–83.

Cullet, P. (2003) *Differential Treatment in International Environmental Law*, Ashgate, Aldershot.

Danielson, L. and Lagos, G. (2001) 'The role of the minerals sector in the transition to sustainable development', Mining, Minerals, and Sustainable Development (MMSD) Project, International Institute for Environment and Development (IIED), London.

Davidson, J. (1993) 'The transformation and successful development of small-scale mining enterprises in developing countries', *Natural Resources Forum*, **17** (4), pp. 315–26.

Davies, V. (2000) 'Sierra Leone: ironic tragedy', *Journal of African Economies*, **9** (3), pp. 349–69.

Davies, V. and Fofana, A. (2002), 'Diamonds, crime and civil war in Sierra Leone', paper prepared for the World Bank and Yale University case study project, The Political Economy of Civil Wars, New Haven, CT.

De Boeck, F. (1998) 'Domesticating diamonds and dollars: identity, expenditure and sharing in southwestern Zaire (1984–1997)', *Development and Change*, **29** (4), pp. 777–810.

de Mowbray, P. (2002) Opening speech at Seminar on 'Small-scale and artisanal mining in Africa: identifying best practices and building the sustainable livelihoods of communities', in B. Labonne, ed., *Seminar on Artisanal and Small-Scale Mining in West Africa: Identifying Best Practices and Building the Sustainable Livelihoods of Communities*, pp. 33–4, Yaoundé.

Delap, E., Ouedraogo, B. and Sogoba, B. (2004) 'Developing alternatives to the worst forms of child labour in Mali and Burkina Faso', Save the Children, UK, available online at: http://www.savethechildren.org.uk/scuk_cache/scuk/cache/cmsattach/1862_child%20labour%20Mali%20&%20BF.pdf (accessed 2 March 2006)

Diamond Development Initiative (DDI) (2005) 'The Diamond Development Initiative' (9 March), Global Witness, London, available online at: http://www.globalwitness.org/press_releases (accessed 24 August 2005).

Dianou, D. and Poda, J.N. (1999) 'Health impacts of mining on communities and human settlements in Burkina Faso', paper presented at the Conference on Mining, Development and Social Conflicts in Africa, Third World Network, Africa Secretariat, Accra (15–18 November).

Dikko, L.S. (2001) 'Nigeria – solid minerals financing: Intercity Bank's perspectives', paper presented at Export financing, administration and practice in Nigeria seminar, Kaduna, Nigeria.

do Nascimento, J.A.S. (2001) 'Project database: documentation of information about small and artisanal mining – Brazilian report', Mining, Minerals, and Sustainable Development (MMSD) Project, International Institute for Environment and Development (IIED), London.

Donkor, A.K., Bonzongo, J.C., Nartey, V.K. and Adotey, D.K. (forthcoming, 2006) 'Mercury in different environmental compartments of the Pra River Basin, Ghana', *Science of the Total Environment.*

Donoghue, A.M. (2004) 'Occupational health hazards in mining', *Occupational Medicine,* **54** (5), pp. 283–9.

Douglas, F. (2001) 'Al Qaeda cash tied to diamond trade', *Washington Post* (2 November).

Dreschler, B. (2001) 'Small-scale mining and sustainable development within the SADC region', Working Paper 84, Mining, Minerals, and Sustainable Development (MMSD) Project, International Institute for Environment and Development (IIED), London.

D'Souza, K. (2002) 'Artisanal and small-scale mining in Africa: a reality check', in B. Labonne, ed., *Seminar on Artisanal and Small-Scale Mining in West Africa: Identifying Best Practices and Building the Sustainable Livelihoods of Communities,* Yaoundé, pp. 45–57.

Eisler, R. (2003) 'Health risks to gold miners: a synoptic review', *Environmental Geochemistry and Health,* **25** (3), pp. 325–45.

Elder, T.G. (2002) 'Mineral legislation of Liberia', *Transactions of the Institution of Mining and Metallurgy B,* **111**, pp. 200–2.

Elias, R. and Taylor, I. (2001) 'HIV, the mining and minerals sector and sustainable development in Africa', report published for the MMSD Initiative (Southern Africa Unit), University of Witwatersrand, Johannesburg.

Ettema, W. and Gielen, G. (1992) *Burkina Faso,* Book Number 26436, Koninklijk Instituut voor de Tropen (Royal Institute of the Tropics), Amsterdam.

Fairbairn, W.C. (1965) 'Licensed diamond mining in Sierra Leone', *Mining Magazine,* **112** (3), pp. 166–77.

Forster, J.J. and Bills, J.H. (2002) 'Comparison of the impact of the fiscal regime on gold projects in Tanzania and Burkina Faso', *Transactions of the Institution of Mining and Metallurgy,* **111**, pp. 195–9.

Fraser, E.D.G., Dougill, A.J., Mabee, W.E., Reed, M. and McAlpine, P. (2006) 'Bottom up and top down: analysis of participatory processes for sustainability indicator identification as a pathway to community empowerment and sustainable environmental management', *Journal of Environmental Management,* 78 (2), pp. 114–27.

French, D. (2005) *International Law and Policy of Sustainable Development,* Manchester University Press, Manchester.

Frery, N., Maury-Brachet, R., Maillot, E., Deheeger, M., de Mérona, B. and Boudou, A. (2001) 'Gold-mining activities and mercury contamination of native amerindian communities in French-Guiana: key role of fish in dietary intake', *Environmental Health Perspectives,* **109** (5), pp. 449–56.

Gberie, L. (2002) 'War and peace in Sierra Leone: diamonds, corruption and the Lebanese', Occasional Paper 6, Partnership Africa Canada, Ottawa.

Gberie, L. (2003) 'West Africa: rocks in a hard place – the political economy of diamonds and regional destabilization', Occasional Paper #9, Partnership Africa Canada, Ottawa.

Gelb, A.H. (1988) *Oil Windfalls: Blessing or curse,* Oxford University Press, New York.

Geo-Jaja, M.A. and Mangum, G. (2001) 'Structural adjustment as an inadvertent enemy of human development in Africa', *Journal of Black Studies,* **32** (1), pp. 30–49.

Ghana Consolidated Diamonds (GCD) (1999) 'A brief profile of Ghana Consolidated Diamonds, Ltd', company document.

GCD (2000) 'Costed reclamation plan for mined-out areas: June 2000–December 2002', company document.

GCD (2001) 'Annual technical report: 2001', company document.

GCD (2002) Annual technical report: 2002', company document.

GCD (2003) 'Mining production: 1959–2002', company document.

Ghanaian Chronicle (2005a) 'Police/Army open fire' (16 June), available online at: http://www.ghanaian-chronicle.com (accessed 18 June 2005).

Ghanaian Chronicle (2005b) 'Mining cripples and illegal miners resist relocation' (7 May), available online at: http://www.theminingnews.org/news.cfm?newsID=803 (accessed 11 September 2005).

Ghana Macroeconomics and Health Initiative (2002) 'Report of the national launch and technical workshop', Accra, 19–20 November.

Ghana Ministry of Health (2001) 'Monthly outpatient morbidity tally sheets – 2001', Ministry of Health, Kwaebibirem District Office.

Ghana National AIDS/STI Control Programme (NACP) (2003) 'The HIV/AIDS epidemic in Ghana: an overview', Ghana National AIDS/STI Programme, Accra.

Ghana News Agency (2005) 'Small-scale miner was shot; surgeon belies AngloGold Ashanti' (1 July), available online at: http://www.ghanaweb.com (accessed 12 September 2005).

Ghana Publishing Corporation (1970) *Mining and Explosives Regulations, L. I. 665*, Accra.

Ghana Statistical Service in collaboration with International Labour Organization (ILO) (2003) 'Ghana child labour survey', International Programme on Child Labour, Accra, available online at: http://www.ilo.org/public/english/standards/ipec/simpoc/ghana/report/gh_rep.pdf#search='Ghana%20Child%20Labour%20Survey (accessed 3 March 2006).

Gilman, J. (1999) *Artisanal Mining and Sustainable Livelihoods*, United Nations Development Programme (UNDP), Geneva.

Gillespie, A. (2001) *The Illusion of Progress: Unsustainable development in international law and policy*, Earthscan, London.

Golow, A.A. and Adzei, E.A. (2002) 'Mercury in surface soil and cassava crop near an alluvial goldmine at Dunkwa-on-Offin, Ghana', *Bulletin of Environmental Contamination and Toxicology*, 69 (2), pp. 228–35.

Golow, A.A. and Mingle, L.C. (2003) 'Mercury in river water and sediments in some rivers near Dunkwa-on-Offin, an alluvial goldmine, Ghana, *Bulletin of Environmental Contamination and Toxicology*, 70, pp. 379–84.

Goreux, L. (2001) 'Conflict diamonds', Africa Region Working Paper Series 13, World Bank, Washington, DC.

Grätz, T. (2000) 'Gold trade in the Atakora region (Republic of Benin): social networks beyond the state', in U. Engel, A. Jones and R. Kappel, *Tagung. Afrika 2000*, VAD. 17, März bis 1, Leipzig: VAD / University of Leipzig /data service (CD-ROM), Leipzig.

Grätz, T. (2003a) 'Gold-mining and risk management: a case study from northern Benin', *Ethnos*, 68 (2), pp. 192–208.

Grätz, T. (2003b) 'Les chercheurs d'or et la construction d'identités de migrants en Afrique de l'Ouest', *Politique Africaine*, 91, pp. 155–69.

Grätz, T. (2004) 'Gold trading networks and the creation of trust: a case study from northern Benin', *Africa*, 74 (2), pp. 147–72.

Greenhalgh, P. (1985) *West African Diamonds, 1919–1983: An economic history*, Manchester University Press, Manchester.

Grootaert, C. (1995) 'Structural change and poverty in Africa – a decomposition analysis for Côte d'Ivoire', *Journal of Development Economics*, 47 (2), pp. 375–401.

Gueye, D. (2001) 'Small-scale mining in Burkina Faso', Mining, Minerals and Sustainable Development (MMSD) Working Paper 73, International Institute for Environment and Development (IIED), London.

Gunson, A.J. and Jian, Y. (2001) 'Artisanal mining in the People's Republic of China', Mining, Minerals and Sustainable Development (MMSD) Working Paper 74, International Institute for Environment and Development, London.

Gyan-Baffour G. (2003) 'Artisanal mining and poverty', Communities and Small Scale Mining (CASM) 3rd AGM and Learning Event, Elimina, Ghana, available online at: http://www.casmsite.org/Documents/Elmina%202003%20-%20Workshop%20-%20Poverty%20Reduction%20-%204.pdf (accessed 3 March 2006).

Gylfason, T. (2001) 'Natural resources, education and economic development', *European Economic Review*, **45**, pp. 847–59.

Hagenaars, A. and Devos, K. (1988) 'The definition and measurement of poverty', *Journal of Human Resources*, **23** (2), pp. 211–21.

Hall, P.K. (1968). 'The diamond fields of Sierra Leone', Geological Survey of Sierra Leone, Freetown.

Harkinson, J. (2003) 'Confessions of a dangerous mine: illegal gold mining in Ghana shafts locals' health and the environment', *Grist Magazine* (24 June), available online at: http://www.google.co.uk/search?hl=en&q=Twyman+livelihoods&meta (accessed 24 October 2005).

Heemskerk, M. and Oliveira, M. (2003) 'Perceptions of small-scale gold mining impacts: results from focus group discussions in mining camps and affected communities', World Wildlife Fund (WWF) Guianas, Paramaribo.

Heemskerk, M. and Oliveira, M. (2004) 'Maroon perceptions of small-scale gold mining impacts, II: A survey in mining camps and affected communities in Suriname and French Guiana', World Wildlife Fund (WWF) Guianas, Paramaribo.

Hentschel, T., Hruschka, F. and Priester, F. (2002) 'Global report on artisanal and small-scale mining', Working Paper 70, Mining, Minerals and Sustainable Development (MMSD) Project, International Institute for Environment and Development (IIED), London.

Herbst, J. (1993) *The Politics of Reform in Ghana, 1982–1991*, University of California Press, Berkeley, CA.

Hilson, G. (2001a) 'Mining and sustainable development: the African case', *Minerals & Energy*, **16** (2), pp. 27–36.

Hilson, G. (2001b) 'A contextual review of the Ghanaian small-scale mining industry', Working Paper 76, Mining, Minerals and sustainable Development (MMSD) Project, International Institute for Environment and Development (IIED), London.

Hilson, G. (2002a) 'Small-scale mining and its socio-economic impact in developing countries, *National Resources Forum*, **26** (1), pp. 3–13.

Hilson, G. (2002b) 'Small-scale mining in Africa: tackling pressing environmental problems with improved strategy', *Journal of Environment & Development*, **11** (2), pp. 149–74.

Hilson, G. (2002c) 'Promoting sustainable development in Ghanaian small-scale gold mining operations', *The Environmentalist*, **22** (1), pp. 51–7.

Hilson, G. (2002d) 'Delivering aid to grassroots industries: a critical evaluation of small-scale mining support services', *Minerals and Energy – Raw Materials Report* **17** (1), pp. 11–18.

Hilson, G. (2002e) 'An overview of land use conflicts in mining communities', *Land Use Policy*, **19** (1), pp. 65–73.

Hilson, G. (2002f) 'Land use competition between small- and large-scale miners: a case study of Ghana', *Land Use Policy*, **19** (2), pp. 149–56.

Hilson, G. (2002g) 'Harvesting mineral riches: 1,000 years of gold mining in Ghana', *Resources Policy*, **28** (1–2), pp. 13–26.

Hilson, G (forthcoming, 2006a) 'Abatement of mercury pollution in the small-scale gold mining industry: restructuring the policy and research agendas', *Science of the Total Environment*.

Hilson, G. (2006b) 'Poverty and artisanal mining in West Africa', in G.M. Hilson, *Small-Scale Mining, Rural Subsistence and Poverty in West Africa*, ITDG Publishing, Rugby, chapter 3.

Hilson, G. and Potter, C. (2003) 'Why is illegal gold mining activity ubiquitous throughout rural Ghana?', *African Development Review*, 15 (2), pp. 237–70.

Hinton, J.J. and Veiga, M.M. (2004) 'Summary report: technical and socio-economic profiles of Global Mercury Project sites', Global Mercury Project, UNIDO, Vienna.

Hinton, J., Veiga, M.M. and Beinhoff, C. (2003a) 'Women, mercury and artisanal gold mining: risk communication and mitigation', *Journal de Physique*, 107, pp 617–20.

Hinton, J.J., Veiga, M.M. and Veiga, A.T.C. (2003b) 'Clean artisanal gold mining: a utopian approach?', *Journal of Cleaner Production*, 11 (2), pp. 99–115.

Hollaway, J. (2000) 'Lessons from Zimbabwe for best practice for small- and medium-scale mines', *Minerals & Energy*, 15 (1), pp. 16–22.

Hopkins, A.G. (1973) *An Economic History of West Africa*, Columbia University Press, New York.

Human Rights Watch (1998) 'Sowing terror: atrocities against civilians in Sierra Leone', *Human Rights Watch*, 10 (3A) (July).

Hutchful, E . (2002) *Ghana's Adjustment Experience: The paradox of reform*, United Nations Research Institute for Social Development (UNRISD), Oxford University Press, London and New York.

Iddirisu, A.Y. and Tsikata, F.S. (1998) 'Mining sector development and environment project: regulatory framework study to assist small-scale miners', prepared for the Minerals Commission, Accra.

Institute of Statistical, Social, and Economic Research (ISSER) (2001) *The State of the Ghanaian Economy in 2000*, University of Ghana, Legon.

International Institute for Environment and Development (IIED) (2002) *Breaking New Ground: Mining, minerals, and sustainable development, the report of the MMSD project*, Earthscan, London.

International Labour Organization (ILO) (1999) 'Social and labour issues in small-scale mines', Report for discussion at the Tripartite Meeting on Social and Labour Issues in Small-scale Mines, Sectoral Activities Programme ILO, Geneva.

ILO (2004) 'Action against child labour in small-scale mining & quarrying: a thematic evaluation', joint thematic evaluation by an independent evaluator, International Programme on the Elimination of Child Labour (IPEC) ILO/IPEC and ILO/SECTOR, Geneva.

ILO (2005) 'Facts on small-scale mining', ILO, Geneva, available online at: http://www.ilo.org/public/english/bureau/inf/download/wssd/pdf/mining.pdf (accessed 8 April 2005).

International Monetary Fund (IMF) (1972 and other years) *Sierra Leone: Recent Economic Trends*, IMF, Washington, DC.

IMF (1994 and other years) *Balance of Payments Yearbook*, IMF, Washington, DC.

IMF and International Development Association (IDA) (2002) 'Heavily Indebted Poor Countries document: Burkina Faso', Enhanced Heavily Indebted Poor Countries Initiative Completion Point Document, IMF and IDA, Washington, DC.

IUCN Members Directory (2004) *IUCN Membership Relations and Governance*, World Conservation Union, Gland, available online at: http://www.iucn.org (accessed 9 October 2004).

Jackson, R.H. and Rosberg, C.G. (1982) *Personal Rule in Black Africa: Prince, autocrat, prophet, tyrant*, University of California Press, Berkeley, CA.

Jaques, E. (2001) 'La mine artisanale en Afrique: aspects techniques et environnementaux', paper presented at Séminaire sur l'exploitation minière artisanale en Afrique (Seminar on artisanal mining in Africa), Ouagadougou (1 March 2000), Occasional Publication 2001/37, International Centre for Training and Exchanges in Geosciences (CIFEG), Orleans.

Jaques, E., Greffié, C., Billa, M., Thomassin, J.F. and Zida, B. (2003) 'Recherche de cibles pour le développement de petites mines d'or au Burkina Faso', Bureau de Recherches Géologiques et Minières (France) (BRGM), Report RC-52143-FR, Orleans.

Jaques, E., Zida, B., Billa, M., Greffié, C. and Thomassin, J.F. (2004) 'La filière artisanale de l'or au Burkina Faso: bilan et perspectives d'évolution et, recherches de cibles pour le développement de petites mines', Occasional Publication 39, CIFEG, pp. 41–59, Orleans..

Jaques, E., Orru, J.F. and Pelon, R. (2005) 'Développement artisanal en Afrique: quelle place pour la mine artisanale?', *Géosciences – La Revue du BRGM pour une terre durable*, 1, pp. 66–71.

Jennings, N.S. (1994) 'Small-scale mining: a labour and social perspective', in A.K. Ghose, ed., *Small-Scale Mining: A global overview*, A.A. Balkema, Rotterdam, pp. 11–18.

Jennings, N.S., ed. (1998) 'Child labour in small-scale mining: examples from Niger, Peru & Philippines', Working Paper 137, ILO, Geneva.

Jennings, N.S., ed. (1999) 'Small-scale gold mining: examples from Bolivia, Philippines and Zimbabwe', Sectoral Activities Programme Working Paper, SAP 2.76/WP.130, International Labour Organization (ILO), Geneva.

Jennings, N.S. (2000) ' Small-scale mining: a sector in need of support', *Mining Environmental Management*, **8** (1), pp. 17–18.

Jennings, N.S. (2004) 'ASM and child labour', presentation at the ILO and Communities and Small-Scale Mining (CASM) meeting on Thematic Evaluation of Action on Child Labour in Artisanal and Small-Scale Mining (Mining Policy Research Initiative), Washington, DC, 28–30 April, available online at: http://www.iipm-mpri.org/biblioteca/index.cfm?action=ficha&lang=eng&cod=249

Jochelson, K., Mothibeli, M. and Leger, J.P. (1991) 'Human immunodeficiency virus and migrant labor in South Africa', *International Journal of Health Services*, **21** (1), pp. 151–73.

Jones, B. (2002) 'Economic integration and convergence of per capita income in West Africa', *African Development Review*, **14** (1), pp. 18–47.

Jutting, J. (2000) 'Transmission of price shifts in the context of structural adjustment: an empirical analysis for staple food after the devaluation of the franc CFA in Ivory Coast', *Agricultural Economics*, **22** (1), pp. 67–74.

Kambani, S.M. (1995) 'The illegal trading of high unit value minerals in developing countries', *Natural Resources Forum*, **19** (2), pp. 107–12.

Kambani, S. (2003) 'Key issues in illegal mining and marketing in the small-scale mining industry', in G.M. Hilson, ed., *The Socioeconomic Impacts of Artisanal and Small-Scale Mining in Developing Countries*, A.A. Balkema, Rotterdam.

Kandeh, J.D. (2002) ,Subaltern terror in Sierra Leone', in T. Zack-Williams, D. Frost and A. Thomson, eds, *Africa in Crisis: New challenges and possibilities*, Pluto Press, London, pp. 179–95.

Karekezi, S. (2002) 'Poverty and energy in Africa – a brief review', *Energy Policy*, **30** (11–12), pp. 915–19.

Keili, A.K. (2003) 'Environmental and sustainable development challenges for Sierra Leone's mining industry', paper presented at the Diamond Sector Workshop organized by DFID, Freetown, Sierra Leone.

Keita, S. (2001) 'Study on artisanal and small-scale mining in Mali', Mining, Minerals and Sustainable Development (MMSD) Working Paper 80, International Institute for Environment and Development (IIED), London.

Kesse, G.O. (1985) *Mineral and Rock Resources of Ghana*, A.A. Balkema, Rotterdam.

Kiétéga, J.B. (1983) *L'or de la Volta noire : archéologie et histoire de l'exploitation traditionnelle*, *Région de Poura, Haute-Volta*, Karthala, Paris.

Kimberley Process (2006) See online at: http://www.kimberleyprocess.com.

Kirscht, H. and Werthmann, K. (2003) *Sanmatenga – Gold-diggers in Burkina Faso*, IWF, Göttingen.

Klein, M. (1998) *Slavery and Colonial Rule in French West Africa*, Cambridge University Press, Cambridge.

Labonne, B. (1996) 'Artisanal mining: an economic stepping stone for women', *Natural Resources Forum*, 20 (2), pp. 117–22.

Labonne, B. (2003) 'Seminar on artisanal and small-scale mining in Africa: identifying best practices and building the sustainable livelihoods of communities, in G.M. Hilson, ed., *The Socioeconomic Impacts of Artisanal and Small-Scale Mining in Developing Countries*, A.A. Balkema, Rotterdam, pp. 131–50.

Labonne, B. and Gilman, J (1999) 'Towards building sustainable livelihoods in the artisanal mining communities', paper presented at Tripartite Meeting on Social and Labour Issues in Small-Scale Mines, International Labour Organization (ILO), Geneva.

Lacerda, L.D. (1997) 'Global mercury emissions from gold and silver mining', *Water, Air and Soil Pollution*, 97, pp. 209–21.

Lacerda, L.D. and Salomons, W. (1998) *Mercury from Gold and Silver Mining: A chemical time bomb?*, Springer-Verlag, New York.

Lavigne-Delville, P (1998) 'Comment articuler législation nationale et droits fonciers locaux: expériences en Afrique de l'Ouest francophone', in *Politique des structures et action foncière au service du développement agricole et rural*, Actes du Colloque de la Réunion, Centre National pour l'Aménagement des Structures des Exploitations Agricoles, Saint-Denis.

Lavigne-Delville, P., Ouedraogo, H. and Toulmin, C. (2002) 'Land tenure dynamics and state intervention: challenges, ongoing experience and current debates on land tenure in West Africa', in 'Making land rights more secure', conclusions of a seminar held in Ouagadougou, Burkina Faso (19–21 March).

Law, R., ed. (1995) *From Slave Trade to 'Legitimate' Commerce: The commercial transition in nineteenth-century West Africa*, Cambridge University Press, Cambridge.

Lawal, M. (2001) 'Constraints to small scale mining in Nigeria: policies and strategies for development', Working Paper, Centre for Energy, Petroleum and Mineral Policy and Law, University of Dundee, Scotland.

Levin, E. (2005) 'From poverty and war to prosperity and peace? Sustainable livelihoods and innovation in governance of artisanal diamond mining in Kono District, Sierra Leone', Master's dissertation, University of British Columbia, Vancouver.

Lewis S.R. (1984) 'Development problems of the mineral-rich countries', in M. Syrquin, L. Taylor and L.E. Westphal, eds, *Economic Structure and Performance: Essays in honour of Hollis B. Chenery*, Academic Press, Orlando, FL, pp. 157–77.

Lewis, S.R. (1989) 'Primary-exporting commodities', in H. Chenery and T.N. Srinivasan, eds, *Handbook of Development Economics*, Vol. 2, Elsevier Science, Amsterdam, pp. 1541–1600.

Logan, M. (2004) 'Making mining work: bringing poverty-stricken, small-scale miners into the formal private sector', Global Policy Forum, available online at: http://www.globalpolicy.org (accessed 12 July 2004).

Logan, I.B. and Mengisteab, K. (1993) 'IMF-World Bank adjustment and structural transformation in sub-Saharan Africa', *Economic Geography*, 69 (1), pp. 1–24.

Lydie, N. and Robinson, N.J. (1998) 'West and Central Africa', *International Migration*, 36 (4), pp. 469–511.

McMahon, G. and Davidson, J. (2000) 'Artisanal and small-scale mining', paper presented at the World Mines Ministry Forum, Toronto, available online at: http://www.wmmf.org/historical/2000docs/b/ASSM.htm (accessed 10 October 2002).

McPhee, A. (1971) *The Economic Revolution in British West Africa*, 2nd edn, Frank Cass, London.

Malm, O. (1998) Gold mining as a source of mercury exposure in the Brazilian Amazon, *Environmental Research*, 77 (2), pp. 73–8.

Management Systems International (MSI) (2004) 'Integrated diamond management in Sierra Leone: a pilot project', report prepared for the United States Agency for

International Development (USAID), Management Systems International, Washington, DC.

Masialeti, M. (2004) 'Small scale mining in Zambia', Southern African Network for Training and Research on the Environment, Harare, available online at: http://www.ies.ac.zw/santren/Projects/ssm/masialeti.htm (accessed 6 April 2005).

Masialeti, M. and Kinabo, C. (2003) 'The socio-economic impacts of small-scale mining: the case of Zambia', in G.M. Hilson, ed., *The Socioeconomic Impacts of Artisanal and Small-Scale Mining in Developing Countries*, A.A. Balkema, Rotterdam, pp 325–34.

Meekers, D. (2000) 'Going underground and going after women: trends in sexual risk behaviour among gold miners in South Africa', *International Journal of STD and AIDS*, 11 (1), pp. 21–6.

Ministère de l'Energie, des Mines et de l'Hydraulique (MEMH), Benin (1992) *Ressources Minières du Bénin*, Benin.

Mikesell, R.F. (1997) 'Explaining the resource curse, with special reference to mineral-exporting countries', *Resources Policy*, 23 (4), pp. 191–9.

MIME Consult (2002) 'Poverty eradication and sustainable livelihoods: focusing on artisanal mining communities', prepared by MIME Consult for UNDP/UNDESA, Accra.

Minerals Commission (2000) *Mineral Production in Ghana: 1980–1999*, Accra.

Mining, Minerals and Sustainable Development (MMSD) (2002a) *Breaking New Ground*, MMSD Group, International Institute for Environment and Development (IIED) and Earthscan, London.

MMSD (2002b) 'Report of the workshop on indigenous peoples and mining, minerals and sustainable development', Perth (4–6 February), International Institute for Environment and Development (IIED), London.

Mobbs, P.M. (1997) *The Mineral Industry of Mali, Minerals Yearbook*, Department of the Interior, Bureau of Mines, Z1-Z4, Bamako.

Morgan, W.B. and Pugh, J.C. (1969) *West Africa*, Butler and Tanner, London.

Moyers, R. (2003) 'The feasibility of establishing a formal credit delivery mechanism for small-scale diamond miners in Kono District, Sierra Leone', consultancy report prepared for Management Systems International, Washington, DC.

Ngugi R.K. and Nyariki, D.M. (2005) 'Rural livelihoods in the arid and semi-arid environments of Kenya: sustainable alternatives and challenges', *Agriculture and Human Values*, 22 (1), pp. 65–71.

Nkrumah, K. (1998) *Dark Days in Ghana*, International Publishers, New York.

Nöetstaller, R. (1994) Small-scale mining: practices, policies and perspectives, in A.K. Ghose, ed., *Small-scale Mining: A global overview*, A.A. Balkema, Rotterdam, pp. 3–8.

Nöetstaller, R. (1996) 'Keynote address', in M. Barry, ed., 'Regularizing Informal Mining: A summary of the proceedings of the international roundtable on artisanal mining', organized by the World Bank (17–19 May 1995), Industry and Energy Department Occasional Paper 6, Washington, DC.

NSR Environmental Consultants (1994) 'Environmental impact assessment of small-scale mining in Ghana: Part I Physical and biological aspects', NSR Environmental Consultants, Melbourne, Australia.

Nugent, P. (2004) *Africa Since Independence: A comparative history*, Palgrave Macmillan, Basingstoke.

Nyame, F.K. and Danso, S.K.A. (2004) *Environmental Implications of the Tributor System of Small-Scale Diamond Mining in the Akwatia Area, Eastern Region, Ghana*, Southern African Network for Training and Research on the Environment (SANTREN) Conference Proceedings, (19–21 May), Gaborone, Botswana.

Ofei-Aboagye, E., Thompson, N., Al-Hassan, S., Akabzaa, T. and Ayamdoo, C. (2004) 'Putting miners first 2004: understanding the livelihoods context of small-scale and artisanal mining in Ghana. Factors involved in increasing the contribution of ASM to poverty reduction targets', prepared for the Centre for Development Studies, University of Wales, Swansea, Wales, UK.

Ogola, J.S., Mitullah, W.V. and Omulo, M.A. (2002) 'Impact of gold mining on the environment and human health: a case study in the Migori gold belt, Kenya', *Environmental Geochemistry and Health*, **24** (2), pp. 141–57.

Okorodudu-Fubara, M. (1998) 'Development and codification of international environmental law: whither Nigeria a quarter of century after Stockholm and half a decade after Rio, in S. Simpson and L. Fagbohun, eds, *Environmental Law and Policy*, Law Centre, Faculty of Law, Lagos State University, Nigeria, pp. 283–96.

Oomes, N. and Vocke, M. (2003) 'Diamond smuggling and taxation in sub-Saharan Africa', IMF Working Paper WP/03/167, IMF, Washington, DC.

Otayek, R. (1992) 'Burkina Faso: la "rectification" démocratique', *Studia Africana*, **3** (February), pp. 11–26.

Owusu, J.H. (2001) 'Spatial integration, adjustment, and structural transformation in sub-Saharan Africa: some linkage pattern changes in Ghana', *The Professional Geographer*, **53** (2), pp. 230–47.

Palmer, K. and Sackey, S. (2004) 'Ghanaian miners risk lives for gold', *Washington Times* (22 September), available online at: http://www.washtimes.com/world/20040921-091541-1701r.htm (accessed 24 October 2005).

PANA (2003) 'Ghana's Ashanti Goldfields steps up HIV/AIDS education', Global Business Coalition on HIV/AIDS, News (27 November).

Partnership Africa Canada and Network Movement for Justice and Development (2004) 'Diamond industry annual review: Sierra Leone 2004', Partnership Africa Canada and Network Movement for Justice and Development, Ottawa.

Paul, R.L., Guest, R.N. and Nel, P. (1997) 'The Mintek small mine case study – Venmag', *Journal of the South African Institute of Mining and Metallurgy*, **97** (1), pp. 1–5.

Peabody, J.W. (1996) 'Economic reform and health sector policy: Lessons from structural adjustment programs', *Social Science and Medicine*, **43** (5), pp. 823–35.

Peace Diamond Alliance (2005) See: http://www.peacediamonds.org

Pegg, S. (2003) *Poverty Reduction or Poverty Exacerbation? World Bank Group support for extractive industries in Africa*, Oxfam America, Boston, MA.

Peters, K. and Richards, P. (1998) '"Why we fight": voices of youth combatants in Sierra Leone', *Africa*, **68**, pp. 184–210.

Piachaud, D. (1987) 'Problems in the definition and measurement of poverty', *Journal of Social Policy*, **16**, pp. 147–64.

Pratt, L.J.T. (2003). 'The contribution of the diamond industry to the economy of Sierra Leone', paper presented at the Diamond Sector Workshop organized by DFID, Freetown, Sierra Leone.

Pugh, M. and Cooper, N. (2004). *War Economies in a Regional Context: Challenges of transformation*, International Peace Academy, Boulder, CO.

Pyatt, F.B. and Grattan, J.P. (2001) 'Some consequences of ancient mining activities on the health of ancient and modern human populations', *Journal of Public Health Medicine*, **23** (2), pp. 235–6.

Raufu, A. (2004) 'Tin mining wreaks havoc on beautiful Nigerian city', Third World Network, Malaysia, available online at: http://www.twnside.org.sg/title/1878-cn.htm (accessed 14 August 2005).

Reno, W. (1995) *Corruption and State Politics in Sierra Leone*, Cambridge University Press, Cambridge.

Reno, W. (1998) *Warlord Politics and African States*, Lynne Rienner, Boulder, CO.

Richards, P. (1996) *Fighting for the Rain Forest: War, youth and resources in Sierra Leone*, James Currey, Oxford.

Riddell, B. (1997) 'Structural adjustment programmes and the city in tropical Africa', *Urban Studies*, **34** (8), pp. 1297–307.

Ridler, N.B. (1993) 'Fixed exchange rates and structural adjustment programs – Côte d'Ivoire', *Journal of Modern African Studies*, **31** (2), pp. 301–8.

Ross, M. (2001) 'Extractive sectors and the poor', Oxfam America Report, Washington, DC.

Ross, M.H. and Murray, J. (2004) 'Occupational respiratory disease in mining', *Occupational Medicine*, **54** (5), pp. 304–10.

Rukuni, M. (2002) 'Africa: addressing growing threats to food security', *Journal of Nutrition*, **132** (11), pp. 3443–8.

Sachs, J. (2005) *The End of Poverty: How we can make it happen in our lifetime*, Penguin, London.

Sachs, J.D. and Warner, A.M. (1995) 'Natural resource abundance and economic growth', National Bureau of Economic Research (NBER) Working Paper 5398, Cambridge.

Sachs, J.D. and Warner, A.M. (2001) 'Natural resources and economic development: the curse of natural resources', *European Economic Review*, **45**, pp. 827–38.

St Dominic's Hospital (2001) Monthly outpatient morbidity tally sheets – 2001, St Dominic's Hospital, Akwatia, Ghana.

Sala-i-Martin, X. (1997) 'I just ran two million regressions', *American Economic Review*, **87** (2), pp. 178–83.

Sands, P. (2003), *Principles of International Environmental Law*, 2nd edn, Cambridge University Press, Cambridge.

Savannah Resources Management Project (SRMP) (2000) 'Medicinal plant conservation management and sustainable utilization in northern Ghana', SRMP Medicinal Plant Survey Report, Upper West Region Forestry Directorate (January).

Save the Children (2003) 'Finding the right tools for the job: lessons learned on the application of ILO Convention 182 on the worst forms of child labour', Save the Children, London.

Search for Common Ground and Talking Drum Studio (2003) 'Diamond area community development fund: report on sensitization activities, 11th to 25th January 2003', Freetown, Sierra Leone.

Seidman, G.W. (1993) 'Shafted: the social impact of downscaling on the Free State Goldfields', *South African Sociological Review*, **5** (2), pp. 14–32.

Sen, A. (2001) 'Why health equity', keynote address to the Third International Conference on 'The economics of health: within and beyond health care', York (23 July).

Serfor-Armah, Y., Nyarko, B.J.B., Adotey, D.K., Adomako, D. and Akaho, E.H.K. (2004) 'The impact of small-scale mining on the levels of mercury in the environment: the case of Prestea and its environs', *Journal of Radioanalytical and Nuclear Chemistry*, **262** (3), pp. 685–90.

Shoko, D. (2004) 'Establishing training guidelines on environmental protection and management for small scale mining (SSM) in Zimbabwe', Southern African Network for Training and Research on the Environment, Harare, available online at: http://www.ies.ac.zw/santren/Projects/ssm/shoko.htm (accessed 5 December 2005).

Sierra Leone, Government of (2004) 'Poverty reduction strategy paper', Government of Sierra Leone, Freetown.

Simpson, J. (2001) 'The Shamva Mining Centre, Zimbabwe', Small-Scale Mining Case Study for Intermediate Technology Development Group (ITDG), ITDG, Rugby: http://www.livelihoodtechnology.org/home.asp?id=csShamva1>,

Smillie, I., Gberie, L. and Hazleton, R. (2000) *The Heart of the Matter: Sierra Leone diamonds and human security*, Insights Series, Partnership Africa Canada, Ottawa.

Smith, I.O. (1998) 'Sustainable development and environmental diplomacy: reconciling economic growth with environmental protection by the year 2000 and beyond', in S. Simpson and L. Fagbohun, eds, *Environmental Law and Policy*, p. 244–82, Law Centre, Faculty of Law, Lagos State University, Nigeria.

Songsore, J., Tsikata, G.K. and Yankson, P.W.K. (1994) 'Mining and the environment: towards a win-win strategy (a study of the Tarkwa-Aboso-Nsuta Mining Complex in Ghana) (final report)', study prepared for the Ministry of Environment, Science and Technology, Accra.

Spiropoulos, J. (1991) *Small-Scale Mineral Industries – Their role in rural development,* *Proceedings of Symposium,* AGID Report Series, A.A. Balkema, Rotterdam.

Steiner, H.J. and Alston, P. (2000) *International Human Rights in Context: Law, politics, morals,* 2nd edn, Oxford University Press, Oxford.

SYSMIN (2003) *Cartographie géologique au Burkina Faso,* No 7 ACP.BK. 074, Notice explicative de la carte géologique, feuille ND-30-XI, 1st edn, Kaya.

Tagoe, K. et al. (2000) 'The Second 5-year District Development Planning, 2001–2005 Profile of Kwaebibirem District Final Report', vol. 1, pp. 1–50, Accra.

Taylor, H., Appleton, J.D., Lister, R., Smith, B., Chitamweba, D., Mkumbo, O., Machiwa, J.F., Tesha, A.L. and Beinhoff, C. (2005) 'Environmental assessment of mercury contamination from the Rwamagasa artisanal gold mining centre, Geita District, Tanzania', *Science of the Total Environment,* **343** (1–3), pp. 111–33.

Temple, H., Levin, E., Turay, A.B. and Renzi, M. (2005) 'Mining the "chaos" in Sierra Leone's diamond fields: policy and program implications of the structure of the artisanal mining sector in Sierra Leone', Management Systems International, Washington, DC.

Thomassin, J.F. (2003) 'Orpaillage et petite mine au Burkina Faso', Bureau de Recherches Géologiques et Minières, Orleans.

Thomassin, J.F. and Toux, L. (1999) 'Projet PRD 519. Rapport de mission Burkina Faso', Bureau de Recherches Géologiques et Minières, Orleans.

Tornell, A. and Lane, P.R. (1999) The voracity effect, *American Economic Review,* **89** (1), pp. 22–46.

Torvik, R. (2002) Natural resources, rent seeking and welfare, *Journal of Development Economics,* **67**, pp. 455–70.

Tráore, P.A. (1994) Constraints on small-scale mining in Africa, *Natural Resources Forum,* **18** (3), pp. 207–12.

Tsikata, F. (1997) 'The vicissitudes of mineral policy in Ghana', *Resources Policy,* **23** (1–2), pp. 9–14.

UNAIDS (2003) 'Ghana epidemiological fact sheet on HIV/AIDS and sexually transmitted: diseases: 2002 update', UNAIDS/WHO, Geneva, Switzerland.

United Nations (UN) (1980) *Report of committee on increased gold output in Ghana,* United Nations, New York.

UN (1996a) *Recent Developments in Small-Scale Mining,* Economic and Social Council, United Nations, New York.

UN (1996b) 'Recent developments in small-scale mining', *Natural Resources Forum,* **20** (3), pp. 215–25.

UN (2003) *Burkina Faso: L'indice de pauvreté est en hausse,* United Nations, New York, available online at: http://www.irinnews.org (accessed 16 February 2004).

United Nations Children's Fund (UNICEF) (2004) See: http://www.unicef.org (accessed 5 October 2004).

UNDESA (2003) United Nations Partnership for Sustainable Development, Division of Sustainable Development, Geneva, available online at: http://www.un.org/esa/sustdev/partnerships/activities_initiate.htm (accessed 17 November 2004).

United Nations Development Programme (UNDP) (2003a) *Human Development Report 2003 – Millennium Development Goals: A compact among nations to end human poverty,* UNDP Human Development Report, UNDP, New York, available online at: http://hdr.undp.org/reports/global/2003 (accessed 14 September 2004).

UNDP (2003b) 'Poverty eradication and sustainable livelihoods: focusing on artisanal mining communities', Final Report, SPPD Project RAF/99/023, UNDP, New York.

UNDP (2005) *International Cooperation at a Crossroads: Aid, trade and security in an unequal world,* UNDP Human Development Report, UNDP, New York.

United Nations Economic Commission For Africa (UNECA) (2002a) 'Recommendations' from Seminar on Small-Scale and Artisanal Mining in Africa: Identifying Best Practices and Building the Sustainable Livelihoods of Communities, Yaoundé, Cameroon.

UNECA (2002b) *Compendium on Best Practices in Small-Scale Mining in Africa*, UNECA, Addis Ababa.

UNEP-UNICEF-WHO (2002) *Children in the New Millennium: Environmental Impact on Health*, United Nations Environmental Programme (UNEP), with inputs from UNICEF and WHO, New York.

United Nations Industrial Development Organization (UNIDO) (2005) 'Pilot project for the reduction of mercury contamination resulting from artisanal gold mining fields in the Manica District of Mozambique', Global Mercury Project, UNIDO, Vienna.

USAID (2001) 'Sierra Leone: conflict diamonds', Progress Report on Diamond Policy and Development Programme, USAID, Office of Transition Initiatives, Washington, DC.

Van der Laan, H.L. (1965) *The Sierra Leone Diamonds*, Oxford University Press, Oxford.

Van Koppen, B. (2003) 'Water reform in Sub-Saharan Africa: what is the difference?', *Physics and Chemistry of the Earth*, 28 (20–7), pp. 1047–53.

Van Oss, H. (1995) *The Mineral Industry of Mali, Minerals Yearbook*, Vol. 3, US Department of the Interior, Bureau of Mines, Washington, DC.

van Straaten, P. (2000a) 'Human Exposure to Mercury due to Small-Scale Gold Mining in northern Tanzania, *Science of the Total Environment*, 259 (1–3), pp. 45–53.

van Straaten, P. (2000b) Mercury Contamination Associated with Small-Scale Gold Mining in Tanzania and Zimbabwe. *Science of the Total Environment*, 259 (1–3), pp. 105–13.

Veiga, M.M. (1997a) *Introducing New Technologies for Abatement of Global Mercury Pollution in Latin America*, UNIDO Report, UNIDO, Vienna.

Veiga, M.M. (1997b) 'Mercury in artisanal gold mining in Latin America: facts, fantasies and solutions', UNIDO Expert Group Meeting, Introducing new technologies for abatement of global mercury pollution deriving from artisanal gold mining, Vienna.

Veiga, M.M., Maxson, P. and Hylander, L.D. (2006) 'Origin and consumption of mercury in small-scale gold mining', *Journal of Cleaner Production*, 14 (3–4), pp. 436–47.

Vieira, R. (2004) 'Mercury-free gold mining technologies: possibilities for adoption in the Guianas', World Wildlife Fund (WWF) Guianas Regional Programme Office Technical Paper Series 1,World Wildlife Fund (WWF) Guianas, Paramaribo.

Villas-Bôas, R.C. and Barreto, M.L. (2002) 'FDI environment and small mining', Working Paper for Discussion, OECD Global Forum on International Investment, Conference on Foreign Direct Investment and the Environment, Paris.

Vincent, P. (1962) 'Rapport d'ensemble sur les prospections et recherches pour or effectuées par le services des mines dans le Nord Dahomey de 1935 à 1942', BRGM, Dahomey, Mission Convention, Benin.

Walker, E.A. (2000) '"Happy days are here again": cocoa farmers, middlemen, traders and the Structural Adjustment Program in southwestern Nigeria, 1986–1990s', *Africa Today*, 47 (2), pp. 151–69.

Walker, R. (1987) 'Consensual approaches to the definition of poverty – towards an alternative methodology', *Journal of Social Policy*, 16, pp. 213–26.

Watts, M.J. (2004) 'Antinomies of community: some thoughts on geography, resources and empire', *Transactions of the Institute of British Geographers*, 29 (2), pp. 196–216.

Weber-Fahr, M. (2002) *Treasure or Trouble? Mining in developing countries*, World Bank/ International Finance Corporation, Washington, DC.

Weissman, S.R. (1990) 'Structural adjustment in Africa: insights from the experiences of Ghana and Senegal, *World Development*, 18 (12), pp. 1621–34.

Werthmann, K., ed. (2000a) 'Ruée vers l'or dans un village au Burkina Faso. Le journal de Dominique Tiendrebéogo', Working Papers on African Societies 48, Das Arabische Buch, Berlin.

Werthmann, K. (2000b) 'Gold rush in West Africa. the appropriation of "natural" resources: non-industrial gold mining in South-Western Burkina Faso', *Sociologus*, 50 (1), pp. 90–104.

Werthmann, K. (2003a) 'The president of the gold diggers: sources of power in a gold mine in Burkina Faso', *Ethnos*, 68 (1), pp. 95–111.

Werthmann, K. (2003b) 'Cowries, gold and bitter money: non-industrial gold-mining and notions of ill-gotten wealth in Burkina Faso', *Paideuma*, **49**, pp. 105–24.

Werthmann, K. (2003c) *Frivolous squandering, comsumption and solidarity among gold and diamond miners in Africa and elsewhere*, Max Planck Institute for Social Anthropology, Halle.

Wels, T.A. (1983) 'Small-scale mining – the forgotten partner', *Transactions of the Institution of Mining & Metallurgy, Section A*, **92** (1), pp. A19–A27.

Williams, J., Sutherland, D., Cartwright, K. and Byrnes, M. (2002), 'Sierra Leone Diamond policy study', report prepared for Department for International Development (DFID), UK.

Wood, G. (2003) 'Staying secure, staying poor: the Faustian bargain', *World Development*, **31** (3), pp. 455–71.

Woolf, L. (1968) *Empire and Commerce in Africa: A study in economic imperialism*, George Allen & Unwin, New York.

World Bank (1993) 'World development report: investing in health', World Bank, Washington, DC.

World Bank (1994) 'Ghana – mining sector management and environment project', Report E0049, Environmental Assessment/Analysis Reports, World Bank, Washington, DC.

World Bank (1995) 'Staff appraisal report, Republic of Ghana, mining sector development and environment project', Report 13881-GH, Industry and Energy Operations West Central Africa Department Africa Region, World Bank, Washington, DC.

World Bank (2002a) 'Sierra Leone: tapping the mineral wealth for human progress – a break with the past', Poverty Reduction and Economic Management Sector Unit, World Bank, Washington, DC.

World Bank (2002b) 'Sierra Leone: public expenditure policies for sustained economic growth and poverty alleviation', World Bank, Washington, DC.

World Bank (2003a) 'Key topics in mining', World Bank, Washington, DC, available online at: http://www.worldbank.org/ogmc/mining_keytopics.htm (accessed 6 October 2003).

World Bank (2003b) 'Project performance assessment report Ghana: mining sector rehabilitation project, mining sector development and environment project', Report 26197, Sector and Thematic Evaluation Group Operations Evaluation Department, World Bank, Washington DC.

World Bank (2004a) 'Understanding and responding to poverty', World Bank, Washington DC, available online at: http://www.worldbank.org/poverty/mission/up1.htm (accessed 4 November 2004).

World Bank (2004b) 'Making services work for poor people', World Development Report 2004, World Bank Group, Washington, DC.

World Commission on Environment and Development (WCED) (1987) *Our Common Future*, Oxford University Press, Oxford.

World Development Indicators (2003) *Measuring Development in 2003, World Development Indicators 2003*, World Bank Statistics/World Development Indicators Office, Washington, DC.

World Health Organization (WHO) (2001) 'Macroeconomics and health: investing in health for economic development. Report of the Macroeconomics and Commission on Health (CMH)', presented by J.D. Sachs to Gro Harlem Brundtland, Director-General of the WHO (20 December), WHO, Geneva.

Yakubu, B.R. (2003a) 'Regularisation of small-scale mining in Ghana: technical approach and its shortcomings', Communities and Small Scale Mining (CASM), 3rd AGM and Learning Event, Elmina.

Yakubu, B.R. (2003b) 'Mercury use in small-scale gold mining in Ghana: an assessment of its impact on the miners', M.Eng. Thesis, Kwame Nkrumah University of Science and Technology, Kumasi.

Zack-Williams, A. (1995). *Tributers, Supporters and Merchant Capital: Mining and underdevelopment in Sierra Leone*, Ashgate, Aldershot.

Zamora, A. (2000) 'International initiatives on small-scale mining: lessons from the Colombian coal experience', *Minerals & Energy*, **15** (3), pp. 31–5.

Zunino, C. and Ki, J.C. (2001) 'Etude hydrologique et d'approvisionnement en eau des régions minières sélectionnées', Assistance technique pour le renforcement des capacités nationales en gestion de l'environnement, Le Projet de Renforcement des Capacités Nationales du secteur Minier et de Gestion de l'Environnement (PRECAGEME), Ouagadougou.

Index